FOREIGN AID

Foreign Aid: Theory and Practice in Southern Asia

BY CHARLES WOLF, JR.

THE *RAND* CORPORATION

PRINCETON, NEW JERSEY
PRINCETON UNIVERSITY PRESS

1960

Charles Wolf, Jr. has served as Vice Consul
and Economic Officer for the United States Foreign
Service in Indonesia, and as Chief of the Asian Program Staff for the Technical Cooperation Administration in Washington. He has taught at Cornell
University and the University of California, both at
Berkeley and Los Angeles, and has been an economic advisor to the President's Committee to
Study the United States Military Assistance Program (the "Draper Committee"). His service with
the Draper Committee and with TCA caused him
to travel widely in South and Southeast Asia. Since
1955, Dr. Wolf has been an economist with The
RAND Corporation.

Printed in the United States of America

by Princeton University Press, Princeton, New Jersey

TO THERESE, TED, AND TIM

PREFACE

FOREIGN AID is a subject that touches the interests of students of international relations, political science, history, military strategy, public administration, psychology, anthropology, and sociology, no less than economics. When foreign aid is considered in relation to a particular country or region, it also comes within the special purview of the "area" expert. Perhaps because of the range of jurisdictions in which it is involved, foreign aid has received relatively little serious analytical treatment. What is everybody's business is often nobody's business. This is not to say that comment and writing on the subject have been scarce. The *Readers' Guide to Periodical Literature*, for example, lists more than 250 articles on "economic assistance" alone for the year March 1957 to February 1958. But much of the writing lacks precise terminology, reliable data, or an agreed set of problems to be considered systematically. It lacks a theory that permits organizing and comparing experience, and, hopefully, profiting from it.

This book is concerned with some of these difficulties. It tries to meet them by describing and organizing the foreign aid record of the United States in terms of the allocation of aid among countries of a particular region (South and Southeast Asia), and between military and economic programs within the region. The central analytical question it raises is how to improve the allocation of foreign aid in a region, once the total amount to be allocated has been determined. In other words, it approaches the problem of foreign aid from the standard economic viewpoint of "optimizing" behavior.

Despite the semantic link, "optimizing" does not imply boundless optimism. One can adopt an optimizing approach and still be acutely aware of the complexity of a problem, the inevitability of making simplifications in trying to treat it analytically, the risks of being rigorous rather than realistic, and the consequent necessity for subordinating analytical results to informed and responsible judgment. Nevertheless, though he usually has abundant reason for humility, the optimizer is optimistic at least to the extent that he believes judgment and understanding can be improved by explicit consideration of major alternatives.

Though this study deals with problems of foreign aid from the standpoint of an economist, an effort is made to render the use of economic tools and reasoning intelligible to non-economists as well.

[vii]

Mathematics is occasionally used to formalize and specify the argument. But, where this occurs, as in Chapters 8, 9, and 10, the mathematical model is relegated to a separate section of the chapter, or to an appendix. These sections can be skipped by non-mathematical readers without losing the continuity of the exposition. In each case, the content and implications of the model are also summarized in non-mathematical terms. Moreover, a summary of these sections, and of their relation to the rest of the book, is presented in Chapter 12.

A comment should be added concerning the general plan of the study, though this is discussed more fully in the first chapter. The book consists of two separate, but related components. The first, Parts I and II, is principally concerned with foreign aid in South and Southeast Asia from an empirical and historical standpoint. This is the "practice" referred to in the book's title. The second, Parts III and IV, is principally concerned with foreign aid from the standpoint of the analysis and theory of aid allocation. This is the "theory" referred to in the title.

The two components can be read alone, since each is more or less self-contained. But I hope that even readers with special interests in one or the other component will be induced to go beyond it. Both were conceived as parts of a whole. The way the history is organized and described in Parts I and II gains in relevance if these parts are read in conjunction with the theoretical analysis. And the analysis of Parts III and IV gains in credibility if read in conjunction with the historical account.

This study was supported by The RAND Corporation as part of its program of RAND-sponsored research. In addition to its work for the United States Air Force and other government agencies, the Corporation regularly sponsors, with its own funds, research projects in areas of importance to national security and public welfare. Such research is considered to be fundamentally the responsibility of the individuals involved in the project, and the conclusions of such projects are not necessarily endorsed by the Corporation. The studies are published in the hope that they may contribute to wider understanding of important national problems.

It is a pleasure to acknowledge the help I have received in preparing this book. Paul Clark, Andrew Marshall, Thomas Schelling, and Lawrence Ebb read over the early chapter drafts and made many helpful comments. Besides writing part of the Appendix to

Chapter 9, Marshall also provided especially useful assistance in connection with the mathematical and statistical sections of the study. Many RAND colleagues, particularly Malcolm Hoag, Oleg Hoeffding, Joseph Kershaw, Harold Lubell, Frederick Moore, and Richard Nelson, commented on parts of the study. I am grateful to William Taylor, Everton Conger, and Brownlee Haydon for editorial help, to Virginia Anderson, Joy Fort, and Herta Horny for research assistance, and to Susan Simek, Lorraine Farr, and Doris Waco for perennially patient clerical assistance.

CHARLES WOLF, JR.

Santa Monica
February 1960

CONTENTS

[xi]

PART II

MUTUAL SECURITY AND SOUTHERN
ASIA, 1951-1957

CONTENTS

TABLES

TABLES

FOREIGN AID:

THEORY AND PRACTICE
IN SOUTHERN ASIA

CHAPTER 1

INTRODUCTION—THE PROBLEM OF
FOREIGN AID ALLOCATION

WHEN Secretary of State George Marshall delivered a Harvard commencement address on June 5, 1947, he initiated a foreign policy debate in the United States that has recurred annually, and shows promise of continuing in the indefinite future. Though the primary stimulus to this debate on foreign economic and military assistance has remained the need for annual appropriations, its scope has fundamentally altered. Instead of Europe, the debate now centers on Asia and the Middle East. Instead of economic recovery, the stress is on local military preparedness and, to an increasing extent, on economic development. Instead of whether the United States should extend foreign assistance, the debate concentrates on how much, to whom, and for what purposes assistance should be extended. These questions of allocation are the core of the continuing debate on foreign aid. They are the questions with which the analytical portions of this study are principally concerned.

Questions of allocation are simply questions of choice: questions that ask how a preferred way of using some given resource can be chosen. As in most frames of reference, questions about allocation in the foreign aid field can be viewed broadly or narrowly. Indeed, the question of whether to have a foreign aid program at all can be viewed as part of the broad allocation question of how to choose an optimal allocation of national (or government) resources as between foreign aid and other uses.

However, as in many other problems, it is also unfortunately true in the case of foreign aid that the broader the allocation question asked, the less reliable the answer that can usually be given to it. Consequently, while we shall comment at the end of the study on the broad question of the over-all size of the foreign aid program, our concern will be mainly with a narrower group of questions of allocation. If one thinks of the allocation alternatives within a given region as various possible *country* combinations (for example, more to Country X, less to Y) and *program* combinations (for example, more to economic programs, less to military programs), then the allocative questions we shall be concerned with ask how an optimal country

[3]

combination and an optimal program combination can be chosen. These questions, of course, raise many subsidiary questions. What meaning, for example, can be attached to "optimality" in the context of regional aid allocation? What are the precise objectives to be maximized, and how can they be related to the aid costs to be incurred? What criteria can guide us in choosing among alternative patterns of allocation?

In examining these questions, we shall be concerned with a particular region: the mainland and island Asian arc stretching from Afghanistan in the West to the Philippines in the East, and including, besides these countries, Pakistan, India, Nepal, Ceylon, Burma, Thailand, Cambodia, Laos, Viet Nam, and Indonesia. In the interest of brevity, rather than precision, we shall refer to this area as Southern Asia.[1] Though the allocation problems that concern us are generic and global, use of the regional framework has several advantages. Southern Asia is one of the two areas in which the grim struggle, euphemistically referred to as "competitive coexistence," is being waged most intensively. It is, consequently, an area on which foreign policy debate in the United States tends to concentrate. Moreover, the complex problems we are interested in are more manageable, both conceptually and empirically, if approached in terms of an area whose component parts are linked by common experiences and interests. These common characteristics will permit us to venture and test generalizations about the entire area using data from only a few of the countries in it with more confidence than if the area chosen were larger and more heterogeneous.

When we consider the intercountry and interprogram allocation of foreign aid in the particular context of Southern Asia, still other questions come to mind, questions that are crucial for American foreign policy and for foreign assistance as an instrument of that policy. What, for example, do we know about such relevant questions as the relationship between external aid and internal economic development, or between economic development, on the one hand,

[1] In terms of more familiar geographic usage, the region we call Southern Asia consists of South Asia and Southeast Asia. Malaya, though a part of Southeast Asia, is excluded from most of the discussion. As a protectorate of Great Britain until August 1957, Malaya did not receive any direct assistance from the United States during the period covered by the empirical portions of this study. In the course of the discussion, it is occasionally necessary to refer separately to each of the two segments of Southern Asia. Where this is done, "South Asia" refers to Afghanistan, Pakistan, India, Nepal, and Ceylon; "Southeast Asia" to Burma, Thailand, Cambodia, Laos, Viet Nam, Indonesia, and the Philippines.

and political stability and vitality, on the other? To shift to another dimension of the problem, what can be said about the relative likelihood of various possible local military aggressions in Southern Asia? More generally, what can be said, or, at any rate, conjectured, about the likelihood of local military aggression and less direct methods of communist penetration? What emphasis, for example, can we expect a resourceful and flexible adversary to assign to external military pressure, to economic aid and trade, to organization and activity by indigenous communist parties, and to the example of Chinese economic development, in pursuing his objectives? And what assessment can be made of the chances of success of any combination of these strategies in the Asian countries, especially, but not exclusively, the "neutralist" countries?

These questions, of course, are not new. They have been with us and will continue to be with us for many years. They endure both because they are important and because they are not answerable in any definitive, "once-and-for-all" sense. They are not strictly answerable because they involve too many uncertainties: not the convenient kind of uncertainty that can be manipulated analytically by means of a known or assumed frequency distribution of possible answers, but the inconvenient kind for which no frequency distribution can be formulated because the chance of different answers being right depends on events that cannot be anticipated.

In raising these questions, our aim is not so much to find answers, but to examine and clarify the questions themselves. Our aim, too, is to suggest certain ways of analyzing them which can be of partial use in improving foreign aid decisions, and hence in increasing the effectiveness of aid as an instrument of United States foreign policy.

The word "partial" should be emphasized. The suggestions made are based on an analysis that admittedly deals with only a part of the complex environment in which foreign aid decisions must be made. Political pressures within the United States, unique and unforeseen emergencies abroad, personalities and publicity at home and abroad, bargaining between agencies and governments, to mention a few of the factors that are excluded from much of our analysis, will, and in varying degrees ought to be highly influential in allocation, as in other major public policy, decisions. For obvious reasons, the probable, no less than the desirable, influence of such factors remains more a matter of judgment than analysis. These and subsequent qualifying remarks that we will make in the study

[5]

should, however, be taken as a counsel of realism, not despair. In solving problems as complex and fluid as those with which we are concerned, analysis can never substitute for responsible judgment. But analysis can help greatly to make judgment, whether of policy-maker or voter, informed and explicit.

As noted in the *Preface*, the book is divided into four parts. Parts I and II (Chapters 2 through 6) are empirical and descriptive. They are devoted to a summary of United States assistance programs in Southern Asia, with two purposes in view. The first is simply to organize the numerical data on aid allocations in a coherent and intelligible manner for convenient reference. Hitherto, these data have been scattered in different sources, confusingly labelled and frequently discrepant. The second purpose is to provide a context and a "feel" for some of the later analytical discussion.

Toward these ends, Chapters 2 and 3 of Part I summarize the pertinent background and precedents to American assistance programs in Southern Asia. Chapter 4 in Part II then reviews the beginning of direct economic and military aid to Southern Asia, which took place almost simultaneously with the onset of the Korean war. Chapters 5 and 6 present the detailed record of allocations of the Mutual Security Program in the region, from July 1, 1951 through the end of fiscal year 1957. Besides ordering the allocations data and interpreting them in terms of the relevant international circumstances and domestic aid legislation, the three chapters of Part II try to clarify the terminological obscurities that have often confused the discussion of foreign aid.

Parts III and IV (Chapters 7 through 12) then considered in more detail some of the analytical issues raised in the first six chapters. In contrast to the earlier chapters, the approach of Parts III and IV is theoretical and abstract. In Chapter 7, the role of foreign aid as an instrument of foreign policy, and the objectives of economic and military aid, are discussed. In view of the particular prominence accorded the objective of strengthening political stability in recipient countries, Chapter 8 tries to analyze the concept of political vulnerability and formulates a model relating it to various measurable indicators of economic and social change. Chapter 9 presents a preliminary statistical test of the model.

In Chapter 10, three specific problems are discussed involving the allocation of aid among the countries of a given region, and between economic and military programs within a region. Heuristic models, which try to reduce these problems to manageable analytical proportions, are formulated with the use of some of the concepts discussed in Part III. Chapter 11 then turns to the specific question of Soviet Bloc economic aid in Southern Asia in the light of the preceding analysis. It considers the extent to which Soviet aid may be not simply a threat to the free world but, from another point of view, perhaps a windfall as well. The final chapter summarizes the entire discussion, and concludes with some general remarks about the role and desirable size of the Mutual Security Program in the competitive coexistence era.

PART I

THE BACKGROUND OF UNITED STATES AID

TO SOUTHERN ASIA

CHAPTER 2

THE ORIGINS OF UNITED STATES AID PROGRAMS IN SOUTHERN ASIA (1)

A. INTRODUCTION

IN THE STUDY of foreign policy, no less than biology, origins tend to be elusive and, if found, are likely to be arbitrary. For foreign policies like biological species, usually evolve gradually and continuously. Whether we view foreign policy as a set of national objectives, or as programs or instrumentalities designed to achieve these objectives, or as a combination of the two, once we look behind the apparent origin of a policy we generally find precedents and prior circumstances that figured prominently in the policy's formulation. In short, origins have a way of receding as we approach them.

Even with the European Recovery Program (ERP), to which we might expect to be able to assign a single point of origin, this difficulty arises. Thus, antedating the historic speech by Secretary Marshall on June 5, 1947, was an equally significant statement by Undersecretary Acheson on May 8, 1947, which officially urged "emergency assistance in areas where it will be most effective in building world political and economic stability."[1] Moreover, the timing and content of both statements were influenced by the earlier efforts and experience of the United Nations Relief and Rehabilitation Administration (UNRRA), the Export-Import Bank, the International Bank for Reconstruction and Development, and wartime Lend-Lease. In part, UNRRA, like ERP, was concerned with providing consumer goods and working capital—mainly in the form of industrial raw materials—for short-term industrial recovery in liberated countries, beginning in 1944 during the war and ending, significantly, in the same month that the Marshall speech was delivered. At the same time, the Export-Import Bank and, to a lesser extent, the International Bank, contributed to longer-term European recovery by a number of loans for industrial reconstruction in Western Europe during the two years immediately following World War II.

[1] *The European Recovery Program—Basic Documents and Background Information*, Senate Foreign Relations Committee and House Foreign Affairs Committee, Washington, D.C., 1947, p. 2.

[11]

And if we wish to go back still farther, we might cite the non-military part of Lend-Lease aid provided to Europe from 1941 to 1945, and the postwar Lend-Lease settlements, as having relevance to the later formulation of ERP. In its concepts and procedures, Lend-Lease "left an impress . . . that is still prominent in the Mutual Security Program."[2]

We find essentially the same fact of historical continuity in tracing the origins of United States economic aid in Southern Asia. If we wished to be exhaustive, for example, we might examine in detail previous United States activities in extending economic and technical assistance to underdeveloped countries, even before Southern Asia became a major recipient. We could go back through more than a century of United States technical assistance missions in which the government, at the request—sometimes elicited—of the host government, provided a variety of advisory services in such fields as agricultural extension, public health, education, transportation, public works, and fiscal and monetary administration. Typically undertaken by the federal government agency operating in the technical field concerned, these missions were concentrated in South and Central America. However, they also included China, and one of the earlier and more successful examples of U.S. technical assistance occurred at the beginning of the Meiji restoration in Japan.[3]

We could go still further back to the first known case of aid by the United States in the form of commodities, as contrasted with technical services, which occurred one hundred and forty-five years ago in Venezuela. Nor are such illustrations as completely incidental to the main interest of this study as their remoteness in time suggests. In the Venezuelan relief aid of 1812, for example, we find the same sort of use of an economic instrument for an avowedly political purpose—in this case the unsuccessful support of a Venezuelan insurrection against Spain[4]—that has characterized, if not

[2] William Adams Brown, Jr. and Redvers Opie, *American Foreign Assistance*, Washington, D.C., 1953, pp. 35ff. This is the best general reference on early foreign aid, especially to Europe. For other references on early postwar aid, see Harry B. Price, *The Marshall Plan and Its Meaning*, Ithaca, New York, 1955; and Raymond F. Mikesell, *United States Economic Policy and International Relations*, New York, 1952.

[3] For an account of these missions, see Merle Curti and Kendall Birr, *Prelude to Point Four*, Madison, Wisconsin, 1954. Another useful reference is Edwin A. Bock, *Fifty Years of Technical Assistance*, Chicago, 1954. Though the latter deals with the experience of private agencies, it contains much that is relevant to the origins, motivations, and operating problems of government technical aid programs, as well.

[4] Harold A. Bierck, Jr., "The First Instance of U.S. Foreign Aid: Venezuelan Relief in 1812," *Inter-American Economic Affairs*, Vol. IX, Number 1, Summer, 1955.

dominated, contemporary United States economic aid programs in Southern Asia. In literally all of the early aid history we also find the same multiplicity, as well as occasional vagueness, of program objectives that has accompanied contemporary aid programs in Southern Asia. Generalizing from case studies of one hundred years of American technical assistance (through 1938), Curti and Birr state, for example, that: "The attempts [at furnishing assistance] grew out of a compound of economic interests, humanitarian sentiment, and strategic considerations. In most of these cases, the motives were so mixed that American aims were never clearly defined beyond a vague desire to maintain a series of reasonably stable republics."[5]

As we shall discuss in Part III, considerations precisely like these also enter into any systematic analysis of contemporary aid allocation problems. Consequently, it can well be contended that the earlier aid experience is relevant to the present study.

Yet, if these earlier examples are not entirely incidental, neither are they fundamental to our present interest in the origins of aid to Southern Asia. In no case did questions of choice among recipients arise. The concept of a sustained economic and technical aid program as a tool of American foreign policy had not been formulated, and the collective size of the various economic aid missions was too small to justify comparison with contemporary economic and technical aid programs.

In the military sphere the relevance of earlier aid experience is perhaps still more tenuous. While the United States sent a number of military training and advisory missions abroad in the four decades preceding World War II, their purposes were limited to such things as training a local constabulary or police force, and, in the case of the Army Medical Corps missions, improving local public health conditions. In view of the special U.S. relationship to the Latin American recipient countries, none of the missions involved the broader questions of strategic objectives and priorities, or military "efficiency," with which contemporary military aid is so closely connected.

Perhaps more relevant was the exprience of the Combined Chiefs of Staff and the Combined Boards during World War II in allocating the military portion of the $40 billion of net Lend-Lease aid extended by the United States from 1941 to 1945. But here, too, the comparison has only limited merit. Allocation of military aid in "hot" war

[5] Curti and Birr, *op.cit.*, p. 205.

differs in some fundamental respects from the same problem in the context of "cold" war or competitive coexistence. In the former, strategic priorities are clearer and firmer. Military considerations dominate, and foreign policy considerations are secondary. Moreover, because the military pie to be allocated is continually growing, misallocations in one period tend to be more easily corrected in subsequent periods.

For these reasons we can confine our historical review to the period since World War II without much fear of overlooking experience that will be essential to our needs.

The following description of the background and origins of United States aid to Southern Asia is divided into two time periods. In the present chapter, we will consider United States war relief during the transitional years from V-J Day to the end of 1947. In Chapter 3, we will summarize U.S. external assistance activities from the Marshall Plan to mid-1950, when the first sustained programs of aid to Southern Asia began. For each period, the relevant international circumstances and domestic aid legislation will be briefly described. For both periods, our concern will be particularly with U.S. aid programs in other parts of Asia that influenced the timing and character of subsequent aid to the countries of Southern Asia. We will also try to keep in view those developments outside the Asian area, and in United States foreign policy generally, which affected the later aid programs in Southern Asia. The latter will be dealt with in detail in Part II.

B. The Postwar Transition, 1945-1947

United States assistance in the Asian area was initiated immediately following World War II, mainly through four programs that differed in administration and legislative authorization, but shared a common purpose. The four programs, in the order of their commencement, were: the United Nations Relief and Rehabilitation Program, administered multilaterally by the UNRRA Council, but financed largely (72 per cent) by United States contributions;[6] the Civilian Supply Program of the War Department, authorized after 1947 by the Congress as a program for Government and Relief in Occupied Areas (GARIOA); the Philippine war damage program, under the Philippine Rehabilitation Act of 1946; and the post-

---

[6] Unless otherwise indicated, all references to UNRRA are taken from Vol. II of George Woodbridge, *UNRRA*, 3 vols., New York, 1950.

UNRRA Relief Program, authorized by the Relief Assistance Act of 1947, which extended limited amounts of aid under direct U.S. administration after the termination of UNRRA in the summer of 1947.

1. The Amount and Purposes of Transitional Aid

Besides the differences in administrative jurisdiction, operationally the four programs related to different—though sometimes overlapping—groups of countries. Thus, UNRRA operated in liberated allied countries, while GARIOA encompassed the occupied belligerents, as well as Korea. In Asia, GARIOA operated in Japan and South Korea, while UNRRA activities centered mainly in China, and to a very limited extent in Korea and the Philippines. UNRRA operations in the Philippines were limited because of the separate and much larger bilateral U.S. war damage program. The limitation in Korea was due partly to Soviet occupation north of the 38th parallel, and partly to the servicing of most relief needs in South Korea by the GARIOA program. The approximate magnitudes of the four programs are summarized in Table 1.

The common purpose of these programs was to provide emergency relief to civilian consumption that had been depressed by the damage and dislocation of war. Thus, the UNRRA program was initiated in order to furnish "imports required to provide the basic essentials of life and to prevent economic retrogression which threatens the supply of these basic essentials."[7] The GARIOA version of the same objective was to provide "such minimum supplies for the civilian populations of such [occupied] areas as may be essential to prevent starvation, disease and unrest."[8]

The essentially similar purpose of the Relief Assistance Act of 1947 was "the provision of relief assistance to the people of countries devastated by war."[9]

Consequently, most of the aid provided under these programs was in the form of consumer goods, especially foodstuffs, clothing, or cotton and wool for local fabrication, and medical and health supplies. Virtually all of the listed GARIOA aid was in this form,

[7] Quoted by Undersecretary Clayton in *Relief Assistance to Countries Devastated by War*, Hearings before the Committee on Foreign Affairs, House of Representatives, 80th Congress, 1st session, Washington, D.C., 1947, p. 2.

[8] Supplemental Appropriation Act, 1948, cited in Brown and Opie, *op.cit.*, p. 109.

[9] Public Law 84, 80th Congress, 1st session, *Documents on American Foreign Relations, 1947*, Princeton, 1949, pp. 130-34. The Act, moreover, explicitly limited relief assistance to "food, medical supplies, processed and unprocessed materials for clothing, fuel, fertilizer, pesticides, and seed."

Table 1

UNITED STATES RELIEF GRANTS IN ASIA IMMEDIATELY AFTER
WORLD WAR II

(millions of dollars)

	UNRRA[a] (1945-47)	Civilian Supply and GARIOA[b] (1946-48)	Philippine Rehabilitation Act[c] (1946-50)	Post-UNRRA Relief[d] (1947-48)	TOTALS
China and Formosa	372.8 (517.8)			45.7	418.5
Japan and Ryukyus		1,200.0			1,200.0
Korea	.6 (.9)	326.0			326.6
Philippines	7.1 (9.9)		520.0		527.1
TOTALS	380.5	1,526.0	520.0	45.7	2,472.2

N.B. Figures are calendar year obligations rather than expenditures, except as otherwise noted. Expenditures typically lagged six months to a year behind obligations. Lend-Lease and surplus property grants and credits extended in the period immediately following the war are excluded both because of difficulties in valuing aid from wartime stocks and because such aid was more a direct war expense than it was civilian relief. Estimated lend-lease aid to China after V-J Day was $769 million (Brown and Opie, *op.cit.*, p. 316), while the surplus property, grants and credits in the Asian region were estimated at a sales value of $390 million, distributed among Burma, China, India, Indonesia, Japan, Korea, Thailand, and the Philippines—the latter under the terms of the Philippines Rehabilitation Act of 1946. See *Report of Activities of the National Advisory Council on International Monetary and Financial Problems*, House Document No. 239, 83rd Congress, 1st session, Washington, D.C., 1951, p. 61. Also excluded are the $70 million budgetary loan by the RFC to the Philippines in 1946, the $120 million used by China during 1945-47 from the U.S. Treasury's Stabilization loan—subsequently a grant—of 1942, and the $84 million in project loans made to China by the Export-Import Bank in 1945-1946, and disbursed over the next four years. *U.S. Relations with China*, Washington, D.C., 1949, p. 1047, and *Report of the National Advisory Council*, 1951, p. 61.

a Woodbridge, *op.cit.*, pp. 378, 460, 464. Figures in parentheses show total UNRRA aid. The U.S. share was arrived at by prorating among the Asian recipients the 72 per cent U.S. contribution to global UNRRA relief outlays. The figures exclude shipping and insurance.

b For the Japanese figure, see Brown and Opie, *op.cit.*, p. 353; GARIOA expenditures in Japan for fiscal years 1946-1948, inclusive, were $925 million. See "Foreign Aid of the U.S. Government, 1940-51," *Supplement to Survey of Current Business*, Washington, 1952, p. 89. Approximately $900 million of additional GARIOA aid was provided between 1949 and the end of 1951. For the Korean figure, see *Seventh ECA Report to Congress* (for the period October 1 to December 31, 1949), Washington, D.C., 1950, pp. 93-94. In Korea, the GARIOA program was superseded by the Korean Aid Program of ECA upon U.S. recognition of the Korean Republic on January 1, 1949.

c Shirley Jenkins, *American Economic Policy Toward the Philippines*, Stanford, 1954, pp. 49-52. $120 million of the aid extended under the Philippine Rehabilitation Act of 1946 was for rehabilitation of public property and services. The remainder was for payment of private relief claims.

d *Aid to China*, Amended Report of the Committee on Foreign Relations, 80th Congress, 2nd session, Washington, D.C., 1948, p. 6.

[16]

as was the post-UNRRA aid in China. In the Philippines, 77 per cent of the aid was provided in the form of cash payments on war damage claims rather than commodities. But here, too, as we shall discuss more fully below, most of the payments actually contributed to increased private imports of consumer goods.

2. Relief Aid to China and Northeast Asia

Only in the UNRRA program in China was the main purpose of relief to consumers supplemented by an attempt to contribute to the rehabilitation of productive plant and equipment. Dollar outlays for agricultural and industrial rehabilitation constituted 46 per cent of the $518 million total UNRRA expenditures in China from 1945-47,[10] although damage to the capital stock caused by China's continuing civil war during this period probably exceeded capital formation financed by UNRRA.

In both content and geographical coverage, United States relief aid in Asia grew out of particular political and economic circumstances existing in the immediate postwar period. On the China mainland and in Northeast Asia (Japan and Korea), U.S. aid was largely an extension or continuation of wartime responsibilities. In China, UNRRA and post-UNRRA aid—like similar aid in Europe—was intended to provide relief to an Allied power whose population as well as productive plant had been badly hurt by World War II. It was not, and was not conceived to be, an instrument of policy for reversing the internal political deterioration that ensued immediately after the war. Even the military aid extended to China, under Lend-Lease and surplus property agreements concluded just after the war, was related largely to the tasks of accepting the surrender of the three million Japanese troops in China and evacuating them from the country, rather than to the task of fighting communist military forces.

It should, of course, be recalled that the 1945-47 period, in Asia as in Europe, was regarded at the time by the United States as marking an abatement of hot war rather than an initiation of cold war. The wartime alliance with the Soviet Union, as well as the psychologically disarming impact of the Sino-Soviet Treaty of August 14, 1945, created expectations of at least a moderately coopera-

[10] Woodbridge, *op.cit.*, pp. 378, 421-47. UNRRA dollar expenditures on rehabilitation were mainly for agricultural, transport, and industrial equipment and construction materials, and, to a lesser extent, for industrial raw materials.

tive resolution of international political problems in the Far East that were not easily dispelled. Only with the growing evidence of intervention in China, of the mass removal of industrial equipment from Manchuria, and of intransigence in Korea, did Soviet intentions become clear in the Far East as they were becoming clear in Europe.

It is neither possible nor necessary here to attempt a review of U.S. relations with China in the early postwar period, a subject on which the literature is already abundant.[11] But to the extent that these relations bear directly on U.S. aid, they are relevant to this study. From this standpoint, it can be said that United States efforts to improve the internal political situation in China relied more on diplomacy, in the form of the Marshall mission of 1946-47 and the Wedemeyer mission of July-September 1947, than on aid. To the extent that aid was used at all, it was only by way of a promise of larger amounts of reconstruction loans from the Export-Import Bank, at such time as reasonable stability would be attained on the mainland and loans would carry with them "reasonable assurance of repayment."[12] In no sense were UNRRA and post-UNRRA aid a carrot tied to the diplomatic stick of the Marshall mission in its effort to bring about an improvement in the internal political situation in China.

We will return to this point later in discussing the China Aid Act

[11] On the various points cited in this and the preceding paragraph, see, for example, *Aid to China*, Senate Foreign Relations Committee Report, 1948, especially pp. 4-5; *Military Situation in the Far East*, Hearings Before the Senate Committee on Armed Services and the Committee on Foreign Relations, Washington, D.C., 1951, especially pp. 2071, 2169-2170, 3238-3242; John C. Campbell and Council on Foreign Relations, *The United States in World Affairs, 1945-1947*, New York, 1947, pp. 281-299; and the same authors' *The United States in World Affairs, 1947-1948*, New York, 1948, pp. 185-202; and *Relations with China*, 1949, pp. 939ff.

[12] The following testimony by the late Clarence E. Gauss, formerly Ambassador to China and President of the Export-Import Bank, is worth noting in this connection:

At the time [April 1946] that we earmarked the $500 million for China at the instance of General Marshall, we had hoped he had been able to perform a miracle; that he had been able to mediate and bring about peace in that country. If we had peace there, we would have had stability, we could have invested our $500 million in China, carefully, project-by-project, following it always to the end use, with a reasonable assurance of repayment. However, when China embarked upon a civil war—and I do not say who was at fault, with reference to the breakdown in negotiations—one could not feel that, if the resources available to China at that time were going to be thrown into that civil war, there was any assurance whatsoever of repayment.

U.S. Foreign Policy for a Postwar Recovery Program, Hearings Before the House Committee on Foreign Affairs, 80th Congress, 2nd session, Part 2, p. 2177, Washington, D.C., 1948. See also Export-Import Bank, *Fourth Semi-annual Report to Congress*, Washington, D.C., 1947, p. 8.

of 1948. Suffice it to say here that U.S. participation in both relief and military aid to China in the postwar period preceding 1948 can be more accurately viewed as an extension of wartime policies and tasks than as an active instrument of United States foreign policy in peacetime. It was not until Greek-Turkish aid and the European Recovery Program that the now-familiar connection between foreign aid and foreign policy was firmly established.

In Northeast Asia, too, U.S. involvement in foreign aid was a direct outgrowth of wartime responsibilities. Korea was in a somewhat anomalous position since it had been promised its independence by the United States, the United Kingdom, and China at Cairo in December 1943, and again at Potsdam in July 1945. However, having been part of the Japanese empire for the preceding thirty-five years, Korea was unable to assume the responsibilities of self-government immediately. Consequently, the United States and the Soviet Union assumed responsibility for occupying the country temporarily and for accepting the surrender of Japanese military forces, agreeing formally to divide this responsibility at the 38th parallel.[18]

In both Korea and Japan, GARIOA relief aid, financed as a part of the Military Establishment's annual appropriations, served as an adjunct to the occupation tasks of pacification, demilitarization, and democratization. Justified under the formula of "preventing disease and unrest," GARIOA aid contained at least a hint of the notion of using economic aid to help build "healthy" political conditions in the occupied countries, a purpose that was to become especially important for U.S. aid in later years. Though the notion was still incomplete, the initial thinking behind the GARIOA "disease and unrest" formula foreshadowed one of the fundamental themes of later U.S. aid policy in the underdeveloped areas of Southern Asia. In its inchoate form, the notion was illustrated by State Department testimony, in support of the GARIOA appropriation for 1947:

". . . the purpose of the State Department appearing today is not so much to explore the logistical details of the War Department's civilian supply program [GARIOA] as to voice the grave concern that the drastic cut made by the House would seriously jeopardize . . . our basic political objectives in the occupied areas. . . . I refer

[18] *Korean Aid,* Hearings Before the House Committee on Foreign Affairs, 81st Congress, 1st session, Washington, D.C., 1949, pp. 37ff.

of course to the policy of our Government to lay the foundation for a healthy growth of democracy in Germany and Japan. This nation, having expended billions of dollars on a war against dictatorships, has committed itself to a foreign policy in which full support will be given to democratic elements and latent democratic tendencies in the ex-enemy countries."[14]

3. Relief Aid to the Philippines

In contrast to the prominent role of U.S. relief aid in Northeast Asia and China, U.S. aid activities in the arc of Southern Asia were confined to the Philippines during this period. Nor are the reasons hard to find.

The political and economic problems of Southern Asia in the immediate postwar period were both numerous and potentially explosive. In most of the area, prewar nationalism had ripened into a popular will that was clear and uncompromising about what it was against, if not about what it was for. Yet opposition to colonialism was not the only characteristic that most of the countries of Southern Asia shared. The damage and dislocation of war, added to the already low levels of technology and productivity throughout the area, confronted the economies of the region with essentially similar economic problems as well.

In all of the countries of Southern Asia, per capita income was below prewar levels, and in most of them aggregate income was less than it had been before the war. Throughout the region, the relatively small amounts of prewar agricultural and industrial capital had been further reduced: in the Philippines, Indonesia, and Burma as the direct result of war damage and Japanese occupation; in India as a result of failure to replant and replace. Only for India was this reduction in capital stock partly counterbalanced by an accumulation of sterling balances in Great Britain as a result of India's wartime services and merchandise exports. Moreover, in all the countries of the area, the money supply had been swollen during the war by the expenditures of the Japanese occupation forces or by the Allied forces, and inflation was widespread. Finally, the international trade network, in which the region figured prominently before the war, had been disrupted. Trade within the region itself, which had pro-

---

[14] Testimony of Assistant Secretary of State Hilldring, *Military Establishment Appropriation Bill for 1947*, Hearings Before the Subcommittee on Appropriations of the Senate, 79th Congress, 2nd session, Washington, D.C., 1946, p. 87.

vided India, Malaya, and the Philippines with much of their marginal rice requirements, and Burma, Thailand, and Indochina with much of their foreign exchange earnings, was at a standstill. The global trade triangle, in which Southern Asia had been a heavy net importer from the European metropolitan powers and Japan, and a net exporter to the United States, was also disrupted.

These generally similar economic circumstances acquired political explosiveness because of the enhancement of economic aspirations throughout the region, both among the elites and, to a lesser extent, among the masses as well. But despite the gravity of both its political and economic problems, Southern Asia was not at first considered an area of primary U.S. interest or responsibility. In Northeast Asia and China, the United States had had a long record of involvement both during and before the war. In the Asian arc, with the exception of the Philippines, U.S. experience and concern were much more limited. Primary responsibility in the postwar, as in the prewar period was presumed to reside with the established colonial powers: with the British in the Indian subcontinent, Burma, and Malaya; the French in Indochina; and the Dutch in Indonesia. Only in the Philippines was the United States immediately and decisively involved during the 1945-47 period. The Philippine Rehabilitation Act of 1946—enacted two months before the Philippine Commonwealth became an independent Republic under the provisions of the Tydings-McDuffie Act of 1934—was a reflection of this involvement.[15]

The Rehabilitation Act was a positive, though limited, response to some of the main problems which the Philippines, no less than the other countries of Southern Asia, faced. Ostensibly, it differed from the GARIOA and UNRRA programs in Northeast Asia and China in that the basic aim of the Rehabilitation Act was to provide compensation for damage to Philippine property incurred during the war, rather than to provide relief to consumers. In practice, however, this distinction was reduced. Except for the $120 million spent for the reconstruction of public buildings and essential services, most of the remaining $400 million of war damage payments were for private claims of less than $500 (a fact that betokened a high marginal propensity to consume). The fact that during the period of the war damage payments total consumption in the Philippines rose substantially while total investment remained low, and that Philip-

[15] The Philippine Rehabilitation Act of 1946, P.L. No. 370, 79th Congress, 2nd session, *Documents on American Foreign Relations, 1945-1946*, Princeton, 1948, pp. 807-810.

[21]

pine imports of consumer goods rose absolutely as well as relative to imports of producer goods, tends to support the view that the major share of war damage aid was actually spent on consumption as in the case of GARIOA and UNRRA aid.[16]

4. Military Aid to the Philippines

Though the emphasis of early aid to the Philippines was thus on relief, mention should also be made of the beginnings of a modest military assistance program in the Philippines during the immediate postwar period. The Philippine Military Assistance Act, approved on June 26, 1946, was the first of the postwar military aid programs undertaken by the United States.[17]

In part, the Military Assistance Act provided evidence of U.S. military support—as the Rehabilitation Act provided evidence of U.S. economic support—for the President's proclamation of Philippine independence on July 4, 1946. However, it also afforded some interesting precedents for the later Mutual Defense Assistance Program (MDAP), which began in 1949. Thus, the Military Assistance Act authorized training and equipping of the Philippine Armed Services, "consistent with military and naval requirements of the United States and with the national interest," and on "such terms and conditions as [the President] shall find proper." The primary condition actually involved was embodied in an agreement, finally concluded on March 14, 1947, to allow the United States to continue to use fifteen military bases for a lease period of ninety-nine years in the interest of "mutual protection and the maintenance of peace in the Pacific."[18] The Philippine bases agreement provided a significant precedent and objective

---

[16] Cf. Jenkins, op.cit., p. 172; *Report of the Economic Survey Mission to the Philippines*, Washington, D.C., 1950, pp. 40, 102-104; and Economic Survey Mission to the Philippines, *Technical Report on Foreign Trade*, Washington, D.C., 1950, pp. 1-2.

[17] On July 16, 1946, an act, authorizing the transfer to China of certain naval equipment excess to U.S. needs, was also approved by the President. More limited in scope than the Philippine Military Assistance Act, the China act did not involve either authorization for new appropriations or for any equipment other than naval "vessels and craft." Actually, the purpose of the China act was to provide a substitute for earlier Lend-Lease military aid to China, authority for which expired at the end of June 1946. Naval equipment with an estimated original procurement cost of $141 million was transferred to China by the time the subsequent China Aid Act of 1948 provided appropriations of $125 million for new military supplies. *Documents on American Foreign Relations, 1945-1946*, Princeton, 1948, pp. 804-805; and Brown and Opie, op.cit., pp. 322-323.

[18] *United Nations Treaty Series*, Vol. 43, p. 272. For the text of the Philippine Military Assistance Act, see *Documents on American Foreign Relations, 1945-1946*, pp. 817-819.

for subsequent Mutual Defense Assistance programs in other areas, notably Western Europe, Saudi Arabia, and Spain. One week after signature of the bases agreement, a Military Assistance Agreement was concluded with the Philippines, establishing a Military Advisory Group and beginning a program of training and equipment assistance involving $19.8 million authorized from the Military Establishment's 1947 appropriation.

5. *Developments in Global United States Foreign Policy*

In both content and geographical emphasis, other United States aid programs in the Asian area continued with little change for the remainder of 1947. But developments in global United States foreign policy during this period were of considerable significance for future aid activities in Asia. With enunciation of the Truman Doctrine on March 12, 1947, the United States recognized the growing threat of Soviet expansion and proposed immediately to meet it by a $400 million program of military and economic aid to Greece and Turkey, in the President's words, "to help . . . to maintain their free institutions and their national integrity against aggressive movements that seek to impose upon them totalitarian regimes."[19]

Passage of the Greek-Turkish Aid Act toward the end of May gave legislative confirmation to the proposed use of military and economic aid as key instruments of U.S. policy in the context of the newly emerging cold war. The Marshall speech of June, and the initial planning for the European Recovery Program by the Harriman, Krug, Nourse, and Herter Committees in the United States and by the sixteen-nation committee for European Economic Cooperation in Paris, were further reflections of this principle.[20] In its focus on the immediately more pressing economic aspects of the threat to Western Europe, ERP itself was, in a sense, a special application of the more general principles underlying Greek-Turkish aid.

Though these developments were global in their implications, they were initially confined to Europe. For the remainder of 1947, only two changes occurred in U.S. aid to Asia. Both concerned China in an incidental way, and both were relatively minor in importance.

In anticipation of the pending dissolution of UNRRA, Congress

[19] *Documents on American Foreign Relations, 1947*, p. 648.
[20] For detailed accounts of the connections among the Truman Doctrine, Greek-Turkish aid, and ERP, see Joseph M. Jones, *The Fifteen Weeks*, New York, 1955; Price, *op.cit.*, pp. 3-48; and Brown and Opie, *op.cit.*, pp. 123-141.

passed the Relief Assistance Act (the so-called post-UNRRA Relief program), approved by the President on May 31, 1947. Of the $332 million subsequently appropriated under the Act, $27.5 million was allocated to China, and the remainder largely to Italy, Greece, Austria, and Trieste. The effect of the Relief Assistance Act was to shift UNRRA aid from multinational to bilateral administration without altering the program's emphasis on providing relief to civilian consumption.

Whereas the Relief Assistance Act was passed in anticipation of UNRRA's termination, the Foreign Aid Act of 1947 was initiated in anticipation of the start of the European Recovery Program. Approved by the President on December 17, 1947, one month after he had summoned a special session of Congress for this purpose, the so-called Interim Aid Program, which was initiated under the Foreign Aid Act of 1947, was originally intended by the Administration to aid France, Austria, and Italy only. Faced with an immediate food and fuel crisis, the three countries required aid before the planning connected with ERP had been completed, and after the funds appropriated under the earlier Relief Assistance Act had already been utilized. The Foreign Aid Act of 1947 was a response to this pressing need. Though authorizing and appropriating the full amount ($597 million) requested by the President for interim aid, the Congress also adopted a House amendment that added China to the three other countries eligible to receive interim aid. Eighteen million dollars from the total interim aid appropriation were obligated for the China Relief Program before the end of the fiscal year 1948.

The addition of China to the countries eligible to receive interim aid under the Foreign Aid Act of 1947 was not without significance from the standpoint of future United States aid programs in Asia. In both the Senate and House Hearings on interim aid, Secretary Marshall had encountered criticism of the Administration's failure to include Asia in general, and China in particular, in its immediate aid plans. Answering the first criticism, he stressed the need to decide about the relative priority of different regions as potential recipients of limited foreign aid funds. In his statement to both the Senate and House Committees, the Secretary argued: "In concentrating upon the problem of aid to Europe, I do not ignore the fact that there are other areas of the world beset by economic problems of tremendous gravity. But the very magnitude of the world problem as a whole requires a careful direction of our assistance to the critical areas where it can be most immediately effective."[21]

The statement was significant not only in its assertion of the actual policy priorities underlying U.S. foreign aid at the time, but in subsequent aid planning as well. It was also significant in its recognition of the basic problem of allocating foreign aid, namely the problem of deciding how to divide limited aid resources among alternative recipients and uses. While the problem was to recur in various forms throughout the subsequent years, Secretary Marshall's statement was probably the first official reference to it in the postwar period.

In response to criticism about excluding China from the interim aid proposals, Marshall stressed the basic differences between the situations in China and in Western Europe. In Europe, he argued, the essential requirement was for dollars "to pay for imports necessary to maintain the ordinary standards of living"; for what, in the later foreign aid vocabulary, was to be called "balance of payments" assistance. "On the other hand," Marshall continued, "when you turn to the Chinese . . . matter, you have quite evident to all of us, and particularly to those who have seen it, a chaotic situation. . . . Also, a very unhappy people. But they are not threatened with a change at the present time in their import procedure. They have resources to continue . . . for quite some months. . . . The character of the emergency we are dealing with is quite different as between the European situation and the Chinese situation."[22] Though indicating that the Administration was then considering a definite proposal for aid to China, Marshall stated that up to that time the China situation provided "no basis to act" and consequently urged its exclusion from the Foreign Aid Act of 1947.[23]

There was considerable opposition to the views expressed by Marshall in both the Senate and House Committees. Congressional inclusion of China among the countries eligible for interim aid, over the Administration's objections, was evidence of this opposition and of the influence of the more Asian-minded members of

[21] *Emergency Foreign Aid*, Hearings Before the House Committee on Foreign Affairs, 80th Congress, 1st session, Washington, D.C., 1947, p. 3.

[22] *Ibid.*, p. 23.

[23] *Interim Aid for Europe*, Hearings Before the Senate Committee on Foreign Relations, 80th Congress, 1st session, Washington, D.C., 1947, pp. 44ff. (As hereafter used, "Senate Hearings" refers to Hearings Before the Senate Foreign Relations Committee, and "House Hearings" refers to Hearings Before the House Foreign Affairs Committee.)

the legislature. Congressman Walter Judd, one of the more persistent, articulate, and influential members of the legislative group pressing for Asian aid at that time, and for the next decade as well, expressed an interesting and different point of view on both issues raised by Marshall. In reply to the Administration's views, Judd said: "I think we have got to win in Asia, too, or we will ultimately lose in Europe. I cannot myself vote . . . [for] holding the line on one front and then ignore another front equally vital to our future. Asia is vital to the program in Europe, because it will be all but impossible for England and France and several other European countries to get back on their feet, despite the assistance of the Marshall plan, unless they are able to return to something like the prewar pattern of trade that they had with Asia. And the key to the situation in Asia is China. If China is taken over by Communists, how long can India, Malaya, the East Indies, even the Philippines, resist the pressures?"[24]

In effect, Judd's argument was that the problem of determining regional aid priorities was more complicated than the Marshall statement implied. If we consider his remarks carefully, we see that Judd was making two points. First, he was contending that Asia and Europe were "equally vital," and hence questioning the policy priorities implicit in Marshall's testimony. Second, he was arguing that economic recovery and a political "win" in Europe required economic recovery and a political win in Asia because of the trade links between the two areas. In reply to Marshall, Judd's second argument urged aid to China on the basis of the then-novel "stack-of-cards" thesis that if China fell to communism, so would the rest of Asia. In effect, the two points advanced by Judd were analytically quite independent. The first said that more U.S. aid and effort were needed in Asia because Asia was as vital to the United States as was Europe. The second point said that more U.S. aid and effort were needed in Asia because of the latter's impact on European recovery, *even if Europe were considered more vital than Asia to U.S. interests.*

History does not entirely corroborate either of these arguments, but they are nonetheless important for their bearing on Asian aid and the problems of allocation we are interested in. Both arguments were to contribute to the development of Asian aid in the ensuing years.

[24] *Emergency Foreign Aid*, House Hearings, pp. 234-235. In a similar vein, see also pp. 27, 69, 253-255.

C. SUMMARY

The main characteristics of economic aid to Asia during the transitional period from 1945 through 1947 can be summarized briefly from the preceding account.

United States economic aid in the Asian area in the two and one-half years after World War II was a response to wartime damage and dislocation. Its principal goal was to provide relief to severely depressed civilian consumption, and it typically took the form of consumer goods and raw materials for local processing into consumer goods.

The programs in China and the Philippines were concerned also, but only to a limited extent, with the repair and rehabilitation of wartime damage to productive plant. Economic development was in no sense conceived as a goal for any of the early Asian programs.

In geographic coverage, Asian aid was initially confined to China, Northeast Asia, and the Philippines. The rest of Southern Asia was excluded largely because of a general U.S. presumption that the European metropolitan powers would resume their prewar responsibilities in the area.

UNRRA, GARIOA, post-UNRRA Relief, and Philippine war damage aid were each financed from different appropriations and administered by different agencies. Though they shared a similar purpose, each was regarded as a special case, unrelated to the others. As a result, questions of how best to allocate aid funds among different countries and alternative programs received little explicit notice during this period.

Conceived largely as an outgrowth of U.S. wartime responsibilities and commitments, the Asian aid programs in the immediate postwar period were not considered to be the active instrument of United States foreign policy that they were later to become. Though the emerging cold war called forth the new foreign policy principles of the Truman Doctrine and the Marshall Plan in Europe, the widely differing international circumstances in Asia delayed their application to that area. Nevertheless, the disease-and-unrest formula of GARIOA aid, the initiation of a Military Assistance Program as a complement to war damage aid in the Philippines, and the sharp disagreements between Congress and the Administration over China aid during this period, contributed to altering the U.S. approach to economic and military aid in the Asian area.

CHAPTER 3

THE ORIGINS OF UNITED STATES AID PROGRAMS
IN SOUTHERN ASIA (2)

A. THE ALTERED INTERNATIONAL CONTEXT, 1948-1950

WHILE the postwar years through 1947 were in general dominated by circumstances and power relationships identified with World War II, the 1948-50 period marked an expansion and intensification of cold war. Developments occurred in the international situation, in United States policy responding to it, and in United States economic and military aid as instruments of this policy, which in combination determined the form and content of the later Mutual Security Program in Asia.[1]

Like many convenient symbols, the term "cold war" is easier to use than to define. As used here, it refers to the existence of conflict, and the absence of a "big" war: conflict between the Soviet Union, its allies and Communist parties in other countries, on the one hand, and the United States and its allies, on the other; and the absence of a war in which the Soviet Union directly commits its own forces against those of the United States and its allies. It has been tersely defined as "the policy of making mischief by all methods short of war involving the Soviet Union in open hostilities."[2]

It is true that "mischief . . . short of war" antedates the 1948-50 period. The Soviet adventure in Azerbaijan in 1945-46, and satellite support for the Greek communists in 1946 and later, are cases in point. Yet the scale of mischief sharply intensified during 1948-50— the period of the iron curtain's descent over Czechoslovakia, East Germany, and North Korea, of the Berlin blockade and airlift, of the first Soviet atomic-weapons tests, of enlarged Soviet aid to and

---

[1] The year 1948 began with the Congressional Hearings on the European Recovery Program. However, ERP had been explicitly foreshadowed in the Hearings on Interim Aid during November 1947, and both programs had their origin in still-earlier changes in the international situation. See Chapter 2, section 5.

[2] *Defence in the Cold War*, Royal Institute of International Affairs, London, 1950, p. 12. The origin of the term "cold war" is hard to place. In October 1947, Walter Lippmann published a little book entitled *The Cold War* (New York, 1947), devoted to a critique of the philosophy of "containment." On January 8, 1948, Senator Vandenberg used the term in interrogating Secretary of State Marshall: "Has the Soviet Union officially, categorically, declared war, let's say declared cold war . . . ?" The response was affirmative, although the exchange did not suggest that the Senator had coined the phrase. *European Recovery Program*, Senate Hearings, 1948, p. 16.

formal recognition of the Chinese Communist regime, and finally of the North Korean attack at the end of June 1950. With this intensification came an increase in the frequency and types of wars "short-of-war," concentrated in the Asian region: the guerrilla wars in Viet Nam, Burma, and Malaya, continuing and rising in tempo throughout the period; the short-lived communist insurrection in Indonesia late in 1948; the larger-scale territorial war in China; and the not-so "short-of-war" hostilities in Korea.

The response of United States foreign policy to these developments in the international situation was a strong and repeated affirmation of the general principles first enunciated in the Truman Doctrine. Besides continued support for the United Nations and "the development of a world order in which each nation feels secure under law," the President in 1948 summarized the aims of U.S. policy:

". . . to assist free nations in creating economic conditions under which free institutions can survive and flourish . . . [and] to help free nations protect themselves against aggression."[3] The same principles were restated frequently in the ensuing years, and became a major and enduring part of American foreign policy.

In his annual State of the Union Message on January 5, 1949, the President, reaffirmed these aims as follows:

"We are following a foreign policy . . . to encourage free states and free peoples throughout the world, to aid the suffering and afflicted in foreign lands, and to strengthen democratic nations against aggression."[4] And toward the end of 1950, five months after the Korean war began, Secretary of State Acheson amplified the same basic ideas in outlining the "Strategy of Freedom." Besides support for the United Nations, the "development of regional groupings," "a readiness to negotiate," and "firm adherence to . . . moral values," he listed as the basic principles of American foreign policy: ". . . economic cooperation . . . [because] it contributes powerfully to the building of our defenses against external attack [and] also is an instrument for helping to build healthy societies in which the vitality and the promise of freedom find practical expression," as well as "the rapid building up of military strength at home and

---

[3] Address on "United States Policy Towards Peace," University of California, Berkeley, June 12, 1948, *Documents on American Foreign Relations, 1949*, p. 17.
[4] *Documents on American Foreign Relations, 1949*, p. 1.

among our allies." These principles, he noted significantly, "constitute a national policy, not a party policy."[5]

This is admittedly only the briefest outline of the far-reaching developments of the 1948-1950 period, both in the international situation generally and in the broad principles of U.S. policy responding to it. But our purpose here is not that of historical description, which would require more extensive treatment of these matters.[6] Instead, our purpose is the limited one of providing perspective for discussing those developments in United States economic and military aid during the period that significantly influenced the scope and character of later aid programs in Southern Asia. This discussion is more directly relevant to our main interests, and the remainder of this chapter will be devoted to it.

We will consider, in turn, the five major bilateral United States assistance programs initiated during this period: the European Recovery Program; the China Aid Program; the Korean Aid Program; the Mutual Defense Assistance Program (MDAP); and the Technical Cooperation (Point Four) Program. Besides giving a summary of the authorizing and appropriations legislation for each program, its influence on later U.S. economic and military aid to Southern Asia will be briefly discussed. What were the declared objectives and operating experience that provided precedents for subsequent aid programs in Southern Asia? What decisions, and methods for arriving at decisions, concerning the allocation of aid funds in 1948-1950, were relevant for later allocation decisions on U.S. aid in Southern Asia?

Admittedly, these questions are broad and imprecise. Our answers to them will be interpretive rather than rigorous. But our aim in this discussion is the limited one of providing background for the later discussion of aid programs in Southern Asia during the period 1951-1957.[7]

---

[5] *Documents on American Foreign Relations, 1950*, pp. 12-15.

[6] For a detailed discussion, see The Council on Foreign Relations volumes *The United States in World Affairs, 1948* (by John C. Campbell), *1949* and *1950* (both by Richard P. Stebbins); and William Reitzel, Morton A. Kaplan, and Constance G. Coblenz, *United States Foreign Policy 1945-55*, Washington, D.C., 1956, especially pp. 99-279.

[7] It should be noted that the preceding chapter dealt mainly with U.S. aid activities in Asia. Two of the five programs to be considered here are almost entirely concerned with aid to Europe. Both ERP and MDAP had significant, if indirect, influences on aid to Southern Asia. Consequently, some discussion of these programs is relevant to our purpose here, whereas relief aid to Europe in the 1945-1947 period was not.

B. FROM RELIEF TO RECOVERY IN EUROPE

1. *The Altered Character of United States Aid*

As previously suggested, U.S. foreign assistance in the immediate postwar period was largely an outgrowth of wartime circumstances and responsibilities. Until the initiation of Greek-Turkish aid in March, 1947, foreign aid tended to be viewed primarily as a temporary means of relieving some of the hardships of war. The ends towards which aid was directed were conceived principally in terms of good-will and friendship in the case of relief aid to our wartime allies and, in the occupied countries, in terms of facilitating the physical tasks of the occupation forces by preventing "disease and unrest."

It is true, of course, that the United States and its wartime allies had anticipated longer-term and larger-scale problems of reconstruction, development, and trade restoration in the postwar period. Extensive planning had been undertaken during the war in anticipation of these problems, culminating in the Bretton Woods agreements. But the terms in which the problems and their solutions were viewed, during the war and throughout most of the 1945-1947 transition, had been essentially multilateral. The use of bilateral, intergovernmental aid as a continuing tool of American foreign policy had been neither desired nor foreseen. Instead, long-term lending by the International Bank for Reconstruction and Development (IBRD), combined with assistance from the International Monetary Fund to relieve temporary balance of payments difficulties, were to be the principal means of rebuilding Western Europe, developing the underdeveloped areas, and supporting the restoration and expansion of international trade.

That these plans were abandoned was due both to miscalculations and to unforeseen circumstances. Not only was the reconstruction task in Western Europe (let alone the development task in the underdeveloped areas) a much larger one than had been originally anticipated; in addition, repayment of much of the resources required for European reconstruction could not be reasonably anticipated. Hence, the role of the IBRD was bound to be more limited than had been hopefully expected. Most important of all, abandonment of the multilateralism of Bretton Woods was due to the profound change in the international environment, more particularly to the breakdown of cooperation with the Soviet Union and the growing threat of communism in Western Europe.

As a consequence, the attitude of the United States toward foreign aid underwent a fundamental change. As first embodied in Greek-Turkish aid in 1947, and as elaborated in the several aid programs of the 1948-1950 period, which are discussed below, bilateral economic and military aid came to be viewed as major instruments of a United States foreign policy whose central objective was to strengthen the will and capacity of free countries to resist communism.

This change in the broad objectives of United States foreign policy was accompanied by basic changes in the character of U.S. aid programs. In Europe, for example, economic aid concentrated on recovery instead of relief. Where earlier aid had focused on consumption, the initial emphasis of ERP, and of other economic aid initiated during the 1948-1950 period under the influence of the ERP precedent, focused on production and investment. Instead of viewing need for aid in terms of essential consumption requirements only, ERP considered need in terms of *total* resources required to raise production sufficiently to attain equilibrium in the recipient country's international payments.

The change of intent and approach was reflected, for example, in the altered provisions of the enabling legislation for European aid drawn up after 1947. The Relief Assistance Act of 1947[8] explicitly limited commodities to be provided under the Act to specific consumer goods (food, medical supplies, clothing, fuel, and pesticides) and certain categories of non-durable producer goods for agricultural use (fertilizer and seed). The Foreign Aid Act of 1947[9] contained the same limitation with the added provision that not more than 5 per cent of the funds made available under the Act could be used to procure other categories of "incentive goods . . . to increase the production or distribution of locally produced commodities." By contrast, the ERP enabling legislation—the Economic Cooperation Act of 1948—asserted the main purpose of assistance under the Act to be "promoting industrial and agricultural production in the participating countries" so that they would "become independent of extraordinary outside economic assistance." The restrictions on the commodity content of the assistance that were

[8] Chapter 2, above, p. 24.
[9] *Ibid.*

contained in the earlier legislation were dropped, and the need for including producer durables as well as any other "commodity, material, article, supply, or goods necessary" was acknowledged.

2. *Some Qualifications: The Problem of Aid Substitutability*

In evaluating these changes, we must avoid the fallacy of identifying the economic impact of aid with the commodity content of aid. Aid provided in the form of consumer goods may, for example, release previously employed productive factors or mobilize unemployed productive factors for purposes of capital formation in the recipient country. Conversely, aid provided in the form of capital goods may release productive factors, which otherwise would have been used to produce such goods, for the production of consumer goods. Substitutability may also operate in terms of the recipient country's international trade, without causing any redirection of internal resources. Aid in the form of consumer goods may substitute in whole or in part for similar imports that the recipient would have financed itself, thereby freeing foreign exchange for importing capital goods. Alternatively, aid in the form of capital goods may simply substitute for a country's planned imports of such goods, thereby freeing foreign exchange for importing consumer goods.

In cases where the interests of donor and recipient diverge, aid substitutability plainly increases the difficulty of effective donor control over the net or "real" impact of aid. The result is to raise a number of interesting questions concerning the effects of aid and the allocation of aid between ostensibly different program uses (for example, between "economic" assistance and "military" assistance) in Southern Asia no less than other areas; questions to which there are no entirely satisfactory answers, but rather alternative assumptions of different plausibility in particular cases. We need not dwell on the substitutability problem here. Appendix I considers it analytically,[10] and we shall return to it in some of the subsequent discussion of interprogram aid allocation in Southern Asia.

However, quite apart from aid substitutability, there are other qualifications that should be added to the sharp distinction we have suggested between the character of economic aid in the 1945-1947 and the 1948-1950 periods. While production and investment, in relation to the achievement of balance of payments equilibrium,

[10] See Appendix I.

became explicit concerns of economic aid programs, providing for minimum essential consumption requirements was hardly less important, though it was less explicit, than in the earlier relief programs. In the calculations of ERP aid requirements, at the program's inception and increasingly in the next two years, stress was laid on relating aid requirements to the amount of investment and production necessary to lower imports and raise exports in order to balance Western Europe's international dollar accounts in four years, without further external assistance. Yet implicit in such calculations were assumptions as to the "minimum," or "reasonable," or "tolerable" levels below which consumption could not be allowed to fall—assumptions that were qualitatively, if not always quantitatively, the same as those underlying the earlier relief programs.[11]

Nevertheless, even after these qualifications are recognized, the shift in emphasis between the two periods remains substantial. Economic aid in Europe faced new and quite different tasks during the 1948-1950 period, and both its objectives and magnitude expanded.

3. The European Recovery Program and Southern Asia

Under the Economic Cooperation Act of 1948, as amended in 1949, $8.7 billion were authorized and appropriated for European recovery grants between April 3, 1948, when the Act became law, and the end of fiscal year 1950. During fiscal year 1951, an additional $2.2 billion were authorized and appropriated.[12] ERP aid far exceeded U.S. aid outside Europe during the 1948-1950 period. Yet planning and operation of aid to Europe actually served to focus U.S. attention on non-European areas, notably on Southern Asia, more sharply than during the immediate postwar period. What accounted for this paradox?

Part of the explanation was that the basic policy behind ERP was so clearly articulated and so highly regarded at the program's inception as to invite application to other areas. ERP, no less than

[11] The quoted terms occur frequently in the requirements discussions. See, for example, "European Recovery and American Aid" by the President's Committee on Foreign Aid (Harriman Report), in *The European Recovery Program—Basic Documents and Background Information*, prepared by the Staffs of the Senate Foreign Relations Committee and the House Foreign Affairs Committee, Washington, D.C., 1947, pp. 113ff.; "Methods and Sources of Estimates for Cost of European Recovery Program," submitted by the Department of State, in *European Recovery Program*, Senate Hearings, Part 3, 1948, Appendix pp. 1456ff.; and Price, *op.cit.*, pp. 43-44, 92-94.

[12] Brown and Opie, *op.cit.*, p. 247. The figures cited are in addition to $1.4 billion in loans and investment guaranties authorized under the ERP legislation.

later Asian aid programs, was motivated by a multiplicity of over-lapping and sometimes conflicting objectives: political, economic, humanitarian, and strategic. But dominant among these objectives was restoration of Europe's social and political strength through the use of economic means. In the ECA Act of 1948, the policy behind ERP was expressed in these terms:

". . . Congress finds that the existing situation in Europe endangers the establishment of a lasting peace, the general welfare and national interest of the United States, and the attainment of the objectives of the United Nations. The restoration or maintenance in European countries of principles of individual liberty, free institutions, and genuine independence *rests largely upon the establishment of sound economic conditions,* stable international economic relationships, and the achievement by the countries of Europe of a healthy economy independent of outside assistance. The accomplishment of these objectives calls for a plan of European recovery."[13]

The statement, of course, applied explicitly to Europe. In the course of the annual ERP Congressional Hearings from 1948 to 1950, the Administration repeatedly expressed its view that the same policy was not necessarily applicable to the Far East and Southern Asia, that conditions there were fundamentally different, in particular that a basis for using economic means to build stronger political communities did not exist.

Nevertheless, Congressional pressure mounted for applying the policy of ECA to Asia. In part, this pressure was due to domestic politics and to special Congressional advocacy of more U.S. assistance to Nationalist China. But Congressional pressure for aid to Southern Asia was also due to the fact that ECA's objectives and premises, as expressed in the ECA Act, seemed to be quite general in their implications. Bipartisan Congressional initiative was in large part responsible for urging and obtaining their application in Southern Asia.[14]

[13] Italics added.
[14] From the standpoint of later Congressional concern for "economy" in foreign aid, the strong Congressional influence to extend the policy implicit in ERP to Southern Asia is of particular interest. To elaborate more fully the statements made in the text would take us too far from our main purpose. The Senate and House Hearings on ERP during the 1948-1950 period are, however, full of illustrations. See, for example, *U.S. Foreign Policy for a Post-War Recovery Program,* House Hearings, 1948, pp. 97, 245, 2174-2175; *Extension of ERP,* Senate Hearings, 1950, pp. 97-101. Interestingly enough, Democratic Congressmen played nearly as active and influential a role in the cited testimony as did Republicans.

Another factor contributing to the influence ERP had in directing attention to Southern Asia was the latter's role in Western Europe's trade. Historically, Southern Asia was (and is) one of Western Europe's important regional trading partners. In 1948, at the start of ERP, merchandise exports from Southern Asia to Western Europe amounted to $1.8 billion, or about 7 per cent of Western Europe's total imports.[15] Europe's pre- and postwar sources of rubber, tin, tea, and copra were in Southern Asia. With the progress of European recovery, Europe's demand for these and other commodities was bound to rise. If the recovery of European industry was not to be hampered by rising import costs, increased output and exports were needed from Southern Asia.

Southern Asia was also traditionally an important market for European manufactures. In 1948, Southern Asia's imports from Western Europe were $2.2 billion, or about 12 per cent of Western Europe's total exports.[16] Increased real income in Southern Asia was therefore likely to contribute to European recovery by raising the demand for European exports.

The importance of Southern Asia for European recovery was a theme that recurred in the Congressional Hearings on ERP, and was one of the more frequently used arguments by which the Asian-minded members of Congress sought, and were able, to direct Administration attention to the needs of Southern Asia.[17]

[15] The export figure is the sum of individual country exports from Burma, Ceylon, India, Indonesia, Malaya, Pakistan, the Philippines, and Thailand to Western Europe, including the United Kingdom. *Economic Bulletin for Asia and the Far East*, November 1956, pp. 77-79. The total imports for Western Europe are from *International Financial Statistics*, April 1957, pp. 22-25. Since the referenced exports and imports are f.o.b. and c.i.f. respectively, the 7 per cent ratio is slightly low. For 1938, the share of the same countries' exports in total Western European imports was just over 6 per cent. *The Network of International Trade*, Geneva, 1942, pp. 46-47.

[16] The import figure is the sum of the same eight countries' imports from Western Europe. See *Economic Bulletin for Asia and the Far East*, November 1956, pp. 77-79. Total European exports are from *International Financial Statistics*, April 1957, pp. 22-25. The 12 per cent figure is slightly high because the Asian imports are c.i.f. while European exports are f.o.b. in the referenced sources. For 1938, Southern Asia's imports were only 6 per cent of total European exports. See *The Network of International Trade*, pp. 46-47.

[17] The following exchange between Secretary Marshall and Congressman Javits during the first ERP Hearings in 1948 is an interesting illustration:

Javits: Is it not a fact also that raw materials supplies must flow to the nations we are trying to aid; in other words, that they need such materials for recovery and that those material supplies would come in part from Asia and the East Indies?

Marshall: I think quite a bit is due from those countries.

Javits: So that stability in that area of the world and some measure of pro-

Western Europe's *political* involvement in Southern Asia was also instrumental in attracting the attention of U.S. policymakers, primarily concerned with ERP, to Southern Asia during the 1948-50 period. One instance of this involvement was the direct use of ERP aid, allotted to the Netherlands, to finance imports into Indonesia. Since Indonesia was then part of the Dutch currency area, its net dollar imports were a charge on Holland's dollar accounts and hence an additional claim on ERP aid. From the start of ERP until December 31, 1950, $101 million of ERP commodity aid went to Indonesia, or about 13 per cent of total ERP grants to the Netherlands.[18] With the exception of earlier aid to the Philippines, ERP aid to Indonesia, extended largely in the form of textiles and foodstuffs unrelated to any internal investment program, was the first U.S. economic assistance to any part of Southern Asia in the postwar period.

In the cases of both the Netherlands and France, political involvement in Southern Asia imposed a direct financial burden on the metropolitan economy, and an indirect burden on the Dutch and French dollar accounts. Although no ERP aid was directly earmarked for Indochina, the ECA mission in Paris estimated that annual French military and civil outlays for Indochina were $475 million during the 1948-50 period, an amount equivalent to roughly half the average annual ERP dollar aid to France.[19] These were franc rather than dollar outlays, and did not entail a commensurate dollar drain on the French economy. Nevertheless, at least some of the resources required by France in Indochina would otherwise have been available for reducing French dollar imports, increasing dollar exports, or increasing domestic investment, thereby sooner or later

---

ductive recovery there is also essential to the success of our plans?

Marshall: It is certainly connected with it. . . .

Javits: Does that lead, Mr. Secretary, to the deduction that to make a success of the ERP, we must immediately proceed to deal with economic rehabilitation problems in both Latin America and the Far East?

Marshall: We certainly have those matters to be considered. We are very shortly going to bring up to the Congress the problem on China. To what extent we would get into the general economic situation in the Far East as it relates to all the other countries concerned out there, I am not prepared to say at the present time.

U.S. Foreign Policy for a Post-War Recovery Program, House Hearings, 1948, Part 1, p. 97.

[18] *Eleventh Report to Congress of the United States Economic Cooperation Administration*, for the quarter ended Dec. 31, 1950, Washington, D.C., 1951, p. 34, and *Operations Report*, International Cooperation Administration, Washington, D.C., March 31, 1956, p. 43.

[19] *Extension of ERP*, Senate Hearings, 1950, pp. 178-81; and *To Amend the ECA Act of 1948 as Amended*, House Hearings, 1950, Part 1, pp. 86-87.

reducing France's need for aid. Dutch expenditures arising from the Netherlands' involvement in Indonesia imposed a similar indirect burden on ERP aid requirements.[20]

The political involvement of the Netherlands in Indonesia also linked ERP to developments in Southern Asia in a unique and interesting way. In mid-December 1948, the Netherlands launched a "police" action against the Republic of Indonesia in violation of a truce agreement between the disputants negotiated under United Nations auspices nearly a year earlier. The United States responded by suspending the Indonesian component of ERP aid to the Netherlands, and in the Security Council strongly condemned the Dutch action. Within two months of the partial suspension of ERP aid, the Dutch resumed the negotiations with the Indonesian Republic that led to Indonesia's independence at the end of 1949. Actually, suspension of ERP aid to Indonesia was less decisive in bringing about this result than the implicit threat that accompanied it of suspending direct ERP aid to the Netherlands, as well.[21]

But both the threat and the actual, if partial, suspension demonstrated a growing concern of U.S. policy with Southern Asia, as well as a willingness to use economic aid—in this case, the denial of aid—as an instrument for achieving political results in Southern Asia no less than in Europe. In this sense, and through their influence on Congressional interest in Southern Asia generally, the events in Indonesia in 1948-49 contributed to the beginnings of direct United States aid in Southern Asia in 1950.[22]

C. THE CHINA AID PROGRAM

1. Objectives and Influence of China Aid

The China Aid Program was initiated as a sequel to and an expansion of Interim Aid and post-UNRRA relief aid to China. Enacted on April 3, 1948, as part of the same omnibus foreign assistance

[20] See, for example, the testimony by the ECA mission chief in the Netherlands, *Extension of ERP*, House Hearings, 1949, Part 1, pp. 260-265.

[21] During September-October 1948, the Indonesian Republic had effectively suppressed an internal communist insurrection. This was one of the reasons for the firmness of U.S. action in December in support of the Republic.

[22] For testimony reflecting the considerable Congressional interest occasioned by the Indonesian situation, see, for example, *Extension of ERP*, House Hearings, 1949, pp. 260-273; and *Extension of ERP*, Senate Hearings, Foreign Relations Committee, 1949, pp. 319-326ff.

legislation which authorized ERP,[23] the China Aid Act authorized $338 million for economic aid to China for fiscal year 1949, of which $275 million was appropriated, and $125 million for military aid, all of which was appropriated.[24]

Aid to the mainland was ineffective in arresting the rapidly deteriorating military and political situation in China. From the standpoint of the broad objectives set forth in the enabling act ("to achieve internal peace and economic stability . . . to maintain the genuine independence and administrative integrity of China, and to sustain and strengthen principles of individual liberty and free institutions in China through a program of assistance based on self-help and cooperation"), there were few, if any, discernible payoffs from the program. After November 1949, the Nationalist Government left the mainland, and all subsequent U.S. aid to China was directed to Formosa.

It is beyond the scope of this study to discuss the China Aid Program in detail.[25] But several facts about the program had a major influence on the initiation and operation of U.S. aid to Southern Asia, and these are relevant.

In a sense, the most significant feature of the 1948-49 China Aid Program was its failure. As previously noted, during the hearings and debates on foreign aid in the immediate postwar years, Congressional criticism of the Administration's alleged neglect of Asia was frequent and mounting in severity.[26] In part, this criticism derived from a concern rather than a lack of concern for recovery in Europe. But, in large part, Congressional criticism was quite independent of events in, and U.S. policy toward, Europe. Besides its direct relation to domestic American politics, Congressional criticism sprang from a mixture of frustration and dismay at the spread of communism in China, and a fear of its spread elsewhere in Asia. Coupled with this criticism was a belief that an expanded program

[23] Title i of the Foreign Assistance Act of 1948 was the Economic Cooperation Act; Title iv was the China Aid Act.

[24] Actually, the Act did not mention military aid explicitly. However, in reporting out the proposed China aid legislation, both the Senate Foreign Relations Committee and the House Foreign Affairs Committee indicated clearly their intent in proposing the "special" $125 million grant. See *Aid to China*, Amended Report of the Senate Committee on Foreign Relations, 1948, pp. 9-10. All of the $125 million was obligated and spent for military items; *U.S. Relations with China*, 1949, pp. 952-953ff.

[25] For detailed accounts, see Price, *op.cit.*, pp. 179-187; and *U.S. Relations with China*, pp. 387-404 and pp. 1006-1042.

[26] See Chapter 2, section 5.

of U.S. economic and military aid to the Nationalist Government could and should, even if at a cost of less aid to Europe, reverse the trend in China. Congressional initiative in including China among the countries eligible for Interim Aid in the Foreign Assistance Act of 1947 was one reflection of this attitude. Another was the repeated Congressional attempt, during the early hearings on Interim Aid and ERP in 1947 and early 1948, to expedite the Administration's submission of a companion aid proposal for China.[27]

Failure of the China Aid Program and the loss of the mainland in the fall of 1949, focused the Administration's attention on other parts of Asia, and especially on Southern Asia. Within five months of the cessation of aid to mainland China, a U.S. mission (the Griffin Mission) was sent to survey the needs of Southeast Asia for economic and technical assistance.[28] It is fair to say that the desire to avoid "another China," no less than the desire of the Administration to avoid further Congressional attacks on its Asian policy, determined the timing of United States aid to Southern Asia.[29]

2. Economic Versus Military Aid:
The "Lesson" of China

Besides its effect on timing, the China Aid Program also influenced the concept behind and the character of subsequent United States aid to Southern Asia. Consideration by Congress of aid to China had, from its inception, occasioned the first discussion of what has been a continuing issue in foreign aid, namely, the relative merits

[27] See *Emergency Foreign Aid*, House Hearings, 1947, pp. 14-15, 23ff.; and *U.S. Policy for a Post-War Recovery Program*, House Hearings, 1948, Part 1, pp. 43-44, 298-299.

[28] The Griffin Mission did not visit the countries of South Asia. See Chapter 4, below, pp. 84-85.

[29] The following exchange between Congressman Judd and an Administration witness testifying in support of the proposed Point Four legislation (see below, pp. 57ff.) is suggestive of the connection between the China experience and the genesis of U.S. aid in Southern Asia:

Mr. Judd: From what you have heard from people who have associated with the Communists, do you think they intend to extend to Southeast [Asia] the same effort they have carried on so successfuly in China?

Mr. Moyer: There is considerable evidence to that effect.

Mr. Judd: Do you see any essential difference between those countries and China which leads you to believe they will be able to resist the kind of thing to which China has succumbed . . . ? If we do not make an effort to do something, it is very unlikely those countries will be able to resist this tide on their own. Would you say that?

Mr. Moyer: I would certainly say that our assistance would be very important. *Act for International Development*, House Hearings, 1950, Part 2, p. 372.

of economic and military aid. The issue involves some of the same analytical considerations we have previously referred to in connection with the problem of aid substitutability. Moreover, in this case, the distinction between economic and military aid may have been more valid than the earlier one between consumer goods and producer goods.[30] We shall return to these and other aspects of the distinction between military and economic aid in later sections of this study.[31] Here, we are interested in the way the issue arose in connection with China Aid.

In the initial discussion of China Aid in Congress, military reverses suffered by the Nationalist forces led to strong advocacy of military aid and of the prospective gains to be derived from it. The argument was not for military aid *instead* of economic aid, but rather for military aid as a *complement* to economic aid. Until reasonable conditions of military security were established in China, programs of economic improvement could not progress very far. By contributing to internal security, military aid was therefore considered likely to increase the gains from economic aid and to be a necessary concomitant of such aid.[32]

By contrast, the official stand of the Administration was that deterioration of the situation in China was not due to military causes, nor could it be reversed by military aid. The inability of the Nationalist government to halt the communist advance was not due to its lack of military hardware. Nationalist reversals, it was suggested, were due instead to the government's lack of administrative capacity and integrity, and to its resulting loss of public confidence. Secretary Marshall, in a statement typical of many, summarized this view as follows: "There has developed in China a very deep feeling on the part of the lowest classes . . . that the Government does not regard their interests as of great importance . . . Particularly in the conduct of guerrilla warfare, the feeling of the population plays a tremendous part in the factors of success of tactics, of strategy and

---

[30] See above, pp. 33-34. Given China's limited production-and-trade possibilities for securing military end items during the 1948-49 period, the end-item content of military aid was very likely to be additional to what otherwise would have been available. The degree of substitutability of military aid was in all probability limited at that time. See the discussion of "Case I" and "Case II" substitutability in Appendix I.

[31] Cf. Chapter 5, section C.3, and Chapter 6, section B.2.

[32] For some statements of this view, see *Emergency Foreign Aid*, House Hearings, 1947, pp. 234-255; *U.S. Foreign Policy for a Post-War Recovery Program*, House Hearings, 1948, 1903-1910, pp. 2068-2069; and *Aid to China*, Senate Foreign Relations Committee Report, 1948, pp. 9-10.

of everything that pertains to it. . . . You can provide unlimited quantities of materiel, but you must have certain fundamental things in that military force, or the materiel is of very moderate importance. . . . You must have effective leadership; you must have a leadership which does not lose morale by its characteristics."[33]

Some advocates of this view even argued that the military position of the Nationalist Government would be *improved* by a reduction in the size of its military forces.[34] In any event, the argument ran, economic aid—if it could contribute to reform and improvement within the government and a lessening of inflationary pressures in the economy—*might* contribute to stability; military aid would certainly not.

The official view was reflected in President Truman's original message on aid to China in February 1948, which requested $570 million for economic aid and no funds for military aid. The Congressional view was reflected and adopted in the China Aid Act of 1948, which provided for military aid in the form of "special" grants to the extent of 27 per cent of the total funds authorized.

Despite legislative enactment of the special grant for military aid, the program's operating experience on the mainland during 1948 and 1949 actually provided some limited evidence in support of the Administration's view of the primacy of economic aid. Thus, the last provinces of the mainland to fall were Kwangsi, Szechuan, and Kwangtung. These were also the provinces in which the community development work of the Joint Commission on Rural Reconstruction, initiated with U.S. economic aid, had progressed the farthest in its efforts "to eliminate some of the root causes of poverty and unrest." Moreover, in several coastal cities, like Canton and Swatow, ECA—the agency responsible for administering China Aid—believed its program had been "an important, and at times crucial, factor in reducing unrest."[35] Clearly, it was not possible in any rigorous way to disentangle cause and effect in this situation. But the particular combination of circumstances suggested a possibility

[33] *U.S. Foreign Policy for a Post-War Recovery Program*, House Hearings, pp. 1562-1563.

[34] See, for example, *ibid.*, pp. 2173ff. The diseconomies of scale implied in this argument involved both intensification of inflation and inability to coordinate and command as large a military force as the Nationalist Government maintained.

[35] *Fourth Report to Congress of ECA, January-April 1949*, Washington, D.C., 1949, p. 77.

of tangible benefits deriving from economic aid which became part of the "lesson" attributed to the China experience.[36]

At the same time, much of the roughly $1 billion of U.S. military equipment, originally provided as Lend-Lease or surplus property grants and credits or as the initial installments on the China Aid Act military grants, increasingly appeared during 1948 and 1949 in the Communists', rather than the Nationalists', arsenal.[37] The obvious inference was drawn that military aid, though seemingly more direct and predictable in its consequences than economic aid, was actually unreliable and inappropriate in the Asian situation.[38] This was another part of the "lesson" of the China Aid experience.

3. A New United States Policy in Asia

Both parts of the China lesson decisively influenced United States policy toward free Asia. In the summer of 1949, while the situation on the China mainland was deteriorating rapidly and Congressional clamor for a U.S. policy for Asia was mounting, the State Department established a panel (the Jessup-Case-Fosdick panel) to review the Far Eastern policy of the United States. Drawing on some of the results of the panel's work, Secretary Acheson in January 1950 made a major statement on the objectives and intended instruments of U.S. policy in Asia.

Although recognizing that "the question of military security . . . is important," Acheson went on to say "we must clearly understand that the military menace is not the most immediate."[39] In dealing with U.S. strategic objectives, the Acheson statement identified "the essential parts of the defensive perimeter . . . [that] must and will be held." West of this Aleutians-Japan-Ryukyus-Philippines perimeter, U.S. objectives were less clearly defined, though they were explicitly limited by the declaration that "no person can guarantee these areas against military attack." Not only were U.S. strategic objectives defined narrowly, but the possible use of military aid in

[36] ECA concluded that the "program in China, despite growing chaos, was constructive and effective within its limited sphere of influence," *ibid.*, p. 77.

[37] *U.S. Relations with China*, 1949, pp. 323, 405-407.

[38] As Congressman Mansfield, another influential participant in the sustained Congressional discussions of Asia, stated later: "One thing that has always bothered me is that in effect our aid to China, at least in a military sense, the materials of war, rifles and what not, have eventually found their way into the hands of the Communists to be used against our friends." See *To Amend the ECA Act of 1948*, House Hearings, 1950, p. 27.

[39] For the text of the Acheson statement, see *Documents on American Foreign Relations, 1950*, pp. 426-433.

helping to achieve them was not mentioned. Instead, U.S. forces and guarantees within the perimeter, and national self-reliance and the United Nations outside the perimeter, were mentioned as the instruments for achieving military security in the free Asian area.

Moreover, the January statement went on to stress that there were other problems more pressing than military ones, problems arising from "the susceptibility of many countries in the Pacific area to subversion and penetration . . . that cannot be stopped by military means." Meeting these problems required, instead, assistance "to develop a soundness of administration of [the] new governments and to develop their resources and their skills so that they are not subject to penetration either through ignorance, or because they believe false promises or because there is real distress in their areas. If we can help that development . . . then we have brought about the best way that anyone knows of stopping this spread of communism."

In both its emphasis on the possibilities of economic assistance, and its implications concerning the limitations of military assistance, the Acheson statement drew heavily on the China Aid experience. In turn, the initiation of U.S. economic and technical aid to Southern Asia during the summer of 1950 was a direct outgrowth of the policy set forth in Acheson's January statement.

China Aid also affected initial United States aid to Southern Asia by providing the latter's financing and, indirectly, its legislative authorization as well. The China Aid Act carried an initial program authorization for one year, through April 3, 1949. By subsequent legislation, the $400 million actually appropriated under the Act were made available through June 30, 1950, for use in areas of China not under communist domination. However, the speed of the communist advance and the move of the Nationalist Government to Formosa delayed obligation of these funds. By the end of June, although all military aid authorized under the Act had been committed, over $89 million of economic aid funds were still unobligated.[40]

In the China Area Aid Act of 1950 (approved on June 5, 1950) the availability of these unobligated funds was continued through fiscal year 1951, and their use in the "general area of China," as well as China proper ("including Formosa"), was authorized. The legis-

[40] *Thirteenth Report to Congress of ECA*, for the quarter ended June 30, 1951, Washington, D.C., 1951, pp. 70-71.

lative history of the Act made explicit that the "general area of China" was intended to include South and Southeast Asia.[41] Moreover, the Act accorded the President wide leeway in the terms and conditions under which economic assistance could be extended to the general area of China, specifying only that it be used in "furtherance of the general objectives of the China Aid Act of 1948."[42] When United States technical and economic aid to Southern Asia began in the summer of 1950, its legislative and financial basis was the China Area Aid Act.

4. Allocation Aspects of China Aid

As previously noted, we are particularly concerned in this study with two types of decisions on allocations in the extension of foreign aid: allocations among countries, and allocations among programs or types of use.

The China Aid experience had some bearing on the latter question, little on the former. Initially aid to China did not involve any direct consideration of intercountry aid alternatives. Aid to Europe did provide ammunition for those in Congress who argued that U.S. policy was concentrating unduly on Europe to the exclusion of Asia. And, in a qualitative sense, this argument implied that United States foreign policy objectives would be better served by more assistance to China. But the implication was not pursued. When the discussion turned, both within the Executive Branch and in Congress, to the desirable amounts of aid, the requirements for and returns from aid to China were considered entirely separately from aid to Europe and other areas—for example, Korea.

A partial exception to this generalization appeared in 1950, after the China Aid Program had shifted to Formosa. Nearly one-third of the $275 million originally appropriated for aid to the China mainland was still unobligated on July 1, 1950. Under the China Area Aid Act of 1950, as described above, these unobligated balances were made available not only for use in Formosa, but in Southern Asia (the "general area of China"), as well. Approximately $70 million

---

[41] See *Foreign Economic Assistance, 1950*, Report of the Senate Committee on Foreign Relations, Washington, D.C., March 1950, Part I, pp. 34-35; and *To Amend the ECA Act of 1948*, House Hearings 1950, pp. 359-369. The China Area Aid Act was Title II of the Foreign Assistance Act of 1950. Use of the term "general area" to encompass Southern Asia followed the practice begun with military aid in the Mutual Defense Assistance Act of 1949. See below, pp. 54-55.

[42] See above, pp. 38-39.

of these funds were obligated for the countries of Southern Asia, including India, during fiscal year 1951. The implication of the legislation and the programming of aid under it was that a reallocation of aid funds from China (Formosa) to Southern Asia would enhance their yield.

As far as the interprogram allocation alternatives are concerned, a distinction needs to be made between the China Aid Program originally submitted by the Administration, and the program that emerged in the China Aid Act of 1948 after Congressional action. The Administration's original proposal in February 1948 involved, as we have seen, $570 million of economic aid funds for a fifteen-month period, and no military aid. The allocation implication of the proposal was, in effect, that marginal returns from military aid were less than those from economic aid.

In fact, the point was made quite explicit. In repeated statements by Secretaries Marshall and Acheson and the chief of the U.S. Military Advisory Group in China, the view was expressed that the Chinese Nationalists had lost no battles for lack of materiel, and that the critical weaknesses of leadership and morale could not be rectified by American aid short of direct intervention by American troops under American command. Since the latter alternative was ruled out, the statements reflected the Administration's position that the returns to be derived from incremental amounts of military aid would be negligible or even negative.[48]

Given the judgment that returns from military aid were negligible, the major part (90 per cent) of the Administration's proposal for economic aid was based on the premise that political unrest and deterioration would be restrained if civilian consumption in urban areas could be maintained at least at its then-current level. With this as the program's objective, the amount of aid required was determined by estimating the imports needed to maintain consumption in seven major mainland cities. Since China's foreign exchange assets were already severely depleted, and since under the circumstances neither export increases nor import reductions were feasible, the requirements for U.S. aid were, in principle at least, uniquely determined.[44]

[48] See above, pp. 41-42, and *U.S. Relations with China*, pp. 358-359, 1053-1054.
[44] See *ibid.*, pp. 1006-1009, for confirmation of the general procedure described. Besides these aid requirements for urban consumption, 10 per cent of the total aid originally proposed included imports for "recovery" projects and for the rural development work of the Joint Commission on Rural Reconstruction; *ibid.*, pp. 1030-1038, and Price, *op.cit.*, pp. 190-194.

In the Congressional review and revision of the Administration's original proposal, quite a different allocation decision was made. After reducing the total authorization from the requested $570 million for economic aid to $463 million,[45] the Congress, as we have seen, provided $125 million of the total for military aid, thereby implying that the Administration's assessment of the relative marginal gains from military and economic aid was in error.[46] The incident was a significant one in that it involved a clear, if implicit, confrontation of the difficult and enduring problem of interprogram aid allocation. The result plainly suggested that Congress accorded the marginal gains from military aid a higher value, at least in China, than did the Administration.

D. THE KOREAN AID PROGRAM

Compared to China Aid and ERP, Korean aid during the 1948-1950 period had a less immediate effect on initial United States aid to Southern Asia. But the communist military attack on South Korea in the summer of 1950 had a profound and increasing effect on U.S. aid in Southern Asia in the following years. By demonstrating that economic and technical aid, no matter how effective,[47] could not be relied on to counter the threat of external attack, the Korean experience exerted a strongly countervailing influence to that associated with China Aid. Over the next five years, the influence of Korea on the allocation of aid between military and economic uses, and among alternative recipients, especially in Southern Asia, became dominant.

1. The Record of Korean Aid

From the end of World War II until the beginning of 1949, U.S. aid to Korea, like aid to Japan, was carried on under the Army's GARIOA program.[48] As already noted, $326 million of GARIOA

[45] Apparently, the figure was arrived at by (inaccurately) prorating the Administration's fifteen-month proposal over a twelve-month period. See Brown and Opie, *op.cit.*, p. 335.

[46] How the precise $125 million figure for military aid was arrived at is not entirely clear, but it apparently had something to do with a request from the Chinese Premier to the American Ambassador in January 1948 for a loan of $100 million to purchase military equipment and ammunition. *U.S. Relations with China*, pp. 376-377.

[47] After a year's operation of the program, ECA termed progress under the Korean aid program "spectacular." See testimony of Paul Hoffman on Korea in *Extension of European Recovery*, Senate Hearings, 1950, p. 366.

[48] See Chapter 2 above, p. 19.

funds, largely for consumption relief, were obligated in this period in Korea, compared with approximately $1.2 billion in GARIOA aid to Japan for similar purposes.[49] On January 1, 1949, the United States extended diplomatic recognition to the Republic of Korea, the military occupation of South Korea was formally terminated, and the President transferred responsibility for U.S. aid from the Army to the Economic Cooperation Administration.[50]

Korean aid under ECA was initiated with $30 million remaining from the GARIOA funds, which were transferred to ECA by the Army. At the same time, the emphasis of aid shifted from relief to recovery or, more precisely, from the limited aim of maintaining minimal civilian consumption to the broader aim of increasing production in order to raise exports, reduce imports, and eliminate the need for external assistance.[51] GARIOA aid had been conceived in terms of the policy objective of facilitating the military occupation by preventing disease and unrest. By contrast, the more comprehensive objective of ECA aid was "to assist the Korean people in establishing a sound economy and educational system as essential bases of an independent and democratic state."[52]

To this end, in the Congressional hearings on Korean aid during the early summer of 1950, ECA proposed a three year recovery-and-development program requiring $350 million in U.S. aid for the fiscal years 1951 through 1953. Besides recovery of the prewar level of per capita food production, the three-year program sought to expand output of coal, tungsten, cement, and textiles with a view to replacing imports or providing exportable surpluses. By the end of the three-year period, Korea's balance of payments deficit was to be reduced by more than 70 per cent. The remainder was considered serviceable through "normal," that is, non-aid, financing. Determination of aid requirements thus followed from the aim of attaining equilibrium in Korea's international accounts. In this respect, planning of Korean aid clearly reflected the ERP precedent.

The three-year assistance program proposed by ECA was not

[49] From the beginning of 1949 to the end of June 1951, additional GARIOA aid to Japan, increasingly oriented toward recovery rather than relief, amounted to $900 million. "Foreign Aid by the U.S. Government," *Supplement to the Survey of Current Business*, Washington, D.C., 1952, p. 89.

[50] *Aid to the Republic of Korea*, Senate Foreign Relations Committee Report No. 748, Washington, D.C., 1949, p. 7.

[51] *Ibid.*, pp. 7-8; *Seventh Report to Congress of ECA*, October-December 1949, Washington, D.C., 1950, pp. 94-95.

[52] *Fourth Report to Congress of ECA*, 1949, p. 87.

accepted. Instead, Congress made two interim appropriations in the fall of 1949 totalling $60 million. Later in the fiscal year, an additional $50 million was appropriated. In fact, the Korean aid proposals for fiscal year 1950 were involved in one of the longest and strangest Congressional actions in the history of foreign aid. After two interim appropriations in October 1949, Congress voted down the Administration's proposed Korean aid bill in January 1950. In February, this defeat was reversed by passage of the Far Eastern Economic Assistance Act of 1950, which authorized Korean aid through the remainder of the fiscal year. No funds, however, were appropriated under this Act until the last day of the fiscal year.

In large part, the legislative opposition and delays encountered by Korean aid grew from the bitter Congressional reaction to the fall of China. Paradoxically, the Asian-minded group in Congress led the attack on Korean aid. Their opposition to Korean aid was motivated by a desire to force the Administration to "clarify" its policy for the Far East as a whole. Yet when this clarification was made, in the Acheson policy statement on Asia in January 1950, it hardly facilitated favorable consideration of Korean aid in Congress. By placing Korea on the far side of the U.S. "defensive perimeter" in Asia, the Acheson statement relegated economic aid to Korea to a considerably lesser importance than the Administration had been previously claiming in its own advocacy of the Korean aid legislation.[53]

A total of $140 million, including the $30 million of transferred GARIOA aid funds, was thus made available for economic aid to Korea between January 1, 1949, and the end of June, 1950.[54] After the communist attack on June 25, 1950, an additional $90 million in economic aid were appropriated under the Far Eastern Assistance Act of 1950, whose duration was extended through fiscal year 1951.[55] By this time, however, war was under way, and the aid program reverted substantially to its pre-1949 orientation. Part of the new

[53] For a fuller account of the legislative history surrounding Korean aid, see *U.S. Code Congressional Service*, 81st Congress, 2nd session, Washington, D.C., 1950, Vol. 2, *Legislative History*, "The Far Eastern Economic Assistance Act," pp. 1910ff.; *Eighth Report to Congress of ECA*, p. 79; *Korean Aid, House Hearings*, 1949, especially pp. 23-29.

[54] Approximately $11 million of military aid were also extended to Korea during the fiscal year 1950 under the Mutual Defense Assistance Act of 1949. See below, pp. 53-54.

[55] *Eleventh Report to Congress of ECA*, p. 97; and *Twelfth Report to Congress of ECA*, p. 81.

funds was transferred to the Army for procuring commodities for civilian consumption, and part was used to meet the short-term needs of agriculture and industry for working capital—for example, fertilizer and cotton. But the program's emphasis on capital formation had to be cut back. In effect, after the outbreak of war, the objective of economic aid reverted from recovery-and-development to consumption relief. In April 1951, economic aid to Korea, apart from relief activities of the UN Command, was formally suspended.

2. Aid Allocation and the Communist Attack

Assessing the factors responsible for the communist decision to attack is an intriguing exercise. The relative influence of the Acheson "perimeter" speech, of the withdrawal of American occupation forces, of dilatory Congressional action on Korean aid, and of internal pressures within communist China, for example, will probably concern students of communist decision-making for years to come. But without entering this debate, certain obvious things can be said about the bearing of the Korean experience on the concepts behind and the allocation of aid to Southern Asia in later years.

Of the intercountry and interprogram allocation questions we have previously mentioned, Korean economic aid did not confront that of intercountry choices.[56] Legislatively and financially Korean aid was considered independently of other U.S. aid. But Korean economic aid was relevant to the question of the relative gains to be derived from military and economic aid. Its relevance derived not from the initial formulation of the Korean program itself, but rather from the circumstances accompanying the program's operation and from the North Korean aggression.

During the eighteen-month operation of the economic aid program, the Korean economy had made notable progress. Agricultural output had risen 11 per cent, and was 20 per cent above the prewar level. Industrial output, though only 10 per cent of South Korea's national product, had risen 50 per cent.[57] In part, of course, the high and rapid returns accompanying aid were due to rehabilitation investment in the small industrial sector, and to the expanded use of fertilizer in the agricultural sector. In both cases, further aid inputs

[56] Despite the fact that the Far Eastern Economic Assistance Act of 1950 authorized continued aid for China (Formosa) as well as Korea, transferability of funds between the two programs was not considered by the Act.

[57] Economic Survey of Asia and the Far East, 1955, Bangkok, 1956, pp. 195, 209; Tenth Report to Congress of ECA, p. 77.

would have met with diminishing returns. Nor does one have to accept entirely the operating agency's evaluation of the program's success before hostilities: "With increased local production and continued American aid, political stability is becoming increasingly evident"[58]—and, after the Korean war was under way: "Assistance to Korea not only brought direct benefits to production and to the economy as a whole, but was instrumental also in generating substantial confidence in their own type of government and good-will towards the United States."[59]

Even if these evaluations are discounted, the inference is warranted that, in terms of the returns that are usually attributed to economic aid, the Korean program had been notably successful by the summer of 1950. Under these circumstances, the June 25th attack plainly signified that economic aid, though perhaps a necessary response, was certainly not a sufficient response to the threats and uncertainties of cold war. This part of the "lesson" of Korea was demonstrable. Parenthetically, one might add that it was also a useful corrective to some of the over-optimistic expectations that had become attached to economic aid as a result of ERP and of the President's proposal of a "bold new program" of technical aid to the underdeveloped areas.[60]

But there was also a tendency to draw another inference that was more debatable, especially when it was applied to judging the relative emphasis to be accorded military and economic aid in Southern Asia. This was the inference that, since economic aid would not deter aggression, military aid would. Hence the returns from military aid must be relatively greater than those from economic aid. Actually, under some circumstances, *neither* military nor economic aid may be a suitable counter to this threat. There are *many* different scales for measuring the returns sought by United States foreign policy. On one scale—deterrence to local aggression, for example—the returns from *both* military and economic aid may be negligible. If this scale is considered of dominant importance, U.S. "aid" may yield higher returns by allocating it to, say, U.S. domestic military outlays for mobile defense forces, than to *either* foreign economic or military aid.[61]

[58] *Fifth Report to Congress of ECA*, p. 83. The date of this evaluation was November 15, 1949.
[59] *Twelfth Report to Congress of ECA*, p. 80.
[60] See below, p. 57.
[61] For elaboration of this point, see Chapter 10, pp. 376-377.

In any event, the influence of the Korean "lesson" on U.S. aid to Southern Asia grew in the following years. The China experience, as previously noted, largely determined the timing of aid to Southern Asia. And by suggesting the inadequacy of limited military aid for meeting one kind of internal communist threat, while at least holding out some promise for the gains to be derived from the contribution of economic aid to political stability, aid to China strongly affected the concept and character of early U.S. aid to Southern Asia, as well. By contrast, the Korean attack, coming in the midst of an evidently successful economic aid program, tended to counter the force of the China lesson and to affect the allocation of later aid to Southern Asia accordingly.

E. The Start of "Coordinated" Military Aid

An important innovation in global U.S. foreign aid during the 1948-50 period was the Mutual Defense Assistance Program (MDAP). We have previously referred to some of the military assistance extended by the United States in the immediate postwar period prior to MDAP, notably in the Philippines, China, Greece, and Turkey.[62] Each of these programs was originally undertaken through separate legislation and appropriations. As the State Department explained in presenting the Administration's proposals to the Congress, the aim of MDAP was "to extend immediate new military assistance to friendly, free nations and to bring together all existing military aid projects into one coordinated Program."[63] The Mutual Defense Assistance Act, approved on October 6, 1949, provided a single enabling act for all military aid programs, and formally asserted their common basis in a foreign policy, one of the instruments of which was "the furnishing of military assistance essential to enable the United States and other nations dedicated to the purposes and principles of the United Nations to participate effectively in arrangements for individual and collective self-defense."[64]

[62] See above, pp. 22-23, 42, 46-47. See also Brown and Opie, *op.cit.*, pp. 440-447ff., for a good summary of "uncoordinated" military aid in the early postwar period, as well as of the beginnings of MDAP.

[63] *The Military Assistance Program*, Department of State, Publication 3563, Washington, D.C., 1949, p. 1.

[64] "The Mutual Defense Assistance Act of 1949," in *Documents on American Foreign Relations, 1949*, p. 626. Actually this "declaration of policy," as it was called in the Act, was a clarification and reaffirmation of previous policy rather than a new departure for the United States. Greek-Turkish aid in 1947, and the "third point" of the President's inaugural address in 1949, were earlier evidences of essentially the same policy.

1. *Mutual Defense Assistance and NATO*

The principal geographic concern of MDAP was, of course, Europe. Timing of the legislation was largely determined by the need to provide tangible support for the North Atlantic Treaty, which was signed on April 4 and came into force on August 24, 1949.[65] In turn, the impetus behind NATO came from the increasing evidence afforded by events in Czechoslovakia, Greece, and Germany, of a rising temperature in the European cold war, and of the unprepared-for possibility of military conflict in Europe. Nonetheless, the MDA Act stated plainly that military assistance, and by inference the benefits to be derived from it, as well, were of lesser priority than ERP. As stated in the Act's initial declaration of policy:

"The Congress hereby finds that the efforts of the United States and other countries to promote peace and security . . . require additional measures of support. . . . These measures include the furnishing of military assistance. . . .

"The Congress recognizes that economic recovery is essential to international peace and security, and *must be given clear priority.*"[66]

The Administration had essentially the same view of the priority of economic recovery over military build-up in Europe as did Congress. Testifying in support of MDAP, Secretary Acheson referred to the responsibility of ECA to:

"Provide the proper coordination [for MDAP] with the European recovery program and safeguard the priority of economic recovery against any tendency of the recipient countries to emphasize military production at the expense of recovery needs."[67]

Of the $1.3 billion authorized and appropriated for the fiscal year 1950 under the MDA Act of 1949, 76 per cent was for the NATO countries and 16 per cent for Greece and Turkey. An additional $28 million (2 per cent of the total) was provided for military assistance to Iran, Korea, and the Philippines.[68] Of this amount, $11 million

[65] See, for example, Acheson's overwhelming stress on support for NATO as the purpose of military aid in his testimony on the Administration's proposed bill, *Military Assistance Program*, Joint Hearings Before the Committee on Foreign Relations and the Committee on Armed Service, U.S. Senate, Washington, D.C., 1949, pp. 5-7 (hereafter referred to as "Joint Senate Hearings").

[66] *Documents on American Foreign Relations, 1949*, p. 626. (Italics added.) The statement is an interesting parallel to the policy on Asia set forth by Acheson in January 1950.

[67] *Military Assistance Program*, Joint Senate Hearings, 1949, p. 12.

[68] *Documents on American Foreign Relations, 1949*, pp. 627-628. The remaining

was obligated in Korea and about $5 million in the Philippines as a continuation of previous U.S. military assistance to these countries.[69] The small amount of Mutual Defense Assistance to both countries was for the limited purpose of helping to strengthen internal security forces, rather than to oppose or deter external aggression. In the MDAP appropriation for the next fiscal year (1951), as formulated *prior* to the attack on South Korea, another $16 million was provided for the Philippines and Korea, or slightly over 1 per cent of the initial MDAP appropriation for that year.[70]

2. *Mutual Defense Assistance and Southern Asia*

Notwithstanding the dominant European focus of MDAP at its inception, several aspects of the MDA Act had considerable influence on the later development of U.S. aid in Southern Asia.

Over the Administration's objections, the Congress, in its "Findings and Declaration of Policy" under the Act, expressed support for "the creation of a joint organization" of the free countries of the Far East. Though the NATO parallel was too obvious to be missed, the statement in the Act included the promotion of "economic and social well-being," as well as military security, as objectives of the proposed regional organization. Formation of the Southeast Asia Treaty Organization (SEATO), five years later, was anticipated by the MDA Act in 1949.[71]

Besides urging the formation in Asia of a regional counterpart to NATO, Congress undertook in other ways to create a more active administration policy in Asia and to stimulate aid for that area. Thus, Title III of the MDA Act authorized $75 million for use in the President's discretion in the "general area" of China to accom-

---

6 per cent ($75 million) of the initial MDA funds was for the "general area" of China.

[69] See above, pp. 22-23, 47-48, and Brown and Opie, *op.cit.*, pp. 380-382.

[70] "General Appropriation Act of 1951," *Documents on American Foreign Relations, 1950*, p. 71. Although passed early in September 1950, the MDAP appropriation for fiscal year 1951 reflected the program as planned before war began in Korea. Later in the month, total MDAP appropriations were supplemented by $4 billion—an increase of nearly 400 per cent over the initial planned program. Of these additional funds, over $300 million, or 7.6 per cent of the total, were allotted to Southern and Eastern Asia. See below, pp. 100-101, and *Second Semi-Annual Report on the MDAP*, House Document No. 119, Washington, D.C., pp. 27-29, 47-50.

[71] See the prideful mention of this fact by the House Foreign Affairs Committee, which had been responsible for inserting the relevant paragraph in the MDA Act of 1949. *The Mutual Security Act of 1954*, House Hearings, 1954, p. 293ff. Also, *To Amend the ECA Act of 1948 as Amended*, House Hearings, 1950, Part 1, pp. 33-35.

plish "the policies and purposes" set forth in the Act, including the promotion of "peace and security." The conditions governing the use of this fund were so flexible that a small portion ($750,000) of the fiscal year 1950 appropriations under Title III was used to initiate the first of the Special Technical and Economic Aid programs in Viet Nam in June 1950. In effect, authority and appropriations under the Mutual Defense Act of 1949 were used in initiating U.S. economic aid in Southern Asia one year later, before separate funds for the latter programs were obtained under the China Area Aid Act.[72]

Actually, this was the only portion of the MDAP "general area" fund obligated before hostilities began in Korea. Once the Korean war started, the remainder of the $75 million general area fund for 1950, together with an additional $75 million appropriated under the same Title of the Act for fiscal year 1951, were used for direct military assistance to the Chinese Nationalist armed forces in Formosa. At the same time, shortly after the outbreak of war, military aid to Korea was removed from MDAP and consolidated with the Defense Department's regular operating budget.

The use of MDAP authority and funds to initiate economic and technical aid in Viet Nam was one of the earliest acknowledgments of a connection between economic aid and change on the one hand, and the requirements of military security on the other. Essentially, the argument was, to the extent that economic aid helped create conditions of internal political stability and public confidence in existing governments, such aid would reduce the need for larger internal military forces in the Asian region. If *internal* military security was the objective of military aid programs, it could be contended that economic development was a better—because more "efficient"—way of realizing gains than materiel.

As we have already seen, this was presumed to be part of the China lesson, and it was to play an important role in the initial justification of economic aid to Southern Asia. In contrast, aggression in Korea provided a different lesson, one that signified the inadequacy of economic aid for meeting *external* military threats. After

---

[72] For the use of MDA authority and funds to finance initial economic aid in Indo-China, see *38th Report of the Public Advisory Board of the Economic Cooperation Administration*, Washington, D.C., 1951, pp. 2ff. For a discussion of Congressional intent, in adding the "general area" provision of Title III to the Administration's proposed Military Assistance legislation, see *Military Assistance Program*, Joint Senate Hearings, 1949, pp. 37-38.

Korea, the objective of military aid in the Asian area increasingly became, as it had been from the outset in the NATO area, the creation of sufficient local military force to resist, and hence to deter, *external* aggression. The objective, in other words, shifted from internal to external military security. At the same time, the connection between internal economic development and external military security seemed more remote, in the light of Korea, than had the connection between development and internal security. Under these circumstances, economic aid for development tended to be viewed increasingly as an alternative to, rather than a source of, military security in recipient countries.

This gradual change in the objectives of military aid in the Asian area had considerable impact on the size and allocation of MDAP in later years. Initially, MDAP allocation in Korea and the Philippines was based simply on estimates by the U.S. Military Assistance Advisory Group (MAAG) of the forces required for maintaining internal order, and security, in the recipient country.[73] The small amount of aid needed was determined by costing the equipment and training requirements of these forces.[74]

Given the objective of *internal* security, intercountry allocation alternatives did not arise in the Korean and Philippine cases. Returns in the form of increased internal security tend to be incommensurable as between different countries. In practice, initial MDAP requirements in the Philippines and Korea were appraised quite independently.

As for interprogram allocation, the use of a small part of the original MDAP funds for economic and technical aid in Viet Nam implied higher marginal gains from this use than from, say, the alternative of increased *military* aid to Viet Nam. This, as we have

[73] In the case of Korea, it was stated, as well, that MDAP was intended to equip "a small force to protect its [Korea's] internal security *and to deter* outside aggression." See *Military Assistance Program*, Department of State, 1949, pp. 23-24. (Italics added.) The small size of the program suggests that the italicized part of the statement had little significance.

[74] The allocation of MDAP aid in Europe was quite another matter. MDAP in Europe was tied to the formulation of a common defense plan and at the outset was directly geared to the attainment of combined and "balanced" force levels needed to resist external aggression. Not only was the task a larger one; it was inherently multilateral, as well. MDAP allocation, consequently, involved not only the costing of the combined NATO forces, but the determination of how the burden of financing these forces was to be shared among NATO members—a problem with which MDAP in Asia has not had to contend. For a discussion of allocation problems in the NATO context, see Malcolm W. Hoag, "Economic Problems of Alliance," *Journal of Political Economy*, December 1957, pp. 522-534.

seen, had been the general implication of the China Aid lesson with respect to the allocation of funds between economic and military assistance programs.

Under the impact of the Korean war, both aspects of the allocation problem were to appear in a different light. In the later Mutual Security Programs, the objective of military aid in Southern Asia increasingly became that of resisting aggression. With this shift in objective, the returns from military programs tended to become more sharply separated from, and gradually to become more highly valued than, the returns from economic programs. As among alternative *country* recipients, those willing to build up forces that might help deter external attack received relatively more military, as well as economic, aid than those which were unwilling.

F. The Technical Cooperation (Point Four) Program

1. *Assistance for Economic Development as a National Policy*

During the 1948-1950 period, concern for the economic development of underdeveloped areas appeared as a final innovation in the concept of United States aid. The initial statement of U.S. concern was, of course, President Truman's inaugural address of January 20, 1949. As the fourth "major course of action" in the U.S. "program for peace and freedom,"[75] the President stated that: "We must embark on a bold new program for making the benefits of our scientific advances and industrial progress available for the improvement and growth of underdeveloped areas."

The President's fourth point was eventually embodied in the Act for International Development (not inappropriately abbreviated A.I.D.), approved on June 5, 1950, as Title IV of the Foreign Economic Assistance Act of 1950. For the first time, it was "declared to be the policy of the United States to aid the efforts of the peoples of economically underdeveloped areas to develop their resources and improve their working and living conditions. . . ."

There had been precursors to the Technical Cooperation Program, notably in the technical assistance activities of the Coordinator of Inter-American Affairs dating back to 1941,[76] and in the *ad hoc* technical assistance missions we have previously referred to. But

[75] The other three were support for the United Nations, continuation of ERP, and military assistance. See *Documents on American Foreign Relations, 1949*, pp. 7-12.
[76] *History of the Office of the Coordinator of Inter-American Affairs*, Washington, D.C., 1947.

the Act for International Development, in the words of Secretary Acheson, "establishes economic development of underdeveloped areas for the first time as a national policy."[77] The mere statement of the policy left unanswered the major and interesting questions of how much and to whom assistance would be provided for economic development. But it at least gave these questions a relevance to United States actions in the cold war which they had not previously had.

In passing, it is worth noting certain connections between the new policy of aid to underdeveloped areas and the earlier changes we have referred to in aid to developed areas during the 1948-50 period.

Both ERP and the Act for International Development were expressions of the same general purpose, originally enunciated in 1947 as part of the so-called Truman Doctrine, to "assist free peoples to work out their own destinies in their own way . . . primarily through economic and financial aid . . . essential to economic stability and orderly political processes."[78] As we shall try to show later in discussing program objectives, this purpose was to recur and to be formulated repeatedly in the course of aid experience in Southern Asia. But throughout its various formulations, the purpose implied essentially a similar connection between economic aid as "inputs" and political consequences as "outputs." This purpose and its underlying implication were part of the concept of initial ERP aid, no less than of later development aid.

Moreover, both programs sought to affect the same economic variables, namely, investment, productivity, and output. In contrast to the initial emphasis on relief and consumption in early post-World War II aid, both recovery and development aid shared a concern for growth.

2. Technical Cooperation, and Aid to Southern Asia: Some Similarities and Differences

In some important respects, the objectives and premises behind the A.I.D. were similar to those underlying early United States aid to Southern Asia. Like economic and technical aid in Southern Asia, the Technical Cooperation Program was based on the premise, which we have previously referred to as part of the China "lesson," that

[77] *Act for International Development*, Senate Hearings, 1950, p. 5.
[78] From the President's message to Congress on Greek-Turkish Aid, March 12, 1947, *Documents on American Foreign Relations, 1949*, p. 649.

economic change in the underdeveloped areas was a necessary—if not sufficient—condition for political stability. Of the many statements of the premise in the hearings on the A.I.D., that by Undersecretary of State Webb is typical:

"The people in the underdeveloped areas are increasingly aware of the possibilities for human advancement through modern technology and economic organization. They have strong aspirations for a better life. They are increasing their pressure on their own governments . . . for action . . . to improve the conditions under which they live. . . .

"It is important to us and to the rest of the world that people in these areas realize that, through perseverance, hard work, and a little assistance, they can develop the means for taking care of their material needs and at the same time can preserve and strengthen their individual freedoms. Democracy is most secure where economic conditions are sound. In the interests of world security . . . this technical assistance program holds great promise."[79]

But besides this "security" objective, which predominated in the initiation of U.S. aid in Southern Asia, the "bold new program" accorded a relatively more important role to "economic" aims and to what, for want of a more precise term, we will refer to as "humanitarian" aims. The former were based on the premise that U.S. trade with the underdeveloped areas would increase as their income levels rose.[80] The latter represented a simple moral proposition that economic development should be aided because it was the "right" thing to do, quite apart from economic or security gains that might result from it.[81]

[79] *Act for International Development,* House Hearings, 1950, p. 5. See also, the similar statement by Secretary Acheson before the Senate Foreign Relations Committee, *Act for International Development,* Senate Hearings, 1950, pp. 4-5.

[80] According to Undersecretary Webb's testimony: "Economic development will bring us certain practical material benefits. It will open up new sources of materials and goods which we need, and new markets for the products of our farms and factories. . . . The volume of trade will inevitably expand." *Act for International Development,* Senate Hearings, 1950, p. 5. See also the statement by the Secretary of the Interior on the gains to be derived from development and expanding trade because of increasing U.S. demand for imported minerals and raw materials. *Act for International Development,* House Hearings, 1950, pp. 298-299.

[81] *Ibid.,* pp. 41-46, 62-64, 91-93. The latter argument, in part, was simply a revised version of the political-stability-hence-security objective with a longer time horizon. See, for example, the previous reference to the Acheson statement in the Senate Foreign Relations Committee. In part, too, it was a moral norm of do-good-regardless-of-the-consequences. In this form, the objective was advanced and the program strongly supported by church, missionary, and charitable organizations.

We shall return to these matters analytically and critically in discussing the objectives of U.S. aid to Southern Asia in Chapter 7. At this point, we need only note that the economic and humanitarian objectives, which were identified with the Technical Cooperation Program under the A.I.D., played a relatively minor role in the case of aid to Southern Asia.

Nevertheless, since technical cooperation and aid to Southern Asia had much in common, the question arises why they were started at different times and under different enabling legislation. In part, the separation was due simply to administrative convenience, rather than to any basic conceptual difference in the two enabling acts or in the programs initiated under them. China's proximity to Southern Asia, especially to South*east* Asia, made its requirements appear more urgent than those of other underdeveloped areas. Moreover, the Economic Cooperation Administration, from its previous operating experience in China and Korea, was ready to administer aid to Southeast Asia rapidly. And, as we have seen, the "general area" provisions of the China Area Aid Act provided authority for doing so immediately in the summer of 1950, at a time when administrative responsibility for the A.I.D. was still under discussion within the Executive Branch.

Actually, global Point Four aid did not become a significant operating program until the following fiscal year, 1951-52, except in Latin America, where technical assistance had been going on since 1941. Beginning in fiscal 1952, Point Four assistance was extended to the western part of the area we have referred to as Southern Asia (the countries of *South* Asia: India, Pakistan, Afghanistan, Nepal, and Ceylon), while the China Area (ECA) programs, which had been started in the previous year, continued in the eastern part (the countries of *Southeast* Asia: Burma, Thailand, Indochina, Indonesia, and the Philippines). For easy reference, we shall refer to the latter group as the "STEM" countries and programs, after the name of the Special Technical and Economic Missions that were set up by ECA to administer the programs in each country.

3. *"Technical" Assistance and "Capital" Assistance for Economic Development*

In part, too, the differing administrative and legislative origins of the STEM and Technical Cooperation Programs reflected an unresolved difference within the Administration concerning the means to be used in providing assistance to underdeveloped areas. This difference was of importance for the later history of U.S. aid in Southern Asia, and is of general analytical interest as well.

Basically, the difference in approach involved the relative stress to be accorded assistance in the form of technical services, emphasized by the Point Four Program under the jurisdiction of the Technical Cooperation Administration, and aid in the form of commodities, emphasized by the STEM programs under the initial jurisdiction of the Economic Cooperation Administration. Given the two programs' common concern for growth, the distinction was essentially one between aid intended to raise output by changing methods of production, and aid intended to raise output by increasing the supply of capital in recipient countries.

Theoretically, the distinction is probably sounder than the distinction previously noted between aid in the form of consumer goods and aid in the form of producer goods. Substitutability of resources and commodities tends to weaken the latter distinction, especially where the commodities provided in the aid program are small in quantity compared to the amounts otherwise available to recipient countries.[82] On the other hand, substitutability between technical aid, narrowly defined, and commodity aid, can more reasonably be presumed negligible in the underdeveloped areas because of the latter's typical reluctance to procure foreign technical services from non-aid sources.

Nonetheless, from an operating standpoint, the distinction between aid in the form of technical services designed to change methods of production, and aid in the form of commodities designed to increase the factors available for production, presents equally difficult problems. In practice, improved technology in underdeveloped areas involves not only the demonstration of more productive methods through assistance in the form of technical services. It usually requires, as well, large inputs of capital associated with the improved technology and necessary for putting it into effect.

In theory, technological change implies a possibility of increasing the productivity of *existing* factors of production. In practice, raising the productivity of existing factors frequently requires substantial amounts of new factors, as well. Technical assistance, viewed as

[82] See above, p. 33, and below, Appendix I.

services only, may change production possibilities in the static sense of what is *known* without providing the means to change what is *done*. New production functions may involve a minimum *scale* of operations beyond the resource capacity of the recipient country. Similarly, the import of capital, *without* technical assistance, may raise output by less than would be possible given knowledge of improved methods of using capital. The answer to the dilemma, of course, lies in achieving an optimum mix, for any given amount of economic aid to a particular country, between technical services and capital assistance, rather than choosing once-and-for-all between them.[83]

Closely related to this conceptual difference between the A.I.D. and STEM programs was the difference in their respective magnitudes. Appropriations for the *global* Technical Cooperation Programs for fiscal year 1951 were $26.9 million, slightly more than 1 percent of total appropriations under the Foreign Assistance Act of 1950.[84] Initial STEM aid in Southeast Asia, under the China Area Aid Act, was $65 million for the same period. The low requirements for Point Four, both initially and in later years as well, were largely due to the program's stress on technical services, rather than capital costs. As repeatedly expressed in the Congressional Hearings on the Act for International Development, Technical Cooperation carried with it the hope that external capital needs could be largely met by investment from private sources, as well as from the International Bank and the Export-Import Bank.[85]

Though much has been written about the limited capacity of underdeveloped countries to "absorb" capital imports,[86] their capacity to absorb foreign technical services is, quantitatively, still more limited. The limitation in the demand for technical services frequently arises because of language differences and organizational bottlenecks in recipient countries. The foreign technician whose

[83] The optimum mix is that which maximizes the present value of the output generated by the given amount of aid. Admittedly, this "answer" raises new questions, for example, measuring future output streams, and determining an appropriate interest rate for discounting them. But it at least offers a guide for finding an answer.

[84] The remainder consisted of $2.25 billion for ERP, $62.5 million for aid to Spain, and $27.45 million for aid to Palestine refugees. See *Documents on American Foreign Relations, 1950*, pp. 69-74.

[85] *Act for International Development*, House Hearings, pp. 8-9; and *Act for International Development*, Senate Hearings, pp. 5-7.

[86] See, for example, Max F. Millikan and Walt W. Rostow, *A Proposal—Key to an Effective Foreign Policy*, New York, 1957, pp. 95-97.

report never reaches the right person is an all-too-frequent phenomenon in the operation of technical assistance programs. But absorption of foreign technical services is also limited on the supply side.
Within a fairly wide price range, the supply of qualified and acceptable American technicians for service abroad is probably inelastic.

Conjoined, the two limitations meant that the dollar cost of technical assistance would be low. By its presumption that the returns
from technical aid would be large, and that requirements for foreign
capital would be met from private sources or public lending institutions, the Act for International Development implied that *total*
aid requirements in the underdeveloped areas would be small. As
an example of the unbridled optimism expressed during the A.I.D.
Hearings concerning the benefit-cost ratios of technical assistance,
the following testimony by then Secretary of Agriculture Brannan
is fairly typical:

> Secretary Brannan: Now, in terms of immediate return as to
> the agricultural aspects, of course, it takes a year for a crop to
> grow in order to test out the theory or idea which has been con-
> ceived for a particular area, but in a relatively short time I would
> say that this program would bring back one-hundredfold what-
> ever we have invested in it. . . .
>
> Congressman Javits: So you have a reasonable expectation of
> getting a one-hundredfold return because you are giving them
> brains, incentive and know-how . . . ?
>
> Secretary Brannan: Yes; that is speculative, but it is certainly
> not unreasonable, in my opinion.[87]

Coming as a sequel to the $10 billion previously appropriated
for the European Recovery Program, the prospect of aid to underdeveloped areas at low cost accounted for no small part of the
initial Congressional, as well as public, enthusiasm for the global
Point Four Program. At the same time, this initial enthusiasm for
Point Four had a significant influence on Congressional reaction to
subsequent aid proposals involving Southern Asia. These proposals,
as formulated by the Administration, included provision for increasing amounts of capital, as well as technical services. Having warmly
accepted the idea of low-cost, high-yielding technical assistance in

[87] *Act for International Development*, House Hearings, pp. 59-60. If the returns
were in fact likely to be this impressive, one might argue that the case for *loan*
financing for technical assistance would be stronger than for capital assistance.

enacting the Act for International Development, Congress reacted sharply against the subsequently proposed aid requirements for Southern Asia. The substantial cuts made in the proposals in later years, as we shall discuss more fully in Chapter 5, resulted in major reallocations of aid among different countries and different uses in the region. In effect, the original "overselling" of technical cooperation militated against subsequent acceptance of a program of development assistance of realistic size and distribution.

4. Point Four's Criteria of Allocation

Before we leave the Act for International Development, brief mention should be made of its bearing on the general problem of intercountry aid allocation. Unlike the legislation authorizing aid to China, the "general area of China," and Korea, the Act for International Development attempted to formulate criteria for allocating technical assistance funds. As set forth in the Act, projects to be financed were supposed to be: (1) "an appropriate part of a program reasonably designed to contribute to the balanced and integrated development of the country or area concerned"; (2) "actually needed in view of similar facilities existing in the area and otherwise economically sound." In the case of projects for which capital assistance was requested, consideration was to be given to (3) "whether private capital is available either in the country or elsewhere upon reasonable terms and in sufficient amounts to finance such projects."[88] For convenient reference, we can call these the "balanced-development," "comparative-advantage" and "alternative-financing" criteria, respectively.

Quite apart from the impreciseness of some of the terms, for example, "balanced," "integrated," "sound," "reasonable," the three criteria had several weaknesses. As formulated in the Act, they were necessary, but insufficient, conditions for allocating the limited amount of funds ($26.9 million) initially appropriated under the Act. Unless the screening of projects by application of the three criteria resulted in a total project bill equal to the appropriations available for financing it, the criteria—even if precisely definable and rigorously applied—were not fully suited to the task of allocation. The likelihood of this result was small indeed. The criteria set forth in the Act for International Development were thus criteria

[88] From Title IV of the Foreign Assistance Act of 1950, *Documents on American Foreign Relations, 1950*, p. 64.

for *elimination* of the least desirable, rather than for *selection* of the most desirable, projects to be aided. In the likely event that the bill of eligible projects exceeded available funds, more stringent criteria were needed to ration the scarce funds.

Moreover, by stressing the allocation of aid to *projects*, rather than country *programs*, the Point Four criteria tended to obscure the problem of substitutability. Actually, financing projects that could qualify under the criteria might simply have the effect of freeing a recipient's own resources to finance other projects which could not qualify.

In practice, the criteria were seldom applied to the allocation of aid among country recipients. In part, this was due to the analytical weakness mentioned above. In part, it was also due to the practical difficulty of applying the three criteria, even to the limited task of screening out less desirable projects.

For example, the balanced-development criterion concealed a variety of knotty problems concerning the meaning and recognition, let alone the ranking, of "integrated and balanced" development plans. If a prospective project, for example, entailed increased farm production without any provision in the country's development plan for farm-to-market transport, presumably one could say the plan was not reasonably "balanced and integrated." But in many, if not most, cases drawing such a conclusion would be considerably more difficult. What form of transport should be provided and to which among alternative markets should the produce be directed for the development to be "balanced and integrated"? And what time period was to be considered in determining adequate balance and integration? What would not be marketable in three years, for example, might very well be marketable in six or ten.

Nor were the conceptual problems involved in applying the comparative-advantage and alternative-financing criteria any easier to answer. For example, how much weight was to be given infant-industry arguments in screening projects involving "similar facilities existing elsewhere," and over what time period? And how was the "reasonableness" of private capital financing—always available, presumably, at some price—to be assessed? By interest rates on IBRD or Export-Import Bank loans, or by interest rates received by private lenders on rural agricultural loans?

Before criticizing the A.I.D. criteria too harshly, and quite apart from the particular weaknesses we have noted in them, we should remember that they at least represented a direct approach to the difficult problem of intercountry allocation of development aid. And in some respects, this problem is inherently more difficult than the comparable problem for aid like ERP, whose aim was economic "recovery." The latter, for example, implies some previously existing standard, such as prewar per capita output, or balance of payments equilibrium, for determining the magnitude and content of aid. However imperfectly, this standard does provide a basis for estimating amounts and kinds and duration of aid in making allocation decisions.

Development aid, on the other hand, provides no such convenient basis for program planning. Similar questions arise as to how to estimate needs, and how to measure progress. But in this case the "recovery" of a previously existing level, however imprecise and fuzzy it may be, cannot be taken either as an answer or as the starting point for finding one.

Moreover, if we try to apply a criterion of maximizing development from *given* aid funds, the problem of planning and allocation remains more complex in the development, than in the recovery, context. The notion of "recovery" implies an existing economic and social structure which, since it previously encompassed the specified ends, can generally be considered to provide a reasonable framework in which aid and domestic resources can be used to reattain these ends. "Developed" countries, in other words, provide a developed economic and social structure for aid planning to work with and within. Given this structure, the allocation of aid can, in principle at least, be based on the maximization of returns from available funds. The relative contribution of each additional aid dollar, in alternative uses, to reaching the stipulated end, can theoretically be estimated, and aid allocations to the preferred uses thereby determined.

However, in the case of underdeveloped countries, there is besides this problem—in practice, it is a far more imposing one than the foregoing remarks suggest—a further one. Many of the requirements for development in the underdeveloped areas involve not only additional resources for use within a given institutional structure, but *changes* in the structure itself. If aid allocation is approached in terms of maximizing the returns from each additional aid dollar, the bigger returns to be had by devoting large blocks of aid to structural changes may be overlooked.

A specific example may help. Each additional dollar of aid spent on fertilizer may raise output more than another dollar spent on salaries and training for an agricultural extension service. Yet several millions spent on the latter may do more to attain stipulated goals than an equivalent outlay on fertilizer. Looking for the "big" returns from structural changes of this type is especially important in planning economic development, and aid directed toward this goal.[89]

It is, of course, true that structural changes can be of major importance in developed, as well as underdeveloped, countries. The European Payments Union, the Coal and Steel Community, and the Common Market are cases in point in Western Europe. Nevertheless, it is fair to say that the big changes are a more typical and more important part of the problem of development in underdeveloped countries than they were of "recovery" in Western Europe.

In practice, the problem of allocating technical cooperation funds among alternative countries was not resolved by attempts to answer these questions, nor by an attempt to apply the broad criteria set forth in the Act for International Development. Instead, intercountry allocations were decisively influenced by bargaining among American ambassadors, administering agencies, and representatives of the recipient countries. Within the amount tentatively allocated to a particular country, sub-allocations to specific projects were largely determined by *ad hoc*, frequently tacit, and generally varying criteria of "general usefulness," applied by the U.S. specialized agencies concerned with the Point Four Program and their field representatives.[90]

This is not to say that the resulting allocation decisions were necessarily poor. But it at least suggests that they were frequently irresponsible, in the sense that the grounds for making them were not clearly stated, and hence were not subject to review. It suggests,

[89] Changes in institutional structure are an example of technological change (see pp. 60-62). Large enough resource inputs may permit an escape from the diminishing marginal returns usually associated with any particular production function by enabling a shift to a new production function. The resulting returns-to-scale may be discontinuous. Between successive "steps," marginal returns may still diminish. If the curve is smoothed, what results is an intermediate region of increasing returns, bounded by regions of diminishing returns. Whether increasing returns can be realized at all depends on the available budget.

[90] The initial administration of the Point Four Program involved the exercise of considerable responsibility by the Departments of Agriculture, Interior, Commerce, and their specialized Bureaus, in project fields within their competence. Standardization of criteria was neither attempted nor facilitated under this decentralized administrative arrangement.

too, that the opportunity to accumulate experience from the decisions that were made was hampered by the *way* the decisions were made. It is indeed hard to avoid the mistakes or repeat the successes of past decisions if the grounds for having made them cannot be ascertained. There are thus several reasons for trying to develop more explicit and testable methods for arriving at decisions on allocation.

Despite their shortcomings and the consequent failure to apply them, the allocation criteria set forth in the Act for International Development at least represented an awareness of this general problem. Moreover, the criteria themselves still remain pertinent. Three years after repeal of the Act for International Development by the Mutual Security Act of 1954, essentially similar criteria were re-enacted in the Mutual Security Act of 1957 to guide the allocation of the new Development Loan Fund, beginning in fiscal year 1958. Thus, the Mutual Security Act of 1957 authorized the President to make loans from the Fund, "taking into account (1) whether financing could be obtained in whole or in part from other free world sources on reasonable terms, (2) the economic and technical soundness of the activity to be financed and (3) whether the activity gives reasonable promise of contributing to the development of economic resources or to the increase of productive capacities. . . ."[91]

The Development Loan Fund criteria share the shortcomings of the earlier Point Four criteria. Like their precursors, the Development Loan Fund criteria are criteria for eliminating the least desirable, rather than selecting the most desirable, projects. Like the earlier criteria, their applicability is limited by their vagueness. And like the earlier criteria, they are *project*, rather than *program* criteria, which neglect the problem of resource substitutability. But, like the earlier criteria, they at least represent clear recognition of one of the continuing problems of foreign aid allocation.

G. SUMMARY

During the 1948-50 period of intensified cold war, United States economic and military aid became major instruments of a foreign policy whose immediate aim, as expressed in the Truman Doctrine early in 1947, was to strengthen the will and capacity of free

[91] Public Law 85-141, 85th Congress, 1st session, August 14, 1957.

countries to resist communism. From the standpoint of their later influence on aid to Southern Asia, the principal aid legislation and appropriations enacted during the period are those summarized in Table 2.

ERP represented a basic change in the scope and content of U.S. aid to Europe. Instead of relief, ERP was concerned with recovery. Instead of consumption, it was concerned with investment, productivity, and output. In part because of the ERP precedent, these were the variables which subsequent U.S. economic assistance to Southern Asia also tried to affect.

Table 2

SELECTED UNITED STATES AID LEGISLATION AND APPROPRIATIONS
January 1, 1948–September 6, 1950[a]
* (millions of dollars)

	1948	1949	1950	Total
Economic Cooperation Act (ERP)[b]	6,196	3,828	2,263	12,287
China Aid Act	400	————————>		400
Economic Aid	(275)	————————>		(275)
Military Aid	(125)	————————>		(125)
China Area Aid[c]			✕	
Korean Aid[d]		90	140	230
Far Eastern Economic Assistance Act[e]			✕	
Mutual Defense Assistance Act[f]		1,314	1,222	2,536
Korea-Philippines		(28)	(16)	(44)
General Area of China		(75)	(75)	(150)
Act for International Development (Technical Cooperation Program)			27	27

Sources are as stated in the text discussion of each program, and Brown and Opie, op.cit., pp. 247, 335, 375-379, 483.

[a] Figures are in millions of dollars appropriated under the indicated authorizing legislation during the calendar year. A cross (✕) indicates authorizing legislation whose funding was from unobligated balances of previous appropriations, rather than from new appropriations. Figures in parentheses are part of the total appropriation under the indicated authorization.

[b] Figures include appropriations for ERP grants, and authorizations for loans and investment guaranties.

[c] The China Area Aid Act superseded the China Aid Act and operated with the latter's unobligated economic-aid balances.

[d] $30 million of the amount shown for 1949 represented unobligated GARIOA funds transferred by the Army to ECA (see above, p. 48). $90 million of the 1950 total was appropriated after the start of the Korean war.

[e] Prior to passage of the Far Eastern Economic Assistance Act, the Korean Aid Program was carried on under the applicable provisions of the Economic Cooperation Act.

[f] MDA appropriations shown for 1950 are the amounts proposed prior to the Korean war, but not actually appropriated until September. See below, pp. 99-101.

There were also other connections between ERP and later aid to Southern Asia. The underlying premise of ERP, that political stability depends on economic improvement, was sufficiently universal in its implications to invite application in other areas. Once the Administration had employed it in Europe, Asian-minded Congressmen had a ready opportunity to press for its use in Southern Asia. Moreover, as a result of the close ties existing between the two areas, political and economic developments in Southern Asia became increasingly relevant to the planning and allocation of aid to Western Europe.

The China experience had a still more direct effect on aid to Southern Asia. The failure of both economic and military aid in China determined the timing of initial aid to Southern Asia, because of a desire to avoid "another China." In addition, the "lesson" inferred from the China Aid experience, concerning both the limitations of military assistance and the possible benefits to be derived from economic assistance in the Asian context, strongly influenced the original operating philosophy of U.S. aid to Southern Asia. As a result of the China lesson, it was initially assumed that higher (total) returns would be obtained by the United States from allocating more aid to economic (or "civilian") uses than to military uses in Southern Asia.[92] Finally, unobligated balances remaining from the China Aid Program provided the initial financing for aid in Southern Asia, while the China Aid legislation provided its initial authorization.

Compared to China Aid and ERP, Korean Aid during the 1948-50 period had a less immediate effect on initial U.S. aid to Southern Asia. But the communist military attack on South Korea in the summer of 1950 had a profound and increasing effect in the following years. By demonstrating that economic and technical aid, even where it had been as effective as in Korea, could not be relied on to counter the threat of external attack, the Korean experience exerted a strongly countervailing influence to that associated with China Aid. In part, the inference drawn from Korea was that since economic aid could not deter external aggression, military aid would. Over the next five years, the influence of the Korean experience on

[92] A presumption of uniformly higher *marginal* returns from economic aid logically would have implied that *no* military aid should be extended at all. As discussed previously, this in fact was what the Administration originally proposed for China Aid (see above, pp. 45-47).

[70]

the allocation of aid among alternative program uses and alternative country recipients grew.

Besides providing a framework for "coordinated" military aid, the Mutual Defense Assistance Program was largely designed to furnish tangible support for NATO. Only a small portion of initial MDAP funds was allocated to Asia, and the only recipient of MDAP aid in Southern Asia prior to the summer of 1950 was the Philippines. In contrast to the objectives of MDAP in Europe, the small programs in both the Philippines and Korea were mainly aimed at strengthening *internal* security. Given this objective, the argument could be made that improving economic conditions was actually an acceptable method for securing military gains. In consequence, the use of a small portion of MDAP funds for strictly economic projects in Viet Nam was considered quite consistent with the objectives of military aid.

With the start of the Korean war, the objective of MDAP in Asia, as in Europe, became that of deterring external aggression and, in the case of Viet Nam, of helping to wage an internal war already underway. Under these circumstances, the gains from military aid became both more sharply distinguished from, and more highly valued than, the gains from economic aid.

MDAP legislation also influenced the course of subsequent aid to Southern Asia by the direct stimulus it provided to formation of the Southeast Asia Treaty Organization (SEATO) five years later.

Finally, the Act for International Development, passed toward the end of the period, established economic development assistance as a national United States policy. Though initially economic and technical aid in Southern Asia was administratively separate from the Point Four Program, the two shared similar objectives, were based on similar premises, and eventually were consolidated administratively, as well. The two programs differed in their relative emphasis on aid in the forms of technical services and commodities. The distinction influenced the later allocation of aid to countries in Southern Asia. Country programs, for which the proposals originally submitted by the Administration included commodity aid, were subsequently cut more sharply by Congress than those involving technical assistance narrowly defined.

The Act for International Development was also of significance for later aid in Southern Asia in that it represented an attempt to formulate criteria to assist in the allocation of aid for economic development. Though the criteria had a number of serious conceptual weaknesses, they reflected an awareness of one of the continuing problems of foreign aid allocation. Though these criteria were not applied initially, essentially similar criteria were re-enacted in the Mutual Security Act of 1957 to guide the allocation of the new Development Loan Fund.

PART II

MUTUAL SECURITY AND SOUTHERN ASIA, 1951-1957

CHAPTER 4

THE FIRST YEAR OF ECONOMIC AND MILITARY
AID IN SOUTHERN ASIA, 1951

A. INTRODUCTION

1. *International Circumstances, Aid Legislation and Aid Allocation*

IN THE TWO PRECEDING CHAPTERS, we have described the international circumstances and the earlier aid programs that influenced the initiation of United States assistance programs in Southern Asia. In this and the next two chapters, our concern shifts from the origin and background of U.S. aid programs in Southern Asia to their record and operation. In the account that follows we shall say something about the changing international circumstances or environment within which the programs operated, but our main concern will be more narrowly and directly with the record of U.S. economic and military aid in Southern Asia from 1951 to 1957. Given our particular interest in the allocation of aid, we shall be especially concerned with (1) the enabling and appropriations legislation under which aid to Southern Asia has been carried on, and (2) the amount and distribution of such aid by country and type of program.

The legislative record bears on the allocation problem in several ways. First of all, it shows the proliferation of aid categories, and hence the widening range of allocation alternatives. Moreover, the legislative history, together with the successive changes made in the enabling and appropriations legislation, provides important clues to the objectives that aid was intended to serve, and to the changing priorities among these objectives. The legislative history is thus indispensable background for the detailed discussion of aid objectives in Part III. In describing the legislative record, we shall also note the terminations or suspensions of aid to particular countries that occurred during the period, in part because of legislative conditions attached to the extension of aid. These conditions, in turn, are suggestive of the objectives attributed to aid.

2. *Ordering the Aid Record: Program, Country, and Project Allocations*

A consideration of amounts of aid, by country and program, is of interest from several points of view. It provides one of the few types of quantitative data available in a field that tends to be dominated by qualitative considerations. While there is certainly more to the relationship between donor and recipient than the transfer of resources, the transfer is certainly an important part of the relationship. By showing the allocation choices that were actually made, the numerical data suggest the changes that occurred in U.S. commitments and interests in the area with which we are concerned. As such, the data are useful for examining aid objectives and the relative weights accorded different objectives and countries from year to year.

In presenting the allocation data for Southern Asia for the seven fiscal years from 1951 to 1957, we shall be interested, first, in the amounts allocated annually to economic and military aid programs within the region, both relative to one another and relative to the foreign aid budget globally. Within the economic aid category, we shall, secondly, be concerned with amounts allocated to the particular *countries* of the region. Insofar as the data permit, we shall, thirdly, consider the pattern of allocation by *project* use.

Where possible, two sets of data will be presented for each of these comparisons: those representing program, country, and project allocations as *proposed* annually to Congress by the Executive Branch; and those representing actual dollar *obligations* after Congressional enactment of authorization and appropriations legislation.[1] The purpose of comparing proposals and obligations is to distinguish allocation decisions made in the proposed programs from those resulting after Congressional action. Not surprisingly,

[1] In U.S. budgetary terminology, "obligations" represent a legal commitment of funds for a specific purpose, incurred between the time Congress appropriates funds and the administering agency finally spends them. The significance of the "legal commitment" is that unexpended funds that are obligated do not revert to the Treasury at the end of the fiscal year, as they would if they remained unobligated.

From the standpoint of the allocation problem, obligations data, though subject to minor errors and corrections, are a more accurate reflection of the annual allocation of funds, to countries and programs, than are expenditures data. Expenditures, in any given year, depend on the type of commodities involved in a particular program, the lead-time on procurement and delivery, and the basis of financing adopted by the United States and the recipient country (for example, direct payment by the United States or reimbursement), considerations that are largely irrelevant to an assessment of donor allocations of aid funds in any given year. Occasionally, obligations are deobligated, but the amount of such deobligations is small. Moreover, deobligations generally lead to reobligations for purposes similar to those for which the original obligations were incurred. Consequently, dollar obligations for a particular period can be presumed to represent equivalent dollar expenditures made over a longer period.

the two sometimes differ markedly. The differences may provide some basis for assessing the differing importance attached to particular countries by the Executive Branch, on the one hand, and Congress, on the other.[2] Alternatively, the differences may simply reflect a change in circumstances after proposals are submitted and before actual obligations are made, rather than a different evaluation of the same circumstances by the Executive Branch and Congress.

From the various statistical comparisons, we shall try to infer something about the relative prominence or priority of different objectives, to the extent that these can be related qualitatively to particular countries and types of aid programs, and about shifts in these priorities over time. Besides providing a convenient way of ordering and presenting the aid record, the purpose of this account is to illustrate the kinds of allocation choices that—implicitly or explicitly—arise in the foreign aid field.

3. Evaluating the Aid Record

In evaluating the allocations data, our approach is to try to uncover some of the assumptions implicit in the allocations actually made. If the actual allocations are considered to have been "optimal," what assumptions—for example, those concerning the physical effects, or "productivity," of economic and military aid in different uses, and the relative "value" of these effects to the United States— are necessary to validate their "optimality"? And how reasonable were these assumptions, in terms of their consistency over time and with prevailing international circumstances?

Obviously, this procedure is contrived. In practice, "optimality" is perhaps the most unrealistic characteristic to assume about actual aid allocations. Aid allocations were affected by too many short-term crises and long-term uncertainties to make optimality a very likely

---

[2] More accurately, obligations figures reflect the allocation judgments of the Executive Branch as *modified* by Congressional action. The sometimes substantial difference between proposals and obligations makes it especially difficult to be precise about the relationship between U.S. foreign policy and aid as an instrument for implementing policy. Frequently, general statements about U.S. policy, which were originally made at the time of submitting foreign aid proposals to Congress, warrant revision in the light of Congressional modification of the proposals. But the original statement of [intended] policy remains on the record. There is, of course, always a problem of defining and determining the consistency between policy and programs intended to implement policy. In the case of foreign aid, the problem is further complicated by the fact that the policy statements frequently refer to programs that may be considerably altered as a result of Congressional action.

result—even if decision-makers had had some way of distinguishing a "better" decision from a worse one, which they did not. But it is precisely to help clarify the yardsticks that may be involved in appraising the returns from alternative allocations that we adopt the procedure described. It is adopted for analytical usefulness, not for historical accuracy. Its purpose is to provide some descriptive content and "feel" for the allocative issues to be dealt with abstractly in Parts III and IV.

Yet we should be clear about the limitations of numerical data for these purposes. Some of these limitations, of course, arise from the incompleteness of the data themselves. This is particularly true, for example, in the case of military aid. Detailed data on military programs, especially with regard to individual countries, are classified. Consequently, the data we use are confined to *regional* figures, for the Asian area as a whole. With only a few exceptions, more detailed comparisons at the country level are precluded. Moreover, the Asian regional grouping for military aid is not congruent with the region of Southern Asia as we have defined it. In the MDAP context, the Asian region includes Formosa, and after 1954, Japan and South Korea, in addition to countries of Southern Asia. Hence, comparisons between military and economic data, even at the regional level, must be treated with particular caution.

The difficulties presented by the numbers themselves are not the whole story. Another difficulty arises from the general problem of substitutability mentioned in Chapter 3 and discussed more fully in Appendix I. How meaningful, for example, are the various aid categories (for example, military and economic) and subcategories (for example, technical assistance, development assistance, defense support) as guides to the objectives and consequences of aid? Not only may recipient countries offset the intended effects of particular kinds of aid through compensating adjustments in their own resource commitments. Equally important, the aid label or category may not clearly define the objective intended by the United States even assuming mutual agreement on objectives between donor and recipient. Aid labelled "defense support," for example, may have been directly related to military objectives in one country, while in another it may simply have served as a convenient way of securing Congressional acceptance for programs whose intended effect was really to add to non-military capital formation.

Moreover, the historical aid allocations themselves imply nothing definite about the factors determining the allocation decisions. Consider, for example, two countries, A and B, in each of which there is a different and clearly established objective of U.S. aid, say, a "military" objective in A and a "political" objective in B. Assume, further, that the two objectives are not only different, but independent of each other. A persistently larger allocation of aid to A than B does not necessarily imply that the military objective is more "important," or of a higher "value," to the United States than the political objective. A larger allocation to A than B may be due to either of two reasons. One is that additions to the military objectives scale in A are more highly valued than additions to the political objectives scale in B.[8] If this is so, more aid will (should) be allocated to A until the surfeit of additions to A has lowered their value, at the margin, to that of an addition to B.

But besides the relative valuation of objectives, there is another factor no less significant in its bearing on aid allocation. Even if each addition to the political objectives scale in B were more highly valued than each addition to the military objectives scale in A, an increment of aid to B might contribute sufficiently fewer such additions than aid to A, to make more aid to A preferable to more aid to B. A larger allocation to A would thus be quite consistent with a lower-valued objective in A. In economic terms, we would expect the physical *productivity* of aid inputs in different uses or activities to be no less important in affecting allocations than the value of the activities.

Another difficulty in evaluating the aid numbers is the fact that the set of countries we have chosen is, from the standpoint of U.S. aid administration, a somewhat artificial one. In the chronology of allocation decision-making, aid to some of the countries in the set, such as India and Pakistan, has not usually been considered as an alternative to aid to others of the set, such as Indochina or Thailand. Nor, typically, was aid of one program type, say, military aid, considered an alternative to aid of another type, such as economic or technical aid. The two sorts of allocation decisions have been usually made from sources of funds which were in practice, and sometimes in law, not considered fungible.

[8] Incidentally, it should be noted that the relative value of *additions* to the objectives scales are decisive here, not the relative value of the objectives themselves in some ultimate sense. In aid, as in trade, we need to look at the *margin* to explain what is meant by the relative value of alternatives.

Moreover, the organization of decision-making has frequently been so compartmentalized, among different administering agencies, that allocations more typically resulted from considering the needs of one problem (for example, country or program) at a time, rather than from comparing alternatives. Consequently, an observed allocation of aid to A rather than B does not necessarily mean that an explicit decision was made, or even considered, to the effect that A represented a higher "valued" or a more "productive" use of aid funds than the alternative of allocating to B.

The point of these qualifications is simply that attempts to infer something about aid objectives from the categories in terms of which the use of aid funds is reported must be recognized to be an interpretive and imprecise undertaking. Though the historical record of aid allocations may be suggestive, it cannot be conclusive. In presenting the numerical side of the aid record, therefore, we are more interested in conveying some sense of the dimensions and complexity of the issues involved than in testing hypotheses or drawing conclusions.

In rounding out the background account of the aid record, we shall briefly note some of the other forms and amounts of assistance extended by the United States in Southern Asia. The Mutual Security Program, to which our previous comments apply, has been and is the main channel for transferring public resources from the United States to the countries of the set we are interested in. It is not, however, the only channel. For example, additional assistance, through the passage of special legislation, has also been provided to India and Pakistan during the period with which we are concerned. Moreover, the Agricultural Trade and Development Act (since 1954) and, to a lesser extent, the Export-Import Bank, have both provided sources of supplementary aid to Southern Asia. To make the quantitative aid data more complete, we shall briefly consider some of the supplementary aid extended outside the Mutual Security Program, though our main concern will be the latter.[4]

[4] How far the account of supplementary aid should be carried is, of course, an open question. Since we are mainly interested in the problem of aid as an instrument of U.S. foreign policy, we shall not discuss aid received from non-U.S. sources, such as the Colombo Plan donor countries, the International Bank, and the UN specialized agencies.

B. The Beginning of Economic Aid[5]

1. *The Griffin Mission to Southeast Asia*

In March 1950, the State Department sent a mission to survey "the kinds and approximate value of assistance needed" in four Southeast Asian countries.[6] Under strong Congressional urging, while the Hearings on ERP for fiscal year 1951 were underway, the Administration had acknowledged its intention to send such a mission to Southeast Asia.[7] Although Secretary Acheson asserted that no decisions or proposals concerning Southeast Asian aid could be made until the mission returned, he assented to a Congressional suggestion "that out of the recommendations of this mission . . . there will come other programs for aid in these various countries."[8] Again at Congressional initiative, the Secretary agreed that it might be helpful to include in the pending foreign aid legislation standby authority to extend aid to the countries concerned at such time as the survey mission had completed its task.[9]

The mission's chief, R. Allen Griffin, a California newspaper publisher and editor, had been deputy chief of the U.S. aid mission to the China mainland. He viewed the mission's task as one of formulating "a constructive program of aid" to help prevent in Southeast

[5] In the two preceding chapters, yearly references have been to *calendar* years, unless otherwise indicated. In this and following chapters, yearly references are to *fiscal* years unless otherwise indicated. The reason for the change is that the numerical data on aid allocations can only be presented on a fiscal year basis, and hence dating of the accompanying descriptive material must be adapted accordingly.

One of the Alice-in-Wonderland oddities about legislative procedures in the foreign aid field is that while appropriations legislation carries a fiscal year title and termination, the corresponding authorizing legislation carries a calendar year title together with either an unspecified *or* a fiscal year termination. The Mutual Security Act of 1958, for example, authorized programs whose funds were appropriated in the Mutual Security Appropriations Act of 1959.

[6] *Ninth Report to Congress of ECA*, for the quarter ended June 30, 1950, Washington, D.C., 1951, p. 99. The countries which the mission visited, at their request, were Burma, Indochina, Indonesia, Thailand, and Malaya. The mission's recommendations on Malaya were subsequently shelved. Aid to Malaya remained the responsibility of the United Kingdom.

[7] For the geographic distinctions between Southeast Asia, South Asia, and Southern Asia, see Chapter 1, p. 4.

[8] *To Amend the ECA Act of 1948 as Amended*, House Hearings, 81st Congress, 2nd session, Washington, D.C., 1950, p. 362. See also *ibid.*, pp. 359-364 for further discussion of aid to Southeast Asia.

[9] As previously noted, the authority was provided by using the precedent of the Mutual Defense Assistance Act of 1949. The China Aid authorization was extended to the "general area of China," and the latter was defined to include Southern Asia. See above, Chapter 3, pp. 40, 50-51. See also, Secretary Acheson's testimony in the House referred to in the preceding footnote.

Asia a repetition of the circumstances leading to the fall of China.[10]

Although the Griffin Mission's written reports have never been declassified, their general orientation may be inferred from the following statements by the Economic Cooperation Administration, commenting on the mission's aims and findings:

"The countries of Southeast Asia are . . . not secure against internal subversion, political infiltration, or military aggression.

"The objective of each [recommended][11] program is to assist as much as possible in building strength, and in so doing . . . to assure the several peoples that support of their governments and resistance to communist subversion will bring them direct and tangible benefits and well-founded hope for an increase in living standards. Accordingly, the programs are of two main types: (1) technical and material aid to essential services and (2) economic rehabilitation and development, focused primarily on the provision of technical assistance and material aid in developing agricultural and industrial output. . . . These activities are to be carried on in a way best calculated to demonstrate that the local national governments are able to bring benefits to their own people and thereby build political support, especially among the rural population."[12]

And, in a similar vein: "The aims of economic assistance to Southeast Asia as proposed by the Griffin Mission are to reinforce the non-Communist national governments in that region by quickly strengthening and expanding the economic life of the area, improve the conditions under which its people live, and demonstrate concretely the genuine interest of the United States in the welfare of the people of Southeast Asia."[13]

The objectives of economic aid, as viewed by the Griffin Mission, were thus broad and far-reaching. But the resource requirements for these objectives were nevertheless considered to be quite limited. Compared to Marshall Plan aid to Europe, for example, the problem in Southeast Asia was considered to be: "not primarily a dollar-shortage, but a shortage of internal revenues and non-dollar currencies, which is coupled with a shortage of trained and experienced technicians and administrators, and a lack of technical skills and equipment—all of these being needed to . . . strengthen the countries' economies as a basis for political stability. The European programs

[10] From a letter to the author, March 26, 1957.
[11] Bracketed word has been added. It is implied in the original.
[12] *Ninth Report of ECA*, pp. 99-100.   [13] *Tenth Report of ECA*, pp. 79-80.

required more dollars and less technical assistance; the Southeast Asian programs generally require fewer dollars and much more technical assistance."[14]

Aid to Southeast Asia was viewed as a "key" resource which, effectively administered in relatively small amounts, could "help unlock the great resources of these countries for their own and the whole world's good."[15] Effective administration meant, moreover, that the "relatively modest net addition to the resources of the [Southeast Asian] countries," provided by the United States, would be extended only "on condition that such additions be supplemented by local resources and directed towards remedying some of the weakest spots in the social and economic structure."[16]

Though "a maximum effort at self-help as a condition of aid"[17] had been no less a principle of European aid, the returns from using this principle in Southeast Asia were, optimistically, conceived to be vastly greater. Aid—heavily weighted by technical services—was viewed as likely to have a catalytic effect on the internal efforts of recipients Southeast Asian countries that would make small amounts of aid extremely productive and large amounts unnecessary. As Secretary Acheson later described the programs: "We provide only a small part of the resources required—but that small part has the effect of a catalyst in making the whole effort of the country succeed."[18] Because of the potentially catalytic effect of aid, its leverage in promoting political stability in recipient countries was believed to be high.

We shall return to both of these notions—of political stability as a "higher level" objective, and the stimulation of internal resources use as an intermediate objective—in our subsequent discussion of aid objectives and aid allocation. Both notions figured prominently in the Griffin Mission's orientation, and exerted a strong influence on the planning of later aid to Southern Asia.

Besides this general orientation, the Griffin Mission had one quantitative guideline for the formulation of specific aid recommendations

[14] *Ninth Report of ECA*, p. 100.
[15] See the testimony by R. Allen Griffin in *Mutual Security Act of 1951*, Joint Senate Hearings, 82nd Congress, 1st session, Washington, D.C., 1951, p. 579.
[16] *Twelfth Report to Congress of ECA*, Washington, D.C., 1951, p. 64.
[17] See Griffin's testimony, *Mutual Security Act of 1951*, Joint Senate Hearings, p. 581.
[18] *Mutual Security Act Extension*, House Hearings, 82nd Congress, 2nd session, Washington, D.C., 1952, p. 13.

in the countries visited. Although the Foreign Assistance Act of 1950 had not yet been passed at the time the mission departed for Southeast Asia, the Congressional Hearings preceding passage strongly implied both Congressional and Administration willingness to use some of the funds authorized by the Act to initiate aid to Southeast Asia. The most promising source of funds discussed in the Hearings were the unobligated balances remaining from previous appropriations for aid to China.[19] In fact, as we have already noted, when the Foreign Assistance Act of 1950 was approved, it contained an authorization to use these funds in Southeast Asia. At the time of the Griffin Mission's departure, the probable availability of from $40 to $60 million from these unobligated China Aid funds provided a rough guide for the mission's quantitative recommendations concerning aid to the particular countries it visited.[20]

2. The Philippines and South Asia

Before turning to the aid figures, a word should be said about those countries, in the region we are concerned with, which the Griffin mission did not visit, namely, the Philippines and the South Asian countries: Afghanistan, Pakistan, India, Nepal, and Ceylon.

In the case of South Asia, there was or seemed to be no immediate likelihood of the type of internal deterioration which had led to China's collapse, and consequently no immediate need for U.S. counteraction. In Indochina and Burma, for example, communist-led insurrections focused the attention of both the State Department and its Asian-minded critics in Congress on the imminent possibility of a repetition of the China debacle. In South Asia, by contrast, there were no such immediate or obvious crises to attract attention. More-

[19] See To Amend the ECA Act of 1948 as Amended, House Hearings, 1950, Part 2, pp. 359-369.

[20] Several factors made the unobligated China Aid funds a somewhat elastic yardstick. Tending to contract the China Aid funds, from the Griffin Mission's standpoint, were the prospective claims of aid for Formosa and the Philippines—the latter not on the Mission's itinerary. Tending to expand the available funds was the possibility of securing a transfer, for use in the "general area of China," of some of the ERP funds to be appropriated for fiscal year 1951. Subsequently, when additional aid requirements arose in India (see below, p. 85), and the Philippines (see below, pp. 85, 95), and when Formosa's aid requirements rose substantially after the start of the Korean war, the Administration secured authority to transfer ERP funds for use under the China Area Aid Act. The authority, provided by the Second Supplemental Appropriation Act of 1951, permitted transfer of up to 3 per cent of the ERP funds. Shortly after enactment, the transfer provision was invoked to make $75 million available for the general area of China (see Thirteenth Report of ECA, Washington, D.C., 1951, p. 70).

[84]

over, with the meeting of the Commonwealth ministers in Colombo in January 1950, consideration of technical and economic aid needs in the South Asian countries, excepting Afghanistan, had already begun without direct U.S. participation.[21] Consequently, there seemed to be little need in South Asia for the type of survey undertaken by the Griffin Mission.

For both reasons, no active program of United States aid to South Asia, comparable to that initiated in Southeast Asia as a result of the Griffin recommendations, was begun in 1951. The nearly negligible assistance that was provided, with one exception, was confined to technical services under authorization of the Act for International Development using appropriations made pursuant to that Act, rather than unobligated China Aid funds as in the case of Southeast Asian aid.[22] The exception involved a special grant of $4.5 million to India in August 1950 to help ease its mounting food shortage. Like Southeast Asian aid, the food grant to India was provided under authorization of the China Area Aid Act.[23]

In the case of the Philippines, a separate Presidential mission was appointed in the summer of 1950 "to consider the economic and financial problems of that country and to recommend measures that would enable [it] to become and remain self-supporting."[24] Headed by Daniel Bell, former Undersecretary of the Treasury, the United States Economic Survey Mission to the Philippines—as the Bell Mission was officially known—played in the Philippines a role parallel to that of the Griffin Mission elsewhere in Southeast Asia.

The problems and weaknesses in the Philippines that led to the

[21] As a result of later meetings, the Colombo Plan was formulated in October 1950. See *Colombo Plan for Co-operative Economic Development in South and Southeast Asia: Report by the Commonwealth Consultative Committee*, London, 1950.

[22] See above, Chapter 3, p. 62.

[23] *Tenth Report of ECA*, pp. 92-93. Later in the year, the Indian food situation deteriorated further. At the beginning of calendar year 1951, the Indian government made a formal request for substantial assistance to increase its grain imports from the United States. After considerable debate and delay—arising in large part from Congressional criticism of India's position on the Korean war—Congress enacted the India Emergency Food Aid Act of 1951, authorizing a long-term loan of $190 million to India to purchase grain from the United States. Though the Act was approved at the end of fiscal year 1951, nearly all obligations and expenditures under the Act were made during fiscal year 1952.

For a more complete account of the special food loan to India, see *Department of State Bulletin*, Vol. xxxiv, 1951, pp. 349-351, 424-428, 591-592, 674, and Vol. xxv, 1951, pp. 37-39; *Thirteenth Report of ECA*, p. 85; *The Mutual Security Program, First Report to Congress*, Washington, D.C., 1951, p. 34; and *The Mutual Security Program, Second Report to Congress*, Washington, D.C., 1952, p. 27.

[24] *Eleventh Report of ECA*, p. 93.

Bell Mission were similar to those in the Southeast Asian countries surveyed by the Griffin Mission. Both politically and economically, deterioration in the Philippines had proceeded rapidly in the year prior to the Bell Mission. Politically, the Presidential elections of 1949 had been accompanied by violence and fraud on such a scale as to arouse deep public resentment against the re-elected government. At the same time, and as a partial consequence, the scale of the communist Hukbalahap insurrection grew, especially in Central Luzon.[25]

Economically, the Philippine predicament was equally discouraging. At the same time that War Damage aid was being received from the United States,[26] the Philippines was experiencing a severe inflation largely as a result of rising budget deficits. Until the imposition of exchange controls at the end of 1949, the inflation was accompanied by a substantial rise in imports and a flight of capital.[27] Notwithstanding War Damage receipts, Philippine foreign exchange reserves fell by more than $180 million, nearly 40 per cent of total reserves, during 1949. Despite the large volume of imports, the Bell Mission found that "inefficient production and very low incomes [kept] . . . the standard of living of most people . . . lower than before the war."[28]

Against this background, the Bell Mission recommended fiscal and monetary measures to control inflation, minimum wage legislation, and certain land reforms to demonstrate the Philippine government's concern for public welfare, and U.S. economic and technical assistance of $250 million in loans and grants over a five-year period to diversify and develop the economy.[29] In November 1950, these recommendations were embodied in a formal agreement between the United States and the Philippines, the Foster-Quirino Agreement. The agreement provided that the President of the United States would recommend to Congress a program of economic and technical assistance "envisioned by the U.S. Economic Survey Mission at $250 million" over a five-year period, *on condition* that the Philippines

[25] For an account of the Philippine elections, the sources of Hukbalahap strength, and its growth in 1949-1950, see Shirley Jenkins, *American Economic Policy Toward the Philippines*, Stanford, 1954, pp. 9-10, 133-139.

[26] See Chapter 2, above, pp. 21ff.

[27] Konrad Bekker and Charles Wolf, Jr., "The Philippine Balance of Payments," *Far Eastern Survey*, February 1950, pp. 41-43.

[28] *Report to the President of the United States by the Economic Survey Mission to the Philippines*, Washington, D.C., 1950, p. 1.

[29] *Ibid.*, pp. 100-106.

enact the tax and minimum wage legislation recommended by the Bell Mission.[30]

The Bell Mission and the Foster-Quirino Agreement differed from the Griffin reports in several interesting respects, all attributable to the long history of United States association with the Philippines. In the first place, the designation of a separate survey mission to the Philippines, for essentially the same task as that with which the Griffin Mission was concerned elsewhere in Southeast Asia, came as a sequel to the two Philippine-U.S. technical missions earlier in the postwar period.[31] Second, the conditions attached to aid in the Philippines as a result of the Bell Mission were considerably more stringent than those invoked by the Griffin Mission.[32] The implication, that "interventionist" conditions are permissible only where one's "friends" are concerned, is as valid in the foreign aid relationship between donor and recipient as it is in other international relationships. Finally, the Bell recommendations differed from the Griffin reports in publicly stipulating a time period and an amount for prospective U.S. assistance, even though these were expressions of intent rather than commitments. Again, the difference was due to the fact that harder bargains can frequently be struck between associates of long-standing than between recent acquaintances. The Philippine government could insist on what the other Southeast Asian governments could not even suggest.

Despite these differences, the two missions and their recommendations had much in common. Both grew out of the same premise that economic and technical aid by the United States was a necessary instrument for increasing political stability in Southeast Asia. Both derived their main impetus from the China experience, which antedated them, rather than the Korean experience, which followed the Griffin Mission and barely preceded the Bell Mission. Both stressed the importance of technical services in United States aid, although both recognized the need for limited commodity or "capital" assistance as well. Both viewed optimistically the catalytic effects on internal development of a judicious combination of capital and

[30] *Eleventh Report of ECA*, p. 95; and Jenkins, *op.cit.*, pp. 159-160.

[31] The Joint Philippine-American Finance Commission and the Philippine-United States Agricultural Mission, both in 1947.

[32] Besides the general "self-help" condition previously mentioned, the only conditions on aid envisaged by the Griffin Mission had to do with publicity, reporting, end-use control, and similar administrative matters.

technical aid.[33] Finally, both missions provided the specific recommendations, concerning the kinds and amounts of assistance needed, on which initial U.S. aid to Southeast Asia was based.[34]

3. Economic and Technical Aid Obligations in 1951

Against this background, Table 3 shows the amounts of aid actually obligated by country and project use, during the first year of United States economic and technical assistance in Southern Asia.

In evaluating the obligations data, we should recall that for fiscal year 1951 no comparisons can be made between obligations and proposals data to see whether changes in the relative importance of particular countries, or types of programs, occurred during these two stages. In contrast with later years, no specific proposals for aid to Southern Asia were made to Congress for 1951. At the time Congressional Hearings on the 1951 foreign aid program began, neither the Griffin nor the Bell Mission had submitted its report—nor, for that matter, had they yet been organized. Consequently, no basis for specific aid proposals existed. In effect, and with a few modifications that were subsequently made within the Executive Branch, the recommendations of these missions, when their reports were completed, were nearly identical to the actual 1951 programs. The resulting aid obligations, incurred under the general area of China authorization, were thus initiated without direct Congressional consideration.

What can be inferred from the data in Table 3 about United States policy in Southern Asia in 1951? More specifically, what do the data suggest about the relative priorities implicitly attached by United

[33] The Bell Mission envisaged that the measures it recommended would eliminate the Philippine budgetary and balance of payments deficits, substantially raise agricultural and industrial output and productivity, and improve land tenure and urban working conditions, *if* the use of the proposed $250 million of aid were made conditional "on the whole range of economic policies of the Philippine government." *Report to the President of the United States by the Economic Survey Mission to the Philippines*, pp. 58-59, 106.

[34] As noted in Chapters 2 and 3, War Damage aid to the Philippines, and ERP aid to Indonesia prior to its independence in 1949, had been extended before 1951. Moreover, after Indonesia became an independent state, the Export-Import Bank established a credit line of $100 million in February, 1950, to finance specific industrial and transportation projects in that country. In each of these cases, however, the aid provided was related to "special" circumstances. There was no implication that aid was to be part of a continuing relationship between donor and recipient. Moreover, aid was extended in such a way, and from such different and non-fungible sources of funds, that the problems of intercountry and interprogram allocation, with which we are concerned, did not arise.

States policy to particular countries in the region, and to particular U.S. objectives identified with the individual countries?

Rigorous answers to these questions cannot be derived from data on aid allocations alone, for reasons previously mentioned. But if we accept something less than rigorous answers, a few interpretive comments can be made. In making these comments, our aim is to suggest some of the assumptions implicit in the allocations, *not* to describe the actual process by which the allocations were decided. It is one thing to suggest, as we will, that certain assumptions were implied by particular decisions of allocation, and that it is useful to examine these assumptions systematically. It is quite another to suggest, as we will not, either that these assumptions were explicitly recognized by the decision makers at the time, or that they "caused" the decisions that were made.

4. An Analytical Interpretation of the Aid Obligations

It is probably fair to say that the percentage distribution of economic and technical assistance among the countries in Table 3 is suggestive of the relative "importance" or "value" implicitly attached by the United States to particular aid objectives in the individual countries in 1951. Several points should be made to clarify and support this conjecture, especially in view of our earlier comments concerning the ambiguities involved in attempting to evaluate the aid record.[85]

The first is that "value" and "importance" are used here in the marginal sense previously alluded to. That is, they refer to the relative value of *additions* to the scales on which objectives are measured in the countries of the region. If, for example, we assume that the physical results or productivity of aid in different uses or countries can be measured in various units—say, x, y, and z—then the "value" measure shows the rates of exchange among these units. The "value" measure is thus a policy "price" indicating how many units of y or z would be accepted as equivalent to a unit of x.

Second, it is assumed that the *physical* productivity of initial aid dollars was not very different in the various countries at the time, but that as more aid was provided (or contemplated), its marginal productivity tended to diminish. Stated more simply, it was probably not hard for the Griffin and Bell Missions to find *some* productive uses for economic and technical aid in each country, but once these had

[85] See above, section A.3.

Table 3

FUNDS OBLIGATED FOR UNITED STATES ECONOMIC AND TECHNICAL ASSISTANCE
TO SOUTHERN ASIA, FISCAL YEAR 1951[a]

(by country and project use)

Country	Project Use (millions of dollars)									Country Total as Proportion of Regional Total (per cent)
	Agriculture	Industry	Transportation	Health	Public Administration	Education	Community Development	General and Miscellaneous	TOTAL	
Afghanistan[b]	–	–	–	–	–	–	–	.06	.06	.1
Burma[c]	1.25	.02	3.62	1.79	.04	.65	.80	2.63	10.80	15.3
Ceylon[d]	–	–	–	–	–	–	–	.04	.04	.1
India[e]	.26	.18	.05	.19	.01	–	–	4.50	5.19	7.4
Indochina[f]	1.62	–	3.32	3.73	.33	.03	–	12.80	21.83	31.0
Indonesia[g]	2.55	1.89	–	2.84	–	–	–	.70	7.98	11.3
Nepal[h]	–	–	–	–	–	–	–	.04	.04	.1
Pakistan[i]	.22	.10	.05	.04	.01	.03	–	–	.45	.6
Philippines[j]	2.79	.81	3.63	.60	.38	.22	–	6.68	15.11	21.5
Thailand[k]	2.32	.62	3.93	2.01	–	–	–	–	8.88	12.6
TOTALS	11.01	3.62	14.60	11.20	.77	.93	.80	27.45	70.38	100.0
Project Total as Proportion of Regional Total (per cent)	15.7	5.1	20.8	15.9	1.1	1.3	1.1	39.0	100.0	

Sources: For the sources to which the footnote letters (in parentheses) refer, see Appendix II, pp. 420-422.
[a] At the level of disaggregation of this and subsequent tables on country and project allocations, the problem of assembling exact statistics on foreign aid obligations is like trying to unravel the Gordian Knot one strand at a time. Country obligations for a given year were subject to modification in later years if the original cost estimates of particular projects turned out to be slightly high or low.

Project obligations sometimes changed both for this reason and because of retroactive, though not always uniformly applied, changes in the category labels; for example, separation of the community development category originally included in the agricultural sector, and elimination of a category originally labelled "emergency relief." Moreover, the program labels attached to particular groups of projects (for example, technical assistance, economic assistance, and, in later years, "development assistance" and "defense support") varied with different administering agencies and were frequently applied retroactively and inconsistently to different countries. For these and other reasons, figures purporting to measure the same thing frequently differ from source to source. Though the discrepancies are usually relatively small, they present the problem of which figures to choose as "best." In general, the rule followed has been to select as the "best" the *most recent* obligations figures of the necessary degree of detail. Where several sources have been used, all are cited. If the sources give differing numbers for the same item, the discrepancies are cited in the footnotes with the corresponding sources.

An explanatory comment on the nine project categories should be made. Each includes *both* technical services and commodity aid, but in degrees varying among countries and among categories. In the case of the Public Administration category, nearly all obligations represent the cost of personnel and travel services required in training nationals of the recipient country. The other categories frequently involve relatively more commodity aid. Only five of the categories correspond to sectors more or less standard in interindustry economics: "agriculture," "industry," "transport," "health and education." "Community Development" refers to the multifaceted extension-type projects involved in raising agricultural productivity and improving health and educational services in rural areas. "General and Miscellaneous" includes some technical services, for example, general engineering advisory services, but consists largely of imports of saleable commodities—usually consumer goods and raw materials—programmed to generate local currency or "counterpart." The real or net economic impact of such aid generally depends on the sector in which the counterpart is spent, not on the character of the initial imports. If, for example, consumer goods imports were additive to a recipient's own imports, and if the resulting counterpart were spent largely on the labor costs of new capital-creating projects (as was the intention of the Griffin Mission's recommendations), the effect of the "general" commodity import category would be to raise consumption of the newly employed labor, and to increase investment in the sector in which the counterpart were spent.

Except as otherwise specifically noted, the project categories will have the same meaning in the subsequent tables.

For Afghanistan, Ceylon, Nepal, and Pakistan, the obligations represent technical services under the Act for International Development (see above, Chapter 3, pp. 57-64). For India, the obligations represent technical services under the Act for International Development, except for the general-and-miscellaneous category (see footnote e to this Table). For the other countries, obligations represent *both* technical services and commodity assistance under the China Area Aid Act.

[b] (j), p. 693; (f), p. 123; and (d), p. 569.

[c] (d), p. 570; (b), p. 909; (c), p. 572; and (f), p. 123.

[d] (j), p. 693; (f), p. 123; and (d), p. 569.

[e] (j), p. 693; (d), p. 570; and (f), p. 123. As already discussed, $4.5 million (that is, the "general and miscellaneous" category) represents special aid financed from China Area Aid Act funds to meet part of the cost of India's purchase of food grains from the Commodity Credit Corporation. See this chapter, above, p. 85.

[f] (d), p. 570; (b), p. 909; and (c), p. 572. (a) and (g'), p. 54, give total obligations of $21.8 million.

[g] (j), p. 693; (d), p. 570; (b), p. 910; (g), p. 123; and (g'), p. 54. The figures shown exclude the Export-Import Bank credit line to Indonesia of $100 million announced in February 1950 (see above, this chapter, p. 88, footnote 32). The Indonesian credit was not fully obligated for specific projects until the end of fiscal year 1953. Subsequently, $15.7 million of the original obligations were deobligated and reobligated for other projects in fiscal years 1956 and 1957. See Export-Import Bank of Washington, *Sixteenth Semiannual Report to Congress*, Washington, D.C., 1953, p. 40; and *Semiannual Report to the Congress*, Washington, D.C., 1957, p. 20.

[h] (j), p. 693; (f), p. 123; and (d), p. 569.

[i] (d), p. 570; and (f), p. 123.

[j] (d), p. 570; (f), p. 116; and (j), p. 676. (g') shows total obligations of $15.0 million, and (a) gives obligations of $8.2 million, which agrees with no other source, but probably refers to project assistance excluding the "general and miscellaneous" category.

[k] (c), p. 573; (b), p. 910; and (g'), p. 54. (a) shows obligations of $7.5 million, which agrees with no other source.

been selected, succeeding candidates tended to be of decreasing "productivity."[36] The assumption about diminishing marginal productivity applies to a particular total aid budget. Conceivably, at a much larger aid budget than that which concerned the Griffin Mission, the administrative and other constraints responsible for diminishing aid productivity might have been removed. Though increasing marginal productivity is thus conceivable, it was quite improbable within the budget ceiling imposed on the Griffin Mission.

The allocation implications of these assumptions can now be derived. Until the productivity of aid starts to diminish, it is obviously preferable to allocate aid dollars to the highest-valued objective or country.[37] As more aid is allocated, assuming no change in the objective values, the marginal productivity of aid in the "first" recipient declines. When the marginal returns from aid—the product of the objective value and the marginal productivity of aid in each use—are no higher in the first recipient than in the highest "excluded" country, aid to the latter will begin. If it is assumed that the marginal productivity of aid follows a similar path in the several countries, the amounts of aid allocated will clearly reflect the relative "value" or "importance" attached by U.S. policy to the objectives of aid in the individual countries.[38]

[36] An exact definition of productivity is not essential here. It can be understood as referring to the internal rate of return on investments of some specified maximum size, or to the *expected* rate of return, that is, the internal rate of return corrected for uncertainty. More loosely, "productivity" can be regarded here as referring simply to reasonably "sound"—in an administrative and technical sense—projects that prospective recipients were not considered able or likely to undertake without assistance.

We shall return to the problem of defining and measuring "productivity" in Chapter 10.

[37] For the present, we are assuming a one-to-one correspondence between objective-values and countries.

[38] Specifically, assume that productivity of aid in a country of the set can be represented by a power function of the form

$$O_i = a\, G_i^{\alpha}, \qquad (1)$$

where O_i is output, G_i is the aid variable, and a and α are constants, with $a > 0$, and $0 < \alpha < 1$.

Assume also that the returns from aid to a country are defined as

$$R_i = O_i \cdot v_i, \qquad (2)$$

where the v_i's are the marginal value parameters for the i countries, with $i = 1, 2, \ldots, n$.

Subject to the constraint that country aid allocations equal total aid available,

$$\sum_{i=1}^{n} G_i = G, \qquad (3)$$

it can be shown that total returns, $(\sum_{i=1}^{n} R_i)$, from aid are maximized when the ratio

How relevant are these assumptions, and the inference drawn from them, to the allocation of initial U.S. economic and technical aid to Southeast Asia in 1951? Of course, the explanatory model we have used simplifies and abstracts from the many factors that influenced the recommendations of the Griffin and Bell Missions. And we should recall the qualifying comments previously made about attempts to evaluate aid allocations from the standpoint of their assumed "optimality." Nevertheless, once these qualifications have been duly noted, it is quite plausible to suggest that the model is not too far removed from the realities of the 1951 situation.

Thus the assumptions mentioned, that the productivity of aid was not very dissimilar among the set countries, and that the aid-production function showed diminishing marginal returns, were at the time reasonable.[39] In all of Southern Asia, there were similar opportunities for technical and commodity assistance in improving meth-

---

between country aid allocations is equal to the ratio of the corresponding value parameters raised to the $\frac{1}{1-a}$ power; that is, when

$$\frac{G_1}{G_2} = \left(\frac{v_1}{v_2}\right)^{\frac{1}{1-a}}, \qquad \frac{G_2}{G_n} = \left(\frac{v_2}{v_n}\right)^{\frac{1}{1-a}}, \dots, \qquad \frac{G_1}{G_n} = \left(\frac{v_1}{v_n}\right)^{\frac{1}{1-a}} \quad (4)$$

The smaller is a, the more nearly will the optimal allocations be proportional to the corresponding value parameters.

The proof arises from the condition that maximization requires equalizing the marginal returns from aid in each country. Hence,

$$\frac{\partial R_1}{\partial G_1} = \frac{\partial R_2}{\partial G_2} = \dots, = \frac{\partial R_n}{\partial G_n} \quad (5)$$

Differentiating, according to (1) and (2),

$$\frac{aa \cdot v_1}{G_1^{1-a}} = \frac{aa \cdot v_2}{G_2^{1-a}} \dots, = \frac{aa \cdot v_n}{G_n^{1-a}} \quad (6)$$

Simplifying (6), gives:

$$\frac{G_1}{G_2} = \left(\frac{v_1}{v_2}\right)^{\frac{1}{1-a}}, \qquad \frac{G_2}{G_n} = \left(\frac{v_2}{v_n}\right)^{\frac{1}{1-a}}, \dots, \qquad \frac{G_1}{G_n} = \left(\frac{v_1}{v_n}\right)^{\frac{1}{1-a}}$$

which is the same as (4).

[39] The resource constraint of the model (see equation [3], footnote 38) was provided by the potential availability of China Aid funds (see Chapter 3, section C.3, and this chapter, p. 84). Unobligated China Aid funds suggested the approximate order of magnitude of total aid likely to be available for allocation by the Griffin Mission, that is the $\sum_{i=1}^{n} G_i$ of the model.

ods of production and developing mineral and agricultural resources. In all, there were also limitations on the amount of aid that could be effectively used in the short-run: limitations imposed by administrative and organizational bottlenecks, sectoral interdependencies, the lack of social overhead facilities, labor shortages and immobilities, and so on.

Consequently, once the more obvious opportunities for assistance were selected, the limitations on absorptive capacity led to rapidly diminishing productivity among the "next-best" projects. How far down the list of illustrative aid projects, suggested by the host governments, the selection proceeded, was crucially—if only tacitly and qualitatively—affected by the missions' judgment of the relative importance or value of U.S. objectives in the countries concerned.[40] In the wording we have used, the allocation of aid thus depended on, and hence reflected, the value parameters implicitly attached by the United States to the productivity of aid to the several countries.

Hence, the aid allocations actually made have some bearing on the problem of evaluating the relative importance of U.S. objectives at the time in the various Southeast Asian countries. In the four countries visited by the Griffin Mission, for example, it is reasonable to contend that the relative importance accorded the objective of increasing political stability and improving governmental performance capabilities in the four recipients, was about the same as the relative amounts of aid allocated to them (see Table 3). To avoid a tautology here, we would have to contend, further, that the relative gravity, need, or urgency—and hence value to the United States—of enhancing political stability in these four countries, could be measured, or at least considered, *independently* of the actual aid allocations made. The allocations could then be attributed to the relative values, rather than being identical with them.

Without pretending that the relative marginal values of this broad objective in the four countries were explicitly considered as such, we can argue that in fact such consideration was an implicit part of the context in which the mission operated. For example, in the Associated States of Indochina, where an active communist-led insurrection involving a U.S. ally was underway, it is reasonable to believe that the need for political stability was the greatest among the Southeast Asian countries. For Burma, also threatened by an internal com-

[40] And, of course, by the judgment of the State Department and ECA after the missions' recommendations were submitted.

munist revolt, a reasonable case could have been made for according the next greatest value to strengthening and stabilizing the established government. In Thailand and Indonesia, the stability needs were qualitatively similar, but less urgent. Thailand's friendly pro-Western government seemed to be fairly secure. In Indonesia, though the new government was not especially secure, its alternatives seemed at the time to be in the nature of a "loyal opposition," rather than something that the United States had reason to view with alarm.

5. Some Complications: The Philippines and South Asia

The Philippine allocation complicates this line of reasoning. Actually, the $15 million allocated from China Aid funds, after the Bell Mission's report, was first proposed in the *middle* of the fiscal year during negotiation of the Foster-Quirino Agreement. Moreover, the funds were not obligated until the last quarter of the year, after "substantial compliance" by the Philippines with the provisions of that agreement.[41] But whether we consider a hypothetical allocation *rate* of $30 million annually, or the actual allocation of $15 million in the last quarter of the fiscal year, the same difficulty arises for the type of allocative reasoning we have advanced.

Disturbing as were the threats to internal stability posed by the Huks and by the corruption and purposelessness of the Quirino administration, the Philippine situation was not nearly as grave as that in Indochina or Burma. If we nevertheless say that a relatively high U.S. aid allocation to the Philippines suggested that a high "value" was placed on the results of such aid, the higher value must be explained by reference to some *other* scale or objective than political stability. In this case, the "other" objective can be traced to the special characteristics of the long-standing relationship between the two countries, including, as part of the relationship, the U.S. strategic stake in its air bases in the Philippines, as well as the close business and trade connections between the two countries.

Put another way, if the chance of Huk success in the Philippines was plainly less than that of the Viet Minh in Indochina, or of the communist insurrection in Burma, the United States had sentimental, strategic, and economic reasons to view the lesser chance in the

[41] See *Thirteenth Report of ECA*, p. 82.

Philippines as its more vital concern. Special concern for one's friends, as well as one's strategic and economic interests, may certainly be influential factors in aid allocation. Whether and how they should be categorized as aid objectives is something we will return to in Chapter 7. Here, at least, we can say that these factors seem to have affected the value attached by United States policy to aid in the Philippines and the amount allocated to it in 1951.

Mention should also be made of the low initial allocation of aid to India, Pakistan, and the other South Asian countries listed in Table 3. For reasons already noted,[42] U.S. aid programs in these countries did not begin in earnest until the following year. With the exception of the Indian food grant of $4.5 million, only a negligible amount of technical assistance was provided South Asia in 1951, from funds authorized by the Act for International Development. By agreement within the U.S. government, the use of China Area Aid funds by ECA in the Southeast Asian countries covered by the Griffin and Bell Missions, was to exclude the use of A.I.D. assistance by the Technical Cooperation Administration, and the use of A.I.D. funds by TCA in South Asia was to exclude the use of China Area Aid funds by ECA.[43] Hence, aid in the South Asian countries was not considered an alternative to aid in the Southeast Asian countries. Though the South Asian countries are included in Table 3, they were not a part of the same allocation system as the Griffin-Bell countries. In part, this separation, as well as the delay in initiating active aid programs in South Asia until the following year, can be viewed simply as an administrative accident within the U.S. bureaucracy. In part, however, it was more than this.

At the start of fiscal year 1951, marginal improvements in governmental performance and internal political stability in the South Asian countries were not valued as highly by the United States as such improvements in the five Southeast Asian countries. Geographically more remote from the center of Chinese communist power, and seeming to be politically less vulnerable to internal communist pressures, the South Asian countries appeared in 1951 to be a stage further removed from the danger zone than the other countries of the set we are concerned with.

The point is *not* that India, even in 1951, was considered to be "worth" less to the United States than Thailand, for example, but

[42] See above, pp. 84-85.
[43] See Chapter 3 above, pp. 60ff. See also, Brown and Opie, *op.cit.*, p. 397.

that the *marginal* improvements which aid might bring about were considered (perhaps quite erroneously) to be more valuable in Thailand. One reason was that conditions were, or seemed to be, relatively stable and promising in India at the time—before, incidentally, the gravity of the Indian food situation was fully recognized, and before the Indian national elections in the following year suggested that internal political conditions were perhaps not as promising as they had seemed.[44] Another reason lay in the hopeful presumption that any Indian requirements for external assistance could be met by the United Kingdom and the Commonwealth. For both reasons, the value to the United States of using aid to bring about further (marginal) improvements in India was, at least implicitly, judged to be low at the time. As in comparing the "worth" of diamonds and water, the relevant comparison for most problems of intercountry aid allocation is at the margin.

6. Sectoral Allocations of Economic and Technical Aid

Before we leave Table 3, an interesting point concerning the amounts allocated to the various project categories might be noted. Leaving the largest category, "general and miscellaneous," aside for the moment, the main project allocations in the region as a whole, and in most of the larger aid recipients individually, are for transportation, health, agriculture, and industry. There is, of course, no way of evaluating the relative productivity of investment in these sectors in precise economic terms in the absence of more information than we have. But it is at least clear that investments in the different sectors usually had quite different time horizons. The typical projects in agriculture—for example, distribution of fertilizer, seed, and small farm tools—and in health, for example, the use of DDT and antibiotics—represented either an increase in investment with a short-run yield, or an immediate increase in consumption. By contrast, projects in transportation—for example, harbor and road development—and in industry, often represented an increase in investment with a smaller annual yield spread over a longer time period.

The relative productivity of projects with differing time horizons depends on the time discount applied. Other things being equal, if the interest rate is high, projects with a high yield over a short time horizon will be relatively more productive. Conversely, if the interest

[44] See Chapter 9, section B.

rate is low, projects with a low yield over a long time horizon will be relatively more productive. That a large share of total project allocations went toward the short-run project categories (agriculture and health) is perhaps suggestive of a high premium attached to short-run yield, that is, an implicitly high interest rate, in the allocation of initial U.S. aid. And the implicitly high interest rate can, in turn, be attributed to the fact that fairly rapid results were considered especially important at the time in order to strengthen the new Southeast Asian governments.[45]

The suggestion is strengthened if one looks at the project categories for which the local currency counterpart funds, generated by the "general and miscellaneous" category,[46] were obligated. Evaluating the counterpart-use data presents difficulties, from the standpoint of the substitutability problem, similar to those involved in evaluating the direct project allocations of dollar aid. Nevertheless, the counterpart-use data at least indicate that substantially more counterpart funds were obligated in 1951 for agricultural and health projects—and other projects with short-term yields—than for transportation and industrial projects, in the Southeast Asian countries for which data are available.[47]

7. Global Aid and Aid in Southern Asia

We conclude this review of the first year of United States economic and technical assistance to the countries of Southern Asia by noting its scale relative to the other bilateral assistance carried on in 1951 under the Foreign Economic Assistance Act of 1950. Table 4 shows the amount of aid in Southern Asia compared to total economic assistance in the Far East, and to global assistance under the Foreign Economic Assistance Act.

[45] That transportation received the largest single sectoral dollar allocation is consistent with this hypothesis. In some cases, rehabilitation investment for transportation facilities damaged during the war (for example, the port of Rangoon) could be expected to yield quick and large returns. Even with an implicitly high time discount, such projects were relatively productive, and hence attractive candidates for economic and technical aid.

[46] See the third paragraph of footnote a in Table 3.

[47] Of the $14.6 million in counterpart funds approved for use in the Southeast Asian countries from June 5, 1950, to November 30, 1951, 47 per cent was for agricultural and health projects, and 36 per cent was for transportation and industrial projects. The remainder of the $27.5 million shown in the general-and-miscellaneous category in Table 3 either had not yet generated counterpart by the end of this period, or represented obligations for types of projects (for example, general engineering advisory services), which did not yield local currency counterpart. The Mutual Security Program, First Report to Congress, p. 71.

Table 4

UNITED STATES ECONOMIC AND TECHNICAL AID TO SOUTHERN
ASIA IN FISCAL YEAR 1951 COMPARED TO TOTAL ASIAN AND
GLOBAL ASSISTANCE UNDER THE FOREIGN ECONOMIC
ASSISTANCE ACT OF 1950

		As Proportion of:	
	Obligations	Total Asian Aid	Global Aid
	(millions of dollars)	(per cent)	
Economic and Technical Aid to Southern Asia, 1951	70.4	43.1	2.7
Economic and Technical Aid to Formosa, 1951	92.9	56.9	3.6
Total Asian Aid	163.3[a]	100.0	6.3
Global Aid Under Foreign Economic Assistance Act of 1950	2,607.1	–	100.0

Sources: Table 3, above, and (g'), p. 54. (See Appendix II.)
[a] Excludes assistance to Korea under the Far Eastern Assistance Act of 1950. Of
the $90 million appropriated for Korean economic aid in fiscal year 1951, the major
part was transferred to the Department of the Army after outbreak of hostilities.
See Chapter 3 above, pp. 49-50.

C. MILITARY ASSISTANCE IN SOUTHEAST ASIA

1. The Melby-Erskine-Craig Mission and the
Mutual Defense Assistance Program

With the start of the Korean war, building up local military forces
became a higher-valued objective of United States foreign policy
in Asia as well as in Europe. In furtherance of this objective, a joint
State-Defense-ECA military survey mission was appointed ten days
after the North Korean attack, with the task of "visiting the principal
countries in Southeast Asia and accurately measuring the specific
needs of each for further military assistance."[48] The mission, under
the direction of John Melby, of the State Department, Major General
Graves Erskine, representing the Department of Defense, and Glenn
Craig of ECA, visited Indochina, the Philippines, Thailand, Indonesia, and Malaya during the next three months. Timing of the
Melby-Erskine-Craig Mission was, thus, as closely related to the

[48] *Second Semi-Annual Report to Congress on MDAP*, Washington, D.C., 1951,
pp. 43-44.

Korean war as the timing of the Griffin Mission was to the fall of mainland China. Like the role of the Griffin and Bell Missions in the initiation of economic and technical assistance to Southeast Asia, the Melby Mission played a significant role in the expansion of the Mutual Defense Assistance Program in the area.

As previously noted, the original MDAP appropriations for 1951, prepared *prior* to the Korean attack, though not enacted until September, 1950, totalled $1.2 billion. Of the total, $1 billion was intended for NATO members, $131 million for Greece, Turkey, and Iran, $75 million for the "general area of China"—including but not confined to Formosa—and $16 million for Korea and the Philippines.[49]

After the Korean attack, the President, on August 1, 1950, submitted to Congress a request for additional MDAP appropriations for 1951 of $4 billion. Of this amount, which was subsequently appropriated in full on September 27, 1950, by the Supplemental Appropriations Act of 1951, $3.5 billion was for the NATO area, $193 million for Greece, Turkey, and Iran, and $303 million for "the Republic of the Philippines and other nations in southern and eastern Asia."[50]

The primary recommendations of the Melby Mission, submitted after its survey had been underway barely two weeks, provided the basis for the Asian portion of the President's supplemental appropriations request. It is interesting, in this connection, to note that the proportion of the supplemental 1951 MDAP funds appropriated for the Asian area was approximately the same as the proportion intended for the Asian area in the initial MDAP appropriation. Of the $1.2 billion initial MDAP appropriation for 1951, $91 million or 7.4 per cent was for the "general area of China," Korea and the Philippines; of the $4 billion supplemental MDAP appropriation, $303 million or 7.6 per cent was for the same area, though now excluding Korea.[51]

Toward the end of 1951, an additional $75 million was transferred

[49] See above, Chapter 3, pp. 53-55, and footnote 70, p. 54. Also see *First Semi-Annual Report to Congress on MDAP*, Washington, D.C., 1950, pp. 50-51; and *Second Semi-Annual Report*, p. 27. Of the "general area" MDAP funds, it was "unofficially reported," before Korea, that Indochina would receive $15 million, Thailand $10 million, and Indonesia $5 million. Richard P. Stebbins, *The United States in World Affairs, 1950*, New York, 1951, p. 179.

[50] *Second Report on MDAP*, p. 29.

[51] Mutual Defense Assistance in Korea was suspended in August 1950. While the war continued, all military expenditures in Korea were financed from the regular Defense Department appropriations. *Ibid.*, p. 38.

from the NATO portion of the MDAP appropriation for use in the Asian area,[52] raising the share of military assistance to the Asian area, excluding Korea, to 9 per cent of total MDAP appropriations for fiscal year 1951.

The foregoing data on MDAP appropriations for 1951 are summarized in Table 5.

2. Objectives and Content of Mutual Defense Assistance

Before commenting on the data in Table 5, a few facts should be noted concerning the content and objectives of MDAP in 1951 in each of the recipient countries we are concerned with.[53] In each case, MDAP took the tangible form of the military end-items and training directly granted to the recipient country, and the intangible form of influence exercised through such grants on the recipient's use of its own resources for military purposes.[54] But beyond this point, the character and aims of the individual country programs varied widely.

In Indochina, for example, MDAP sought to strengthen fairly extensive, conventional capabilities suited to fighting a major "one-country" war in which the Viet Minh adversary had large-scale, well-equipped ground forces, trained and increasingly supplied by China. Initial military aid to Indochina consequently involved several dozen fighter planes, a number of B-26 light bombers, light naval vessels, and napalm weapons. In Thailand, the capabilities sought were "effective front line troops" and a small, well-trained air

[52] *Fourth Semi-Annual Report to Congress on MDAP*, Washington, D.C., 1952, p. 99, footnote 4. The Mutual Defense Assistance Act of 1949 authorized the President to transfer up to 5 per cent of the funds authorized for any one region for use in any other region covered by the Act.

[53] The following information on military aid in particular Southeast Asian countries in 1951 is taken from the *Third Report on MDAP*, pp. 22-25, and the *Fourth Report on MDAP*, pp. 57-65. The quoted phrases in the following two paragraphs are from these sources.

[54] Nearly all MDAP dollar expenditures were for military end-items: to reimburse the U.S. military departments for items furnished from stock; to meet charges for repair of equipment supplied; to procure new equipment; and to meet costs of packing, crating, handling and transport. Training, provided in the recipient country by the U.S. Military Assistance Advisory Group, or in the United States at service training schools, accounted for a small share of MDAP dollar costs. In the first years of the program, relatively little financing was provided for troop rations, POL, and other "consumables." Besides the costed items, some end-items were initially provided under MDAP without any dollar costs. Materiel declared excess to U.S. needs was, within stipulated limits, furnished without reimbursement to the military departments under Title IV of the Mutual Defense Assistance Act of 1949. See *Fourth Report on MDAP*, p. 67.

Table 5

MUTUAL DEFENSE ASSISTANCE APPROPRIATIONS,
FISCAL YEAR 1951[a]

Source of Funds ——— Region	Initial (Pre-Korea) Appropriations[c]	Supplemental Appropriations[d]	Inter-regional Transfers[e]	TOTALS	Proportion of Total
	(millions of dollars)				(per cent)
NATO Area	1,000.0	3,504.0	—90.3	4,413.7	84.5
Greece, Turkey, and Iran	131.5	193.0	14.8	339.3	6.5
Asian Area[b]	91.0	303.0	75.5	469.5	9.0
Korea and Philippines	(16.0)			(16.0)	
General Area of China	(75.0)			(75.0)	
Southern and Eastern Asia	–	(303.0)	(75.5)	(378.5)	
TOTALS	1,222.5	4,000.0	0	5,222.5	100.0

[a] In describing MDAP allocations, appropriations data are preferable to obligations data for our purposes. MDAP financial records involve a complex sequence from appropriation to "allocation" or allotment (by the Budget Bureau to the Defense Department), to "commitment," to "obligation" and finally, expenditure of funds. The "commitment" stage is additional to the categories used in recording utilization of non-military aid funds. It represents an administrative reservation of funds (for countries and equipment classes) which subsequently leads to obligations, the latter representing orders placed and contracts awarded.

Because contracting time for many military end-items has been long, and because annual MDAP appropriations have, nearly automatically, involved a reappropriation of "unobligated" (and hence of "uncommitted") funds from preceding appropriations, commitments and obligations have both lagged far behind annual appropriations. Appropriations, therefore, represent a more satisfactory indicator of the changing annual pattern of MDAP allocations among regions than either commitments or obligations.

Since appropriations are made on a regional, rather than country, basis, intercountry appropriations comparisons are impossible. In the case of economic and technical aid data (see above, Table 3), we use obligations, rather than appropriations, because obligations are made on a *country* basis, appropriations usually on a *regional* basis. In the case of MDAP, however, intercountry comparisons of *obligations* are precluded by the security classification of the relevant obligations data. Consequently, we use appropriations, rather than obligations, for the MDAP data, because at the regional level, the appropriations figures are more complete.

[b] The "Asian Area" category, which does not appear in the MDA Act or appropriations as such, is a composite of the indicated sub-headings which do appear in the legislation. It is used to facilitate comparisons with appropriations in later years when the sub-headings were changed. As already noted, MDAP aid to Korea was discontinued shortly after the Korean war began. The data include military aid to Formosa.

[c] Appropriated in the General Appropriation Act of 1951. The amount appropriated, in total and for each region individually, represented the full amount requested by the Executive Branch. See *Second Report on MDAP*, p. 27.

[d] Appropriated in the Supplemental Appropriation Act of 1951. The amount appropriated, in total and for each region individually, represented the full amount requested by the Executive Branch. *Ibid.*, p. 29.

[e] A transfer of the indicated NATO funds, for use in Greece, Turkey, and the Asian area, was made on June 11, 1951. See *Fourth Report on MDAP*, footnote 4, p. 99.

force to meet "the threat of communist aggression." In the Philippines, the relevant capability was an additional group of ten mobile constabulary units "to rout the Huks from their strongholds and break up their forces into small, scattered elements."

In Burma and Indonesia, the force goals were more limited. MDAP in Burma was confined to ten coast-guard patrol vessels to prevent smuggling and "to deter insurgents from attacks against river craft and towns in the [Irrawaddy] delta area." In Indonesia, vehicles, ordnance and signal items, as well as training, were provided to help develop "a trained national constabulary, amounting ultimately to two mobile police brigades."

In summary, among the military aid programs initiated or expanded as a result of the Melby Mission recommendations, two (Indochina and Thailand) were concerned with building capabilities for relatively "big" local wars;[55] and three (the Philippines, Indonesia and Burma) were primarily concerned with enhancing capabilities to maintain internal order against small-scale insurrectionary threats.

From Table 5, it can be seen that *total* MDAP appropriations for 1951 represented a fourfold increase over the first year of the program, that is, from $1.3 billion in 1949-50 to $5.2 billion in fiscal year 1951.[56] As a result of the Korean attack, total military assistance in 1951 was thus clearly and understandably accorded by the United States a substantially higher relative value—compared, for example, with "non-military" assistance and with most other government programs as well—than during the first year of MDAP operations. While appropriations for MDAP in fiscal year 1950 had been about one-third of global economic aid obligations, in 1951 MDAP appropriations became twice as large as global economic aid obligations.[57]

Also of interest are the changes in MDAP aid shares received by the regions shown in Table 5. The NATO area's share rose from 77 per cent in 1950 to over 84 per cent of total MDAP appropriations in 1951, the Asian share rose from 7 per cent to 9 per cent, and the

[55] The Formosa program, too, was directed "toward increasing the capabilities of the Chinese Nationalist armed forces to defend the island against hostile attack," *ibid.*, p. 64.

[56] For the 1950 figures, see pp. 53-54.

[57] Economic aid obligations for ERP and Greek-Turkish aid were $3.6 billion in fiscal year 1950, while MDAP appropriations were $1.3 billion. In 1951, economic aid obligations under the Foreign Economic Assistance Act were $2.6 billion and MDAP appropriations $5.2 billion. For the economic aid obligations, see *Operations Report*, International Cooperation Administration, data as of December 31, 1956, Washington, D.C., 1957, p. 54.

share received by Greece, Turkey, and Iran fell from over 16 per cent to less than 7 per cent.[58] It might therefore be reasonable to infer that, within MDAP itself, the returns to the United States from increments in military strength rose relatively more in Europe than Asia—excluding Korea, of course—and more in Asia than in the Greek-Turkish-Iranian area. Here, again, we risk the tautology that arose in assessing intercountry allocations of economic and technical assistance. If the inference is drawn that a shift in interregional (or intercountry) shares of MDA appropriations signifies a corresponding shift in the relative returns to the United States from military aid to these regions, *and* if we wish this inference to be more than simply an identity, we need to define returns in terms other than the observed allocative shares.

3. Evaluating Returns from Military Aid

Though it is a difficult problem and one we shall have occasion to return to later, a few observations can be made here to clarify some of the difficulties involved in the notion of returns from military aid.

One component of the returns from military aid is the estimated likelihood of various local conflicts whose favorable resolution would require the availability of additional local military strength. What are some of these conflicts? They can be thought of as a more or less continuous spectrum of possible local wars varying in their geographic scope, the complexity of weapons systems involved, and the level of organization and types of military units used. The possible alternatives are many. Some of them are illustrated by the differing military capabilities that were sought by MDAP in the several Southeast Asian countries.

Geographically, the possible alternatives range from small-scale civil uprising in a single country, to two-country conflicts not involving a communist country, to small-area and theatre wars involving participation by minor communist countries (North Korea or North Viet Nam) or major communist powers (China or the Soviet Union). In their weapons dimension, they extend from primitive hand weapons, to automatic infantry and artillery weapons, to ground armor, to air fighters and bombers, and from high explosive to nuclear weapons—the latter over a fairly continuous range as wide

---

[58] For comparison, see Chapter 3 above, pp. 53-54. The 7 per cent attributed to Asia in 1950 is arrived at by adding approximately $16 million of previous MDAP obligations in Korea and the Philippines to the $75 million for the general area of China.

as that of all the preceding stages. And in their organizational dimension, the range is from small guerrilla units to fully-mobilized national forces.

Conceptually, as the likelihood of one such local war situation rises in a particular region, *other things being equal,* the returns to the United States from using aid to increase the appropriate type of local military strength in that region may be expected to rise also. The italicized qualification is, unfortunately, crucial. What if the estimated probabilities change in more than one region at a time— as did occur, for example, following the Korean attack? In this case, assessing the relative returns to the United States from military aid in the various regions requires some way of measuring the relative disutility or gravity of the local war alternatives whose associated probabilities have changed.

What, for example, is the relative disutility to the United States of a given increase in the probability of internal insurrection in Indonesia compared with a similar change in Burma, or of external aggression of a certain scale in Southeast Asia compared with a similar change in the Middle East? The answer is even more difficult than estimating the changes in probabilities themselves. For the disutility of a particular local war contingency depends on such a variety of conjectural interactions—strategic, political, and economic— as to place it more in the realm of judgment and intuition than quantitative estimation.

Analytically, this is something less than a satisfactory answer. Two slightly more hopeful comments can be added. First, the disutility, or "worth," of a possible local war situation might be estimated in terms of the costs which the United States would be willing to incur to counter the situation if it arose. For example, the disutility of a North Korean attack on South Korea (*ca.* 1965), might be considered more or less than the disutility of a Viet Minh attack of equivalent scope on South Viet Nam, depending on the relative costs we would be prepared to incur to counter each of the two situations.

Second, even if disutility, in the sense that we have used it, remains largely a matter of intuitive judgment, it is perhaps worthwhile to make such judgment explicit. For example, a relative "gravity" or disutility measure on a pure numerical scale might be assigned at least to the major alternative war situations under consideration. By combining such a policy parameter with the no-less intuitively based probability estimates already mentioned, one might then approach an expected-*value* estimate for the corresponding local war situations.

Nor do the problems of estimating disutilities (or worths) and probabilities exhaust the difficulties of dealing with military aid allocation in the future, or of inferring anything meaningful from observed changes in MDAP allocations in the past. Allocations of military aid, besides being affected by the disutility and probability components of "value," will be affected by the varying capacity of military aid in different uses to produce desired increases in military strength. Allocating additional military aid to a lower-valued use may be warranted if the physical effects produced by aid in this use are large enough to compensate for the lower *unit* worth of these effects. By the same token, allocating additional military aid to a higher-valued use may be eschewed because its effectiveness is limited.

Limitations on the effectiveness of military aid in a potentially high-valued use may, in turn, arise from two different causes. If the non-aid services, experience, and facilities required for the effective employment of military end-items are absent, hardware itself may have little effect. Bottlenecks in organization, logistics, and "infrastructure" of various kinds may impose limits on the capacity to absorb military hardware effectively that are essentially similar to absorptive limitations in the case of economic aid.[59]

The other limitation on effectiveness arises from the fact that certain highly valued contingencies may not be susceptible of influence by additional military aid. The physical effectiveness of military aid is usually measured in terms of increases in the level of particular forces which such aid makes possible. But certain kinds of possibly highly valued local war contingencies may not be affected at all by continuous, relatively small force increments. If the contingency were, for example, a mass Chinese attack against Burma, the number of divisions in Burma's army—over the feasible range imposed by budget constraints—might make little or no difference, either in terms of delaying the Chinese advance or making it more costly to the aggressor. The *marginal* effectiveness of military aid, from the standpoint of this contingency, might be too small to justify aid.

While the "effectiveness," or productivity, of military aid will thus be an important variable in the allocation of military aid, it should be clear that it is not wholly independent of the "probability" and "disutility" variables already discussed. The latter variables will define, or, more realistically, suggest, the most highly valued local

[59] See above, p. 94.

war contingencies. And it is in terms of these contingencies that the appropriate scales or units (for example, air, ground, or naval forces, police units, bases, etc.) for measuring the effectiveness of additional military aid must be determined.[60]

It should be noted that no military aid was intended or proposed in the South Asian countries in 1951. The returns to the United States from a military buildup in this area were thus considered to be small. Notwithstanding the Korean war, there seemed little probability of a local war situation developing in South Asia which could be favorably affected by additional military strength. The obvious possibility of an Indo-Pakistan war over Kashmir was quite consistent with this judgment. Favorable resolution of the Kashmir dispute, from the U.S. standpoint, would hardly have been helped by additional military strength on one side *or* the other.

Besides presenting some of the facts concerning MDAP in the Asian area, the preceding discussion has tried to suggest some of the conceptual problems involved in evaluating "returns" from military aid, as well as in inferring anything meaningful from historical allocations of such aid. Although much has been written about the shortcomings of the military mind where civilian policies are concerned, the shortcomings of the civilian mind where military matters are concerned is perhaps less frequently noted. There is, for example, a natural tendency for the civilian, be he Congressman or voter, to view the determination of military aid needs and shares as relatively clear, precise, and dependable. In fact, the analytical complexities that are involved in military aid allocation are no less troublesome than those involved in the allocation of economic and technical aid. Perhaps they are more so. The estimation of local war probabilities and the judgment of their worth or disutility to the United States (the two components of the "value" of local military buildup), and the assessment of whether military aid can contribute to altering

[60] Since the relevant effectiveness units will still be diverse, the problem of inter-country and interregional allocations is likely to result in a comparison of fish and fowl; for example, constabulary units in the Philippines and jet fighters in Thailand. Conceptually, at least, this problem is not as intractable as some of the other problems. One solution is to make the comparison in terms of the alternative costs to the United States of providing similar capabilities in other ways. The differing units can then be compared in terms of relative dollar costs. Another solution is simply to focus responsible judgment on the need to establish a substitution or exchange rate between the differing units. If a "technical" substitution rate cannot be calculated by alternative costing, the best procedure may be to establish an explicit "policy" rate which specifies the number of units of X to be considered of equivalent value to a unit of Y.

these contingencies and by how much (the "productivity" of military aid), are questions as complex and difficult as any of the analytical problems connected with economic aid.

We shall return to these questions in Chapters 7 and 10. Here the point is simply that military aid allocation is emphatically not the cut-and-dried and unassailable process it is sometimes believed to be.[61]

D. SUMMARY

In this and the two following chapters, our aim is to order the record of United States aid in Southern Asia, both for its own sake and to provide a context for the analytical discussion in subsequent chapters. The record of U.S. economic and military aid in Southern Asia in the period from 1951 through 1957 is to be presented in terms of the international circumstances and aid legislation affecting the programs, and the dollar allocations to particular countries and programs. Primary stress is to be placed on the allocation aspects of the record. In assessing the aid data, the general approach set forth is to treat allocations in any one year as though they were "optimal," and then to see what assumptions seem necessary to validate this premise, whether these assumptions seem realistic, and, indeed, what useful meaning can be attached to the concept of "optimality" in analyzing foreign aid problems.

Economic and technical assistance in Southern Asia was initiated at the start of fiscal year 1951 as a result of the recommendations of the Griffin Mission to Southeast Asia in March and April 1950. The Griffin Mission was strongly influenced by the China experience. It viewed U.S. economic and technical aid as a key resource which could stimulate internal development and contribute to political stability. The Griffin Mission did not visit the Philippines. Aid to the

[61] Although there have been several dozen public and private surveys, commissions and reports dealing with foreign economic and technical aid in the underdeveloped areas over the past decade, it is interesting that only a few studies have considered in any detail the problems of military aid in the same areas. (The formation in November 1958 of a Presidential Committee, The Draper Committee, to study the military aid program, was in part a response to this neglect.) For the few useful, if not exhaustive, studies of military aid, see *The Military Assistance Program of the United States*, Two Studies and a Report Prepared at the Request of the Special Committee to Study the Foreign Aid Program, U.S. Senate, Committee Print, Washington, D.C., 1957; Paul H. Nitze, "The Policy Background of Military Assistance," in *International Stability and Progress*, The American Assembly, New York, 1957; and Edgar S. Furniss, Jr., *Some Perspectives on American Military Assistance*, Center for International Studies, Memorandum Number Thirteen, Princeton University, 1957. For the Draper Committee Report, see *Composite Report of the President's Committee To Study the United States Military Assistance Program*, Vols. I and II, Washington, D.C., 1959.

Philippines was initiated as a result of the recommendations of a parallel U.S. survey mission (the Bell Mission) which visited that country. No active program of U.S. aid in South Asia was begun until the following year, both because South Asia seemed less threatened by the communist victory on the China mainland, and because aid requirements in South Asia were initially considered to be the responsibility of the British Commonwealth.

Actual economic and technical aid obligations in 1951 totalled $70.4 million, provided under authority of the China Area Aid Act. The intercountry breakdown of this total can be interpreted in terms of a simple model whose main parameters are the physical productivity of aid in different countries and the marginal "values" attached by the United States to these countries. The model interprets allocations to Indochina, Indonesia, and Thailand fairly plausibly, but it runs into difficulties, and requires further elaboration, in interpreting allocations to the Philippines and the South Asian countries.

A brief inspection of the sectoral composition of obligations in 1951 suggests an implicitly high time-discount attached to the allocation of initial aid. In turn, the implicitly high discount rate can be attributed to the fact that rapid returns were considered by the United States to be especially important to strengthen the new Southeast Asian governments quickly.

The Mutual Defense Assistance Program, which was originally planned for Southeast Asia in fiscal year 1951, was expanded as a result of the recommendations of a State-Defense-ECA military survey mission, shortly after the North Korean attack. Mutual Defense Assistance in Southeast Asia was directed toward creating quite different military capabilities in different countries: to help meet relatively "big" local war contingencies in Indochina and Thailand; and to help maintain internal order in the Philippines, Indonesia, and Burma.

The "returns" from military aid in different uses can be conceived in relation to the relative *probabilities* of a wide spectrum of possible local wars, the relative *"disutilities"* attached by the United States to these contingencies, and the capacity or *productivity* of military aid to produce increments in military strength relevant to these contingencies. Even though some useful things can be said about these matters, it is evident that the problem of evaluating returns from military aid is no less complex and difficult than the corresponding problem in the case of economic assistance.

[109]

CHAPTER 5

THE MUTUAL SECURITY PROGRAM IN
SOUTHERN ASIA, 1952-1954

A. THE BEGINNING OF MUTUAL SECURITY

1. *The Foreign Aid Budget Cycle*

TO A CONSIDERABLE EXTENT, the size and composition of foreign assistance programs in any particular fiscal year depend on circumstances and judgments made in the preceding year. The budget cycle for a given year's foreign aid program gets underway with the Bureau of the Budget's call for "estimates" from the administering agencies, at the beginning of the prior fiscal year. Once the Bureau has started the process, plans, recommendations, and decisions begin to be made: by the U.S. Operations Missions and Military Assistance Advisory Groups (MAAG) early in the fall, in response to requests from their Washington agencies—the International Cooperation Administration and the Defense Department, respectively; by ICA, and the State and Defense Departments in December, when hearings are held by the Budget Bureau on prospective appropriations requests to the pending Congressional session; by the Budget Bureau and the White House in January, when the President's State of the Union and Budget messages to the Congress are presented, and again in the early spring, when Congressional hearings usually begin; and, finally, by Congress, in the summer, when program authorizations and appropriations are enacted.

Decision-making is a continuous process in which the early stages, though preparatory and preliminary, significantly constrain the decisions subsequently made. In the case of foreign aid, initial judgments about aid needs and shares can be overturned if later circumstances are sufficiently compelling. The fourfold increase in the supplemental MDAP appropriation for 1951, after the Korean attack, was a case in point. And smaller adjustments to less compelling circumstantial changes can be made on the discretionary authority of the President. But these tend to be exceptions. In general, aid allocations in any given year reflect more accurately the judgments and circumstances of the preceding year than those currently prevailing. Consequently, to record the circumstances—international and domestic—relevant to foreign economic and military assistance in 1952, for example, we need to look mainly at 1951.

2. The International Context
Preceding Mutual Security

During fiscal year 1951, hostilities in Korea continued, but prospects for their termination improved. In the fall of 1950, when preparation for fiscal year 1952 foreign aid programs actively began, the rapid recovery and advance of United Nations forces strengthened these prospects. Though Chinese intervention at the end of November threatened to prolong the war, conditions improved again in the spring of 1951. In a costly military deadlock established below the 38th parallel, both sides indicated in June that an armistice might be acceptable. Early in July the first armistice discussions began at Kaesong.

In Europe, the impact of the Korean war on aid planning was profound and pervasive. Not only did the example of Korea suggest a possibility of similar aggression against Western Europe. Another possibility was that the Korean attack might be a deliberate feint to engage U.S. forces in the Far East in preparation for a Soviet attack against Western Europe. Beginning in the fall of 1950, NATO planning "centered on a single problem: how to defend the NATO area from an aggression similar to that which had taken place in the Far East."[1] Initially, the buildup of NATO forces proceeded rapidly, "galvanized by the shock of the aggression in Korea."[2] Between December 1949, when NATO planning began, and December 1951, the forces available to NATO rose from "about 12 divisions, 400 aircraft and a proportionate number of naval vessels" to "approximately 35 divisions, in varying states of readiness, slightly less than 3,000 aircraft and 700 naval vessels."[3]

As a consequence, the planning and allocation of both economic and military assistance to Europe was, in fiscal year 1952 and subsequently, largely determined by the requirements of expanding European defense outlays. As the end of the Marshall Plan approached, the justification for economic assistance to Europe became that of financing imports "necessary to permit a country to make its

[1] Lord Ismay, *NATO, The First Five Years, 1949-1954*, North Atlantic Treaty Organization, Paris, 1955, p. 32.
[2] *Ibid.*, p. 101.
[3] *Ibid.*, p. 102. NATO force goals were raised further at the Lisbon conference of the NATO Council in February, 1952.

contribution of manpower, construction and military supply to the NATO plan."[4]

Paradoxically, perhaps, the Korean experience had a less dominant influence on United States assistance to Asia than to Europe in 1952. In part this was due to the fact that other circumstances, associated with what we have referred to as the China "lesson," impinged on and influenced the planning of aid to Asia. In part, too, it was due to the fact that the physical possibilities of increased military preparedness in Asia, and hence of aid specifically directed to this goal, were limited in the short run. In the terminology of the previous chapter, military aid to China was limited by the fact that its marginal physical *productivity* was small, however large its marginal *value* might have been.[5]

During fiscal year 1951, the Gray and Rockefeller Reports to the President on economic assistance programs were completed.[6] Both strongly reiterated the vital interest of the United States in enhancing political stability in the underdeveloped areas by increased aid for economic development. Though the Gray Report was firm in advocating the primacy of rearmament among the objectives of U.S. assistance in Europe, its view of problems in the underdeveloped areas was quite different:

"These countries no longer accept poverty as an inevitable fact of life. The contrast between their aspirations and their present state of unrelieved poverty makes them susceptible to domestic unrest and provides fertile ground for the growth of Communist movements. Some of these countries, in addition, are geographically close to Soviet dominated countries.

". . . In the present state of world tension, the urgency of our interests in these areas has greatly increased. First, we must help them strengthen their ability to maintain their independence. Second, we must secure the cooperation of their peoples and their government in an effective system of mutual defense. Third, we must help bring about in these areas increasing production and mutually

---

[4] *The Mutual Security Program*, First Report to Congress, December 31, 1951, Washington, D.C., 1952, p. 14.

[5] Chapter 4, above, pp. 78-79. Also compare Secretary Marshall's statement in 1948 concerning the limited productivity of military aid in the China context, Chapter 3, pp. 41-42.

[6] *Report to the President on Foreign Economic Policies* (Gray Report), Washington, D.C., 1950; and *Partners in Progress—A Report to the President by the International Development Advisory Board* (Rockefeller Report), Washington, D.C., 1951.

beneficial exchange of materials. . . . Finally, we must assist in bringing them increasingly into a network of international trade which will promote a more effective use of the economic resources of the free world."[7]

The Gray Report, in considering assistance for economic development, stressed the importance of increasing production and trade in basic materials to a greater extent than had previous Congressional and Executive discussions of aid to the underdeveloped areas. The Report stated, for example:

"The requirements of collective security demand a more vigorous effort than has yet been made to bring about a rapid expansion in the output of these materials. *This is a vital part of a program of economic development.*"[8]

The reason for this increased emphasis is evident. Between June and November 1950, when the Report was presented to the President, the prices of the major raw materials traded internationally rose by 40 per cent.[9] They were to rise another 20 per cent before the end of the Korean war boom. Though the deteriorating terms of trade posed a more serious immediate problem for Western Europe than for the United States, the sharp rise in materials prices dramatized the longer-run requirements for the United States as well. One of its consequences was the Gray Report's emphasis on economic development abroad as a source of higher output and exports of basic materials.[10] Nevertheless, the Report's primary stress was political stability as the rationale for increased development aid.

In the light of the several aims mentioned, the Gray Report recommended increased technical and capital assistance "up to $500 million a year for several years."[11] For essentially similar reasons, the Rockefeller Report specifically endorsed this recommendation.[12] The amount recommended was not adopted. Nevertheless, both Reports had considerable influence on the Administration's planning of assistance programs for 1952. Both influenced the increased scale of aid for economic development, to the underdeveloped areas generally and more specifically to Southern Asia, that was enacted by the Mutual Security legislation.

[7] Gray Report, p. 49.　　　　　　　　[8] *Ibid.*, p. 60 (Italics added.)
[9] *The Mutual Security Program*, First Report, p. 10.
[10] Another consequence was the report of the President's Materials Policy Commission eighteen months later. See below, pp. 140-141, footnote a, and *Resources for Freedom: A Report to the President by the President's Materials Policy Commission*, 5 Vols., Washington, D.C., 1952.
[11] Gray Report, p. 69.　　　　　　　　[12] Rockefeller Report, pp. 61-62.

3. *The Mutual Security Act of 1951*

The Mutual Security Act of 1951 provided the name and, until 1955, the legislative model for United States foreign assistance in ensuing years. In the preceding year, military and economic assistance had each been authorized and administered independently. Military assistance was provided, as we have seen, under authorization of the Mutual Defense Assistance Act and directly administered by the Defense Department. Economic assistance, defined as all assistance other than the military end-items and training comprised in the MDAP, was provided under the Foreign Economic Assistance Act of 1950, the latter containing separate sections covering aid to Europe under the Economic Cooperation Act, aid to the "general area of China" under the China Area Aid Act, and global technical assistance under the Act for International Development. Technical assistance was administered by the Technical Cooperation Administration; all other economic aid by the Economic Cooperation Administration.

Coordination among the several component programs had been previously undertaken by an interagency committee, the International Security Affairs Committee (ISAC), under the direction of the Department of State. Although the Executive Branch proposed continuation of this arrangement, Congress demurred.

Reporting to the Senate on the Mutual Security Act, the Joint Senate Foreign Relations and Armed Services Committees said it was "not satisfied with the present coordination by the ISAC," and that its subcommittee on military assistance "had found evidence among field representatives of dissatisfaction with the multiheaded command in Washington."[13] In its place the Mutual Security Act fixed "responsibility for the coordination and supervision of these programs in a single person, . . . [the] Director for Mutual Security."[14] The Defense Department, the Technical Cooperation Administration in the State Department, and the Mutual Security Agency— established by the Act as the successor to ECA—were to administer the component programs, subject to the "coordination and supervision" of the Mutual Security Director.

In part, this change was designed for administrative efficiency and

[13] Report of the Senate Committee on Foreign Relations and the Committee on Armed Services, *The Mutual Security Act of 1951*, Washington, D.C., 1951, p. 36.
[14] *The Mutual Security Act of 1951*, Public Law 165, 82nd Congress, 1st session, Title v, in *Documents on American Foreign Relations, 1951*, Vol. xiii, Princeton, 1953, pp. 131-132.

simplicity.[15] In part, it grew from a substantive policy decision by the Congress that the international situation required a more strongly military orientation in foreign assistance programs than the previous legislative and administrative arrangements had provided for. To this end the Mutual Security Act accorded the strengthening of defense forces the leading role in its statement of legislative purpose.

"The Congress declares it to be the purpose of this Act to maintain the security and promote the foreign policy of the United States by authorizing military, economic and technical assistance to friendly countries to strengthen the mutual security and individual and collective defenses of the free world, to develop their resources in the interest of their security and independence and the national interests of the United States, and to facilitate effective participation by those countries in the United Nations system for collective security."[16] To this end, also, the Act abolished ECA one year before the scheduled end of the Marshall Plan, integrated the authorization for military aid for the first time in the same legislation authorizing economic and technical assistance, and legislatively instructed the new Director for Mutual Security to exercise his coordination and supervisory responsibilities "so as to assure that the defensive strength of the free nations of the world shall be built as quickly as possible. . . ."[17]

The altered orientation and the administrative modifications adopted by the Mutual Security Act of 1951 had their primary immediate application in the European context. As we have seen, the impact of Korea in Europe had been to raise and accelerate NATO force goals. Even if country contributions typically lagged behind the plans, defense expenditures in the NATO countries were rising substantially. In absolute terms, total defense expenditures by the European NATO countries[18] rose by more than 50 per cent between 1950 and 1951 from $5.2 billion to $8 billion. As a fraction of gross national product, total defense expenditures rose by over 40 per cent, from 5.3 per cent in 1950 to 7.6 per cent in 1951.[19]

[15] However, it was questionable in principle, and proved so in fact, that overall program coordination by an official (the Director for Mutual Security) junior in rank to the administrators of portions of the program (the Secretaries of State and Defense) could be considered either efficient or simple.

[16] *Documents on American Foreign Relations, 1951*, p. 128.

[17] *Ibid.*, p. 132.

[18] Excluding Greece and Turkey, which did not formally join NATO until February 1952.

[19] *The Mutual Security Act of 1951*, Joint Senate Hearings, Washington, D.C., 1951, p. 185.

The increase in Western Europe's output and exports, during the first years of the Marshall Plan, had been so impressive that the need for further United States assistance in fiscal year 1952 would have been substantially reduced, if not eliminated, had not the growing defense requirements intervened. Consequently, the Executive Branch, as well as Congress, justified the continued economic assistance in terms of the additional burden placed on the Western European economies by rearmament. Higher military outlays, not covered by reductions in other government outlays, or by increased taxes or private savings, meant higher money income; and higher income meant increased dollar imports which the NATO countries were not able to finance themselves. Secretary Acheson's testimony on European economic aid before the Senate Foreign Relations and Armed Services Committee summarized the point:

> The Chairman (Senator Connally): Mr. Secretary, it has been the opinion around here that the money heretofore appropriated for the ECA would largely, if not entirely, now be devoted to the military program; is that not true?
>
> Secretary Acheson: Yes, sir; I think that the whole impact of the economic assistance is . . . to carry out the rearmament program and to a very large degree the ECA's original task has been accomplished.[20]

4. Economic Assistance in Europe and in Southern Asia

As a result, economic assistance to Europe was renamed "defense support," reflecting not so much its altered content as its altered justification and purpose. In Europe, beginning in 1952, rearmament was the rationale of economic assistance, or defense support, no less than of military end-item assistance. The main changes enacted by the Mutual Security Act of 1951 were intended to assure that this rationale would guide the operation and administration of the program.

By contrast, the rationale for economic and technical assistance in Southern Asia in 1952 was as far removed from rearmament as was the provision of military end-item aid in that region from the NATO joint defense plan in Europe. The circumstances in which the Griffin and Bell Missions had recommended economic and tech-

[20] *Ibid.*, p. 10.

nical aid to Southeast Asia in the preceding year were basically unchanged. In Indochina, the Viet Minh continued to receive increasing military aid from China.[21] Although French Union forces, with considerable MDAP equipment, were able to turn back Viet Minh attacks in the Red River delta region throughout 1951, the position of the Vietnamese government remained precarious. The Vietnamese government's need both to demonstrate to the people its independence from France, and to identify itself with war relief and at least limited economic improvement programs, made the case for U.S. technical and economic assistance seem as strong in 1952 as it had seemed at the time of the Griffin mission's survey.

In Burma, Thailand, and Indonesia, the Korean war boom in export prices of rice and raw materials had resulted in current account surpluses and windfall accumulations of foreign exchange, but the need for United States aid in these countries, to perform the "catalytic" role which the Griffin mission had originally stressed as a means of enhancing internal political stability,[22] remained pressing. In the Philippines, runaway inflation had been slowed down as a result of the Bell Mission's tax recommendations, and Hukbalahap activity was less intense than it had previously been. But public discontent, from which the Huk movement derived its main support, remained acute.

In South Asia the need for U.S. assistance appeared more compelling than it had in the previous year. India's First Five-Year Plan had begun on April 1, 1951. Though actually quite modest in size,[23] the Plan appeared likely to require assistance beyond what could be expected from within the Commonwealth alone. The basis of U.S. interest in providing such assistance—a subject that was to be actively debated and constantly reviewed in Congress and the Executive Branch over the ensuing years—at least came prominently to the attention of the State Department and the Congress during 1951. Passage of the $190 million Indian Food Loan in June 1951, represented a somewhat ambiguous initial judgment concerning the basis of U.S. interest. With Indo-American diplomatic relations at one of their periodic low points, as a result of India's strong opposition to U.S. conduct of the Korean war, Congressional enactment of the

[21] *The Mutual Security Program*, First Report, p. 30.
[22] Chapter 4, above, pp. 82-84.
[23] India's First Five-Year Plan involved an intended public investment program of less than $4 billion, about 4 per cent of cumulative net national product over the five-year period.

food loan after three months of debate and delay was as much a reflection of humanitarian interest in relieving a temporary famine as of interest in India's long-term economic development.[24]

In Pakistan, the need for U.S. aid was essentially similar to that in Burma, Indonesia, and Thailand. Like them, Pakistan was a temporary beneficiary of the rise in jute and cotton prices induced by the Korean war. Like them, too, Pakistan was considered to be in need of assistance in order to catalyze the use of the country's internal resources, including its accumulated foreign exchange balances, in the interest of economic growth and, hopefully, of internal political stability.

In no country of Southern Asia was rearmament the rationale of United States economic and technical aid in 1952. Not even in Indochina was the need to provide support for an internal military effort, larger than permitted by the country's own savings and taxes, the rationale of economic and technical aid in 1952. The major purposes of U.S. aid in Southern Asia were, in 1952, essentially what they had been in 1951. In presenting the fiscal 1952 programs for the area he referred to as "the vital crescent," from Afghanistan to Japan, Secretary Acheson stated the case for economic aid to Southern Asia as follows:

"Poverty, disease, illiteracy and resentments against former colonial exploitations are our enemies. . . . They represent turbulent forces which the Communist exploits at every opportunity. To achieve our objective of helping the people of this area maintain independent governments friendly to us, we must understand these forces at work in Asia, and we must assure that the forces of nationalism and of the drive for economic improvement are associated with the rest of the free world instead of with communism.

"That is why an essential part of the Mutual Security Program for this area is designed to help the people of Asia to create social and economic conditions that will encourage the growth and survival of non-Communist political institutions dedicated to the honest fulfillment of their basic needs and aspirations."[25]

These were, essentially, the same objectives which the Griffin Mission had formulated and the Gray and Rockefeller Reports had

---

[24] See, for example, Acheson's stress on the humanitarian theme in his statement on behalf of the Administration's proposal. *India Emergency Assistance Act of 1951*, House Hearings, Washington, D.C., 1951, p. 5.

[25] *Mutual Security of Act of 1951*, Senate Hearings, p. 5. In the same vein, see the testimony of Assistant Secretary Dean Rusk, pp. 530ff.; and of R. Allen Griffin, pp. 577ff.

endorsed. In contrast to the altered orientation of aid to Europe, the basic reason for economic and technical assistance to Southern Asia in 1952 remained that of enhancing political stability through economic improvement.

5. Program Operations Under the Mutual Security Act

Though the contrast between the Mutual Security Program in Southern Asia and in Europe is valid from the standpoint of program objectives and, as we shall see below, of program allocations, a qualification needs to be added about program *operations*. The European rearmament goal was of such influence in the Mutual Security Act that procedures and program labels, devised primarily for the European phase of the program, occasionally carried over into the operation of the programs in Southern Asia. One significant example concerned Indonesia.

Under the Mutual Security Act of 1951, a country receiving military assistance was required to pledge "the full contribution permitted by its manpower, resources, facilities and general economic condition to . . . its own defensive strength and the defensive strength of the free world." Countries receiving only non-military aid were asked merely to agree to "join in promoting international understanding and good will."[26] The strong pledge was fundamentally intended for, and relevant in, the European context of common force goals and burden-sharing.

In nationalist and hypersensitive Asia, the pledge had explosive effects. When, in February 1952, the terms of the agreement between Indonesia and the United States, which included the strong pledge, became known, public reaction was so intense that the Indonesian cabinet was obliged to resign, the agreement was withdrawn, military aid was terminated, and the economic aid program was suspended for eight months. The incident suggests some instructive facts of life about foreign aid operations: the need to discriminate between the major and minor goals of aid; the need for flexibility in determining when and what conditions should be attached to aid; and the shortcomings of written agreements for stipulating conditions.

For reasons illustrated by the Indonesian example, the "Mutual Security" label was not exactly warmly regarded in Southern Asia.

[26] *Documents on American Foreign Relations, 1951*, p. 134.

In Asian minds, it tended to be associated with a military point of view that some Asian leaders believed misconceived their countries' problems and might even compromise the independent foreign policies they wished to maintain. It is, therefore, notable that, labels aside, the Mutual Security Program in its first year actually involved a substantially larger *absolute* and *relative* allocation of funds to Southern Asia than in the preceding year, and for essentially the same purposes quite unrelated to rearmament.[27]

6. Economic Aid Allocations to Southern Asia, 1952

The point is illustrated by a comparison of Table 6 below, and Table 4 in Chapter 4. Economic and technical aid to Southern Asia doubled between 1951 and 1952. Moreover, it rose to 65 per cent of total Asian economic aid (including aid to Formosa) under the Mutual Security Program, and to 8 per cent of global economic aid, compared to 43 per cent and 3 per cent respectively in 1951.

Turning from the global and regional allocations summarized in Table 6 to those at the country and sector level, Table 7 shows the *proposed* country and project allocation of economic and technical assistance to Southern Asia submitted by the Executive Branch to Congress for 1952. Table 8 shows actual *obligations* by the administering agencies[28] during the fiscal year 1952, after Congressional enactment of the Mutual Security Act of 1951 and the Mutual Security Appropriation Act of 1952.

7. Comparison of Proposals and Obligations for 1952

Comparison of the two tables, and of both with the prior year's obligations data, shown in Table 3, suggests some interesting things. It is, first of all, clear that the differences between Tables 7 and 8 are small. The $10 million reduction in the regional total (from $160

[27] "Unrelated" is, perhaps, too strong. As previously noted, enhanced political stability, to some extent, can be considered a substitute for the strengthening of local military forces *to the extent the latter are needed for preserving internal order.* In the specific case of Indochina, the relationship was closer. The effort to strengthen the national Vietnamese government's position among the public, hardly less than the MDAP effort to train and equip local forces to take over from the French forces, was hopefully aimed at a reduction in France's commitments in Indochina and hence a greater French contribution to NATO force goals.

[28] In the Southeast Asian countries, the Mutual Security Agency—the successor agency to ECA—administered economic and technical aid in 1952. In the South Asian countries, TCA was the administering agency. In principle, both were subject to the "supervision and direction" of the Director for Mutual Security.

Table 6

UNITED STATES ECONOMIC AND TECHNICAL AID TO SOUTHERN ASIA
IN FISCAL YEAR 1952 COMPARED TO TOTAL ASIAN AND
GLOBAL ECONOMIC ASSISTANCE UNDER THE MUTUAL
SECURITY ACT OF 1951

| | Obligations | As Proportion of: | |
		Total Asian Aid	Global Aid
	(millions of dollars)	(per cent)	
Economic and Technical Aid to Southern Asia, 1952	149.7	64.9	7.9
Economic and Technical Aid to Formosa, 1952	81.0	35.1	4.3
Total Asian Aid	230.7	100.0	12.2
Global Economic Aid Under the Mutual Security Act of 1951	1,887.2	–	100.0

Sources: Table 8 below, and (g'), p. 54. (See Appendix II.)

million proposed to $150 million obligated) for Southern Asia was
negligible compared to Congressional cuts in other portions of the
Mutual Security Program. By contrast, of the original Executive
Branch proposal for slightly over $2 billion in global economic and
technical assistance, Congress appropriated only $1.4 billion, a re-
duction of 30 per cent. Looking only at the overall cut made in the
Executive Branch proposals, one might say that it reflected a Congressional judgment that the benefits to the United States from
marginal Mutual Security aid were less than those from the same
resources in other uses, government or private. Of course, one can
draw the same inference from *any* Congressional cut in any proposed
appropriation.

More interesting and relevant to this study, however, is the relatively small reduction in the funds made available for economic
and technical assistance to Southern Asia. Whereas the amount proposed by the Executive Branch for economic assistance to Europe
was reduced by 36 per cent, the amount proposed for aid to the
countries of Southern Asia was reduced by only 6 per cent. What
significance can be ascribed to this difference?

Using the terminology discussed in the preceding chapter, we can

[121]

Table 7

FUNDS PROPOSED BY THE EXECUTIVE BRANCH FOR UNITED STATES
ECONOMIC AND TECHNICAL ASSISTANCE TO SOUTHERN ASIA, FISCAL YEAR 1952[a]

(by country and project use)

Country	Project Use									Country Total as Proportion of Regional Total
	Agriculture	Industry	Transportation	Health	Public Administration	Education	Community Development	General and Miscellaneous	TOTAL	
	(millions of dollars)									(per cent)
Afghanistan[b]	–	–	–	–	–	–	–	.31	.31	.2
Burma[c]	2.80	1.00	2.55	3.75	–	1.40	.70	1.80	14.00	8.8
Ceylon[d]	–	–	–	–	–	–	–	.24	.24	.1
India[e]	28.00	19.92	.58	1.94	.48	.28	–	3.37	54.57	34.2
Indochina[f]	2.49	.51	2.95	6.44	–	.40	–	16.51	29.30	18.3
Indonesia[g]	3.24	.50	.41	2.60	.40	.30	–	.55	8.00	5.0
Nepal[h]	–	–	–	–	–	–	–	.06	.06	.0
Pakistan[i]	2.10	.35	1.43	.89	.15	2.10	–	3.76	10.78	6.8
Philippines[j]	10.05	.45	3.45	2.25	.50	.50	–	18.20	35.40	22.2
Thailand[k]	2.31	.65	.25	2.86	–	.93	–	–	7.00	4.4
TOTALS	50.99	23.38	11.62	20.73	1.53	5.91	.70	44.25	159.66	100.0
	(per cent)									
Project Total as Proportion of Regional Total	31.9	14.6	7.3	13.0	1.0	3.7	.4	28.1	100.0	

(continued)

Sources: For the sources to which the footnote letters refer, see Appendix II.

a The problem of securing a "best" set of proposals figures is no less difficult than the comparable problem for obligations (See Table 3, footnote a.) Usually, the Executive Branch proposals are scattered among various volumes of the Congressional Hearings and the Committee Reports. Frequently, the proposals are changed between the initial presentation to the authorizing committees (the Foreign Relations Committee in the Senate, and the Foreign Affairs Committee in the House) and the later presentation to the Appropriations Committees. In selecting from the alternative proposals data, the rule followed in this study has been to select as the "best" the *earliest* available proposals submitted by the Executive Branch. In general, these reflect most accurately the decisions on allocation reached within the Executive Branch, prior to any Congressional consideration. Consequently, the "early" proposals are the most appropriate ones to compare with the obligations figures (see Table 8 below), arrived at *after* Congressional action has been completed, from the standpoint of assessing the allocation changes that have occurred between the planning and implementation of programs.

The project categories have the same meaning as in Table 3 above.

b (d), p. 569.
c (b), p. 913, and (e), p. 182.
d (d), p. 569.
e (d), p. 570, and (j), p. 693.
f (b), p. 912.
g (b), p. 913; (c), p. 576; and (d), p. 570.
h (d), p. 569.
i (d), p. 570, and (j), p. 693.
j (b), p. 912; (c), p. 575; and (d), p. 570.
k (b), p. 914; (c), p. 577; and (d), p. 570.

Table 8

FUNDS OBLIGATED FOR UNITED STATES ECONOMIC AND TECHNICAL ASSISTANCE TO SOUTHERN ASIA, FISCAL YEAR 1952[a]

(by country and project use)

Country	Project Use									Country Total as Proportion of Regional Total
	Agriculture	Industry	Transportation	Health	Public Administration	Education	Community Development	General and Miscellaneous	TOTAL	
	(millions of dollars)									(per cent)
Afghanistan[b]	.34	.10	–	.03	–	.17	–	–	.64	.4
Burma[c]	3.75	1.53	3.40	2.10	1.12	.48	–	1.29	13.67	9.1
Ceylon[d]	.01	–	–	–	–	–	–	–	.01	.0
India[e]	33.89	8.58	.06	.77	–	.46	–	8.95	52.71	35.2
Indochina[f]	.85	.02	2.58	2.86	.88	.27	–	17.14	24.60	16.4
Indonesia[g]	2.85	.89	.56	1.22	.23	2.00	–	.31	8.06	5.4
Nepal[h]	.08	–	–	.12	–	–	–	–	.20	.1
Pakistan[i]	1.66	4.18	1.10	.47	.04	.75	–	2.40	10.60	7.1
Philippines[j]	14.04	6.88	3.93	5.86	.34	.95	–	.10	32.10	21.5
Thailand[k]	2.94	.85	.19	2.49	.12	.47	–	.04	7.10	4.8
TOTALS	60.41	23.03	11.82	15.92	2.73	5.55	0	30.23	149.69	100.0
	(per cent)									
Project Total as Proportion of Regional Total	40.4	15.4	7.9	10.6	1.8	3.7	0	20.2	100.0	

(continued)

Sources: See Appendix II.

ᵃ See footnote ᵃ of Table 3 for explanation of categories and terms used in this table.

ᵇ (k), pp. 59, 147 and 189.

ᶜ (k), pp. 60, 143 and 189. (g'), p. 54, and current reports of ICA show obligations of minus $154,000 for 1952. This figure represents a small deobligation of 1951 funds, and excludes the actual obligation of 1952 funds. The exclusion is misleading but understandable. In fiscal 1953, administrative responsibility for the Burma program was transferred from MSA to TCA. Because TCA operated with different obligating procedures, the transfer of administrative jurisdiction was followed by a reobligation of the 1952 funds using the TCA procedures. TCA records henceforth showed the funds as 1953 obligations even though the original source of funds was the Mutual Security Appropriation Act of 1952. The record-keeping problem was further complicated by termination of the Burma program toward the end of fiscal 1953, and the subsequent retroactive deobligation of 1952 and 1953 funds. For clarification, see Table 11, footnote ᶜ, below.

ᵈ (o), p. 887, and (n), p. 241.

ᵉ (l), p. 189, and (a).

ᶠ (n), p. 530.

ᵍ (k), p. 189 and (a). (g'), p. 54, and current ICA reports show obligations of minus $1,874,000. The figure represents a deobligation of 1951 funds, and excludes the obligation of 1952 funds. The explanation is the same as that for Burma, described in footnote ᶜ, above.

ʰ (o), p. 881, and (n), p. 241.

ⁱ (k), p. 190.

ʲ (k), p. 74. In addition, the Export-Import Bank authorized a credit to the Philippines of $20 million for hydroelectric power at the end of January 1952. See Export-Import Bank of Washington, *Report to the Congress for the Period July-December 1956*, Washington, D.C., 1957, p. 24.

ᵏ (o), p. 887. In addition to Mutual Security aid, the Export-Import Bank authorized a loan to Thailand for $1.1 million in August 1951 for the purchase of cargo vessels in the United States. See the Export-Import Bank report cited in footnote ʲ, above.

say that the relatively small reduction in aid obligations in Southern Asia was due to one or both of two implicit Congressional judgments. One judgment was that the physical effects or "productivity" of aid to Europe diminished more rapidly at the margin than the productivity of aid to Southern Asia. The other was that the "value" of the United States of the physical effects of aid to Europe was smaller, *relative* to the value accorded the effects of aid to Asia, than the Executive Branch presumed.

It is probably a reasonable assumption that in the case of foreign aid, as in most other government programs, Congress tends to concern itself more with the "higher-level" value judgments than with the "lower-level" productivity judgments: more with the desirability of A, B, C . . . as effects or consequences of proposed government programs, than with their physical effects. If this assumption is made, we can then infer from the relatively small reduction in aid to Southern Asia a Congressional value judgment quite different from that implicit in the Executive Branch proposals.

Despite the reasons previously noted for caution in making inferences from observed differences between proposals data and obligations data,[29] the above inference is sufficiently in accord with other evidence to make it reasonable in this instance. Thus, the "Asian-minded" Congressmen, to whom we have previously alluded, had become even more influential in the Congressional committees as a result of the Korean war.[30] Not only did their counsel increasingly affect regional allocation decisions made within the Executive Branch itself, but their influence within the Congress tended to protect proposals for aid to Southern Asia from receiving proportionate cuts. The inference of a Congressional value judgment relatively more favorable to Southern Asia than to Europe is simply a different way of expressing the result of this influence on Congressional decision-making.

Returning to Tables 7 and 8, we find that not only were the regional reductions relatively small, but that the project and country proportions (the last row and column, respectively, in both tables) are very similar. The obligations figures (Table 8) shown after Congressional action thus reflect essentially similar judgments on the

[29] See Chapter 4, section 3.
[30] See, for example, the statements by Congressmen Judd, Javits, and Roosevelt. *The Mutual Security Program*, House Hearings, 1951, pp. 26-27, 178-179.

desirable distribution of aid among countries and projects, as did the original proposals (Table 7).[81]

8. *Intertemporal Comparison of Allocations, 1951 and 1952*

A comparison of the 1952 allocations with those for 1951 is also of interest. Perhaps the most striking contrast between obligations for economic and technical aid in Southern Asia in 1951 (Table 3) and 1952 (Table 7) is the change in the country composition of aid.

Obligations in India, which in 1951 were just over $5 million or 7 per cent of the regional total, in 1952 were nearly $53 million or 35 per cent of the regional total. In Pakistan, obligations rose from under $.5 million to over $10 million, or from less than 1 per cent of the regional total to over 7 per cent. At the same time as the amount and share received by the *South* Asian countries rose substantially—excluding Ceylon which received negligible technical aid in both years—the *Southeast* Asian share, though not its absolute amount, declined. Of the Southeast Asian countries, only in the Philippines did the amount of aid obligated in 1952 rise enough to maintain its share of the total as high as in 1951. Even in Indochina, the share declined from 31 per cent to 16 per cent, though the amount obligated rose. In Thailand, alone among the larger recipients in the region, the absolute amount obligated dropped below the 1951 level, while in Indonesia the amount of aid remained approximately constant, the *share* falling from 11 per cent to 5 per cent.

Interpretation of these intertemporal changes is hazardous but nonetheless interesting. The trouble, of course, is that so many incidental imponderables intrude: the personality of an ambassador in Indonesia; the surmounting of the 1951 administrative and legislative barriers to TCA operations in the South Asian countries; the

[81] In Table 8, the agricultural share of total obligations is 40 per cent, while that for "general and miscellaneous" commodities and services is 20 per cent. The comparable figures in the proposals (Table 7) are 32 per cent and 28 per cent respectively. However, these two differences between Tables 7 and 8 are more apparent than real. Congressional sentiment against "general" commodity imports emerged quite clearly during the Mutual Security Hearings. Consequently, an attempt was made by both MSA and TCA, as the administering agencies, to attribute as large a share as possible of programmed commodity imports to the sectors in which their immediate impact might be expected. Substitutability complications aside, dollars used to pay for fertilizer imports could be attributed either to general commodity imports or to agriculture. In large measure, the change in project shares shown by Tables 7 and 8 is due to a modification of recording procedures, rather than a shift in the character of the proposed and obligated programs.

difficulty of persuading technicians to go to landlocked and remote Afghanistan and Nepal, or of transporting supplies to these distant places. Admittedly, the accidents and incidents affecting the changes in allocation are numerous. Nevertheless, besides these important but analytically unhelpful chance events, a general pattern can be found in the intertemporal allocation data.

The substantial rise in the shares received by India and Pakistan was, in the analytical terminology previously described, a plausible reflection of a United States policy judgment that the productivity of aid for their economic development and its value to the United States were relatively higher than had appeared in the prior year. The reason for the altered judgment concerning productivity lay in the evidence accumulated in the Colombo Plan that Commonwealth resources would not be adequate to fill the resource gaps in Indian and Pakistani investment planning. The serious Indian food shortage during the calendar year 1951 provided further evidence of the same sort. Since, by 1952, Commonwealth resources—including private savings and taxes within India and Pakistan themselves—seemed less likely to be adequate than they had in 1951, prospective U.S. aid in 1952 could be regarded more reasonably as an addition to, rather than a substitute for, possible assistance from within the Commonwealth. Consequently, the *net* productivity attributable to United States aid to India and Pakistan might reasonably be considered higher in 1952 than in 1951.

There were also at least impressionistic reasons for concluding that the "value" to the United States of the stabilizing benefits ascribed to economic growth in India and Pakistan would be relatively higher in 1952 than had seemed to be the case in 1951.[32] The rise in communist agitation and strength in Madras, Bombay, and Travancore Cochin, as well as the prospect of India's first national elections at the end of calendar year 1951, contributed to this altered judgment. And in Pakistan the congenital instability of a geographically and culturally divided country was dramatized in 1951 by the discovery and aborting of a planned communist *coup*.[33]

[32] As we have previously noted, it is difficult to define, let alone measure, what we mean by "value" in this sense, independently of the observed changes in allocation shares themselves. We shall return to this problem in detail later (Chapters 8-9). For the present we will simply assume that the value to the United States of the physical effects of aid in different countries can be distinguished from the country aid shares themselves.

[33] See Stebbins, 1951, *op.cit.*, p. 252, and the *New York Times*, March 22, 1951, cited therein.

In the Southeast Asian countries, the tendency toward diminishing marginal productivity of aid, which we have previously explained in terms of absorptive limitations,[34] is probably a sufficient explanation for the fall in aid *shares*. Even in Indochina and Burma, where the value of political strengthening was especially high under the prevailing circumstances, the opportunity to use additional aid productively was severely limited. Consequently, the absolute increases in country allocations in these two cases were relatively small.

In Thailand and Indonesia, the tendency toward diminishing aid productivity was accentuated by the windfall gains realized from the rise in materials prices already mentioned. Between 1950 and 1951, gold and foreign exchange holdings of the Thai and Indonesian central banks rose by 25 per cent and 44 per cent respectively. Though the "catalytic" effect attributed to United States aid may have been especially applicable to aid under these circumstances, there was also a likelihood that *additional* amounts of aid might simply substitute for liquid resources already and increasingly available to Thailand and Indonesia. Consequently, the net productivity of additional aid could be judged zero or low, and the case for at least avoiding any increased aid to Thailand and Indonesia seemed a reasonable one.[35]

[34] Chapter 4, above, pp. 93-94.

[35] The fact that the Thai allocation in 1952 was *less* than that in 1951, while the Indonesian allocation was approximately the same, is not explainable in these terms. One can argue, in fact, that, *given* similar production functions with diminishing marginal aid productivity, and similar value parameters in the two cases, equalizing the marginal returns from aid would have warranted a much larger allocation to Indonesia because of wide differences in the size of the two countries. Presumably, the availability of more resources complementary to aid in the larger economy (for example, underemployed labor, administrative and organizational facilities and skills) would permit absorption of more aid at any given marginal productivity.

If the Indonesian economy were, let us say, equivalent in every respect to three Thai economies, and assuming the same linear and homogeneous production functions for both countries, then the marginal productivity of aid in the two cases would be equalized at an aid ratio of 3 to 1. From this standpoint, the fall in aid to Thailand relative to Indonesia in 1952 was a step, and a very small one at that, toward adjusting the initial (1951) imbalance in aid allocations. In the value-and-productivity terms used here, the *relative Indonesian aid allocation from 1951 through 1957 would seem to have been unusually and persistently small*.

Against this judgment must be placed the Export-Import Bank's $100 million credit to Indonesia of February 1950 (see above, Table 3, footnote *g*), which, in effect, represented an additional U.S. aid allocation, though outside the Mutual Security Program. If, however, one makes a further allowance for the loans ($25 million) made by the International Bank to Thailand in 1951 (see International Bank for Reconstruction and Development, *Twelfth Annual Report, 1956-1957*, Washington, D.C., 1957), the underlined judgment in the previous paragraph is strengthened. Though IBRD loans are even more remote from the allocation of

Philippine aid remains something of an oddity in the 1952, as in the 1951 allocations.[86] Despite the reasons we have suggested for the intertemporal changes in country shares, obligations in the Philippines for 1952 rose at the same rate as those for the region as a whole, leaving its share of the total constant for the two years. One partial explanation is that the Philippines did not share in the improved terms of trade resulting from the Korean boom to the same extent as Indonesia or Thailand. Consequently, the assumption that marginal aid productivity would be relatively low because of the substitutability of resources did not have the same force in the Philippines. But this hardly suffices to explain a doubling in the Philippine allocation compared, for example, with the modest increase in that for Indochina.

The circumstantial explanation of the relatively high Philippine allocation in 1952 is the five-year aid target specified by the Bell Report and reiterated in the Foster-Quirino agreement.[87] The more general explanation is the one previously mentioned in discussing the Philippine allocation in 1951: the long-standing and intimate ties between the United States and the Philippines, and the resulting premium placed on political strengthening, and the "showcase-of-democracy" theme in the Philippines. In 1952, too, this factor tended to raise the Philippine aid allocation.

9. Sectoral Allocations

Before we leave Tables 7 and 8, a comment concerning the project composition of economic and technical aid should be added. As previously mentioned,[88] part of the decrease in the "general and miscellaneous" category, and part of the increase in the agriculture category, shown in Table 8, were due to one of the occasional changes in the meaning of the project labels. If allowance is made for this, the generalization previously made, in connection with the sectoral allocations shown for 1951 in Table 3, applies in 1952 as well.[89] Though the share of total services and commodities allocated

---

Mutual Security funds than are Export-Import Bank loans, the official U.S. stand on prospective IBRD loans (like those in Thailand) is influenced by some of the same productivity-and-value considerations affecting MSP allocations. And, in practice, the "position" adopted by the U.S. governor of the IBRD is likely to influence the Bank's action on a pending loan to a significant extent.

[86] Cf. Chapter 4, above, pp. 95-96.
[87] See above, Chapter 4, pp. 86-87.
[88] See above, footnote 31.   [89] Chapter 4, section B.6.

to industrial projects rose from 5 per cent to 15 per cent, that for transportation projects fell. The sectors with relatively short-term investment returns, agriculture and health, continued to receive a larger share of the increased aid allocations in 1952 than did the categories with a longer-term yield, transportation and industry. Thus, a premium on short-term yield, or, stated differently, an implicitly high time-discount, continued to be a characteristic of United States aid programming in 1952 as in 1951.

10. Appropriations for Military Assistance

Turning now to the MDAP component of the Mutual Security Program, we find it notable that the regional distribution of direct military aid remained approximately the same as in the previous year. A comparison of Table 9, below, and Table 5,[40] shows that, though the amount of MDAP appropriations in 1952 for the Asian area, including Formosa, rose by $66 million over 1951, the Asian share of the total remained nearly constant: 9 per cent in 1951 and 9.3 per cent in 1952. When we recall that the Asian share of total economic and technical aid in 1952 nearly doubled compared to 1951, while that for Southern Asia nearly tripled,[41] an interesting conclusion emerges. In Southern Asia, the Mutual Security Program in 1952, despite the military orientation commonly attributed to it, actually accorded considerably more emphasis to non-military, economic development-and-political stability considerations than did the 1951 aid program.

For reasons previously noted, detailed quantitative data on military aid must be confined to the regional level. However, there are a few comments on the country composition of MDAP in Southern Asia which can be made.

In large part because of the eligibility conditions imposed on recipients of military aid by the Mutual Security Act of 1951,[42] Burma and Indonesia terminated their participation in MDAP. Delivery of vehicles and light arms, already programmed under the 1951 pro-

[40] See Table 5, above. The altered row headings in Table 9 represent the new regional titles introduced by the Mutual Security Act of 1951. Except for the fact that aid to Spain was included in the European title in 1952, the countries included in the new regional titles of Table 9 were the same as those covered by the regions shown in Table 5, with the addition of a new title covering military aid to Latin America.

[41] See Tables 4 and 6, above. In these tables, "Southern Asia" represents the "Asian Area" minus Formosa.

[42] See Chapter 5, section A.5.

[131]

gram for the Indonesian police force, continued during 1952, but no new funds were programmed for either Indonesia or Burma. Consequently, only three countries in the area we are primarily concerned with—the Associated States of Indochina, Thailand, and the Philippines—continued as recipients of direct military aid. The half-billion dollars of equipment and training, shown in Table 9 for Asia and

Table 9

MUTUAL DEFENSE ASSISTANCE APPROPRIATIONS,
FISCAL YEAR 1952

	Appropriations[a] (millions of dollars)	Proportion of Total (per cent)
Europe	4,818.9	83.2
Near East and Africa	396.3	6.8
Asia and the Pacific	535.3	9.3
American Republics	38.2	.7
TOTALS	5,788.7	100.0

[a] *Mutual Security Appropriations Act, 1952*, Public Law 249, 82nd Congress, 1st session, Washington, D.C., 1951. The total appropriation represented an 8 per cent reduction from the Administration's original proposals of $6.3 billion. Within the total, the Asian segment was reduced by less than 4 per cent: from $555 million in the original proposals to the $535 million shown in Table 9. See *The Mutual Security Act of 1951*, Report of the Senate Committees on Foreign Relations and Armed Services, Washington, D.C., 1951, p. 6.

the Pacific, were divided among these three countries and Formosa.[43] The major share of the total went to meet the more pressing requirements of Indochina and Formosa, with Thailand and the Philippines receiving substantially smaller amounts. An indication of the order of magnitude involved in the largest of these programs is provided by one estimate which placed the value of end-item *deliveries* to Indochina at $228 million by the middle of fiscal 1952 and an additional $500 million one year later.[44]

[43] Actually, the amount of assistance extended was larger than the dollar appropriation. The MDA Act of 1949, as amended in 1950 and 1951, provided that a total of $1 billion of equipment excess to the requirements of the U.S. armed services could be furnished under MDAP without any charge against the appropriation, except "the gross cost of repairing, rehabilitating or modifying such equipment." A portion of this excess equipment was provided the Asian MDAP recipients in addition to the amounts of the new 1952 appropriation.

[44] Cited in Richard P. Stebbins, *The United States in World Affairs, 1952*, New York, 1953, p. 201.

11. MDAP Force Goals in Southern Asia

The military capabilities which the 1952 MDAP sought to build in Indochina, Thailand, and the Philippines followed essentially the lines set during the first year of the program.[45] In Indochina, MDAP had two major goals: to provide fighter aircraft and light bombers for the French air force and naval air force to use in mountain and delta fighting; and to equip and train over 200,000 Vietnamese, Cambodian, and Laotian ground troops to assist the French forces, and eventually to relieve them, in the war against the Viet Minh. In Thailand, the objective of MDAP continued to be mainly the equipping of several army battalions ostensibly for service in defending its borders against possible Viet Minh or Chinese attack through Laos.[46] In the Philippines, the military objective sought by MDAP continued to be the equipping of ten mobile and lightly-armed constabulary units to strengthen internal security against the slowly waning Huk threat.

In each case, the MDAP country force goals were established through bilateral discussions between the MAAG and the Service staffs of the recipient country. Once the country goals had been accepted by the Joint Chiefs of Staff in Washington, MDA requirements were largely determined by costing the end-item components of the goals. Such considerations as the composition of "balanced" forces and financial "burden-sharing," which dominated the multilateral planning of military aid in the NATO areas, did not enter into the formulation of MDAP goals in Southern Asia. Nor did an explicit evaluation of the probabilities of alternative local wars, their relative disutility to the United States, or the ability of MDAP to provide the military capabilities necessary to deal with them,[47] enter into the formulation of MDAP goals. Though 20-20 hindsight is less creditable than 20-20 foresight, it is fairly evident that in Indochina these problems warranted more explicit attention in MDAP planning than they received. Thus, the likelihood of massive Chinese assistance to the Viet Minh, if and as hostilities in Korea slackened, was a prominent and rising one. And the limited ability of MDAP to provide a counter to trained and hardened Viet Minh guerrilla

[45] See *First Mutual Security Report*, pp. 30-31, and *Second Mutual Security Report*, pp. 24-25. See, also, Chapter 4, above.

[46] MDAP aid to Thailand also enabled it to provide one battalion for service in Korea under the UN Command, *ibid.*, p. 25.

[47] See the discussion of these three problems, Chapter 4, section C. 3.

forces, as long as the domestic political climate favored them, should perhaps have figured more directly in MDAP planning.

This is not to say that military aid planning should necessarily regard the internal political climate as a variable. It is rather to suggest that in a guerrilla-type local war, the existing political environment has an important bearing on the productivity or effectiveness of end-item aid, and hence on its justification and allocation. Where, as in Indochina in 1952, the prevailing political environment favored the mobile, dispersed guerrilla force and was hostile to the conventionally armed pursuing force, logistics and intelligence constraints sharply curtailed the effectiveness (or productivity) of additional air and ground equipment. Under such circumstances, the point of zero return from additional allocations of such end-item assistance tends to be reached fairly rapidly. It is quite likely that MDAP aid to Indochina in 1952 reached this point well before the amounts that were actually allocated. In such a situation, of course, improved allocation of military aid cannot alter the unfavorable outcome that is pending. But it can at least reduce the waste of additional resources on the outcome.[48]

One might even argue that recognition of the limited effectiveness of military aid in the existing political environment might have had a positive influence on the outcome. By focusing attention on the need to *alter* the political environment, if the effectiveness of additional military aid were to be increased, such recognition might have encouraged a stronger effort to use diplomacy to alter the constraining environment than was in fact made.

The observation about zero returns should be understood in terms of the *relevant range* over which additional amounts of aid are considered. In an Indochina-type situation, for example, there may be discontinuities in the relation between end-item aid and military returns. Beyond some point, additional aid may yield no returns and this relation may prevail over a fairly wide range. But at a considerably higher level of aid, a new relationship may apply. Total returns may be greater and marginal returns positive.

The point is that the additional amounts of end-item aid actually provided by the United States in Indochina may have had zero military effect, as suggested above. At the same time, an all-out commitment of U.S. support, including perhaps U.S. forces or nu-

[48] For further discussion of the productivity of different types of end-items in the Indochina situation, see below, pp. 176-177.

clear weapons, might have had a decisive military effect. For reasons that are obvious, though possibly debatable, this level of aid was considered to be beyond the relevant range. It can, thus, be argued that military aid to Indochina from 1951 through 1954 was either too much *or* not enough.

B. MUTUAL SECURITY IN 1953

1. *The International Context*

The international circumstances affecting the Mutual Security Program for 1953 were not essentially changed from the preceding year. As planning of the 1953 Program proceeded through fiscal year 1952, the Korean armistice negotiations continued. Broken off in the late summer of 1951, negotiations were resumed in the fall and agreement on a provisional cease-fire line was reached soon after. When the MSP proposals were being put in final form within the Executive Branch in February and early March 1952 for presentation to Congress, prospects for a permanent cease-fire and a restoration of the *status quo ante* seemed reasonably good.

Congressional Hearings on the Mutual Security Program were already well underway by the time the armistice negotiations foundered, principally over the issue of prisoner repatriation. At the end of June, after communist rejection of the "final" U N proposals at Panmunjom, and with an acceleration of the buildup of communist ground forces, the U N command launched its heaviest air attack against North Korea in an effort to exert military pressure toward securing acceptance of the armistice proposals. At the time, the Mutual Security Appropriation Act was still under Congressional consideration. The sharp modifications made by the Congress in the original Executive Branch proposals for Southern Asia were, as we shall see below, directly affected by these circumstances.

As in 1952, the European segment of the Mutual Security Program in 1953 continued to be largely the result of a costing and phasing of NATO force goals, combined with a politically determined assumption concerning feasible levels of savings and taxes in the NATO countries. As previously noted, the NATO force goals themselves had been directly affected by the Korean war. As established by the NATO Council at Lisbon in February 1952, these goals provided the basis for most of the military end-item aid and defense-support proposed for Europe in 1953 and, with modifications which we shall refer to later, in the following three years as well. In presenting the program to the Congress, Mutual Security Director Harriman stated that, of the funds proposed for Europe, "over $5 billion (or 85 per cent) is intended to help implement the Lisbon plan of action."[49]

In Indochina, the annual offensive of the Viet Minh in the Tonkin delta area had resulted in French evacuation of one major salient in February 1952. Nevertheless, precluding a step-up in Chinese support for the Viet Minh, the position of the French Union forces seemed no less tenable during 1952 than it had when the prior year's Mutual Security Program was being formulated. Mounting French casualties were, at least in part, compensated for by increased participation of the national forces of the three Associated States in the conflict.[50] The possibly optimistic inference drawn from the military situation was that approximate maintenance of the level of U.S. MDAP aid in Indochina might permit a favorable resolution of the conflict. Toward the end of June 1952, Secretary Acheson confidently stated: "The Communists have made a most determined effort in Indochina. Their aggression has been checked and recent indications warrant the view that the tide is now moving in our favor."[51]

If the threat of external communist *military* aggression in Southern Asia seemed no graver than in the preceding year, the internal *political* threat to the countries of the region did appear more pressing. By dramatizing the pertinence—even in the midst of the Korean and Indochinese wars—of this political threat, the Indian national elections of 1951-52 exercised a strong influence on Executive Branch planning of the 1953 Mutual Security Program.

Testifying on the 1953 Program, Secretary Acheson acknowledged the influence of the Indian elections on the planning of aid to Southern Asia:

"The Indian people have just completed their first national elections. These elections have shown some very startling and revealing and important things. Although the Congress Party won by a substantial majority, the Communist Party showed unexpected strength, especially in certain localities. This showing is essentially attributable

[49] *Mutual Security Act Extension*, House Hearings, Washington, D.C., 1952, p. 4. The Lisbon goals consisted of 50 divisions, 4,000 combat aircraft, and "substantial naval forces." *Ibid.*, p. 3, and Ismay, *op.cit.*, p. 47.
[50] *Report to the Congress on the Mutual Security Program, June 30, 1953*, Washington, D.C., 1953, p. 38; and *Department of State Bulletin*, Vol. xxvii, July 21, 1952, p. 99.
[51] *Department of State Bulletin*, Vol. xxvi, June 30, 1952, p. 1010.

to the discontent of many over the abject poverty and hopelessness of their lives. This discontent is being fanned by a constant flow of communist propaganda and subversion. The advice of all our observers on the ground is that, unless the newly independent government under Prime Minister Nehru can show substantial progress in economic development over the next five years, the likelihood is that in the next elections the democratic forces will be endangered either by the extremists of the right or by the communists."[52] Within the Executive Branch, there was no more articulate or persuasive "observer on the ground" than the then-new U.S. Ambassador to India, Chester Bowles. In effect, Bowles' insights and arguments were responsible for applying to South Asia the same reasoning and experience we have previously associated with the China "lesson," and with the Griffin and Bell Missions in Southeast Asia.

2. Mutual Security Legislation

Though these views strongly influenced Executive Branch planning of aid to Southern Asia, they had less influence on the Mutual Security authorizing legislation, and still less on the appropriations legislation actually enacted by the Congress. Congressional unwillingness to accept these views accounted, in part, for the sharp reductions that were made in the economic and technical aid proposed for Southern Asia. Of the $408 million originally proposed by the Administration for "Asia and the Pacific," that is, Southern Asia *and* Formosa,[53] only $270 million, or 66 per cent, were finally appropriated in the Mutual Security Appropriation Act of 1953. As we shall see below, the legislative cuts made in the Indian segment of the regional aid proposals were still deeper.

Before we compare the proposals and obligations data for the individual countries, one other aspect of the Mutual Security legislation should be mentioned. In its basic features, the Mutual Security Act of 1952 followed identically the Act of the preceding year: in broad program objectives, in the closer administrative integration of military end-item assistance (MDAP) and non-military aid, in the

---

[52] *Mutual Security Act Extension*, House Hearings, 1952, p. 13.

[53] Besides the figures shown in Table 10, the $408 million proposed for "Asia and the Pacific" included $115 million for Formosa, $35 million for "direct military support" in Indochina (see footnote f to Table 10), and a $13 million fund for "Basic Materials Development," unallocated by country (see footnote a, Table 10). See *Mutual Security Act of 1952*, Report of the House Committee on Foreign Affairs, Washington, D.C., 1952, pp. 50, 55.

regional grouping of aid recipients, and in the conditions imposed on aid recipients.[54] However, one administrative change made by the legislation had some bearing on the future course of aid to Southern Asia.

As a result of the difficulties that had arisen in Indonesia from the conditions imposed on recipients of military aid under the Mutual Security Act of 1951,[55] Congress sought to clarify the distinction between countries receiving *only* economic and technical aid, and those receiving military end-item aid as well. Administratively, the distinction was made by restricting the responsibility of the Mutual Security Agency for administering economic and technical aid programs to countries also receiving military end-item aid. In countries receiving only economic and technical aid, TCA's administrative responsibility, under the Act for International Development, was to be mandatory. Legislatively, the distinction was established by confining MSA's authorization to administer non-military aid solely to countries where such aid was "necessary for carrying out mutual defense (that is, MDAP) programs."[56] In Southern Asia, this meant that, for 1953, TCA was to be administratively responsible for aid to all countries except Indochina, the Philippines, and Thailand.

Two paradoxical implications followed from this Congressional action. The first was an oblique confirmation of the view that the United States did indeed have non-military objectives that warranted economic and technical aid to countries not receiving MDAP aid; the transfer to TCA of responsibility for administering aid to Burma and Indonesia underscored this implication. In this case, however, aid was to emphasize technical service, in accord with the original intent of the Act for International Development, and "capital" as-

---

[54] For a discussion of these points in the Mutual Security Act of 1951, see above, pp. 114-116. The Mutual Security Act of 1952 was passed as a series of lengthy amendments to the Act of 1951 leaving the basic provisions of the previous Act intact. One exception to the statement made in the text above involved a modification of program objectives in Europe. In the Mutual Security Act of 1952, Congress expressed the intention that the Act "be so administered as to support concrete measures for political federation, military integration and economic unification of Europe." The "concrete measures" envisaged were—besides NATO—the Coal and Steel Community, and the European Defense Community.

[55] See above, Tables 7 and 8, and pp. 119-120.

[56] The quotation is from Section 503 of the Mutual Security Act of 1951. The intent of Congress that this provision, beginning in fiscal 1953, required administration of economic and technical aid by TCA under the Act for International Development in all non-MDAP countries, was affirmed in the House Committee's Report on the Mutual Security Act of 1952, which was subsequently accepted by the Senate as well. See U.S. Congressional Code, 82nd Congress, 1952, Vol. 2, p. 1595.

sistance was to be generally confined to demonstration purposes.[57]

The second implication was that in countries which were receiving military aid, the sole justification for non-military aid was to be its contribution to the military program itself, that is, its "defense support." While United States non-military objectives were thus recognized as warranting economic and technical aid in non-MDAP countries, these same objectives were evidently to be discarded in MDAP countries.[58]

In effect, the European precedent—of using and justifying economic aid, primarily if not exclusively, as a means for increasing internal defense efforts—was applied to the MDAP countries in Southern Asia as well. One result was that economic aid proposals for MDAP countries in Southern Asia, for example in the Philippines and Thailand in 1953, were sometimes misleadingly labelled "defense support," even though the underlying objective, as well as the project composition of such aid, remained what they had been *before* enactment of the Mutual Security Act of 1952. In these circumstances, the label tended to obscure rather than clarify the relevant objective.

Besides this modification in the administration of the program, the Mutual Security authorizing and appropriations legislation for 1953 substantially altered country and project allocations of aid to Southern Asia. The extent of this change can be seen by comparing the proposals and obligations figures in Tables 10 and 11 below.

3. Economic Aid Allocations to Southern Asia for 1953

In comparing Tables 10 and 11 with each other and with the corresponding tables for the preceding year,[59] several points stand out. In the first place, the regional total for Southern Asia, which the Executive Branch proposed to *increase* more than 50 per cent above the 1952 proposals,[60] was actually *reduced*, on an obligations basis, 12 per cent below the 1952 level.[61]

---

[57] See above, Chapter 3, pp. 60-64.
[58] We shall consider more fully in Chapter 7 what meaning can be attached to "military" and "non-military" objectives. For illustration and simplification, in the present context military objectives can be thought of in terms of the local force goals, established by the MAAGs and by the Joint Chiefs of Staff, and non-military objectives as enhancing internal political stability, in the sense argued by the Griffin, Gray, and Rockefeller Reports.
[59] See above, pp. 122-125.
[60] From $160 million in 1952 (above, Table 7) to $245 million for 1953 (Table 10, above).
[61] From $150 million in 1952 (above, Table 8) to $132 million (Table 11, above).

Table 10

FUNDS PROPOSED BY THE EXECUTIVE BRANCH FOR UNITED STATES
ECONOMIC AND TECHNICAL ASSISTANCE TO SOUTHERN ASIA, FISCAL YEAR 1953[a]

(by country and project use)

Country	Project Use								TOTAL	Country Total as Proportion of Regional Total
	Agriculture	Industry	Transportation	Health	Public Administration	Education	Community Development	General and Miscellaneous		
	(millions of dollars)									(per cent)
Afghanistan[b]	.22	–	.34	.13	–	.04	–	.07	.80	.3
Burma[c]	4.55	1.40	2.57	3.36	.50	1.62	–	4.00	18.00	7.3
Ceylon[d]	.20	.03	.15	–	–	.03	–	.04	.45	.2
India[e]	37.53	30.80	37.88	4.00	.14	4.36	–	.29	115.00	46.9
Indochina[f]	3.22	.50	3.38	4.39	1.20	.40	–	16.91	30.00	12.2
Indonesia[g]	2.33	.95	.17	1.70	1.15	1.20	–	.50	8.00	3.3
Nepal[h]	.13	–	–	.06	.02	–	–	.04	.25	.1
Pakistan[i]	11.08	8.67	10.40	2.16	.13	.24	–	.82	33.50	13.7
Philippines[j]	12.63	.78	4.93	5.19	.99	1.48	–	6.00	32.00	13.1
Thailand[k]	2.13	.59	.80	2.38	.30	.80	–	–	7.00	2.9
TOTALS	74.02	43.72	60.62	23.37	4.43	10.17	–	28.67	245.00	100.0
Project Total as Proportion of Regional Total	30.2	17.8	24.7	9.6 (per cent)	1.8	4.2	–	11.7	100.0	

(continued)

[140]

Sources: See Appendix II.

a For further explanation of the problems involved in assembling the proposals data, see above, Table 7, footnote a. Besides the amounts shown in Table 10, the Executive Branch proposals for 1953 included $13 million for an Asian Basic Materials Development Fund, unallocated by country. The Fund was an outgrowth of the work of the President's Materials Policy Commission (Paley Commission) in 1952, and of the earlier Gray Committee on Foreign Economic Policies. It reflected the Administration's view that growth of free world requirements for basic materials warranted the use of economic assistance to develop additional supplies. See above, pp. 112-113, *Mutual Security Act of 1952*, House Committee Report, p. 54; and *Monthly Operations Report*, July 31, 1954, Foreign Operations Administration, Washington, D.C., p. 69. For Mutual Security Director Harriman's testimony on development of basic materials as an objective of aid to the underdeveloped areas, see *Mutual Security Act Extension*, House Hearings, 1952, p. 8.

After the deep Congressional cuts in the 1953 MSP proposals, only $259,000 was actually obligated under the material development program in Southern Asia.

b The country total is from (i), p. 50. The project breakdown is estimated from (i), p. 51, and (f), p. 128.

c (g), p. 841, and (i), p. 55.

d Same as footnote b, above.

e Same as footnote b.

f (g), p. 831; (h), p. 56; and (i), p. 55. In addition, "direct military support" amounting to $35 million was proposed for financing under the economic aid authorization. The commodities comprised in this category represented military "software," for example, P.O.L. and military medical supplies, to be furnished directly to the French Union forces in Indochina. The decision to include these civilian-type, or "common use" items in the economic aid proposals was based in part on the relative simplicity of using existing MSA procurement channels, rather than Defense Department channels. See the text below, pp. 154-155.

g (g), p. 841; and (i), p. 55.

h Same as footnote b, above.

i Same as footnote b.

j (g), p. 836; and (h), p. 56.

k (g), p. 849; and (h), p. 56.

Table 11

FUNDS OBLIGATED FOR UNITED STATES ECONOMIC AND TECHNICAL ASSISTANCE TO SOUTHERN ASIA, FISCAL YEAR 1953[a]

(by country and project use)

Country	Project Use (millions of dollars)								TOTAL	Country Total as Proportion of Regional Total (per cent)
	Agriculture	Industry	Transportation	Health	Public Administration	Education	Community Development	General and Miscellaneous		
Afghanistan[b]	.34	.10	–	.03	–	.17	–	1.50	2.14	1.6
Burma[e]	2.27	.21	.33	2.72	–	1.28	–	.12	6.93	5.3
Ceylon[d]	–	–	–	–	–	–	–	–	–	–
India[e]	33.27	.70	.02	5.85	.04	1.46	2.24	–	43.58	33.1
Indochina[f]	1.31	–	3.21	.68	.03	–	.68	18.07	23.98	18.2
Indonesia[g]	1.04	.33	.09	.48	.28	.49	–	.85	3.56	2.7
Nepal[h]	.34	.04	–	.07	–	–	–	–	.45	.3
Pakistan[i]	6.97	3.05	–	–	–	–	.75	16.03	26.80	20.3
Philippines[j]	4.86	.57	6.71	2.43	.68	3.35	–	(.68)	17.92	13.6
Thailand[k]	1.64	.82	1.87	1.80	.13	.73	–	(.03)	6.46	4.9
TOTALS	52.04	5.82	11.73	14.06	1.16	7.48	3.67	35.86	131.82	100.0
Project Total as Proportion of Regional Total	(per cent)									
	39.5	4.4	8.9	10.6	.9	5.7	2.8	27.2	100.0	

(continued)

[142]

Sources: See Appendix II.

a See Table 3, footnote a, for explanation of categories and terms used in this table.

b (q), p. 160, and (a). The $1.5 million general-and-miscellaneous item in Table 11 represents a long-term loan (40 years at 2½ per cent interest) extended to Afghanistan in January 1953, for the purchase of wheat, under the Mutual Security Act and using MSP appropriations.

c (k), pp. 60, 143, and 189; (l), p. 923; (m), p. 540; and (n), p. 241. The figures shown represent obligations made through March 1953. At that time, the Burmese government (for reasons discussed in the text below, pp. 150-151) requested that the program be terminated. As a result, nearly all of the 1953 obligations shown in Table 11 were subsequently deobligated, either later in fiscal 1953 or in the following two years. This was, consequently, one of the exceptional instances in which initial obligations did not lead to equivalent expenditures subsequently.

There is another complication about the Burma figures for 1953. As previously noted (see Table 8, footnote c), administrative responsibility for the Burma program shifted to TCA in 1953. Because of the reobligation of 1952 funds, using TCA obligating procedures, subsequent records (for example, [g'], p. 54) show 1953 obligations of $12.8 million. This sum represents the reobligation of 1952 funds under the TCA procedures, plus new obligations made during 1953 funds, minus deobligations made during 1953 after termination of the Burma program.

d Technical assistance to Ceylon was discontinued because of Ceylon's rubber exports to Communist China which began in 1953. The Mutual Defense Assistance Control Act of 1951 (the Battle Act) prohibited assistance to countries exporting "items of primary strategic significance" to the communist bloc and discouraged assistance to countries exporting "other commodities." Rubber was considered in the latter category. See (l), pp. 93-95,

and The Strategic Trade Control System 1948-1956, Ninth Report to Congress, Washington, 1957, pp. 51-62.

e (s), p. 376; and (a).

f (q), p. 283. In addition, $30.1 million of direct military support, or "common-use" items (see above, Table 10, pp. 140-141, footnote f) were provided to the French Union forces in Indochina.

g (q), p. 290. Later records (for example, [g'], p. 54) show 1953 obligations of $13.2 million which actually represent the reobligations of previous years' funds using TCA obligating procedures, as well as the obligation of newly appropriated funds. Administrative responsibility for the Indonesian program, like that for Burma, was transferred to TCA in 1953. Consequently, the same explanation for the recording anomaly in Burma applies in Indonesia, as well. See footnote c, above.

h (q), p. 216.

i (k), p. 190. Of the general-and-miscellaneous items, $15 million is a long-term Mutual Security loan, made early in fiscal 1953, for the purchase of wheat to help reduce the threat of famine brought on by successive crop failures. See Report to the Congress on the Mutual Security Program, June 30, 1953, Washington, D.C., 1953, p. 46. Later in the year, Congress authorized an additional grant of wheat to Pakistan. Under the Pakistan Food Act (see below, footnote 73), $65 million worth of wheat was shipped in the following fiscal year, of which $15 million represented freight costs financed from MSP 1953 funds (see [r], p. 160). Consequently, some reports on the Pakistan 1953 program show total obligations for the year of $42 million (the $26.8 million shown in Table 11, plus $15 million ocean freight). See, for example, (p), p. 55; and (g'), p. 55.

j (q), p. 315. The figure in parentheses represents a net deobligation of prior years' funds.

k (q), p. 325; and (g'), p. 54. The figure in parentheses represents a net deobligation of prior years' funds.

The extent of the reduction in the 1953 proposals for Southern Asia can also be viewed in relation to *global* aid, other than MDAP, under the Mutual Security Program for 1953. Whereas the original Executive Branch proposals for Southern Asia (Table 10) comprised 9.9 per cent of global economic aid proposed in the 1953 Mutual Security Program (excluding MDAP),[62] actual obligations in Southern Asia amounted to 7 per cent of global obligations. The obligations figures, comparable to Table 6 for 1952, are summarized in Table 12 below.

Table 12

UNITED STATES ECONOMIC AND TECHNICAL AID TO SOUTHERN ASIA
IN FISCAL YEAR 1953 COMPARED TO TOTAL ASIAN AND
GLOBAL ECONOMIC ASSISTANCE UNDER THE MUTUAL
SECURITY ACT OF 1952

	Obligations	As Proportion of:	
		Total Asian Aid	Global Aid
	(millions of dollars)	(per cent)	
Economic and Technical Aid to Southern Asia, 1953	131.8a	55.5	7.0
Economic and Technical Aid to Formosa, 1953	105.5	44.5	5.6
Total Asian Aid	237.3	100.0	12.6
Global Economic Aid Under the Mutual Security Act of 1952	1,876.4	–	100.0

Sources: Table 11, above, and (g'), p. 54.
a The total excludes $30 million of common-use items supplied directly to French Union military forces, but financed under the Mutual Security appropriation for economic aid.

4. A Comparison of Proposals and Obligations

To clarify some of the reasons behind the $113 million (or 46 per cent) reduction in the 1953 proposals for Southern Asia, we need to look at the individual country amounts and shares shown in Tables 10 and 11. The Congressional cuts in the *regional* total are to be understood in terms of considerations relating to the individual countries affected.

[62] The Administration's original proposals for 1953 amounted to $2.47 billion for European defense support and all other non-MDAP aid. See *Mutual Security Act of 1952*, Report of the Senate Committee on Foreign Relations, pp. 4-6.

Of the $113 million reduction in the regional proposals, $71 million, or over 60 per cent, was accounted for by the India program. Two considerations, both perhaps of historical rather than analytical interest, were responsible for this heavy cut.

The first consideration concerned India's foreign policies, and more particularly its policy on Korea. Assertively independent in its foreign policies generally, India had abstained from the original Security Council resolution of June 27, 1950, that recommended UN military assistance to the Korean Republic to help it deter aggression. India had officially criticized MacArthur's crossing of the 38th parallel, and Nehru and India's UN delegates repeatedly called for Communist China's admission to the UN, both before and after its intervention in Korea. As might have been expected, India's reaction to UN resumption of the air war in Korea in the summer of 1952 was sharply critical, and came at precisely the time when the Mutual Security Appropriation Bill was under debate in the Congress.

To some in the United States, and especially in the Congress, this record, coming as a sequel to the $190 million food loan of 1951-52, seemed more like partisan belligerence than neutrality. The Congressional reaction was to discount the Administration's arguments for expanding aid to India, and to reduce it instead. If India showed neither understanding nor sympathy toward America's international problems, what was the value to the United States of showing sympathy and ever-rising generosity to India's domestic problems?

The other consideration affecting aid to India arose from the constraints imposed by the legislation under which the program was authorized. Unlike the economic and technical aid programs in Southeast Asia, those in South Asia were carried out under the continuing authorization of the Act for International Development repeated each year in the annual Mutual Security Act. As we have previously discussed, the A.I.D. had been enacted and the original Point Four program launched with unrestrained optimism concerning the returns to be expected from low-costing technical services.[63] When the Administration's 1953 proposals plainly showed that the Act was to be used, at least in the special case of India and Pakistan, for undertaking programs of substantial capital assistance as well, Congressional reaction was sharply adverse.

In part, Congressional reaction was to be explained by the Ad-

[63] That is, from technological change rather than increased investment. For further discussion of the point, see Chapter 3, section F.3.

ministration's unwillingness to admit it had oversold the returns to be derived from technical assistance alone. If "hundredfold" returns were still to be expected from technical aid,[64] the case for capital assistance could hardly be as pressing as the Administration claimed. In part, too, the Congressional reaction arose from doubts about the returns to the United States from larger amounts of aid, *even if* technical services were not as panacean as had been originally hoped.[65]

The influence of these two considerations on the deep Congressional cuts made in the proposed aid to India is suggested by the following excerpt from the debate on the India program.[66]

> *Congressman Davis of Georgia:* . . . [this] is not a technical assistance program. [It] carries $50 million for steel . . . $10 million for fertilizer . . . 2,000 deep wells in the Ganges Delta. It is full of items like that. They jumped from $5 million (for India) in 1951 to $77 million in this bill.
>
> *Congressman Smith of Virginia:* . . . They talk about the fact that this is to make friends, this is to help keep our friends. If there is anybody in the House who has ever seen or heard that Nehru has ever made a statement favorable to the United States, I would like him to say so now.
>
> *Congressman Fulton of Pennsylvania:* I will say it; yes.
>
> *Congressman Smith:* I deny the statement. I do not believe he ever did. I never did see it.[67]

a. The Comparison for India and Pakistan. What analytical significance can be attached to the sharp reduction in the 1953 proposals for India from the standpoint of the broader allocation issues which concern us? Clearly, emotional factors that are hard to place in neat

[64] See above, Chapter 3, pp. 63-64.

[65] For a clear expression of these views, see *The Mutual Security Act of 1952*, House Report, 1952, *op.cit.*, pp. 49, 52; and *The Mutual Security Act of 1952*, Senate Report, Washington, D.C., 1952, p. 37.

[66] *Congressional Record*, Vol. 98, No. 115, June 28, 1952, pp. 8551-8552. The debate came in connection with a proposed amendment, made on the floor of the House, to reduce the appropriation for the TCA countries in Southern Asia by another $50 million, after the authorizing and appropriations committees had already made cuts that lowered the *proposed* program for India from the $115 million, shown in Table 10, to $77 million, the figure referred to by Congressman Davis in the cited quotation.

[67] Congressmen Fulton, Kennedy, and Javits all contested the views of Davis and Smith in later portions of the debate, *ibid.*, pp. 8552-8553. Nevertheless, the Davis amendment, which proposed the cut, was adopted and retained in the final appropriations act.

analytical categories affected Congressional action. If, however, we try to fit the considerations discussed above into the analytic terms we have previously used, two observations can be made. The first is that, to the extent India's less-than-friendly foreign policy pronouncements influenced the cuts, the latter proceeded from a basic "value" judgment by the Congress at variance with that reflected in the Administration's original proposals.

The Administration's proposals had been based on the fact that Indian democracy was new and, in a sense, on trial, and the premise that the success of the Five-Year Plan would improve the chances of a favorable verdict. Given the fact and the premise, the Administration's judgment was that India's accelerated economic development had a high value to the United States. The Congressional action didn't necessarily conflict with the fact or the premise. Instead it implied a difference in interpretation. In effect, Congressional action amounted to a further and different evaluation of the fact and premise: India's development had a high value to the United States *if* India's verbal pronouncements and international conduct were friendly, or at least not unfriendly, toward the United States.

The second observation relates to the misgivings expressed by the Congressional Committees concerning the growing size of Point Four aid in general, and to India in particular. In the terms we have previously used, it is reasonable to attribute these misgivings in large part to a Congressional judgment, concerning the physical productivity of capital assistance, which was fundamentally different from that of the Executive Branch. The Congressional Committees argued that, under the most generous assumptions, U.S. capital assistance to the countries of Southern Asia could do no more than "scratch the surface" of their "needs." Consequently, their development "depends to a large extent upon the willingness of the host countries to help themselves." The programs "will not succeed if they are financed . . . by the United States."[68]

The Committees contended, further, that the financial contribution made by the recipient countries to their own development could and should be increased if U.S. capital assistance were reduced.[69] In recommending a reduction in the aid proposed for India and Pakistan, the House Foreign Affairs Committee stated that it was: ". . . impressed by the heavy outlays for supplies and equipment in

[68] *The Mutual Security Act of 1952*, Senate Report, p. 37.
[69] *Ibid.*, pp. 38-39.

[the aid programs of] some countries, notably India and Pakistan. . . . The Committee expects that those administering TCA programs will show a firm determination that supplies and equipment, even though supporting technical assistance programs, will be reduced. There is little evidence . . . that [the Executive Branch] has weighed too carefully the absorptive capacity. . . . The basis for technical assistance should not be what a country wants or needs. . . . The criterion must be what a country can absorb. A country may enthusiastically embark upon an array of programs it needs and wants but that it cannot maintain without continued assistance from external . . . sources. A half loaf is better than no bread. The same satisfaction is not derived from half an irrigation system."[70]

In economic terms, the Committees' reasoning can be expressed in the following propositions: (1) the major investment requirements for Asian economic development must be met from internal savings and taxes; (2) capital assistance from the United States might obscure this fact, and hence simply substitute for savings or taxes that recipient countries would otherwise provide themselves; (3) where capital assistance was not substitutive, it would not be large enough to overcome the discontinuity or "lumpiness" involved in the necessary social overhead investment projects.[71]

This line of reasoning led to the conclusion that the net physical productivity of capital assistance, unlike technical services alone, was likely to be small. Given adequate internal tax and savings efforts by recipient countries, capital assistance would be unnecessary (that is, substitutive). Without such efforts, it would be insufficient. The sharp Congressional cut in the Indian aid proposal derived, in part, from this view. Though the physical productivity of technical services, supplemented by only limited supplies and equipment for "demonstration purposes," was high, that from additional capital assistance was regarded—correctly or not—as low or nil. Consequently, the prospective "returns" to the United States did not justify the large increase in aid to India proposed by the Executive Branch.

The same considerations also applied to Congressional action on aid to Pakistan. As a result of Congressional action on the Executive

[70] *The Mutual Security Act of 1952*, House Report, p. 52.

[71] Strictly speaking, the introduction of discontinuities means that the *marginal* productivity of aid is generally zero, occasionally infinite. If the discontinuous jumps are precluded by constraints on the permissible *total* amount of assistance, the zero productivity conclusion follows.

Branch proposals for 1953, it was intended that aid to Pakistan would also be reduced substantially. However, in the summer of 1952 a serious food shortage developed in Pakistan from two successive crop failures. To meet the threat of famine, a long-term Mutual Security loan of $15 million was extended early in fiscal 1953.[72] For this reason, Pakistan's share of total obligations in Southern Asia in 1953 rose to 20 per cent, compared to 14 per cent in the original 1953 proposals and only 7 per cent in the 1952 obligations.[73] While aid obligations to India fell from $53 million in 1952 to $44 million in 1953, obligations in Pakistan rose from $11 million to $27 million.

The significance of this sharp change in the amount and share of aid to Pakistan can only be translated into the value-and-productivity terms we have previously used with difficulty. It can be more readily understood as the result of exogenous factors impinging on and altering the allocation of aid after both Executive Branch planning and Congressional appropriations had been completed.[74] The exogenous factors—Pakistan's critical food shortage, and the humanitarian impulse of the United States to respond generously to economic emergencies in the free world[75]—rather than altering the value-and-productivity calculations implicit in the previous aid allocation, represented essentially different and noncommensurable dimensions for making these calculations.[76]

[72] *Mutual Security Report, June 30, 1953*, p. 46.
[73] See Tables 11, 10, and 8, for the cited figures. As Pakistan's food situation continued to deteriorate, President Eisenhower requested, and Congress authorized, a grant to Pakistan of up to one million tons of wheat from stocks of the Commodity Credit Corporation. The Pakistan Food Act which resulted was approved by the President at the end of June 1953. In the following fiscal year, over 600,000 tons were shipped to Pakistan before an improvement in the food situation made further shipments unnecessary. The value of the wheat shipped under the Act amounted to $65 million, of which $15 million represented freight costs which were financed from MSP 1953 funds. None of this $65 million is shown in Table 11. Like the Indian food loan of 1951 it is excluded from the MSP obligations figures because it was provided under a separate legislative authorization. The reason for this exclusion is simply that the motives—heavily dominated by humanitarian considerations, which prompted the wheat grant—were different from those determining the allocations of MSP aid to Southern Asia generally. See *Report to the Congress on the Mutual Security Program, June 30, 1954*, Washington, D.C., 1954, p. 31; and *Mutual Security Act of 1954*, House Hearings, Washington, D.C., 1954, p. 160.
[74] The funds required for the emergency food loan to Pakistan were transferred from the Title I (European) portion of the Mutual Security Appropriation under the provision of the authorizing legislation which permitted interregional transfers up to 10 per cent of the funds appropriated.
[75] The "humanitarian" impulse should perhaps not be overstressed. Pakistan's subsequent adherence to SEATO, and its increasingly close ties to the United States, may have been in part related to the generous U.S. response to the 1953 food crisis.
[76] The same explanation applies to the increase in aid obligations in Afghanistan

b. The Comparison for the Southeast Asian Countries. The reductions made in the 1953 proposals for Indonesia and Burma were based on essentially the same considerations involved in the Indian case. No "exogenous" factors intervened, as in the case of Pakistan, to offset the reductions made by Congress in the Administration's proposals for these two countries. Consequently, the amounts and shares allocated to Burma and Indonesia were reduced in the 1953 obligations (Table 11) substantially below the original 1953 proposals as well as the 1952 obligations.

In the case of Burma, the latter statement needs to be amplified. During 1953, new aid obligations were as shown in Table 11. However, at the end of March 1953, the Burmese government requested that the program be terminated. As a consequence, toward the end of fiscal 1953 and retroactively during fiscal 1954, most of the Burma obligations shown in Table 11 were cancelled.[77]

The reasons behind termination of the program are interesting, though not entirely relevant to the main concern of this study. After the Communist victory in China in 1949, several thousand Chinese Nationalist troops were driven from Yunnan across the Burmese border. During 1952 and 1953, the Burmese allegedly found evidence that these troops were linking their guerrilla activities with the internal rebellion in Burma. The Burmese also believed the Nationalist guerrillas were being given logistic support from Formosa. Since Formosa was, in turn, receiving heavy financial, as well as political, support from the United States, the Burmese viewed the presence and activities of the Nationalist guerrillas as a responsibility of the United States as well. Previous complaints to the United States (Burma did not have diplomatic relations with Nationalist China) brought no response considered satisfactory by the Burmese. Either the United States was unable or unwilling to take measures that would alter the situation. Consequently, before pursuing their

---

as well as Pakistan. Though scheduled for a reduction in aid as a result of the Congressional cuts, obligations were increased as a result of altered circumstances later in the year. As in Pakistan, a food shortage threatened in Afghanistan due to drought conditions. The United States responded to an Afghan request for assistance with a $1.5 million long-term Mutual Security loan in January 1953. *Mutual Security Act of 1953*, Senate Hearings, Washington, D.C., 1953, p. 540.

[77] See Table 11, footnote c. In effect the 1953 obligations shown for Burma represent largely "paper" obligations. Unlike the other obligations data for 1953, and for the preceding and subsequent years as well, the Burmese obligations did not lead to corresponding expenditures. The Burmese obligations are, however, retained in Table 11 because they reflect the decisions on allocation made at the time (that is, during 1952).

charges in the United Nations against Formosa, and if need be against the U.S., the Burmese felt morally and practically bound to divest themselves of the close politico-economic relation with the United States implied by the existing aid program. Termination of the program was the result.

Two implications of the incident are worth noting. First, it should be recalled that the obligated 1953 program in Burma was just half that of 1952. Consequently, prior to terminating the program, Burma had reason to anticipate, if not a decreasing, then at least a highly unstable amount of aid in future years. With rice prices at an all-time high, and Burma's foreign exchange holdings continuing to rise during 1953, termination of aid may have seemed a small price to pay for enhanced moral stature, as well as an improved bargaining position.

The incident suggests, too, a more general lesson. While the aid-giving relationship may involve some political opportunities and gains for the donor, it may involve political risks and losses as well. If the donor acquires potential influence over the recipient, he also acquires a potential obligation to respond to the recipient's influence over him.

Returning to Tables 10 and 11, we find it clear that the reductions made in the Executive Branch proposals for aid to Indochina and Thailand, and to a lesser extent the Philippines, were small relative to those made for India, Indonesia, and Burma. In explanation it should be recalled that Indochina, Thailand, and the Philippines were countries in which MDAP was also underway. Economic and technical aid in these countries was justified by the Executive Branch not only in terms of the political-stability objective adduced to justify aid to the "neutralist" countries. It was also justified as providing support for military outlays in the recipient countries. In fact, as we have already seen, "defense support" was the sole *legal* basis for non-military aid to these countries after 1953.

From the Congressional viewpoint, there was thus reason for relatively smaller cuts in the aid appropriation for these countries.[78] The existence of a military aid program in itself was evidence of closer cooperation with the United States and, in contrast to the Congressional animus against Indian neutralism, a reason for tacitly

[78] In the Supplemental Appropriations Act of 1953, funds for Indochina, Thailand, and the Philippines (and Formosa)—the "MSA countries"—were appropriated separately from those for the rest of Southern Asia, that is, the "TCA countries."

according non-military aid a higher "value" to the U.S. in the three MSA countries. Moreover, in the MSA countries, even if commodity assistance did substitute for internal savings and taxes that could otherwise be devoted by the recipients to the projects receiving such aid,[79] the aid might still be physically productive. It might still permit the recipient country to divert internal savings and taxes to military outlays, thereby reinforcing the MDA program. In the MSA countries this, too, could be considered a "productive" consequence of non-military aid. From the *Congressional* standpoint, there were plausible reasons for attributing higher value-and-productivity to aid in the MSA countries than the TCA countries, and for reallocating accordingly.

The Philippines was a partial exception to these observations. So small was the MDA program in the Philippines compared to the originally proposed non-military aid, that the case for attributing military benefits to non-military aid was particularly weak. In effect, the implication of the substantial Congressional reduction in Philippine aid was this: *where nonmilitary aid was large relative to MDAP, the former could not be adequately justified by its contributions to the latter.* Stated more generally, the justifiable amount of non-military "defense support" depended on the amount of military aid received, other things being equal. "Defense support" required evidence of an additional "defense" burden to support. The evidence could be provided by a large military end-item program. In Indochina, the large and rising MDAP represented such evidence. In Thailand, though MDAP wasn't large absolutely, it was still sufficiently large relative to proposed non-military aid so that the latter was accepted by Congress as "defense support." In the Philippines, no warrant for the amount of "defense support" proposed could be provided by the size of MDAP itself. Consequently, non-military aid in the Philippines was reduced by more, absolutely and proportionally, than in Indochina or Thailand.

5. Sectoral Allocations

Before leaving Tables 10 and 11, a final comment on the project composition of economic and technical aid in 1953 is in order. It can be seen from Table 10 that the share of aid allocated for the relatively long-term industrial and transport sectors, 42.5 per cent, in

---

[79] This, it will be recalled, was one reason for presuming that commodity assistance in the TCA countries had a low physical productivity.

the original 1953 *proposals*, for the first time exceeded the share proposed for the shorter-term agricultural and health sectors, 39.8 per cent. In the obligations actually made after Congressional action (Table 11), the quicker-yielding sectors represented by far the larger share (50.1 per cent compared to 13.3 per cent). Moreover, while obligations for the shorter-term sectors in 1953 were approximately the same as in 1952, obligations for the longer-term sectors were substantially cut (from 23.3 per cent in 1952 to 13.3 per cent in 1953).[80] Hence, the implicitly high discount on future yields, which we previously attributed to the 1952 allocations, applies *a fortiori* to the 1953 obligations.

6. Military Aid in 1953

During 1953, the size and content of military assistance in Southern Asia followed closely the lines set in the preceding year. As in 1952, Indochina, Thailand, and the Philippines were the only countries in the region which received Mutual Defense Assistance. MDAP appropriations for the four Asian recipients (including Formosa) were $541 million, approximately the same as in 1952.[81] However, as a fraction of global MDAP appropriations, the Asian share rose from 9 per cent in 1952 to nearly 13 per cent in 1953. The MDAP appropriations data are summarized in Table 13.

It is notable that the total appropriation for MDAP fell from $5.8 billion in 1952 to $4.2 billion in 1953. In large measure, the drop was due to Congressional cuts, rather than to cuts made by the Executive

Table 13

MUTUAL DEFENSE ASSISTANCE APPROPRIATIONS,
FISCAL YEAR 1953

	Appropriations[a] (millions of dollars)	Proportion of Total (per cent)
Europe	3,128.2	74.2
Near East and Africa	499.1	11.8
Asia and the Pacific	540.8	12.8
American Republics	51.7	1.2
TOTALS	4,219.8	100.0

[a] *Mutual Security Appropriation Act of 1953*, Public Law 547, 82nd Congress, 2nd session, 1952.

[80] See Table 8.   [81] See above, Table 9.

Branch in its original 1953 proposals. In contrast to the earlier years, when MDAP appropriations either equalled or closely approached Executive Branch proposals,[82] in 1953 Congress made appreciable reductions in the MDAP proposals. Compared to the appropriations shown in Table 13, the original Executive Branch proposals had been $5.4 billion—only slightly below the 1952 appropriation—consisting of $4.1 billion for Europe, $.6 billion each for the Near Eastern and Asian regions, and $62 million for Latin America.[83]

On a global basis, Congressional reductions in the Executive Branch military aid proposals were approximately in the same proportion as Congressional reductions in the non-military aid proposals. MDAP proposals were reduced by 22 per cent, from $5.4 billion to $4.2 billion; non-military aid proposals by 24 per cent, from $2.5 billion to $1.9 billion.[84]

But on a regional basis, incidence of the cuts was markedly different. For Southern Asia, economic and technical aid, as we have seen, was reduced by $113 million or 46 per cent,[85] while for the Asian area as a whole (including Formosa), MDAP was reduced by $70 million, or 11 per cent.[86] The implication of this difference is that the "returns" to the United States per marginal aid dollar were considered higher in military than non-military uses. To minimize the "losses" resulting from cutting the programs, relatively more was thus cut from the non-military than from the MDAP programs.

Of course, this is *not* to say that an explicit "rate of exchange" between MDAP and non-MDAP aid was consciously formulated, nor that the problem was actually viewed in these terms, at the time Congress acted. (One might even argue that had it been so viewed, the results might have been different.) The point is *not* that it is historically accurate, but rather that it is analytically useful, to view Congressional decisions in these terms.

Within the three countries of Southern Asia that participated in MDAP in 1953, the amount and content of end-item aid continued

[82] See Table 9, footnote ᵃ, and Table 5, footnotes ᶜ and ᵈ.
[83] *The Mutual Security Act of 1952*, Senate Committee Report, pp. 5-6.
[84] See above, Table 12, footnote ᵃ.
[85] Above, Tables 10 and 11. The original 1953 non-military aid proposals and obligations for Formosa were $115 million and $105 million respectively. If these figures are added to the corresponding totals for Southern Asia, then the amount of the reduction in non-military aid for the Asian region becomes $125 million or 34 per cent.
[86] From $611 million proposed to $541 million appropriated. See *Mutual Security Act of 1952*, Senate Committee Report, pp. 5-6.

along the lines of the previous year. In its sixth year, the war in Indochina was demonstrating the considerable scope and intensity that even a "one-country" war can reach. Under MDAP, deliveries of fighters, bombers, artillery, tanks and other combat vehicles, as well as lighter infantry weapons, rose above the prior year.[87] Other than military end-items, most of the costs of maintaining French Union forces in Indochina—estimated at over $1 billion a year[88]—continued to be borne by the French government. But in 1953, for the first time, the United States also began to bear a small portion of the "software" costs of conducting the war. Besides the costs of MDAP and of economic and technical aid, U.S. assistance to Indochina in 1953 included $30 million of "direct military support."[89]

Comprising military "consumables," like petroleum, medical supplies, textiles for uniforms, etc., as distinct from military hardware, direct military support entailed a further U.S. contribution toward meeting the cost of the war, which was to grow dramatically larger in 1954. Though technically financed under non-military appropriations for the Mutual Security Program, direct military support was considered, by both the Administration and Congress, to be justified on grounds quite different from those justifying economic and technical aid. Direct military support in Indochina represented an attempt to maintain a distinction between "economic" and "military" aid, *not* in terms of the types of commodities involved (that is, military hardware as against all other commodities), but in terms of the differing and competing objectives for which additional aid was required.

In the Philippines, mobile constabulary units, equipped and trained to meet small-scale guerrilla threats to internal security, continued to be the primary capability sought by MDAP. End-item deliveries continued to reflect this emphasis. However, as Huk disturbances were brought increasingly under control, the Philippine Armed Forces and the MAAG turned their attention toward developing complementary military capabilities which would further contribute to internal security. During 1953, for example, the capabilities of the Philippine Navy to prevent smuggling and infiltration of agents and weapons from the Chinese mainland to the Huk guerrillas "in-

[87] See above, this chapter, p. 130. Also *Mutual Security Program Report*, June 30, 1953, pp. 37-38.
[88] *Ibid.*, p. 37.
[89] See above, Table 10, footnote ⁱ, and Table 11, footnote ⁱ.

creased materially with [MDAP] deliveries of coast guard patrol craft."[90]

In Thailand, during the latter part of 1953, one military threat became apparent with the invasion of Laos by Viet Minh guerrillas. With the onset of the rainy season in the summer, the Viet Minh guerrillas withdrew to the Laotian side of the North Vietnamese border after announcing plans for setting up a "Federation of Free Thai" peoples.[91] Though these plans aborted with the Viet Minh withdrawal, a possible move against Thailand through Laos became a more prominent threat than it had previously seemed. In response to this contingency, higher priority was accorded MDAP shipments of combat and training aircraft and end-items for the Thai ground forces, with the aim of providing Thailand a limited capability to withstand external attack.[92]

C. MUTUAL SECURITY IN 1954

1. The International Context and the Change in U.S. National Administration

At the end of fiscal year 1953, as the 1954 Mutual Security legislation was being enacted, the first signs of an easing of international tensions appeared. The death of Stalin in March, the resumption of Korean armistice negotiations in April, and the armistice agreement at the end of July were the beginnings of what later came to be known, though somewhat ambiguously, as the period of "peaceful," or "competitive," coexistence. Nevertheless, the existence of limited war, rather than the possibility of limited *détente*, continued to dominate the international environment while the 1954 Mutual Security Program was being formulated.

If the possibility of *détente* influenced planning of the 1954 Program, the influence was in Europe rather than Asia. From 1950 through 1952, the buildup of NATO forces had been rapid. As an indirect measure of the buildup, annual defense expenditures of European NATO members nearly doubled between the calendar years 1950 and 1952.[93] Rising output had made possible a sufficient increase in tax receipts and savings so that a number of NATO countries were able to reduce their requirements for U.S. aid at the

[90] *Mutual Security Program Report*, June 30, 1953, p. 41.
[91] The *New York Times*, June 2, 1953.
[92] *Mutual Security Program Report*, June 30, 1953, p. 42.
[93] Ismay, *op.cit.*, p. 11.

same time that they were increasing defense outlays. As a result, at the end of fiscal year 1953 the Mutual Security Agency announced the suspension of direct non-military aid in eight NATO countries.[94]

At the same time, it became clear that domestic political pressures would make it increasingly difficult for the European NATO countries to sustain the rate at which defense expenditures had been growing. Consequently, they were predisposed to accept any suggestion of an easing in the international environment which might justify a slow-down of the Lisbon force schedule.

In the United States, the new Administration was also under pressure to reduce government expenditures generally and foreign aid expenditures particularly. It was hardly more willing than its NATO partners to insist on the Lisbon schedule, lest this entail a rise in foreign aid requirements. As a result largely of these circumstances, and only to a lesser extent of convincing evidence of a relaxation of international tensions, the NATO Council in April 1953 decided to emphasize "quality rather than . . . quantity," to "stretch-out" the original Lisbon targets, and to seek their realization over the "long haul" rather than as originally planned.[95] Easing of the pace of NATO buildup in Europe had a moderate effect on the size and character of the Mutual Security Program in 1954 and an increasing effect in subsequent years.

If the signs of communist *détente* had, however, some influence on the European segment of MSP, they had little influence on the program in Asia. When the Eisenhower Administration took over the formulation of the 1954 program in January 1953, two broad considerations guided the MSP proposals it made for the Asian area. The first was the continuing war in Korea and Indochina. Even though armistice negotiations were underway in Korea, the military conflict persisted. In fact, a fortnight before the armistice agreement was signed on July 27, 1953, the communists launched their heaviest offensive in two years.

In Indochina there was no sign of abatement in Viet Minh intentions or ability to pursue the military conflict. With something approaching 400,000 "regular" and "local" troops under arms, and with continued if still limited logistic support from China, the Viet Minh

[94] The eight countries were: Belgium, Denmark, Iceland, Ireland, the Netherlands, the Luxembourg, Portugal, and Sweden. Cited in Stebbins, 1953, *op.cit.*, p. 171.
[95] The Council's communique, which confirmed this decision, nonetheless recognized that "despite recent Soviet moves and gestures . . . there had not in fact been any change in the fundamental threat to the security of free peoples." Ismay, *op.cit.*, p. 197.

was probably stronger militarily at the end of 1953 than it had ever been previously. The invasion of Laos in April 1953, and again in December after an initial withdrawal, were evidences of this strength.

The second consideration, which prominently influenced the 1954 MSP proposals for Asia, was the new Administration's firm intention—in part the result of domestic no less than international politics —to give relatively more attention to Asia in formulating United States foreign policies than had the previous Administration. As the Republican Party's 1952 platform had stated: ". . . we shall end neglect of the Far East which Stalin has long identified as the road to victory over the West. We shall make it clear that we have no intention to sacrifice the East to gain time for the West."[96] Characterizing U.S. foreign policy, after the new Administration had been in office for three months, Secretary Dulles asserted: "A new order of priority and urgency has been given to the Far East."[97]

2. Global and Asian Non-MDAP Obligations in 1954

What bearing did these considerations have on the Mutual Security Program for 1954? The change in regional priorities meant that, to the extent the returns from aid in different regions could be compared, those in Asia were to be more highly valued.[98] At the same time, continuation of the fairly extensive "limited" wars in Korea and Indochina, throughout fiscal year 1953, focused the Administration's attention on the returns, and hence on the uses and forms of aid, most directly relevant to meeting or relieving *military* threats in Asia. Additional aid to Asia, and especially additional aid to meet directly military needs and objectives, were consequently prominent characteristics of the Mutual Security Program proposals for 1954.

The extent to which these considerations governed the actual 1954 program, *after* enactment of the authorization and appropriations legislation, is suggested by Table 14 below, showing *non*-MDAP aid obligations globally and in the Asian area in 1954.

Comparing Table 14 with Table 12, which contains similar data for 1953, two points stand out: the substantial absolute and relative

[96] Cited in *Mutual Security Act of 1953*, House Committee Report, 83rd Congress, 1st session, Washington, D.C., 1953, p. 2.

[97] *Department of State Bulletin*, xxviii, April 27, 1953, p. 605.

[98] And, within Asia, more particularly in the Western Pacific defense perimeter, that is, among "our Eastern friends from Japan, Korea, and Formosa to Indochina and Malaya." *Ibid.*, p. 605.

increase in the amount of aid obligations in the Asian area (from 12.6 per cent of global aid in 1953, to 54.5 per cent in 1954);[99] and the overwhelming concentration of this increase in Indochina, Korea, and Formosa where predominantly military objectives determined the amount of *non*-MDAP aid no less than they determined the amount of MDAP aid.[100]

3. *"Military Aid," "Economic Aid," and "Military Support":* Labels and Contents

The latter point warrants further comment. It will be recalled that the historical account we have presented so far has maintained a consistent distinction between "military" assistance (MDAP) on the one hand, and "economic and technical" assistance on the other. Conceptually, the distinction has been based on the differing purposes or objectives motivating the two categories of aid: military capabilities, conceived primarily in terms of force goals relevant for meeting various local war contingencies or actualities, in the case of military aid; and political stability, and, occasionally, political loyalty and friendship, in the case of economic and technical aid. In the area with which we are principally concerned, each of these broad objectives has applied fairly generally to the corresponding aid category for all recipient countries. In physical content, the distinction has been between military hardware and training allocated to particular types of forces, and civilian "software"—producer and

---

[99] A less sharp, but similar, contrast in regional emphasis results if we compare *proposals*, rather than obligations. Global non-MDAP aid proposals submitted by the Executive Branch for fiscal 1954 amounted to $1.80 billion. Proposed aid to Asia, including military support in Indochina but excluding MDAP, represented 36.7 per cent of this total. (For fiscal year 1953 the comparable figures were $2.47 billion and 16.6 per cent, respectively.) Aid proposed for *Southern* Asia alone (that is, excluding Formosa from "Asia") represented 33 per cent of global non-MDAP proposals. (See *Mutual Security Act Extension*, House Committee Hearings, 1953, p. 191; Table 15 below; and *Mutual Security Act of 1952*, Senate Committee Report, pp. 4-7.)

[100] As far as increased aid to Indochina is concerned, it should be borne in mind that a large part (perhaps as much as half) of the apparent increase represented "repackaging" rather than reallocation. To a considerable extent, what had been proposed and obligated in 1953 as defense support aid to France was, in 1954, proposed and obligated as defense support for Indochina, though used to reimburse France for franc outlays on the Indochina war. While non-MDAP aid to Indochina rose to $679 million in 1954, from $60 million in 1953 (including the so-called "common-use" items for 1953), recorded defense support aid to France fell from $397 million in 1953 to $85 million in 1954. See International Cooperation Administration, *Monthly Operations Report*, June 1957, Issue No. 4, p. 59.

Table 14

UNITED STATES ECONOMIC AND TECHNICAL ASSISTANCE AND
MILITARY SUPPORT TO SOUTHERN ASIA IN FISCAL YEAR 1954 COMPARED
TO TOTAL ASIAN AND GLOBAL NON-MDAP ASSISTANCE UNDER
THE MUTUAL SECURITY ACT OF 1953[a]

	Obligations	As Proportion of:	
		Total Asian Aid	Global Aid
	(millions of dollars)	(per cent)	
1. Economic and Technical Aid to Southern Asia	164.6	14.0	7.7
2. Military Support for Indochina	678.6	57.9	31.5
3. Total Non-MDAP Aid to Southern Asia (1+2)	843.2	71.9	39.2
4. Military Support for Formosa, Korea, and Japan[b]	330.2	28.1	15.3
5. Total Asian Non-MDAP Aid (3+4)	1,173.4	100.0	54.5
6. Global Non-MDAP Aid Under the Mutual Security Act of 1953[c]	2,151.9	–	100.0

Sources: Table 16 below, and (h'), p. 46.

[a] The term "non-MDAP," as used in this table, refers to *all* aid other than the military end-items, NATO infrastructure, and training provided under the Mutual Defense Assistance Program. See the discussion that follows (subheading 3.) for an explanation of the ambiguity involved in cases, like Indochina, where nearly all "*non*-MDAP" aid was no less directly related to military objectives than MDAP aid itself. For MDAP appropriations in 1954, see Table 17 below.

[b] Of the total, $111.6 million represents obligations in Formosa, $208.6 million obligations in Korea, and $10 million obligations in Japan. Toward the end of fiscal 1954, aid to Korea, which had been provided from regular Defense Department appropriations during the war (see above, Table 5, fotnote [b]), began to be provided under the Mutual Security Program.

[c] The $2.1 billion total for non-MDAP aid obligations was $800 million more than the amount of new funds originally appropriated for such aid. The difference was made up by transfers from MDAP appropriations (see Table 17 below) and, to a lesser extent, by obligation of deobligated funds from prior years.

consumer goods—allocated directly or indirectly[101] to particular sectors of the economy. In an economic sense, the distinction has been between the share of gross national expenditure, inclusive of foreign aid, devoted to defense, and the share devoted to investment by recipient countries. Legislatively, the distinction derived from the

[101] "Indirectly," in some cases, through the generation of counterpart funds and their allocation to particular sectors. See above, Table 3, footnote [a].

separate legislative histories of the Mutual Defense Assistance Act of 1949 in the case of military aid, and of the Act for International Development and the China Area Aid Act in the case of economic and technical aid.[102]

With passage of the Mutual Security Act of 1953, it became more difficult and less meaningful to maintain the same distinctions. Mutual Defense Assistance retained its previous orientation and content. But the problem of identification of objectives and interpretation of allocations could no longer be based simply on a distinction between "military aid" (MDAP), involving hardware and training, and economic and technical aid, involving all other software and services. For, beginning in fiscal 1954, increasing amounts of *non-MDAP* aid acquired objectives virtually identical to those associated with MDAP aid; namely, reaching or maintaining particular force levels in order to provide certain indicated military capabilities. In their effect on the share of gross national expenditure devoted to defense, such non-MDAP aid was indistinguishable from direct end-item aid. Beginning with Tables 14, 15, and 16, we shall henceforth use the term "military support" to refer to such non-MDAP aid.[103]

In the area we are primarily concerned with, Indochina is, of course, the prominent example. The expansion in non-MDAP aid to Southern Asia in 1954, shown in Tables 14 and 16, is largely to be understood in terms of the increased share borne by the United States of the rising total costs of the Indochina war, over and above the costs of military equipment.[104] Beginning in 1954, *operating* costs,

[102] See above, Chapter 3, pp. 33-41, 47-62.

[103] For a further discussion, see Chapter 6, section B.2. For glossary purposes, the term "military support," as we shall use it, includes what was called "direct forces support" (that is, the former "common-use items" category) and that part of what was labeled "defense support" which was more or less clearly intended to help maintain or raise internal military outlays. As previously noted, there were cases where the defense-support label did *not* accurately convey the objectives or the impact of aid. Its application to economic and technical aid in the Philippines and Thailand in 1953 (see above, pp. 138-139) was one example; its application to "development" assistance in Pakistan in 1955 was another (see below, Chapter 6, pp. 188-189). For a discussion of the impossibility of precisely identifying the "military support" component of "defense support," and of the procedure we have followed for doing so imprecisely, see below, pp. 190-191.

[104] Explicit authorization for more extensive U.S. participation in meeting the direct and indirect costs of the Indochina war was provided in Chapter II, "Mutual Defense Financing," of the Mutual Security Act of 1953. The Act provided for the "procurement of equipment, materials and services . . . which are required by and are to be made available to, or are necessary for the support of the forces of the Associated States of Cambodia, Laos and Vietnam and the forces of France located in the Associated States." *Mutual Security Act of 1953*, Public Law 118, 83rd Congress, 1st session.

as distinct from equipment costs, of the French Union forces in Indochina became the major claimant on "non-MDAP" aid to Southern Asia.

In Indochina, then, the labels "direct military support" and "defense support," which were used in presenting the 1954 program to Congress, accurately described the purpose of nearly all *non*-MDAP aid, and this purpose was in large measure identical to that of MDAP aid itself: to provide or maintain certain military capabilities defined in terms of specified force units. In effect, the two types or programs of aid differed only in that the one (military support) was identified with the operating or current costs of these capabilities, while the other (MDAP) continued to be identified with their equipment costs.

An inference important for the allocation of foreign aid follows from these considerations. If we grant the shared objective of MDAP and what we are calling "military support," both categories of aid should be considered part of the same allocation system. The same probability-productivity-and-worth (disutility) considerations, affecting the intercountry allocation of MDAP aid, should apply no less to the allocation of military support aid. Thus, the returns from additional military *"support"* in country (1) should be evaluated in relation to the returns from additional military *end-item* aid in countries (1), (2), . . . (n), in order to arrive at optimal country allocations of militarily-oriented assistance. We shall try to apply this reasoning in our discussion of the intercountry allocation of military aid.[105]

In presenting the historical aid data, however, we shall continue to observe the distinction between military end-item (MDAP) aid and "other" aid, including military support, in Southern Asia. The reasons for doing so are reasons of convenience rather than substance. From the standpoint of separating dollar allocations into categories having similar objectives, it would make more sense to group what we are calling military support with MDAP rather than with economic and technical assistance. However, accounting difficulties make this procedure confusing. MDAP accounting records were maintained and reported by the Defense Department. Until fiscal 1957, nearly all other aid allocations were recorded by the successive "civilian" agencies administering foreign aid: the Economic Cooperation Administration through 1951, the Mutual Security Agency

---

[105] See below, Chapter 10.

through 1953, the Foreign Operations Administration through 1955, and the International Cooperation Administration since 1955. Since "obligations" have a different meaning in Defense Department accounting than in the accounting systems of the civilian agencies, the attempt to group military support with MDAP aid would lead to awkward aggregation problems, for example, combining MDAP *appropriations* for the entire Asian *region* with military support *obligations* for individual countries in the region.[106] To avoid these problems, military support allocations, clearly designated as such, will be grouped with economic and technical aid allocations in our subsequent tables. In evaluating and interpreting the allocations data, however, we will try to distinguish clearly the objectives affecting military support allocations from those affecting economic and technical aid allocations.

4. "Special Economic Aid" Under the Mutual Security Program

Before turning to the country allocations for 1954, we should note one other legislative provision of the Mutual Security Act of 1953 because of its bearing on future aid in Southern Asia. In 1954, a new aid category, "special economic assistance," was authorized by the Act to permit additional assistance to India and Pakistan over and above what could reasonably be provided under the Act for International Development. Special economic assistance—in 1955 it was renamed "development" assistance (see Chapter 6)—was, in the words of the authorizing legislation, intended "to promote economic development . . . , [and] to assist in maintaining economic and political stability." Thus, it shared the basic purpose of previous economic and technical assistance. The Administration's reason for introducing the new category was to avoid the severe Congressional criticism of the preceding year, when the Administration had tried to include substantial commodity or "capital" assistance in programs labelled and authorized as "technical cooperation" under the Act for International Development.[107] "This year," said Mutual Security Director Stassen in presenting the special economic assistance proposal to the Senate Foreign Relations Committee, "we have separated out the technical-aid program from the economic-aid program. We

---

[106] See Table 5, above, footnote a.
[107] See above, pp. 145-146.

do not lump them together, so that you can separately pass each item."[108]

How effective the tactic was, from the standpoint of moderating the deep cuts and reallocations made by the Congress in the Administration's aid proposals in 1953, is suggested by Tables 15 and 16 showing the proposals and obligations data for non-MDAP aid to Southern Asia in 1954.

5. Non-MDAP Aid Allocations to Southern Asia, 1954

Whereas the comparable Executive Branch proposals for economic and technical assistance in 1953 were reduced by Congressional action from $245 million to $132 million (or 46 per cent),[109] Tables 15 and 16 show that the 1954 proposals of $190 million (excluding military support in Indochina) were reduced to $164 million (or less than 14 per cent). The smaller absolute and relative reduction in 1954 is mainly accounted for by the doubling of aid obligations in India over the prior year. How can this sharply increased amount of aid to India in 1954 be explained?

6. The Inconsistency of Allocation Decisions
   in 1953 and 1954

It will be recalled that we interpreted the severe absolute and relative cuts in the 1953 Executive Branch proposals for Southern Asia in general, and India in particular, in terms of (1) a differing Congressional judgment concerning the "value" to the United States of accelerating economic development in countries like India, which were not unequivocally "friendly" to the United States; and (2) a differing Congressional judgment concerning the productivity of commodtiy assistance over and above technical services.[110] For both variables, the "differing" Congressional judgment implicitly involved a substantially lower estimate than the corresponding judgment by the Executive Branch. The relatively small reduction in the Executive Branch proposals for 1954 suggested that Congress had changed its value or productivity estimates, or both, of the previous year.

That Congress raised its estimate of the *value* to the United States of accelerating development in neutralist India is a reasonable,

[108] *Mutual Security Act of 1953*, Senate Hearings, 83rd Congress, 1st session, Washington, D.C., 1953, p. 51.
[109] Above, pp. 140-144.   [110] See above, pp. 146-147.

though not demonstrable, inference from the legislative record in 1954. In commenting on the question of aid to neutralist countries, for example, the House Foreign Affairs Committee stated:

"In the newly independent nations . . . there is a hostility toward the western countries, including the United States. . . . Their fear of domination by foreign powers and their suspicions and hostility must be overcome by reassuring cooperation. *It is important to our own security*, therefore, to do everything possible to prevent any weakening of their governments. . . ."[111]

That Congress altered its judgment concerning the *productivity* of commodity assistance is even clearer. We have previously referred to the adverse Congressional estimate of the productivity of commodity assistance when it was proposed as part of the technical cooperation program under the Act for International Development.[112] By contrast, in 1954, when substantially similar amounts of commodity assistance for similar projects were proposed by the Executive Branch for India (and Pakistan),[113] but were separately identified as "special economic assistance," the Congressional productivity estimate was favorable. "Special economic aid programs," noted the House Foreign Affairs Committee, "are required to help the countries of the region to help themselves in accelerating development possibilities where other funds are not available. . . . The [combined] economic and technical assistance program for India . . . is largely an extension and acceleration of the program already underway, and will constitute a relatively small, but vital contribution to India's own development program."[114] Especially striking is a comparison of this statement with one previously quoted by the same committee in the preceding year.[115]

One is left with a strong impression that the altered productivity estimate in the case of Indian aid was based on the *label*, rather than the amount, content, or purpose of the proposed aid. It is laboring the obvious to note that, from the standpoint of preferred aid allo-

[111] *The Mutual Security Act of 1953*, House Report, Washington, D.C., 1953, p. 7. (Italics added.)

[112] See above, pp. 145-149, including footnote 65 on p. 146.

[113] While the Eisenhower Administration's formal proposals for aid to India and Pakistan in 1954 (see Table 15) were only slightly below those of the preceding Administration in 1953 (see Tables 10 and 11), the *original* proposals of the Truman Administration for 1954, before it left office, were $112 million above those made by the new Administration for aid to India and Pakistan. (See *Mutual Security Act of 1953*, Senate Report, pp. 452-453.)

[114] House Report, 1953, *op.cit.*, pp. 42-43.

[115] See above, pp. 147-148.

Table 15

FUNDS PROPOSED BY THE EXECUTIVE BRANCH FOR UNITED STATES
ECONOMIC AND TECHNICAL ASSISTANCE AND
MILITARY SUPPORT TO SOUTHERN ASIA, FISCAL YEAR 1954[a]

(by country and project use)

	(1)	(2)	(3)	(4)	(5)	(6)	(7)
				Project Use			
Country	Agri-culture	Industry	Trans-portation	Health	Public Adminis-tration	Educa-tion	Commu-nity Develop-ment
			(millions of dollars)				
Afghanistan[b]	.87	.10	.02	.18	–	.17	–
Burma[c]	–	–	–	–	–	–	–
Ceylon[d]	–	–	–	–	–	–	–
India[e]	25.58	61.15	.64	8.51	.08	5.03	8.76
Indochina[f]	1.34	.33	5.00	2.02	.67	.08	–
Indonesia[g]	1.32	.57	–	.66	.06	.53	–
Nepal[h]	.46	–	–	.08	.02	–	–
Pakistan[i]	13.22	3.05	.75	1.46	–	–	4.82
Philippines[j]	10.98	.83	.90	2.14	1.00	1.15	–
Thailand[k]	2.10	.24	.78	1.21	.14	.53	–
TOTALS	55.87	66.27	8.09	16.26	1.97	7.49	13.58
Project Total as Proportion of Regional Total	29.3	34.8	4.3	(per cent) 8.6	1.0	3.9	7.1

Σ Col (1)/ Σ Col (9), Σ Col (2)/ Σ Col (9), etc.

(continued)

Sources: See Appendix II.

[a] For further explanation of the data problems involved in assembling Executive Branch proposals, see above, Table 7, footnote [a].

[b] (k), pp. 59, 147, 189.

[c] The Burma program was terminated at the end of 1953. See Chapter 5, section B.4(b).

[d] Technical assistance to Ceylon was discontinued in 1953. See above, Table 11, footnote [d].

[e] (k), p. 189, and (a). The figures shown represent *both* technical assistance ($30.1 million) and special economic assistance ($79.9 million). For an explanation of the special aid category, see Chapter 5, section C.4. The sectoral breakdown of the special aid was: $18.5 million for agriculture; $54.7 million for industry; and $6.7 million for health projects.

[f] (1), p. 771; (n), p. 530; and (a). The $400 million for military support represents

Table 15 (continued)

(8)	(9)	(10)	(11)	(12)
	Project Use		Country Total as Proportion of Regional Total	
General and Miscellaneous	Total Excluding Military Support	Military Support	Excluding Military Support Col (9)/Σ Col (9)	Including Military Support Col (9) + Col (10) Σ Col (9) + Σ Col (10)
(millions of dollars)			(per cent)	
.06	1.40	–	.7	.2
–	–	–	–	–
–	–	–	–	–
.25	110.00	–	57.8	18.6
15.56	25.00	400.00	13.1	72.0
.86	4.00	–	2.1	.7
.04	.60	–	.3	.1
4.20	27.50	–	14.5	4.7
–	17.00	–	8.9	2.9
–	5.00	–	2.6	.8
20.97	190.50	400.00	100.0	100.0
(per cent)				
11.0	100.0			

proposed dollar reimbursement to France for part of the real costs of the Indochina war. As distinct from MDAP end-items, military support provided "software" and "consumables" required for maintenance of French Union forces in Indochina. For reference to the procedure by which dollar transfers to the French were made, see (1), p. 112.

g (k), pp. 68, 167, 189; (n), p. 347; and (1), p. 1072.

h (k), pp. 174, 189; and (a).

i (k), pp. 180, 190; and (n), pp. 340, 344. The figures shown represent *both* technical assistance ($13.0 million) and special economic assistance ($14.5 million). For an explanation of the special aid category, see above, pp. 162-164. The sectoral breakdown of the special aid was: $9.8 million for agriculture; $2.5 million for industry; $.7 million for transportation; and $1.5 million for health projects.

j (k), p. 74; and (a).

k (1), p. 779; (m), p. 486; and (o), p. 868.

Table 16

FUNDS OBLIGATED FOR UNITED STATES ECONOMIC AND TECHNICAL
ASSISTANCE AND MILITARY SUPPORT TO SOUTHERN ASIA,
FISCAL YEAR 1954[a]

(by country and project use)

	(1)	(2)	(3)	(4)	(5)	(6)	(7)	(8)
					Project Use			
Country	Agri-culture	Indus-try	Trans-portation	Health	Labor[b]	Public Adminis-tration	Educa-tion	Commu-nity Develop-ment
	(millions of dollars)							
Afghanistan[c]	.78	.09	–	.12	–	–	.37	–
Burma[d]	–	–	–	–	–	–	–	–
Ceylon[e]	–	–	–	–	–	–	–	–
India[f]	17.35	35.33	21.97	5.01	.10	.01	.86	5.74
Indochina[g]	.93	–	4.27	1.36	–	.63	.10	.48
Indonesia[h]	.10	1.34	.08	.40	–	1.17	.48	–
Nepal[i]	.24	.03	–	.10	–	.01	.22	.14
Pakistan[j]	16.62	1.23	.07	.14	–	.02	1.68	1.83
Philippines[k]	3.82	.04	4.97	1.39	.35	1.68	2.45	–
Thailand[l]	1.64	.14	3.78	2.06	.02	.09	.96	–
TOTALS	41.48	38.20	35.14	10.58	.47	3.61	7.12	8.19
Project Total as Proportion of Regional Total	(per cent)							
	25.2	23.3	21.4	6.4	.3	2.2	4.3	5.0

Σ Col (1)/Σ Col (10), Σ Col (2)/Σ Col (10), etc.

(*continued*)

Sources: See Appendix II.

[a] See above, Chapter 4, Table 3, footnote a, for explanation of categories and terms used in this table.

[b] Beginning in 1954, technical assistance obligations for training and education in trade union work was listed as a separate category.

[c] (k), pp. 59, 147 and 189. The $1.15 million for "general and miscellaneous" represents 12,000 tons of surplus wheat provided under Section 550 of the Mutual Security Act of 1953 to help Afghanistan meet a food shortage. See *Report to the Congress on the Mutual Security Program, June 30, 1954*, Washington, D.C., 1954, p. 31. Under Section 550, a stipulated portion ($100-$250 million) of the appropriations authorized by the Act was required to be used for purchasing surplus agricultural commodities from the Commodity Credit Corporation for resale to recipient countries in exchange for local currency. The local currency proceeds, like previous counterpart funds, were to be used for the same general purposes as those governing other appropriations authorized by the Mutual Security Act.

The Section 550 provision, renewed subsequently as Section 402 of the Mutual Security Acts of 1954 through 1957, is of interest and significance as the first explicit legislative requirement directly linking foreign assistance under the MSP and agricultural surplus disposal. With enactment in July 1954 of Public Law 480, the Agricultural Trade and Development Act, agricultural surplus disposal was to become a major instrument of U.S. foreign assistance. In several countries of Southern Asia, for example, assistance later provided under this Act was several times larger than assistance provided directly under the Mutual Security Act. See below, Chapter 6.

[d] The Burma program was terminated at the end of 1953. See Chapter 5, section B.4(a). Negative obligations shown in later reports, for example, (i'), p. 57, for the fiscal years 1954 through 1956, represent deobligations from 1951-53 obligations, after termination of the program.

Table 16 (continued)

(9)	(10)	(11)	(12)	(13)
	Project Use		Country Total as Proportion of Regional Total	
General and Miscellaneous	Total Excluding Military Support	Military Support	Excluding Military Support Col(10)/Σ Col(10)	Including Military Support Col(10) + Col(11) / Σ Col(10) + Σ Col(11)
(millions of dollars)			(per cent)	
1.15	2.51	–	1.5	.3
–	–	–	–	–
–	–	–	–	–
.48	86.85	–	52.8	10.3
16.68	24.45	678.57	14.9	83.4
.34	3.91	–	2.4	.5
–	.74	–	.5	.1
1.14	22.73	–	13.8	2.7
(.25)	14.45	–	8.8	1.7
.04	8.73	–	5.3	1.0
19.58	164.37	678.57	100.0	100.0
	(per cent)			
11.9	100.0			

e Technical assistance to Ceylon was discontinued in 1953. See above, Table 11, footnote d.

f (u), p. 227; and (a). Later records, for example, (i'), p. 58, show total obligations of $87.2 million without a breakdown by project-use. The figures shown in Table 16 cover both technical assistance ($26.35 million) and special economic assistance ($60.5 million). The sectoral breakdown of the special aid was $8.5 million for agriculture (for tubewells and fertilizer); $32.0 million for industry (largely for unfinished steel to be processed in India); and $20.0 million for transportation (for locomotives and freight cars).

g The non-MDAP aid originally obligated in the Associated States for 1954 totalled $769.45 million, consisting of: $745 million for what is referred to in various reports as "direct forces support," "direct military support," and "defense support"; and $24.45 million for the continuing developmental program [See (u), p. 323, and (j'), p. 70.] Subsequently, savings were realized in the military support obligations through the use of franc counterpart funds to reimburse the French, and through a scaling down of military expenditures in Indochina, after hostilities ceased in the summer of 1954. [See (u), pp. 320, 321.] As a result of these savings, net dollar obligations, after deobligations, for 1954 amounted to only $703.02 million [in Table 16, the sum of columns (10) and (11) for Indochina] see (i'), p. 57.

h (u), p. 270; and (a).

i (u), p. 236; and (a).

j (u), p. 246; and (a). The figures shown cover both technical assistance ($8.23 million) and special economic assistance ($14.50 million). The sectoral breakdown of the special aid was: $12.72 million for agriculture (mainly fertilizer, agricultural implements, and tubewells); $.28 million for industry; and $1.5 million for community development.

k (u), p. 304. The figure in parentheses represents a net deobligation of prior years' funds.

l (u), p. 314; and (a).

cation, if alternatives (A) and (B), and the environments in which they are considered, are essentially identical except for the numerical labels, decisions to choose one and not the other cannot both be equally valid. With only a little less certainty, it can be asserted that the substantially different (absolute and relative) allocations of aid to India in 1953 and 1954 were not equally valid. At least one of them was, in a meaningful sense, something less than "optimal."

This is not to disparage the importance of aid labels under all circumstances. From the standpoint of operating flexibility, different labels, even for programs that are similar in purpose and content, have some advantages. In negotiating with some recipient countries, for example, aid carrying one label may have a higher "exchange" value than aid carrying a different label. Moreover, if the donor subsequently wishes to exercise a modicum of pressure on a recipient by withholding aid, the existence of several categories of aid may permit the donor to apply "graduated" pressure, rather than confronting him with the choice of terminating aid completely or refraining from exercising any pressure whatsoever.[116] Nonetheless, it is not at all clear that the "special economic assistance" label used in 1954 provided any advantages that could not have been obtained in 1953 without it.

7. Economic Assistance and Military Support

Returning to Tables 15 and 16, the overwhelming quantitative importance of Indochina in 1954, in both the proposals and obligations figures *inclusive* of military support, is evident. Before commenting on the preponderant Indochina share in the 1954 totals for Southern Asia, the increase in military support obligations (Table 16, Column [11]) for the Associated States, by $279 million above the original proposals (Table 15, Column [10]), requires explanation.

During the summer of 1953, when the 1954 Mutual Security Program was in its final stage of enactment, the French Government advised the United States of its plan to increase Vietnamese national ground forces by 70 per cent (about 125,000 troops) in two years' time, in order to bring the Indochina war to a successful conclusion.

[116] The previously cited example of U.S. suspension of aid to the Netherlands East Indies in 1948, rather than a total suspension of aid to the Netherlands itself, is a case in point. See Chapter 3, pp. 37-38. For other examples and refinements of this point, see the discerning discussing by Thomas C. Schelling, "American Aid and Economic Development: Some Critical Issues," in *International Stability and Progress*, The American Assembly, New York, 1957, pp. 145-147.

This so-called "Navarre Plan" was estimated to entail additional costs to the French of over $500 million a year for training and maintenance expenditures during the buildup period, apart from direct military equipment costs. To permit the Plan to go ahead, without a reduction in France's NATO commitments, the United States agreed early in the fall of 1953 to make available up to $385 million from 1954 MDAP funds, *in addition* to the $400 million, shown in Table 15, which was previously proposed and appropriated for military support in Indochina. Like the $400 million originally proposed, the additional funds were to be used to reimburse France for franc outlays on the Indochina war.[117] For several reasons (referred to in Table 16, footnote *), only $279 million of the additional $385 million were actually obligated during 1954.

But whether the proposals or obligations data are used, it is clear that the overwhelming Indochina share of the totals[118] is to be explained by the same military objectives associated with MDAP aid, rather than by the objectives associated with economic and technical assistance. In the terminology we have used before, Indochina's dominant share of 1954 non-MDAP aid to Southern Asia suggests *not* that the "value" or the "productivity" of "economic" aid was judged higher in Indochina than in other countries of the region or than in prior years, but that "military" returns in Indochina were considered to have a higher rate of exchange, in terms of "political" returns elsewhere in the region, than in prior years.[119] Given the policy judgment, the extension of aid in the form of software rather than hardware, implied that such aid would have a larger yield, in terms of the relevant force goals required by the planned buildup of national Vietnamese forces, than additional end-item aid.

This roundabout interpretation of Indochina aid in 1954 reinforces what we have previously noted about the intimate connection between non-MDAP aid and directly military objectives. Where, as

[117] See "Joint Communique Issued by the Governments of France and the United States Relative to French Aims and American Aid in Indochina, September 30, 1953," in *Documents on American Foreign Relations, 1953*, New York, pp. 350-351; and Stebbins, 1953, *op.cit.*, pp. 274-275.

[118] Columns (12) of Table 15 and (13) of Table 16.

[119] This conclusion should be qualified by the fact, mentioned in the preceding paragraph, that U.S. aid to Indochina in 1954 was significantly affected by political and military considerations relating to *France* and *Europe*, rather than *Indochina* and *Asia*. Nevertheless, recognizing that the total amount of Indochina aid was part of a many-sided bargain between the United States and France, the conclusion remains a reasonable statement of some of the considerations affecting the U.S. position in the bargain.

in Indochina in 1954, such a connection existed, intercountry allocation comparisons of non-MDAP aid entail comparisons *not* of similar objectives in different countries, but of qualitatively differing objectives in different countries.

8. Sectoral Allocations in 1954

The project composition of Tables 15 and 16, *excluding* the dominant Indochina military-support aid, shows an interesting and sharp change from the prior years. Allocations for the sectors likely to yield returns over a longer period, namely industry and transportation, rose absolutely and relatively compared to 1953.[120] For the first time, in the four years of United States aid obligations in Southern Asia, combined allocations for industrial and transport projects in 1954 (45 per cent of the total in Table 16) exceeded those in the quicker-maturing sectors of agriculture and health (32 per cent of the total). The excess of the longer-term sectoral allocations persists even if obligations for community development are added to the agricultural and health sectors.[121] In comparison with the sectoral or project allocations of earlier years, a lower implicit discount on future yields is suggested by the 1954 project allocations in Southern Asia.

It is clear from Table 16 that the change in intersectoral allocations is entirely due to the relatively large Indian obligations in the industry and transport fields. Whereas in the preceding year, similar sectoral allocations in these fields had been *proposed* by the Executive Branch,[122] they were eliminated from the actual obligations as a result of the subsequent Congressional cuts in 1953. In 1954, Congressional reaction to the Indian aid proposals was, as we have already seen, more favorable. When commodity assistance for Indian industry and transport was labelled "special economic assistance," rather than "technical" assistance, a different judgment about its productivity was reached by the Congress. As in the case of the increase in *total* Indian aid for 1954, the increase in allocations for the later-maturing industry and transport *sectors* in 1954 was largely due to the new label attached to these allocations when they were initially proposed. There is, in other words, a fairly clear presumption that Congress accepted in 1954 the same time-discount which was

[120] Cf. Table 11 above and pp. 152-153.
[121] The larger relative and absolute figure for community development in 1954 was due mainly to the inclusion in that category of some projects, for example, fertilizer distribution, which in previous years had been included in the agricultural sector.
[122] See above, Table 10.

implicit in the Executive Branch proposals that it had rejected in 1953.

9. Appropriations for Military Assistance in 1954

In our discussion of aid to Indochina in 1954, the intimate connection between non-MDAP aid and the directly military objectives of MDAP itself has been stressed. For this reason, in 1954 and subsequent years, separate consideration of MDAP and non-MDAP aid allocations in Southern Asia becomes more artificial than in prior years. Analytically, we should first consider allocations among alternatives (for example, countries or programs) which are related to the same objective, and then consider the rate of exchange (or substitution) among the different objectives, each with its own set of alternatives. For neither of these tasks is the MDAP *versus* non-MDAP, or military-hardware *versus* "all other"-aid, distinction entirely appropriate, for reasons already noted. Consequently, in discussing non-MDAP allocations in 1954, we have tried to indicate the portion, namely military support in Indochina, which was more closely related to the objectives of direct military aid than to the objectives of economic and technical aid. The same procedure will be followed for later years as well.

In reviewing MDAP allocations in the Asian area in 1954, it should therefore be kept in mind that we are considering only a *part* of the aid actually allocated in that year for military purposes. The relevant data on MDAP appropriations in 1954 are summarized in Table 17 below.

At the same time as total MDAP appropriations in 1954 fell by $1 billion from the 1953 level,[123] appropriations for the entire Asian area nearly doubled from $541 million or 13 per cent of the total in 1953, to $1,035 million or 32 per cent of the total in 1954.[124] A relatively small portion of this increase was due to the inclusion of Japan in the program for the first time.[125] In large measure, however, the

[123] See Table 13 above.

[124] Since global MDAP appropriations fell, from $4,220 million in 1953 to $3,230 million in 1954, the Asian *share* of the total increased 2½ times, while the *absolute amount* of Asian MDAP doubled. (See Table 13 above.)

[125] Under the terms of the 1951 Security Treaty between the United States and Japan, the signatories expressed their intention that Japan would "increasingly assume responsibility for its own defense." To this end, Japan formed a "National Safety Force" in October 1952 with an authorized strength of 110,000 men. In fiscal year 1953, equipment for these limited forces was provided directly from Defense Department appropriations. Beginning in 1954, the costs of additional equipment for

new appropriation applied to equipment costs for the same Asian countries which received Mutual Defense Assistance in 1953: Formosa, Indochina, Thailand, and the Philippines.

Among the countries in the Asian set we are concerned with,

Table 17

MUTUAL DEFENSE ASSISTANCE APPROPRIATIONS,
FISCAL YEAR 1954

	Appropriations[a] (millions of dollars)	Proportion of Total (per cent)
Europe	1,910.0	59.1
Near East, Africa, and South Asia	270.0	8.4
Asia and the Pacific	1,035.0	32.0
American Republics	15.0	.5
TOTALS	3,230.0	100.0

[a] *Mutual Security Appropriation Act of 1954*, Public Law 218, 83rd Congress, 1st session, August 7, 1953. The amounts shown are in addition to $1.9 billion of unobligated funds remaining from the 1953 appropriation which were specifically reappropriated for use in 1954. Some of the MDAP appropriations for 1954 were subsequently transferred to *non*-MDAP uses, under the intertitle transfer provisions of the Mutual Security Act of 1953. These transferred funds are included in the non-MDAP obligations data shown in Table 14 above, as well as in Table 17. (See Table 14, footnote c.)

The appropriations in Table 17 compare with the following MDAP proposals originally submitted by the Administration (millions of dollars):

Europe	2,497.0
Near East, Africa, and South Asia	425.0
Asia and the Pacific	1,082.0
American Republics	20.0
	4,024.0

See *Mutual Security Act Extension*, House Hearings, 1953, pp. 191, 336. The figures for Europe include $311 million for infrastructure and administrative expenses.

Pakistan was one significant addition to the participants in MDAP during 1954. Funds for end-item aid to Pakistan, however, were charged to the appropriation shown for the Near East, Africa, and South Asia in Table 17, rather than for Asia and the Pacific. Pakistan's participation grew from the new Administration's desire to extend the concept of regional security arrangements, already represented by NATO in Europe, into other areas, as a deterrent to communist aggression. To this end, a formal alliance between Pakistan and

Japan were included in MDAP. See *Mutual Security Act Extension*, House Hearings, 1953, pp. 1050-1051; and *Mutual Security Report*, June 1954, pp. 43-44.

Turkey—a NATO member—was encouraged by the United States. MDAP aid was both an inducement to and a consequence of this alliance. While negotiations between Pakistan and Turkey were underway, Pakistan formally requested military aid on February 22, 1954. President Eisenhower publicly granted the request shortly thereafter, "to increase the defense potential in this area."[126] By the end of fiscal year 1954, a Mutual Defense Agreement between the United States and Pakistan was signed stipulating that aid furnished under the Program would be used "solely for the purpose of internal security and legitimate self-defense."[127]

10. The Regional Shift in MDAP Appropriations

Table 17 clearly shows a substantially larger absolute and relative allocation of 1954 MDAP funds to the Asian area than occurred in 1953.[128] (If Pakistan were included in the Asian appropriation, the increase would be still larger, since Pakistan did not participate in MDAP in 1953.) Implicitly, this reallocation was equivalent to a judgment that the ratio between the returns from incremental military aid to the Asian area, and the returns from incremental military aid to the other regions concerned, notably Europe, was higher in 1954 than it had been in 1953. To what circumstances can this judgment be attributed?

It is perhaps reasonable to assume that, as a result of the Korean armistice,[129] the probability of a Soviet attack in Western Europe in the near term diminished somewhat while the probabilities of various near-term local war contingencies in Asia, including an intensification of the ongoing Indochina struggle, increased. On the one hand, the pending disengagement of some U.S. forces from Korea might have been expected to increase the likelihood of a U.S. response to limited aggression in Europe, as well as to increase the forces that could be applied to make such a response militarily effective. If the probability of aggression in Europe is, and was, presumed to depend inversely on the probability of an effective U.S.

---

[126] *Documents on American Foreign Relations, 1954*, New York, 1955, p. 373. For a fuller account of the initiation of MDAP in Pakistan, see James W. Spain, "Military Assistance to Pakistan," *American Political Science Review*, September 1954, pp. 738-751; and Richard P. Stebbins, *The United States in World Affairs, 1954*, New York, 1956, pp. 321-324.

[127] *Mutual Security Report, June 30, 1954*, p. 22.

[128] See Table 14.

[129] Signed on July 27, 1953, eleven days before the Mutual Security Appropriations Act of 1954 became law.

response, it is reasonable to conclude that the former probability diminished with the approach and consummation of the Korean armistice.

On the other hand, the disengagement of Chinese resources in Korea might have been expected to increase the force China could bring to bear elsewhere in Asia. Indochina and Formosa were obvious opportunities. The Viet Minh invasion of Laos in April 1953 suggested another. True, disengagement of United States forces from Korea would also tend to increase the forces available to oppose possible Chinese aggression in these countries. But this may well have been an insufficient counter to the added power and maneuverability afforded the Chinese by the Korean armistice. Geographic proximity to these potential Asian trouble spots may well have conferred on China a net advantage from the bilateral disengagement of U.S. and Chinese forces. At least some of the U.S. forces would presumably be sent home. By contrast, the Chinese volunteers returning from Korea could be redeployed for quicker and cheaper access to other potential Asian trouble spots. If, then, its geographical proximity to these areas conferred on China a *net* advantage from the joint disengagement of U.S. and Chinese forces in Korea, it is reasonable to conclude that the probabilities of local wars in these areas rose after the Korean armistice. The reasoning is speculative, but not implausible.

As to the disutility or worth to the United States of local war contingencies in the four MDAP regions, it can be presumed that the disutility parameters in the Asian region rose in 1954 over 1953. Such a rise was a corollary of the new Administration's explicit aim to accord a higher priority to, and end "neglect" of, the Asian area.

It is less clear that the rise in the relative marginal returns from military aid to Asia can be attributed to a rise in the physical effectiveness or productivity of such aid in Asia relative to its effectiveness in other regions. Granted, the stretch-out of NATO force goals suggested that the extent to which additional end-item aid could contribute to strengthening military capabilities in Europe was likely to diminish. Clearly, additional planes or tanks or artillery are not a potent deterrent if unmanned.

At the same time, we can argue that additional military equipment in the Asian area, notably Indochina, was already approaching a point of extremely low effectiveness from the standpoint of increasing the relevant military capabilities. Consequently, a further expansion of MDAP in Indochina could only with difficulty be justified by the presumed reduction in the effectiveness of MDAP in Europe. If the effectiveness of MDAP in Europe had decreased by 1954, it did not necessarily follow that the *relative* effectiveness of MDAP in Asia had risen. In the specific case of Indochina, for example, much of the heavy high-cost equipment provided under MDAP probably had little net effect on the capabilities required to defeat the Viet Minh. Additional bombers, jets, and artillery were of little consequence against an adversary as mobile and dispersed as the Viet Minh. Under the prevailing circumstances, their wider use was as likely to increase support for the adversary as to weaken him. This is not to say that additional amounts of some types of equipment—for example, transports for airlift, light reconnaissance planes, and automatic ground weapons for the expanding Vietnamese national ground forces—might not have been considerably more effective in Indochina than some of the equipment actually provided. The opportunities for such substitutions were probably considerable. But here, too, one has the impression that the opportunities for effective substitutions could have been exploited well within the amounts of aid actually disbursed under MDAP in Indochina.[180]

The point admittedly is not conclusive. Even if the effectiveness of additional end-item aid in 1954 was lower in Asia than in Europe, offsetting changes in probability and worth parameters *might* have warranted a regional reallocation of MDAP funds in favor of Asia. One is left, however, with a strong impression that, at least in Indochina, the reallocation that actually occurred went beyond the limits imposed by the negligible productivity of incremental MDAP aid.

11. Military Programs in Southern Asia

For reasons previously described, the amounts and detailed content of the MDA programs in Southern Asia are unavailable. However, a few general comments on the programs can be made.

Of the total increase in end-item aid to the Asian region in 1954, the bulk was accounted for by the programs in Indochina and Formosa,[181] together with the requirements for Japan, previously noted. In Indochina, the expansion in MDAP was intended to provide the combined and growing French-Vietnamese forces with enough

---

[180] For a listing of the types of equipment delivered to Indochina under MDAP, see *Mutual Security Report, December 31, 1953*, p. 5; and *June 30, 1954*, p. 37.
[181] *Mutual Security Act Extension*, House Hearings, 1953, p. 340.

equipment to "retake the offensive" from the Viet Minh, and, hopefully, to bring the war to a successful conclusion within two years.[132]

In Thailand, the buildup of army and air forces continued. The MDAP program in 1954, as in prior years, was directed largely to creating capabilities for meeting external aggression, rather than preserving internal security. By 1954, the Mutual Security Progress Report referred to the "real combat potential" of the Thai air force, and offered the possibly optimistic conclusion that Thailand's combined forces "should be able successfully to ward off any military incursions, unless direct participation by Communist China is involved."[133] Perhaps the key question suggested by the conclusion was how direct the hypothetical Chinese participation would have to be to negate the effectiveness of Thailand's enhanced defensive capability.

In the Philippines, the force goals to which MDAP was addressed in 1954 continued to be those of internal security. By 1954, the Philippine constabulary units, which had been the main recipients of MDAP training and equipment in prior years, were so effective that the Huk guerrillas were reduced to negligible numbers.[134] In the spring of 1954, the Huk leader, Luis Taruc, surrendered to the government forces. In effect, the Huk guerrilla threat, which four years earlier had been grave, was ended. Though MDAP was only a part of the reason for this striking improvement in the Philippine situation, it was an important part. It is fair to say that military aid in the Philippines through 1954 provided an example of one of the more effective uses of this instrument of United States foreign policy in Southern Asia.

Finally, in Pakistan, military assistance requirements were formulated in terms of the broader objective of creating an effective multiservice capability to resist external aggression. Early reports, accompanying initiation of the program in 1954, estimated the end-item costs of bringing "Pakistan's fighting forces up to full potential" at

[132] *Mutual Security Report, December 31, 1953*, p. 39. See also, above, pp. 165-171. The size of the expanded end-item program in Indochina for 1954 was suggested by one Administration official during testimony on the Mutual Security Program in May 1954: ". . . there is estimated an end-item program [for Indochina] financed from military assistance funds of $530 million for the fiscal year 1954." *The Mutual Security Act of 1954*, House Committee Hearings, 83rd Congress, 2nd session, Washington, D.C., 1954, p. 980.

[133] *Mutual Security Report, June 30, 1954*, p. 40.

[134] *Ibid.*, p. 39.

$250-$500 million. The initial "slice" of these requirements, to be met from part of the 1954 appropriation for the Near East, Africa, and South Asia, was estimated between $25 and $40 million.[185] Later, when Pakistan joined the Southeast Asia Collective Defense Organization, the time period for achieving the originally formulated force goals was shortened, and the annual end-item program raised accordingly. This acceleration of MDAP in Pakistan did not get underway until the following fiscal year. It will be discussed in connection with the Mutual Security Program for 1955, together with the general problem of assessing the probability and "disutility" of differing local war contingencies confronting Pakistan, and the effectiveness of end-item aid in helping to meet these contingencies.[186] In anticipation of this discussion, we can say that, whether or not the force goals implicit in the level of end-item aid planned for Pakistan were large enough for meeting possible *external* attack, they were clearly too large from the standpoint of maintaining *internal* security.

D. Summary

The Mutual Security program began, *in fiscal year 1952*, in an international environment dominated by the Korean war. Besides attempting to centralize foreign aid administration, the program's authorizing legislation—the Mutual Security Act of 1951—generally asserted the primacy of military considerations among the objectives of foreign assistance. Paradoxically, however, the Korean experience, and the Mutual Security Act's military orientation, had less influence on initial MSP aid in Southern Asia than in Europe. The reasons behind the paradox concerned the still vivid recollection of the China "lesson," the limited physical productivity of incremental military aid in Southern Asia, and the recommendations of the Gray and Rockefeller Reports.

In fact, in no country of Southern Asia—unlike Europe—was a buildup of military forces the rationale of U.S. economic aid in 1952. Actually, the Mutual Security Program, despite its military orientation in other areas, in Southern Asia in 1952 accorded considerably more emphasis to non-military, economic-development-and-political-stability considerations than did the 1951 aid program. Thus, the Mutual Security Program in its first year brought a substantial in-

---

[185] See Spain, *op.cit.*, pp. 747-748; and Stebbins, 1954, *op.cit.*, p. 326.
[186] See below, Chapter 6.

crease in both the absolute amount and the proportion of economic aid allocated to the countries of Southern Asia. Most of this increase was due to the start of economic and technical aid programs in India and Pakistan. In turn, the initiation of the programs in these countries can be understood credibly in terms of the increased "productivity" of aid, and of its "value" to the United States, in 1952 compared with the previous year.

As in 1951, the *sectoral* allocation of economic aid in 1952 entailed relatively larger allocations to sectors with shorter maturing periods, suggesting that an implicitly high time-discount entered into the programming of U.S. aid in Southern Asia.

While the Asian regional share of total *economic* aid under the Mutual Security Program doubled over the previous year, its share of *military* assistance remained approximately constant. In turn, *country* allocations of Mutual Defense Assistance in Southern Asia continued to be arrived at by costing the military equipment components of the country force targets which were submitted by the MAAG's and approved by the Joint Chiefs of Staff. MDAP force goals in Southern Asia, for 1952, followed closely those set in the previous year.

At least in the case of Indochina, there seem to be reasons for believing that the military productivity of MDAP reached a point of negligible marginal returns well within the amounts and types of equipment provided.

In 1953, the Mutual Security Program, as *proposed* by the Executive Branch, called for a further increase in economic aid to Southern Asia of over 60 per cent above the level during 1952. But the program, as *obligated* after Congressional enactment of authorizing an appropriations legislation, was substantially altered. Congressional cuts in the original proposals for Southern Asia were relatively more severe than those made in other parts of the Mutual Security Program. In consequence, economic aid obligations in Southern Asia in 1953 were well below those of the previous year.

The heaviest Congressional cuts were made in the aid proposed for India. Influencing Congressional action was a resentment against Indian foreign policy in the Korean war, combined with a judgment that the productivity of "capital," as distinct from "technical," assistance was likely to be small. In effect, the Mutual Security legislative record for fiscal year 1953 implied that the productivity of "capital" assistance for economic development was low, that capital assistance should generally be confined to countries receiving military aid, and that in these countries the primary justification for such assistance should be its contribution to "defense support," not economic development.

By contrast, 1953 appropriations for MDAP, in the Asian region as a whole, actually *rose* above the prior year. Though the original Executive Branch proposals for MDAP were cut, the cuts were light compared to those made in non-military aid—a further indication of the altered character of MSP in 1953.

In 1954, the Mutual Security Program reflected the new Administration's explicit emphasis on the Asian region, as well as a growing concern, already evidenced in the previous year, for the military objectives of foreign aid. This concern began increasingly to blur the distinction between "military" and "economic" assistance, as more and more "soft" aid began to be provided (notably in Indochina) to help achieve objectives virtually identical to those associated with "hard" military-end-item aid (MDAP).

At the same time, the distinctly *non*-military component of United States aid to Southern Asia rose appreciably in 1954: on an obligations basis by 20 per cent above 1953. This increase was due entirely to increased obligations for economic aid in India, combined with *reduced* obligations in most of the other countries of Southern Asia. The sharp increase in Indian aid over 1953 suggested markedly altered Congressional judgments concerning the value-and-productivity of such aid. In turn, these altered judgments seemed to arise more from the altered *label* attached to Indian aid in 1954 (that is, "special economic aid" rather than "technical assistance") than from any change in relevant circumstances. The conclusion seems warranted that the Indian allocations of 1953 and 1954 were, from the standpoint of allocation optimality, mutually inconsistent.

Closely related to the altered scale of Indian aid was the altered *sectoral* composition of economic aid obligations in 1954. For the first time in the four years of aid to Southern Asia, the later-maturing industry and transport sectors received larger allocations than did the quicker-maturing sectors.

MDAP appropriations for Asia doubled in 1954 over 1953. The increase largely resulted from increased end-item aid to Indochina, which perhaps extended well beyond the point when positive returns might have been expected from further increments.

Pakistan became a participant in MDAP in 1954. The capabilities and force goals associated with military aid in Pakistan were concerned with resisting overt external aggression, as were MDAP goals in Indochina and, to a lesser extent, in Thailand. In this respect, MDAP objectives in the three countries differed from the primary internal-security objective in the Philippines.

CHAPTER 6

MUTUAL SECURITY AND COMPETITIVE
COEXISTENCE, 1955-1957

A. INTRODUCTION

THERE are two ambiguities about the term "competitive" or "peaceful" coexistence that make one hesitate to use it to characterize a particular period in international affairs. One concerns its meaning; the other its beginning. The latter is a problem confronting any attempt to tidy history by dividing it into discrete periods. Events develop continuously rather than discretely. More or less abrupt changes occur, but they usually have definite antecedents. And the more the antecedents are investigated, the less abrupt the changes appear.

Certainly, there were indications of the international *détente* we associate with coexistence as early as 1953, though their significance was diminished by the subsequent intensification of the Indochina war.[1] With the Geneva conference in the spring and summer of 1954, prospects for an easing of tensions again improved. Granting the arbitrariness of assigning exact dates in these matters, perhaps the best argument for identifying the period covered by fiscal year 1955 as the beginning of coexistence is that it was the first year after the start of the Mutual Security Program that no large-scale "local" war was underway.

Once we have assigned a beginning to coexistence, it is tempting to argue that the start of the new period warranted a major reallocation of resources under the Mutual Security Program. In Southern Asia, for example, the probability of local war somewhere in the area was obviously less after the Indochina armistice in July 1954 than before, when the Indochina conflict was still actively under way. If the returns from military aid are conceived in terms of the expected-value concepts previously suggested, we can argue that good grounds existed for (1) lowering the policy rate of exchange between political returns and military returns, and (2) reallocating accordingly in favor of programs and recipients yielding non-military returns.

Despite its appeal, the argument is one that rests on an unwar-

[1] See above, Chapter 5, section C.1.

ranted assumption that coexistence carries with it an unambiguous meaning concerning the reduced probability of various local war contingencies. If we assume that the term, and hence the period with which we've identified it, really "stands for peaceful coexistence of the two systems,"[2] then the inference about a lowering of the probabilities of various local war contingencies seems reasonable. More realistically, however, the meaning of coexistence was and is ambiguous. Rather than signifying the compatibility of conflicting systems, coexistence has signified the compatibility of political *détente* and military threats, of velvet glove and mailed fist, of thaw and freeze in the Soviet Bloc's international moves. At precisely the time the siege of Dienbienphu was actively underway and the Viet Minh invaded Cambodia in April 1954, Communist China signed a three-year trade agreement with Burma.[3] At the same time as Chou En-lai's peregrinations to Rangoon and New Delhi in June 1954 led to enunciation of the "five principles of coexistence," China repeated its military threats against Formosa; and, at the same time as the Soviet Union was conducting tests of nuclear weapons in September and October 1954, it offered to provide a fifteen-year credit to finance the equipment costs of an Indian steel plant—the first major offer of Soviet economic aid outside the Bloc.[4]

Coexistence has, in other words, meant vastly more *flexible* Sino-Soviet behavior in international affairs, beginning while the Mutual Security Program for 1955 was in its final stages of formulation, and becoming increasingly evident while the Program was underway. Coexistence has *not* meant that military moves and threats have been eliminated or that the likelihood of *all* local war contingencies has been reduced. Actually, the likelihood of some local wars may well have increased during the coexistence period.

If, for example, local wars in an area like Southern Asia are engendered and supported by the Soviet Bloc, they are likely to compete with each other for scarce resources. A conflict in Indochina or Korea may mean that less logistic support and "volunteer" manpower will be available for a possible war in Burma. Hence, the latter's occurrence may become less probable. Termination of the initial

[2] The quotation is from Malenkov's address to the Supreme Soviet of the U.S.S.R., August 8, 1953. See *Documents on American Foreign Relations, 1953*, New York, 1954, p. 146.

[3] *Soviet Technical Assistance*, Senate Committee on Foreign Relations, Washington, D.C., 1956, p. 26.

[4] *Ibid.*, p. 16.

conflict disengages an aggressor's resources for mischief elsewhere. While countervailing U.S. resources may be disengaged to oppose the subsequent mischief, the result may not be symmetrical. Redeployment of U.S. forces, for example, may make them less accessible to subsequent trouble spots than are the redeployed Chinese forces, and consequently embolden the latter for another try.[5]

On the other hand, ongoing wars may create certain inducements to wage additional local wars. A conflict in Indochina may make the returns from military resources invested in a collateral Cambodian or Thai adventure appear relatively large, and hence increase the probability that the latter will occur. Moreover, even if these inducements are not perceived, other conflagrations may be ignited by an ongoing war. Other local conflicts may arise not from calculation, but from a general increase in tensions and sensitivities.

Admittedly, the picture is not entirely clear. But it is at least plausible that the probability of a particular local war depends partly on whether a "competing" war is already underway. From this standpoint, it can be argued that the probability of *some* local war contingencies in Southern Asia may actually have increased as a result of termination of the Indochina hostilities by the Geneva armistice agreement in July 1954. With regard to the country and program allocations of Mutual Security Aid to Southern Asia during the 1955-57 period, it cannot, therefore, be simply assumed that "military" returns acquired a uniformly lower exchange value in relation to "political" returns as a result of peaceful coexistence.

In approaching the allocations for 1955, one should also recall the lag between program formulation and implementation, to which we have previously referred. Quite apart from the implications concerning allocation that may be associated with the coexistence period, the Mutual Security Program for 1955 actually depended in considerable measure on circumstances prevailing in the preceding year. The siege of Dienbienphu in the spring of 1954, the serious consideration by the United States of intervention against the attacking forces, and, in this connection, the then active U.S. effort to promote in Southeast Asia an association of friendly Asian and Western nations to undertake such intervention collectively, directly influenced the Mutual Security Program for 1955. Against this background, the Mutual Security Act of 1954 formally expressed Congressional support for the creation by the free Asian countries "of

[5] See above, Chapter 5, pp. 175-176.

a joint organization to develop their economic and social well being
. . . and to protect their security and independence."[6] This reaffirmation of a policy first enunciated in the Mutual Defense Assistance
Act of 1949[7] foreshadowed the formation of the Southeast Asia Collective Defense Organization (SEATO) in September 1954.[8] In its
turn, SEATO significantly affected intercountry and interprogram
allocations of Mutual Security aid not only in 1955, but in subsequent
years as well.

B. THE 1955 PROGRAM IN SOUTHERN ASIA

1. The New Mutual Security Legislation

The Mutual Security Act of 1954 was an attempt to embody in a
single enabling law the relevant provisions of the nine predecessor
statutes under which the Mutual Security Program had been operating.[9] Because the new Act provided the framework for aid allocations
in the next two years as well, a brief description of its provisions is
in order.

Viewed analytically, each of the major titles or sections of the
Mutual Security Act of 1954 implicitly represented a separate sub-
system for allocating aid among countries.[10] The first title, Mutual
Defense Assistance, authorized "measures in the common defense."
The second title, Development Assistance, authorized capital "as-

[6] "The Mutual Security Act of 1954," Chapter 1, in *Mutual Security Legislation
and Related Documents*, Foreign Operations Administration, Washington, D.C.,
1954, p. 1.

[7] See above, Chapter 3, pp. 54-55.

[8] For a full discussion of the circumstances surrounding the formation of SEATO,
see *Collective Defence in Southeast Asia: The Manila Treaty and Its Implications*,
Royal Institute of International Affairs, London, 1956.

[9] For a listing of the various statutes which had been incorporated in the previous
Mutual Security Acts, see *Mutual Security Act of 1953*, Report of the House Committee on Foreign Affairs, *op.cit.*, p. 9. The Mutual Security Act of 1954 explicitly
repealed all of the prior aid legislation, including the Mutual Defense Assistance
Act of 1949, the Act for International Development, and the Mutual Security Acts
of 1951, 1952, and 1953. See *Mutual Security Legislation and Related Documents*,
1954, p. 46.

[10] The Act also provided that transfers of funds could be made, at the discretion
of the President, among any provisions (sections) of the Act, subject to certain
constraints. The constraints: that no more than 10 per cent of the funds appropriated
under a particular provision could be transferred *from* that provision; and that no
more than the equivalent of 20 per cent of the funds appropriated under a particular
provision could be transferred *to* that provision. By implication, the three subsystems
were thus part of a *single* system of allocation at a higher objectives level, that is,
assuming some known or intuited rates of exchange between the returns identified
with the separate subsystems. The notion of "lower" and "higher" level objectives
will be discussed more fully later. See below, Chapter 7, section A.1.

sistance designed to promote economic development, and to assist in maintaining economic and political stability." The third, Technical Cooperation, authorized "aid [to] . . . the peoples of economically underdeveloped areas to develop their resources and improve their working and living conditions by encouraging the exchange of technical knowledge and skills. . . ."[11]

The two latter categories corresponded, respectively, to the "special economic assistance" and "technical assistance" categories of the prior year.[12] The first category, Mutual Defense Assistance, represented a more complicated relabeling. Though the term applied to the first title was taken from the Mutual Defense Assistance Act of 1949, it was redefined and given broader scope than in the parent legislation.

As we have previously seen, the original MDA legislation encompassed military end-item aid nearly exclusively.[13] In the new legislation, Mutual Defense Assistance was redefined to include "military assistance," "direct forces support," *and* "defense support." The military assistance component represented the same type of military hardware that previously had comprised MDAP, and was now redesignated the Military Assistance Program (MAP).[14] Direct forces support represented software provided directly to and for the exclusive use of the military forces of recipient countries. In concept and commodity content, direct forces support corresponded identically to what in previous years was called "common use items" or "direct military support."[15] Like the latter, it was as much motivated by, and represented as direct a contribution to, military force goals as did end-item aid. Defense support, finally, represented all other aid "designed to sustain and increase [the] military effort" of a recipi-

---

[11] The quotations in this paragraph are from the indicated titles of the Mutual Security Act of 1954. See *Mutual Security Legislation and Related Documents*, pp. 14, 15.

[12] Above, Chapter 5, pp. 162-163.

[13] See above, Chapter 3, section E, and Chapter 5, section C.3.

[14] The Mutual Security Act of 1954 included, as part of the military assistance (end-item) program, an explicit dollar authorization for U.S. contributions to NATO "infrastructure." A French-devised Anglicism, infrastructure represented military public works—air bases, naval installations, telecommunications, SHAPE headquarters, and other capital facilities—required for NATO operations in Europe. In the three preceding years, U.S. contributions to infrastructure had been financed either from MDAP funds (1952 and 1954), or the regular Defense Department appropriations (1953). See the *Mutual Security Act of 1954*, House Hearings, pp. 757-760.

[15] See above, Table 10, footnote f, and Table 16, footnote g. Also, *Mutual Security Act of 1954*, House Hearings, pp. 28ff.; and Foreign Operations Administration, *Monthly Operations Report*, Washington, D.C., July 1954, p. 5.

ent.[16] In principle, if textiles were provided directly to a recipient's armed forces for fabrication into uniforms, they were called direct forces support. If the same kind of textiles were imported and sold in the open market, they were called defense support, *regardless* of whether the proceeds from sale were devoted to military or non-military outlays in the recipient country.

2. Semantics and Mutual Security

The semantics of foreign aid is not the least obscure aspect of the subject, and the labeling distinctions described in the previous paragraph provide an illustration. Viewed in economic terms, the distinction between direct forces support and defense support, for example, is either meaningless or misleading. Whether particular commodities are earmarked for the use of a country's armed forces or for the civilian sector tells us nothing about the actual or the intended economic impact of the resources furnished.

As we have previously noted, substitutability of resources weakens any attempt to equate the actually benefiting sector with the ostensibly recipient sector, if the interests of recipient and donor countries diverge.[17] Assuming divergent interests between donor and recipient, neither direct forces support nor defense support may make a net contribution to the recipient country's military capabilities. On the other hand, if we assume convergent interests between donor and recipient, both forms may make such a contribution and with equal effectiveness. From the standpoint of *actual* aid impact, the labeling distinction is meaningless in case of convergent interests. In case of divergent interests, it is misleading.

But quite apart from the difficulty of determining from the labels themselves the actual impact of incremental aid, the distinction between defense support and direct forces support was misleading because it did not accurately reflect the *intentions* or objectives underlying the two sorts of aid in a number of recipient countries in Southern Asia. In some countries, Indochina for example, the objectives behind defense support and direct forces support were identical: to increase or sustain a given military capability by assuring that a cer-

[16] The quotation is from Chapter 3 of the Mutual Security Act of 1954. For a similar statement of the purpose of defense support, see also *Monthly Operations Report*, July 1954, p. 6.

[17] Except under the circumstances that the aid resources provided to the ostensibly recipient sector are large relative to the amounts that might otherwise be available to it. See above, Chapter 3, pp. 33-34, and below, Appendix I, pp. 417-419.

tain portion of the recipient country's gross national expenditure, including foreign aid, was devoted to military outlays. In such a case, the distinction went too far by implying that different categories of aid were intended to yield different kinds of returns.

In other countries—the Philippines, Thailand, and Pakistan, for example—defense support, in whole or in large part, was intended to contribute to economic development and political stability by adding to the share of the recipient country's gross national expenditure devoted to investment and technical training. In these cases—assuming convergent interests between donor and recipient—different returns were attributable to defense support and direct forces support: the former more closely identified with the returns from technical and development aid; the latter identified with the returns from military end-item aid. Under these circumstances, the legislative distinction did not go far enough in separating the defense support and direct forces support categories. In effect, "defense support" was—to a considerable extent—simply the name applied to development aid extended to countries which were also receiving military end-item aid. By including defense support within "mutual defense assistance," rather than within "development assistance," the Mutual Security Act of 1954 obscured the allocation choices that were involved, for example, between "defense support" in Country A and development aid in Country B, in both of which the relevant returns were conceived in the same units.

The point, to which we have alluded before and will return again,[18] is that the *initial* or "lower-level" problem of foreign aid allocation is to group and compare the available alternatives in terms of reasonably homogeneous objectives. Admittedly, since widely different objectives are served by the program, the "higher"-level problem then involves comparison of objectives, and determining rates of exchange among them. Of course, the latter must eventually depend on hunch, intuition, and judgment concerning national "interests" or preferences. But something is to be gained by making the judgments conscious and explicit. The least to be gained is more responsible judgments. The most to be gained is more accurate judgments. To this end, the labeling of foreign aid categories (or "subsystems") should be determined by the initial need to identify the primary objectives that each program category seeks to advance.

These considerations create numerous difficulties for presenting

[18] See above, Chapter 5, pp. 138-139, and below, Chapter 7, pp. 254-255.

the 1955 data for Southern Asia in a form that is both accurate and comparable to prior years. For reasons already noted, a strong argument can be made for including both direct forces support and the validly designated portion of defense support (if we could determine it) in the same table in which data on military end-item aid are presented. Correspondingly, it would make sense to include the residual portion of defense support in the data on economic and technical aid allocations. However, for convenience we shall continue to maintain the distinction between end-item aid, and "other" aid, including defense support and direct forces support as well as development aid and technical assistance.[19]

End-item aid to Southern Asia will be shown in one table; all other aid to Southern Asia, in a separate table. The latter table will distinguish economic and technical aid from military support (that is, "direct forces support" and *part* of the so-called "defense support"), and we will continue to assume that the net or real impact of economic and technical aid is in the sector ostensibly receiving it. Where aid commodities are imported for local sale, the sector in which the derived counterpart is spent will generally determine whether the aid is labeled military support or economic assistance. For example, saleable commodity imports in Indochina in 1955 are classified as military support, while in Pakistan they are classified as economic assistance.[20] Where data on the sectoral allocation of counterpart funds are not available, other evidence will be relied on to estimate the portions of so-called defense support that can appropriately be regarded as "military support," and economic and technical assistance, respectively. The main "other evidence" used is the amount of a recipient's internal military outlays and its changing share in total public expenditure. In general, where internal military outlays are large or growing, defense support will be attributed to this use and labeled military support. Where military outlays are small or rapidly diminishing, defense support will be attributed to the economic assistance category.[21]

To summarize the semantic conventions adopted in the following tables, the term "military support" will refer to both direct-forces support and that part of so-called defense support which can be reasonably considered to have contributed to higher outlays in the

---

[19] See above, Chapter 5, section C.3.
[20] See below, Table 19, footnotes g and j.
[21] See below, Table 24, footnotes i and k.

military sector, according to the foregoing criteria. The residual portion of defense support will be included in economic and technical assistance. If the distinction between the categories remains somewhat arbitrary, it is to be hoped that it is the less so for being explicit.

3. Allocations for Economic Assistance and Military Support

The non-end-item aid proposals and obligations for 1955 in Southern Asia are summarized in Tables 18 and 19 below.

Viewed from a global standpoint, the data shown in Tables 18 and 19 reflect the increasing prominence of the Asian area in the Mutual Security Program as a whole. Thus, the proposals data for Southern Asia shown in Table 18 represented 51.4 per cent of global Mutual Security proposals for 1955, excluding military end-items, compared with 33 per cent in 1954.[22] In terms of obligations, the data shown in Table 19 for Southern Asia represented 41.8 per cent of global Mutual Security obligations in 1955, exclusive of military end-item aid, compared to 39.2 per cent in 1954. Obligations for the *entire* Asian areas (that is, including Korea and Formosa, as well as Southern Asia) represented 63.6 per cent of global non-end-item aid in 1955, compared to 54.5 per cent in 1954. The relevant global and regional obligations data for 1955 are shown in Table 20 below.[23]

4. Some Implications of the Data

It is reasonable to interpret the rising share, represented by obligations in Southern Asia, of the declining Mutual Security budget in 1955 in the same terms previously used to explain the still sharper rise of the corresponding share in 1954.[24] Notwithstanding the end of the Korean and Indochina wars, the marginal effects of aid were relatively more highly valued, by both the Executive Branch and the Congress, in the Asian area than in the other major regions receiving Mutual Security aid. Given this higher regional "policy" value, the allocation of a reduced global Mutual Security budget implied relatively smaller reductions in aid to the Asian area than in the program globally.

The point applied both to the program proposed by the Executive

[22] See above, Chapter 5, footnote 99. Global MSP proposals for 1955, exclusive of military end-items, amounted to $1.9 billion. Inclusive of end-items, the MSP proposals for 1955 amounted to $3.5 billion. See below, Table 21, footnote b.

[23] For the corresponding data in 1954, see Table 14.

[24] Above, Chapter 5, pp. 157-158.

Table 18

FUNDS PROPOSED BY THE EXECUTIVE BRANCH FOR UNITED STATES
ECONOMIC AND TECHNICAL ASSISTANCE AND MILITARY SUPPORT
TO SOUTHERN ASIA, FISCAL YEAR 1955[a]

(by country and project use)

	(1)	(2)	(3)	(4)	(5)	(6)	(7)
				Project Use			
Country	Agri-culture	Indus-try	Trans-porta-tion	Health	Public Adminis-tration	Educa-tion	Commu-nity Develop-ment
	(millions of dollars)						
Afghanistan[b]	.84	.11	.12	.15	.10	.30	–
Burma[c]	–	–	–	–	–	–	–
Ceylon[d]	–	–	–	–	–	–	–
India[e]	15.57	19.11	15.12	6.68	.17	1.50	6.35
Indochina[f]	.72	.11	4.08	1.56	.80	.33	.40
Indonesia[g]	.98	.59	.10	.41	.36	.29	–
Nepal[h]	.33	.03	.01	.15	.01	.04	.21
Pakistan[i]	18.38	4.05	.06	.41	.09	.30	3.41
Philippines[j]	3.74	6.28	5.80	2.12	1.08	.98	–
Thailand[k]	.93	.34	.84	1.32	.42	.90	.25
TOTALS	41.49	30.62	26.13	12.80	3.03	4.64	10.62
Project Total as Proportion of Regional Total	(per cent)						
	22.1	16.3	13.9	6.8	1.6	2.5	5.7

Σ Col (1)/Σ Col (9), Σ Col (2)/Σ Col (9), etc.

(*continued*)

Source: Appendix II.

[a] For further explanation of the data in Table 18, see above, Table 7, footnote [a].

[b] (q), p. 160; and (t), p. 68.

[c] See above, Table 15, footnote [c].

[d] *Ibid.*, footnote [d].

[e] (r), p. 536; (t), p. 68; and (a). The figures shown represent *both* technical assistance ($19.5 million) and development assistance ($85.0 million). For an explanation of the development assistance category, see above, pp. 252-254. The sectoral breakdown of the proposed development assistance was: $10.5 million for agriculture; $16.0 million for industry; $15.0 million for transportation; $3.5 million for health; and $40.0 million for general and miscellaneous. The latter represented surplus agricultural commodities to be sold for Indian rupees with the proceeds to be used for internal development outlays under Section 402 of the Mutual Security Act of 1954, as amended. See above, Table 16, footnote [c].

[f] (q), p. 283; and (r), pp. 251-252. The $800 million listed in column (10) represented "direct forces support" to reimburse France for part of the franc costs

Table 18 (continued)

(8)	(9)	(10)	(11)	(12)
	Project Use		Country Total as Proportion of Regional Total	
General and Miscellaneous	Total Excluding Military Support	Military Support	Excluding Military Support Col (9)/Σ Col (9)	Including Military Support Col (9) + Col (10) Σ Col (9) + Σ Col (10)
(millions of dollars)			(per cent)	
–	1.62	–	.9	.2
–	–	–	–	–
–	–	–	–	–
40.00	104.50	–	55.7	10.6
17.00	25.00	800.00	13.3	83.5
1.27	4.00	–	2.1	.4
–	.78	–	.4	.1
–	26.70	–	14.2	2.7
–	20.00	–	10.7	2.0
–	5.00	–	2.7	.5
58.27	187.60	800.00	100.0	100.0
(per cent)				
31.1	100.0			

of the Indochina war. See above, Table 15, footnote ^{f}. Of the remaining $25 million, $3.5 million was for technical assistance and $21.5 million for so-called "defense support." Since the latter consisted almost entirely of the foreign exchange or local costs of projects in the civilian sector of the economy, it is included under economic and technical assistance. For clarification of the semantics, see the discussion in the text aboxe, pp. 189-191.

^{g} (q), p. 290; (t), p. 68; and (a).
^{h} (q), p. 216; (t), p. 68; and (a).
^{i} (s), p. 376; (t), p. 68; and (a). The figures shown represent *both* technical assistance ($6.7 million) and development assistance ($20.0 million). For an explanation of the development assistance category, see above, pp. 186-187. The sectoral breakdown of the proposed development assistance was: $14.3 million for agriculture; $3.3 million for industry; and $2.4 million for commodity development.
^{j} (q), p. 315; (r), p. 253; and (a).
^{k} (q), p. 325; (s), p. 376; (t), p. 68; and (a).

[193]

Table 19

FUNDS OBLIGATED FOR UNITED STATES ECONOMIC AND TECHNICAL
ASSISTANCE AND MILITARY SUPPORT TO SOUTHERN ASIA,
FISCAL YEAR 1955[a]

(by country and project use)

	(1)	(2)	(3)	(4)	(5)	(6)	(7)	(8)
				Project Use				
Country	Agri-culture	Indus-try	Trans-porta-tion	Health	Labor[b]	Public Admin-istra-tion	Edu-cation	Com-munity Devel-opment
				(millions of dollars)				
Afghanistan[c]	.72	.07	–	.09	–	–	.81	.14
Burma[d]	–	–	–	–	–	–	–	–
Ceylon[e]	–	–	–	–	–	–	–	–
India[f]	7.80	17.42	18.55	7.73	.70	.04	.73	.28
Indochina[g]	1.68	.63	3.25	1.10	–	1.90	.96	17.25
Indonesia[h]	1.35	1.30	.12	2.13	.30	.75	.71	.10
Nepal[i]	.08	.03	–	.06	–	.01	.11	.14
Pakistan[j]	8.72	5.42	3.21	4.56	–	.10	.81	.93
Philippines[k]	4.17	1.17	3.99	1.80	.16	1.72	1.56	.01
Thailand[l]	1.01	.32	9.68	1.27	.03	.63	1.20	–
TOTALS	25.53	26.36	38.80	18.74	1.19	5.15	6.89	18.85
Project Total as Proportion of Regional Total				(per cent)				
	10.1	10.5	15.4	7.4	.5	2.1	2.7	7.5

Σ Col (1)/Σ Col (10), Σ Col (2)/Σ Col (10), etc.

(continued)

Source: Appendix II.

[a] See above, Chapter 4, Table 3, footnote **a**, for explanation of categories and terms used in this table.

[b] See above, Table 16, footnote **b**.

[c] (a); and (z), pp. 39, 48-49.

[d] See above, Table 16, footnote **d**.

[e] Ibid., footnote **e**.

[f] (u), p. 227. Later reports, for example, (g'), p. 55, show total obligations in 1955 of $85.7 million, but without a sectoral breakdown. The figures shown for India in Table 19 represent *both* technical assistance ($15.2 million) and development assistance ($69.2 million). For an explanation of the development aid category, see above, pp. 186-187. The sectoral breakdown of the development

assistance was: $15.8 million for industry; $18.5 million for transportation; $4.7 million for health; and $30.2 million for general-and-miscellaneous. The "general and miscellaneous" category represented obligations for surplus agricultural commodities imported for sale in India with the rupee proceeds to be used for internal development outlays. (See [i'], p. 76.) The surplus commodity component of Indian development aid was financed pursuant to Section 402 of the Mutual Security Act of 1954 which, like Section 550 of the Mutual Security Act of 1953, required that a stipulated portion of new Mutual Security appropriations be used to purchase surplus agricultural commodities in the United States for sale to recipient countries

Table 19 (continued)

(9)	(10)	(11)	(12)	(13)
	Project Use		Country Total as Proportion of Regional Total	
General and Miscellaneous	Total Excluding Military Support	Military Support	Excluding Military Support Col (10)/Σ Col (10)	Including Military Support Col (10) + Col (11) Σ Col (10) + Σ Col (11)
(millions of dollars)			(per cent)	
.18	2.01	–	.8	.3
–	–	–	–	–
–	–	–	–	–
31.18	84.43	–	33.5	12.0
–	26.77	435.82	10.6	65.6
.24	7.00	–	2.8	1.0
1.94	2.37	–	.9	.3
47.61	71.36	–	28.4	10.1
5.06	19.64	9.50	7.8	4.1
24.02	38.16	8.37	15.2	6.6
110.23	251.74	453.69	100.0	100.0
(per cent)				
43.8	100.0			

in exchange for local currency. See Chapter 5, Table 16, footnote c. Of the total development assistance, $45 million was provided as a forty-year Mutual Security loan, inclusive of the $30 million for surplus commodities already mentioned.

g Categorizing and quantifying aid to Indochina in 1955 is not only difficult, but bound to be more or less inaccurate, as well. In the middle of the fiscal year, France recognized the sovereignty of Cambodia, Laos, and Viet Nam, and U.S. aid began to be channeled to each sovereign state individually. The figures shown in Table 19 represent a consolidation of obligations which subsequent records show separately for Cambodia, Laos, Viet Nam, and "Indochina Undistributed."

Distinguishing between economic and technical assistance (columns [1] and [10]) and military support, (column [11]), presents still another problem. In Table 19, estimated obligations for *specific project* expenses are included in columns (1) through (10), and all other aid, excluding military end-items, is included in column (11). Of the latter, part represented reimbursement in dollars to France for franc outlays on the Indochina war, part represented saleable commodity imports to Indochina, and part represented U.S. purchases of piastres, kips, and riels. In turn, these local currencies were used to provide general budgetary support
(Continued on following page)

Branch and the program resulting after Congressional appropriations. Illustrative of both Congressional and Executive Branch judgment in this regard was the following statement by Congressman Walter Judd, commenting on the prominence of Asia in the 1955 Mutual Security proposals: "It is very late, but it is a good thing to have a better balance between East and West and give more aid to

---

(Notes to Table 19 continued)

for the expenditures of the governments of Viet Nam, Laos, and Cambodia respectively. Inasmuch as 70 to 80 per cent of the budgetary outlays of these countries represented direct military costs, and the bulk of counterpart withdrawals was for military uses, attribution of all non-project dollar aid to military support (column [11]) is reasonable, though certainly not exact.

The project obligations shown in columns (1) to (10) are from (a). The military support figure (column [11]) is derived by subtracting the total *project* obligations (column [10]) from total obligations shown in (i'), p. 57.

The large obligations figure shown in column (8) under "community development" represented housing materials and consumer goods for the relief of refugees from North Viet Nam.

[h] (a). Later reports give slightly different obligations figures without a sectoral breakdown, for example, (c'), p. 73; and (g'), p. 54.

[i] (z), pp. 40, 48-49; and (a). The general-and-miscellaneous category includes $1.6 million of "development assistance" for consumer goods to provide emergency flood relief.

[j] (a); and (z), p. 40. Categorizing 1955 aid to Pakistan is about as difficult and arbitrary as in the case of Indochina (see footnote [g] above). Originally the Executive Branch proposed development assistance for Pakistan in 1955. (See Table 18 above.) However, the Mutual Security Act of 1954 provided that development assistance be confined to countries *not* receiving military end-item aid, while similar assistance in MDAP countries be construed as supporting the military effort and hence termed "defense support." With initiation of MDAP in Pakistan at the end of fiscal year 1954, the categories of assistance to Pakistan were accordingly changed. What had been proposed as development assistance was relabeled de-

fense support, and is so recorded in current government reports. At the same time, the total amount of aid obligated was substantially increased over the amount originally proposed. It is impossible to determine with any confidence how much of the increase can be reasonably attributed to the subsequently increased costs of Pakistan's military buildup, hence *validly* designated as defense support. In Table 19, *none* has been so designated, and consequently column (11) shows no entry for Pakistan. The reason for adopting this procedure is that *none* of the sales proceeds (counterpart) derived from the large commodity imports shown under column (9) was directly used for meeting defense expenditures in the Pakistan budget (see [e'], p. 8). Moreover, total Pakistan defense outlays actually declined during fiscal year 1955. Though not exact, the procedure followed in Table 19 is probably more accurate than the alternatives that are available, for example, listing all aid in 1955, or even the "general and miscellaneous" portion alone, as "military support."

[k] (a), and (z), p. 39. The $9.5 million shown in column (11) as military support represented both software supplied directly to Philippine military forces, and estimated current military expenditures financed from the peso proceeds of saleable commodity imports.

Besides Mutual Security aid to the Philippines, the Export-Import Bank authorized credits of $4.6 million to public and private corporations in the Philippines during fiscal 1955. Export-Import Bank of Washington, *Report to Congress*, Washington, D.C., July-December 1956, p. 24.

[l] (a); and (z), p. 39, which shows slightly different totals. The $8.4 million shown in column (11) as military support represented both software supplied directly to the Thai military forces, and estimated current military expenditures financed from the baht proceeds of saleable commodity imports.

Table 20

UNITED STATES ECONOMIC AND TECHNICAL ASSISTANCE AND
MILITARY SUPPORT TO SOUTHERN ASIA IN FISCAL YEAR 1955
COMPARED TO TOTAL ASIAN AND GLOBAL NON-MAP ASSISTANCE
UNDER THE MUTUAL SECURITY ACT OF 1954[a]

	Obligations	As Proportion of:	
		Total Asian Aid	Global Aid
	(millions of dollars)	(per cent)	
1. Economic and Technical Aid to Southern Asia	251.7	23.4	14.9
2. Military Support for Southern Asia	453.7	42.2	26.9
3. Total Non-MAP Aid to Southern Asia (1+2)	705.4	65.6	41.8
4. Non-MAP Aid to Formosa and Korea	368.9	34.4	21.8
5. Total Asian Non-MAP Aid (3+4)	1,074.3	100.0	63.6
6. Global Non-MAP Aid Under the Mutual Security Act of 1954[b]	1,688.0	–	100.0

Sources: Table 19, above, and (i′), p. 57.

[a] The term "non-MAP," as used in this table refers to *all* aid other than the military end-items, NATO infrastructure, and training provided under the renamed "Military Assistance Program" (MAP). For clarification, see the discussion in the text above, pp. 186-191, and below, pp. 201-203.

[b] Of the amount shown in (4), $131.6 million represented obligations in Formosa, and $237.3 million, obligations in Korea.

the areas where we have been losing, rather than to follow the traditional pattern of more and more aid to . . . Europe. More than half the aid in this whole program is for Asia, which I think is a great advance. Not less emphasis on Europe, but more on the area where failure to get emphasis previously led to disaster."[25]

Tables 18 and 19 suggest some interesting changes in non-MAP allocations to Southern Asia between the proposals and obligations stages, as well as changes in intercountry allocations within the region.

In comparing Mutual Security proposals and obligations in previous years, we have usually interpreted reduced obligations as indicative of Congressional judgments, concerning the productivity or the value of aid in different countries, differing from the Executive

[25] *The Mutual Security Act of 1954*, House Committee Hearings, pp. 44 and 236.

Branch judgments on which the proposals were originally based. In 1955, this interpretation is not valid. Instead, the 29 per cent reduction in total non-MAP allocations to Southern Asia[26] is attributable to the altered international circumstances arising between the time proposals and obligations were made.[27] The armistice in Indochina at the end of July 1954 meant that military support requirements in the Associated States were substantially reduced: in part because French troops began to be repatriated during 1955, and in part because the cost of maintaining the remaining national armies was less in peace than in war. Actually, the bulk of the military support funds requested by the Executive Branch for Indochina were appropriated by the Congress; of the $800 million requested, $700 million was appropriated. Subsequently, the transfer provisions of the Mutual Security Act[28] were invoked by the Administration, after consultation with Congress, to move funds from their originally intended use in Indochina to other uses judged of higher yield.

These transfers appear in Tables 18 and 19 as a reduction in military support obligations for Indochina and as a partly compensating rise in economic assistance and military support in Pakistan, Thailand, and the Philippines.[29] How is the substantial increase in obligations to the three latter countries, relative both to obligations in 1954 and to aid proposals in 1955, to be explained? What factors would account for the attribution of relatively higher returns to aid in these countries in 1955?

Pakistan, Thailand, and the Philippines were the three Asian signatories of the SEATO agreements in September 1954.[30] Yet, in economic terms, there is no apparent reason why participation in SEATO in itself would tend to raise the marginal physical productivity of aid. Even if we consider productivity in military terms,[31] the argu-

[26] From $987.6 million proposed, to $705.4 million obligated. The figures are the sums, respectively, of columns (9) and (10) in Table 18, and columns (10) and (11) in Table 19.

[27] See above, Chapter 4, pp. 76-77.   [28] See above, footnote 10.

[29] The remainder of the Indochina "savings" was used in Korea, Formosa, and other parts of the Mutual Security Program.

[30] Although Cambodia, Laos, and South Viet Nam were not members of SEATO, a protocol to the Southeast Asia Collective Defense Treaty designated them as part of the area to which the provisions of the Treaty applied. Consequently, any aggression or threat against the Associated States was to be regarded in the same light as an aggression or threat against a SEATO member country, and hence to require the members "to consult immediately in order to agree on the measures which should be taken for the common defense." See *Collective Defence in Southeast Asia*, pp. 169-171.

[31] On the ground that the substitutability between non-MAP aid, and other

ment that the military "output" per unit of additional aid tended to increase as a result of SEATO membership is not entirely persuasive. We might argue, for example, that prior to a country's membership in SEATO, the marginal claimant for additional resources may have been private consumption, while afterwards the military sector became the marginal claimant. Under these circumstances, the military productivity of non-military aid might be considered to have risen as a result of SEATO membership.

The flaw in the argument is factual rather than analytical. Annual military outlays in the three Asian countries participating in SEATO actually *fell* or, in the case of the Philippines, increased by an amount that was small relative to the rise in annual U.S. non-MAP aid. Annual defense outlays in the three countries, immediately before and after formation of SEATO, were as follows, in millions of dollars:[32]

	1954	1955	1956
Pakistan	$253.7	$225.3	$185.6
Thailand	45.3	41.0	39.4
Philippines	80.0	74.0	76.5

Consequently, it is not convincing—at least, not in the short-run—to argue that the *military* productivity of *non-military* aid rose appreciably in the SEATO countries because of their greater propensity to divert internal resources to military uses as a result of the pact.

One is left with the conclusion that the sharply increased absolute and relative allocations of aid to the SEATO members, especially Pakistan and Thailand, reflected the relatively higher policy "value" attached to the essentially unchanged productivity of aid in these countries. Because the SEATO countries became more closely allied *with* the United States, the results of aid in these countries became more highly valued *by* the United States. In effect, the gains (to the donor) from aid seemed to depend, to a greater extent than in prior years, on the degree of association between recipient and donor.

---

resources available to recipient countries, may have permitted an intentional diversion of these resources to direct military uses.

[32] *Economic Survey of Asia and the Far East, 1956*, Bangkok, 1957, p. 190. The figures have been converted to dollars at official exchange rates. The Thai figures cover calendar years, those for the Philippines and Pakistan cover fiscal years. Pakistan devalued its currency in August 1955 from 3.3 rupees per dollar to 4.8 rupees per dollar. The pre-devaluation rate has been used in converting the 1955 figure (covering the period April 1, 1954, to March 31, 1955) to dollars. The post-devaluation rate has been used to convert the 1956 figure. If the pre-devaluation rate were used for 1956, the figure for defense outlays would be $267.9 million instead of $185.6 million.

Institutionalized cooperation with the West, through SEATO, became a more prominent part of the objectives of U.S. aid than it formerly had been.

In turn, of course, SEATO was a *means* to "higher level" U.S. objectives in the area: for example, deterrence against overt communist aggression, and legitimization of U.S. intervention in the event of such aggression. We shall return in Chapter 7 to a consideration of SEATO in relation to U.S. objectives in Southern Asia, and of the analytical implications of these objectives for aid allocation. Here it is sufficient just to note the prominent influence exercised by SEATO on intercountry allocations in 1955.

5. Sectoral Allocations in 1955

Before leaving Tables 18 and 19, we should note the altered sectoral shares of the regional aid total. Allocations to the longer-term transportation and industrial sectors, in both the proposals and obligations tables, continued to be larger than those to agriculture and health in 1955 as in 1954.[33] But the more impressive fact about the 1955 allocations is the dominant increase in regional allocations to the "general and miscellaneous" category. Obligations for this category, largely for saleable commodities and especially surplus agricultural commodities, rose from about $20 million, or 12 per cent of the regional total in 1954, to $110 million, or nearly 44 per cent of the total in 1955. In the three countries in which general and miscellaneous allocations were concentrated—Pakistan, India, and Thailand—it is difficult to determine with any precision the sectors on which these additional resources impinged. Not only is there the difficulty presented by resource substitutability to which we have repeatedly alluded. In addition, the records of local currency use do not provide sufficient data to attribute the sales proceeds to specific sectors.[34]

[33] See above, Tables 15 and 16.

[34] Through fiscal 1956, local currency proceeds from the sale of agricultural surpluses in India (see above, Table 19, footnote f) were reported as programmed for "development assistance," without any specific sectoral designation. See International Cooperation Administration *Counterpart Funds and ICA Currency Accounts*, Washington, D.C., June 30, 1956, p. 46. In Pakistan and Thailand, though the sectoral use of counterpart funds was reported in more detail, only a small part of the total sales proceeds resulting from the 1955 Mutual Security Program was actually withdrawn. Of the funds withdrawn from the counterpart accounts in these two countries during 1955 and 1956, the agricultural and health sectors were the preponderant beneficiaries (*ibid.*, pp. 26, 37). It seems likely that most of the remaining counterpart was intentionally held as a deflationary cushion against rising total government

Nevertheless, two conjectural explanations for the substantial increase in the saleable commodity allocations in 1955 may be advanced. One explanation is that by 1955 the rising scale of national development outlays in India, Pakistan, and Thailand was, to an increasing extent, confronted by a shortage of *total* savings, rather than just a shortage of foreign exchange to meet the external costs of the direct import component of investment projects. Where the direct dollar costs of producer goods were a pressing obstacle to increased investment, Mutual Security aid could properly concentrate on meeting these costs. Aid allocations would tend, in this case, to be mainly for producer goods for specific sectors, and internal savings could be relied on to cover other costs. As total investment rose, the level of total internal savings tended to become no less an obstacle than foreign exchange[35] to further increases in investment. Aid allocations had then to provide for meeting the local costs no less directly than for meeting the foreign exchange costs of investment projects. The increased allocation of aid dollars to the "general and miscellaneous" category can be partly understood in these terms.

Another partial explanation may lie in the anticipated contribution of sales proceeds to prospective increases in defense costs in the SEATO countries. In other words, a portion of the "general and miscellaneous" allocations shown in Table 19 perhaps ought to be listed as military support. Although direct counterpart withdrawals in 1955 and 1956 for military purposes were zero or negligible in Pakistan, Thailand, and the Philippines,[36] and although military outlays in these countries actually fell below the 1954 levels, the financing of saleable commodity imports may have provided—and been intended to provide—the SEATO recipients with greater fiscal flexibility to meet defense costs in subsequent years.

6. *Military End-Item Aid*

Turning now to military end-item aid in 1955, we summarize the relevant data on the Military Assistance Program (MAP)[37] in Table 21, below.

---

expenditures in both Pakistan and Thailand. Between 1955 and 1956, for example, budget deficits in both countries approximately doubled. See *Economic Survey of Asia and the Far East, 1956*, p. 186.

[35] The distinction is between total savings, and that portion of savings readily convertible or transferable into foreign exchange by lowering imports or increasing exports.

[36] International Cooperation Administration *Counterpart Funds*, June 30, 1955, pp. 26, 38-39; and *Counterpart Funds*, June 30, 1956, pp. 26, 36-37.

[37] See above, pp. 187-188.

Table 21

MILITARY ASSISTANCE APPROPRIATIONS,
FISCAL YEAR 1955[a]

	Appropriations and Regional Obligations Ceilings[b] (millions of dollars)	Proportion of Total (per cent)
Europe	(414.9)	34.8
Near East, Africa, and South Asia	(181.2)	15.2
Far East (Asia) and the Pacific	(583.6)	48.9
American Republics	(13.0)	1.1
TOTALS	1,192.7	100.0

[a] Beginning in 1955, funds for military end-item assistance were appropriated on a global, rather than regional, basis. The total amount ($1,192.7 million) shown was the amount appropriated globally, including $100 million for European infrastructure. (See *Mutual Security Appropriation Act of 1955*, in *Mutual Security Legislation and Related Documents*, p. 75.) Instead of specific regional appropriations, as in prior years, the Mutual Security Act of 1954 specified obligations ceilings for the separate regions. The dollar figures shown in parentheses in Table 21 are the regional ceilings specified in the Act, except in the case of Europe. Because of the large amount of unobligated MAP funds for Europe, remaining from prior years and reappropriated in 1955 (see footnote [b], below), we assume that the entire difference between the sum of the regional ceilings ($1,192.7 million), and the total amount originally proposed by the Administration for MAP ($1,580.0 million), represented a reduction in available funds for Europe. See *House-Senate Conference Report on the Mutual Security Act of 1954*, p. 58.

[b] The amounts shown in Table 21 represent only *new* appropriations. They are in addition to $2,422.5 million of unobligated funds remaining from prior years which were specifically reappropriated for use in 1955. The figures shown above compare with the following MAP proposals, originally submitted by the Administration (millions of dollars):

Europe	$ 802.2
Near East, Africa, and South Asia	181.2
Far East (Asia) and the Pacific	583.6
American Republics	13.0
TOTAL	$1,580.0

The Mutual Security Act of 1954, House Hearings, pp. 37, 214, 256, 366.

In relation to the corresponding data for 1954,[38] total MAP appropriations in 1955 represented a reduction of over 60 per cent. Even in relation to the original proposals made by the Executive Branch for end-item aid in 1955, the figures shown in Table 21 represented a reduction of nearly 25 per cent.[39] In both cases, the reason for the reduced appropriations was the same. Unobligated balances, amount-

[38] See above, Table 17.   [39] See Table 21, footnote [b].

ing to nearly $2.5 billion and concentrated largely in the European segment of the program, remained from prior years' appropriations for end-item aid. As distinct from unexpended but obligated military funds,[40] the large amount of unobligated funds could not properly be explained by the lead-time of end-item deliveries. Their explanation lay, rather, in the stretch-out of NATO force goals previously mentioned.[41] Effective absorption of end-item aid was sharply restricted by European defense outlays. The estimated marginal contribution of end-item aid to European defensive strength consequently tended to decline more rapidly than in the earlier, precoexistence years. A sharply reduced MAP appropriation for Europe in 1955 was the result.

Within the Asian area, a major shift occurred in the allocation of end-item aid. The Administration's proposals for military aid to Asia had originally included a large share to continue the force buildup envisaged by the Navarre Plan in Viet Nam, Cambodia, and Laos.[42] With signature of the Geneva agreements in July 1954, the purpose of the Indochina force buildup was dissipated. Though costs of maintenance and training of the existing national forces of Viet Nam, Cambodia, and Laos continued to exercise a strong claim on military-support aid, the need for additional military end-items was considerably reduced by the ending of hostilities.[43] At the same time as termination of the Indochina war led to reduced MAP allocations to Viet Nam, Cambodia, and Laos, the formation of SEATO resulted in substantially increased end-term aid to the Asian members of the pact.[44]

[40] See Chapter 4, above, Table 5. Obligated, but unexpended, military aid funds were over $9 billion at the end of fiscal 1954. See *The Mutual Security Act of 1954*, House Hearings, pp. 33-34.

[41] See above, Chapter 5, section C.1.

[42] Testifying on the Mutual Security Program for 1955 in April 1954, the Deputy Assistant Secretary of State for Far Eastern Affairs stated that the proposed program "provides $308 million for mutual defense assistance in the form of military supplies and equipment for the forces in the French Union and the Associated States of Indochina which are essential for them to withstand and defeat the Communist Viet Minh." *The Mutual Security Act of 1954*, House Hearings, pp. 251-252.

[43] Although neither the United States nor the Vietnamese Governments were signatories, the Geneva armistice agreements forbade the introduction of additional military equipment into Viet Nam, except for replacement on a "piece-for-piece . . . basis." See *Documents on American Foreign Relations, 1954*, New York, 1955, pp. 291-292.

[44] Military end-item aid to the non-SEATO countries in Asia (namely Japan, Formosa, and Korea), with which the United States had mutual defense treaties, also rose in 1955. *Report to Congress on the Mutual Security Program*, December 31, 1954, pp. 12-18, and in the same source, June 30, 1955, pp. 2, 11-14.

In Pakistan and Thailand, especially, increased end-item aid was ostensibly related to enhancing military capabilities to resist possible direct external attack, presumably by or with support from Communist China. In the case of Pakistan, it can be argued that the country's geographic and social cleavages would have tended to make the costs of *internal* security—or what we have referred to previously as a "one-country" war— relatively high, and hence warranted an expansion of end-item aid, quite apart from the requirements for resisting *external* aggression. Nevertheless, the size and character of the expanded MAP was, in fact, related to the external attack contingency (that is, a "two-or-more-country" war).[45] And for this type of contingency, it is by no means clear that the expanded program made sense. Actually, there is only one contingency involving external attack against Pakistan to which a reasonably high probability could be assigned: an attack by India. And it is highly questionable whether additional military strength could be expected to contribute anything toward meeting this contingency.

More specifically, it is not at all clear that the possibility of an Indian attack was made less likely as a result of additional military aid to Pakistan, or even that such an attack, if it did occur, would be more effectively met by Pakistan. Instead, diversion of additional Indian resources to military uses was likely to result, leaving the relative strength of the two countries' military forces unaffected. It can be argued, however, that the same relative military strength at a higher *absolute* level might reduce the chance of a war. Assume, for example, that the potential gains to either India or Pakistan from initiating war against the other are unaffected by an increase in the military strength of both. If the bilateral increase in military strength leaves *relative* strengths unaffected, the costs to each of waging a war are likely to go up. A ten-division war is likely to be more costly than a five-division war. If the likelihood of an Indo-Pakistan war is presumed to depend on the relation between gains and costs to either side from initiating war, the higher costs of a possible war may reduce its likelihood.

The argument is intriguing and is perhaps one of the more persuasive reasons for expanded end-item aid to Pakistan in 1955. Yet the argument also entails some major difficulties. For one thing, the pro-

[45] See above, Chapter 4, pp. 104-105. The expressed aim of the expanded end-item program in Pakistan was "to enable Pakistan to increase the effectiveness of its army, navy and air forces and substantially strengthen its defenses against external aggression." *Report to Congress on the Mutual Security Program*, June 30, 1955, p. 20.

spective diminution in the gain-cost ratio might actually trigger a "preventive" war. India, for example, might prefer to initiate war rather than to face a continuing rise in the costs of maintaining a military balance with Pakistan. Moreover, it can be contended that, in a situation as unstable as Kashmir, the likelihood of an Indo-Pakistan war arising from "rational" gain-cost calculations is small, while the likelihood of its arising from a random "incident" is relatively large. If incidents are more probable where more troops on both sides are in contact, a bilateral military buildup would enhance the chance of an accidental war. On balance, it is not clear that stepped-up military aid to Pakistan in 1955 reduced the chance of an Indian attack or, if it did, that this reduction was greater than the increased chance of an Indo-Pakistan war arising, not from an Indian attack, but from incidental causes.

As far as the possibility of a Chinese attack against Pakistan is concerned, there are several reasons why it seems of sufficiently low likelihood to be set aside. In the case of an attack on East Pakistan, the intervening Indian border would seem, paradoxically enough, to be a fairly reliable deterrent. Given the negligible gains from such an attack in the first place, the inconvenience costs to China of violating the Indian border would probably reduce the likelihood of such an attack to negligible proportions, unless China were to attack East Pakistan as a follow-up to a direct attack against India. In the case of West Pakistan, some of the highest mountains in the world traverse the 200-mile common border between it and China. Logistically, an attack across this segment of the Himalayas would be costly to conduct. It would, too, be quite unambiguous. There is no local irredentism that China could use as a pretext for supporting a local insurrection with Chinese "volunteers." Because a Chinese attack would tend to be unambiguous, it would increase the attacker's costs still further by adding the costs of occupation in a hostile country to those of the attack itself. Finally, the need to conduct an unambiguous attack would confront the attacker with a stronger prospect of U.S. intervention, and hence discourage the initial attack. For these reasons, it would seem that the probability of a Chinese attack may have been too small to warrant expanded end-item aid to Pakistan.

In the case of Thailand, the likelihood that an external attack would be ambiguous was perhaps greater than in Pakistan. The creation of a "Free Thai" government—presumably a potential source of ambiguity—in Yunnan was, for example, explicitly cited as one threat to Thailand's security which MAP sought to meet.[46] But whether a potential attack were directly and unambiguously started by China, or, more ambiguously, by the "Free Thai" and by North Viet Nam with Chinese support, the same question arises. In the range over which military aid to Thailand was considered, it is doubtful that it was sufficient to contribute to Thailand's ability to meet either contingency.

As with allocations of non-MAP aid to Thailand,[47] it would seem that validation of increased military end-item aid in Thailand in 1955, as in the other Asian SEATO countries, requires the assumption of a rise in the relative disutility or "worth" parameters for given contingencies associated with those countries, as a result of the Manila agreements. In effect, the "value" of the SEATO members to the United States seems implicitly to have been increased by virtue of the pact itself, resulting in substantially increased MAP allocations to these countries.

At issue here are the larger questions of what benefits the United States derives from its SEATO alliance, and how or whether these benefits should affect the allocation of military aid, questions which we shall take up in discussing the objectives of military aid in Chapter 7.

7. Surplus Agricultural Commodity Assistance

In concluding this summary of the Mutual Security Program in Southern Asia in 1955, brief mention should be made of a related program of bilateral United States assistance which began during the period. The Agricultural Trade and Development Act, approved in July 1954, established as United States policy ". . . the maximum efficient use of surplus agricultural commodities in furtherance of the foreign policy of the United States."[48] Title I of the Act authorized the sale abroad for foreign currencies of surplus agricultural commodities from stocks of the Commodity Credit Corporation. In turn, the local currency proceeds were to be used for certain stipulated purposes, including "loans to promote multilateral trade and eco-

---

[46] *Report to Congress on the Mutual Security Program, December 31, 1954*, Washington, D.C., 1955, pp. 19-20. There is, however, some question how "ambiguous" a "Free Thai" attack on Thailand across intervening Laos could be.

[47] See above, pp. 199-200.

[48] Public Law 480, 83rd Congress, see *Mutual Security Legislation and Related Documents*, pp. 131-138.

nomic development." While administrative responsibility for Title I was delegated by the President to the Department of Agriculture, responsibility for the use of local currency proceeds for this particular purpose was vested in the agency administering the Mutual Security Program: the Foreign Operations Administration until fiscal year 1956, later the International Cooperation Administration.

By July 1956, Congress had increased the $700 million authorization originally specified in the Act to $3 billion. Use of the Title I authority in Southern Asia did not get underway until the following fiscal year.[49] When it did, it provided a source of development assistance in Southern Asia on a scale considerably larger than economic aid available under the Mutual Security Program, and for an essentially similar purpose.[50]

C. The Second Year of Coexistence

While the Mutual Security Program for 1956 was in preparation, the same paradoxical circumstances we have previously associated with "coexistence" continued to dominate international affairs. Smiles and threats were both in evidence. On the one hand, for example, the protracted meetings of the five-nation UN Disarmament Sub-committee took a more encouraging turn. In May 1955, the Soviet Union made proposals which seemed to contain a number of concessions to Western views concerning both disarmament and nuclear weapons control. It appeared to some "that negotiations had been budged from dead-center and the foundation for a new approach had been laid" by the Soviet proposals.[51]

Similarly tending to support the "peaceful" element in coexistence was the growing evidence of Soviet readiness to provide credits and technical aid to the underdeveloped and neutralist countries in Southern Asia and the Middle East. Besides moving expeditiously to implement its earlier (1954) credits to Afghanistan for grain ele-

[49] Title II of the Agricultural Trade and Development Act authorized grants of up to $300 million in surplus commodities for famine and other urgent relief requirements abroad. Surplus foodstuffs, valued at $10 million, were provided to Pakistan under Title II during 1955. See International Cooperation Administration, *Operations Report*, June 30, 1957, p. 80.

[50] See below, pp. 221, 232. For a fuller account of Public Law 480, and the use of agricultural surpluses to raise internal investment in underdeveloped countries, see B. F. Johnston, "Farm Surpluses and Foreign Policy," *World Politics*, October 1957, pp. 6, 18-20; and F.A.O., *Uses of Agricultural Surpluses to Finance Economic Development in Underdeveloped Areas—A Pilot Study in India*, Rome, June 1955.

[51] H. W. Barber, *The United States in World Affairs, 1955*, New York, 1957, p. 273.

vators and petroleum storage tanks, the Soviet Union made additional aid offers to India, Indonesia, and Burma, as well as Afghanistan, during the period that the 1956 Mutual Security Program was in preparation. This facet of the Soviet Union's conciliatory policy was underscored by the signature in February 1955 of a credit agreement with India to cover the direct foreign exchange costs of a steel plant at Bhilai.[52]

Yet, on the other hand, some developments in the Soviet Union had a harsher quality. Soviet tests of nuclear weapons, for example, increased both in frequency and in the size of weapons tested.[53] And the change in Soviet leadership in February 1955, with its accompanying reemphasis on heavy industry, was no more reassuring.

Moves by the Communist Bloc in Asia showed similar flexibility and ambivalence. China's threats against Formosa were intensified by occupation of the Tachen Islands and raids against Quemoy and Matsu in February and March 1955. In Laos, the Pathet-Lao, with support from China and North Viet Nam, effectively partitioned the country by forcibly preventing the return of the Laotian civil administration.[54] At the same time, Chou En-lai participated in the Afro-Asian Conference in Bandung, blandly and effectively reiterating China's support for the "five principles" of peaceful coexistence.

In effect, "coexistence" meant that a wider range of foreign policy choices was open to the Sino-Soviet Bloc than formerly. As circumstances varied, different choices could be made. Covert military support might be extended to local guerrilla forces, like the Pathet-Lao, with the possibility of more extensive support later. Burma, hardly less than Laos, provided such an opportunity. At the same time, faithful application of the "five principles" could be adopted by the Bloc in other countries in which the internal difficulties encountered by new and inexperienced governments, attempting to generate economic development, might give local communist parties a growing

[52] See *Soviet Technical Assistance*, Technical Assistance Programs, Senate Foreign Relations Committee, Washington, D.C., 1956, pp. 10, 17-20, 26-33. For a discussion of the scope and implications of Soviet Bloc economic aid to Southern Asia, see below, Chapter 11.

[53] On September 17, 1954, for example, TASS announced that "a new type of atomic weapon" had been tested, and again on November 27, 1954, that tests of "new types of atomic and thermonuclear weapons recently (were) carried out." *Current Digest of the Soviet Press*, Vol. vi, No. 37, p. 23, and Vol. vii, No. 48, p. 30. In February 1955, Deputy Premier Molotov claimed that the Soviet Union had a "lead" over the United States in nuclear weapons development. The *New York Times*, February 9, 1955, p. 1.

[54] Barber, *op.cit.*, pp. 115-116.

chance to come to power, perhaps directly through the electoral process. In Asia, given adequate time, India and Indonesia seemed to provide examples of the latter possibility.

The Mutual Security Program for 1956 was affected by these changes in the international context in two principal ways. It placed greater allocation emphasis on the Asian area, where the opportunities for and evidence of Soviet Bloc maneuvering seemed most worrisome. And it accorded more prominence to the political dangers of economic malperformance in the Asian countries—to what we earlier referred to as the "lesson" of China.

1. Allocation Emphasis on Asia

The emphasis on the Asian area, already marked in 1954 and 1955, is suggested by the following table summarizing regional obligations, other than those for MAP, under the 1956 program. It is hardly necessary to recall the previous comments we have made about the diversity of U.S. objectives underlying the non-MAP obligations shown in Table 22. Though the table records non-MAP allocations in 1956, it does *not* record allocations for "non-military" objectives alone. Military objectives, conceived mainly in terms of reaching or maintaining stipulated country force levels, affected the allocations shown in Table 22 directly and significantly.

If we make some simple, but not unrealistic, assumptions about the allocations shown in Table 22, we can attribute those in Indochina, Korea, and Formosa, for example, primarily to military objectives.[55] As a first approximation, it can be said that not only did the Asian share of global aid rise slightly over the preceding year (from about

[55] In Formosa and Viet Nam, for example, internal military expenditures represented, respectively, 83 per cent and 73 per cent of total budgetary outlays in 1955-1956. See *Economic Survey of Asia and the Far East, 1956*, pp. 189-190. If we assume that the *net* resources contributed to a given sector by U.S. aid depend on that sector's share in total government outlays, we can identify the military sector as the predominant beneficiary of U.S. aid in these countries. We can then attribute military objectives, in the sense indicated above, to aid allocations to these countries by assuming that the sector actually benefiting from aid was the sector *intended* to benefit.

The initial assumption, that a sector's *net* receipts from aid are a function of the sector's share in total budgetary outlays, is probably reasonable when the amount of aid is large relative to total government outlays and when the amount of "non-project" aid is large relative to total aid. Both conditions applied in the countries mentioned. Aid obligations in both Formosa and Viet Nam in 1956 represented almost half of total government outlays, and the bulk of the aid provided consisted of "general and miscellaneous," that is, largely "non-project," rather than project, assistance. See *ibid.*, and (i'), p. 57.

Table 22

UNITED STATES ECONOMIC AND TECHNICAL ASSISTANCE AND
MILITARY SUPPORT TO SOUTHERN ASIA IN FISCAL YEAR 1956
COMPARED TO TOTAL ASIAN AND GLOBAL NON-MAP ASSISTANCE
UNDER THE MUTUAL SECURITY ACT OF 1955[a]

	Obligations	As Proportion of:	
		Total Asian Aid	Global Aid
	(millions of dollars)	(per cent)	
1. Economic and Technical Aid to Southern Asia	266.5	27.8	18.7
2. Military Support for Southern Asia	297.9	31.0	20.8
3. Total Non-MAP Aid to Southern Asia (1+2)	564.4	58.8	39.5
4. Non-MAP Aid to Formosa and Korea[b]	395.7	41.2	27.7
5. Total Asian Non-MAP Aid (3+4)	960.1	100.0	67.2
6. Global Non-MAP Aid Under the Mutual Security Act of 1955	1,428.1	–	100.0

Sources: Table 24, below, and (i'), p. 57.

[a] Beginning in 1956, obligations for "direct forces support," that is, software provided directly to the military forces of recipient countries, were consolidated in a subcategory called "construction and consumables" as part of MAP. (See below, Table 25, footnote [a].) Consequently, "non-MAP" assistance, as used in Table 22, refers to a somewhat smaller segment of the over-all Mutual Security Program than what we have referred to as "non-MAP," or "non-MDAP," assistance in prior years. (See Table 20, footnote [a].)

[b] Of the amount shown in (4), $69.9 million represented obligations in Formosa and $325.8 million, obligations in Korea. Only $250 thousand of the newly appropriated $100 million Asian Economic Development Fund was obligated in 1956. (See below, p. 213.)

64 per cent in 1955 to 67 per cent in 1956).[56] But, in addition, the share allocated for primarily military objectives in Asia remained

[56] See Table 20, above. As a comparison of Tables 20 and 22 shows, the absolute amount of non-MAP obligations in the Asian area appears to have dropped slightly in 1956. Actually, the reduction was more apparent than real. Because of changes in aid labels, the data in Table 22 don't mean exactly what they say, and don't say exactly what they (should) mean. Part of the apparent reduction represents simply a relabeling of the "direct forces support" component of what we have called "military support," and its consolidation with the MAP. (See Table 24, footnote [a], below.) The rest of the apparent reduction reflects the $100 million Presidential Fund for Asian Development which was appropriated, but not obligated, in 1956. (See the discussion in the text below, pp. 212-213.)

approximately constant (military support obligations in Southern Asia, together with obligations in Korea and Formosa, were about 49 per cent of global aid, excluding MAP, in 1955 and in 1956); and the share allocated for primarily "non-military" objectives in Southern Asia (economic and technical aid obligations) rose from 15 per cent in 1955 to nearly 19 per cent of global aid in 1956.

The objection can be raised that the distinction between military and non-military objectives is misleading. What we have called "military objectives" entailed important non-military considerations as well. The survival of free government in Viet Nam, for example, was—at a higher objectives level—the reason for maintaining Vietnamese force goals. To liquidate the remnant Viet Minh guerrillas, as well as to absorb or liquidate the private military forces of the "loyal" politico-religious sects in South Viet Nam, required large Vietnamese national military forces. The point, however, is that the latter was a major, if *intermediate*, objective of U.S. aid to Viet Nam. From this standpoint, the objectives of aid to Viet Nam can be distinguished from those, for example, of aid to India.[57]

2. *The Objective of Political Stability*

As might have been expected from the increased relative and absolute allocations for economic and technical aid shown in Table 22, the non-military, "political-stabilizing" objective of aid to Southern Asia received added emphasis in the Administration's presentation of the Mutual Security Program for 1956. In testifying on the program, Secretary Dulles stated:

"International communism is pressing hard to extend its influence in Asian countries which lack the economic strength to support an adequate defense establishment and to provide the necessary foundation of political stability and steadily improving living conditions. By means of the Manila Pact and other defense treaties, we have placed the communists on notice regarding the danger to them of further armed aggression in that area. But this is not all we can and should do. We know that nations which are economically weak find it difficult to become politically strong and nationally secure. We believe that an increase in free Asia's economic strength can be another effective resistant to communism."[58]

[57] See the discussion of objectives levels, below, Chapter 7.
[58] *Mutual Security Act of 1955*, Hearings before the House Committee on Foreign Affairs, 84th Congress, 1st session, Washington, D.C., 1955, p. 3.

And in response to a specific question concerning the relative "need for financial and military aid in Asia" compared to prior years, the Secretary replied:

"The need for economic aid is, I think, very much greater; and the need for military aid is about the same as it was last year. . . . One half of all the [Mutual Security] funds sought is for straight military assistance; . . . another quarter is for defense [military] support. . . . And then the balance . . . is economic assistance, which is not directly related to any military operation. Of that, almost all is in Asia and is designed to help promote the over-all economies of Asia, so as to give the people there hope that out of a free economy they can have some sort of capital development comparable to what is going on in the Soviet and Chinese communist world."[59]

Assistant Secretary George Allen expressed a similar view of the updated China "lesson" in the period of coexistence:

"What is the impact of communism upon these [South Asian] countries and their people? I think we must all recognize the fact that if these governments are unable to carry out their plans for economic development, and if they are unable to bring tangible benefits to their people under a democratic system, then the claim of the communist Chinese that they alone possess the formula for bringing rapid economic development . . . will sound increasingly convincing. Our programs aid materially in the achievement of economic improvement and in this way serve the national interest of the United States."[60]

Another indication of this view was the new "President's Fund for Asian Economic Development," an addition to the categories of assistance in previous Mutual Security Programs. Two hundred million dollars were originally proposed for the Fund, to be used exclusively in the "arc of free Asia . . . for financing economic development projects of importance to the programs of two or more countries."[61]

Criteria for allocating the proposed regional Fund among recipient countries were not clearly specified, either in the Administration's original proposals or in the authorizing legislation as finally enacted. Besides specifying that not less than 50 per cent of the Fund should

[59] *Mutual Security Appropriations for 1956*, Hearings before the Committee on Appropriations, 84th Congress, 1st session, Washington, D.C., June 1955, pp. 6-7.

[60] *Mutual Security Act of 1955*, House Hearings, *op.cit.*, pp. 112-114.

[61] Foreign Operations Administration, *Mutual Security Program*, Fiscal Year 1956 Estimates, Congressional Presentation Book, Washington, D.C., Vol. II, p. 343. As originally proposed, use of the Fund was, "to the maximum extent feasible, . . . [to] be on the basis of repayment to the United States in dollars or local currency." See also, *Mutual Security Act of 1955*, House Hearings, pp. 90, 99-100, *et passim*.

be extended as (dollar or local currency) loans, the authorizing legislation stated that preference should be given "to projects or programs that will clearly contribute to promoting greater economic strength in the area *as a whole*, or among a *group* or *groups of countries* of the area." Beyond this, the President was given complete discretion in allocating the Fund within the area over a three-year period.[62] Despite this latitude, the size of the proposed Fund was large relative to the amounts proposed for the individual countries of the region.

3. *Economic Assistance and Military Support in 1956*

Table 23 shows the 1956 country proposals for Southern Asia, together with the unallocated Asian regional Fund. The total amount of economic and technical aid—excluding military support—specifically proposed for individual countries in 1956 was $271 million compared to the unallocated regional Fund of $200 million.

By contrast, actual obligations from the regional Fund in fiscal 1956 were negligible in comparison with obligations for bilateral economic and technical assistance from regular Mutual Security appropriations. Table 24 shows the relevant aid obligations in 1956. Although appropriations for the proposed Fund were reduced by the Congress to $100 million, the Fund's limited use in 1956 was not due to this reduction. Rather, it was due to the fact that appropriations for the regional Fund were authorized by the Mutual Security Act of 1955 to be available over a three-year period. Consequently, there was less pressure than usual on the administering agency to obligate available funds during the year of appropriation (1956). This, together with the lack of explicit allocation criteria governing the Fund's use, and the inherent difficulty of formulating projects that would be acceptable to the "group or groups of countries" affected by them, accounted for the lag of obligations under the Asian regional development Fund.[63]

4. *Changes in Country Proposals and Obligations*

In the individual country proposals and obligations figures shown in Tables 23 and 24, respectively, two of the larger absolute differ-

---

[62] Italics added. See *Mutual Security Act of 1955*, Public Law 138, 84th Congress, 1st session, July 8, 1955, Sec. 418.

[63] Besides the obligations from the Fund shown in Table 24, 1.9 million was obligated in 1957 for a Telecommunications Survey in Southeast Asia. Thus, at the end of fiscal 1957, nearly all of the original $100 million Fund was still unobligated. International Cooperation Administration, *Operations Report*, June 30, 1957, p. 25.

Table 23

FUNDS PROPOSED BY THE EXECUTIVE BRANCH FOR UNITED STATES
ECONOMIC AND TECHNICAL ASSISTANCE AND MILITARY
SUPPORT TO SOUTHERN ASIA, FISCAL YEAR 1956[a]

(by country and project use)

	(1)	(2)	(3)	(4)	(5)	(6)	(7)	(8)
				Project Use				
Country	Agri-culture	Industry	Trans-porta-tion	Health	Labor	Public Admin-istra-tion	Edu-cation	Com-munity Devel-opment
				(millions of dollars)				
Afghanistan[b]	.86	.07	—	.14	—	.08	.69	.16
Burma[c]	—	—	—	—	—	—	—	—
Ceylon[d]	—	—	—	—	—	—	—	—
India[e]	10.04	23.19	6.15	7.91	.27	.14	1.62	1.43
Indochina[f]	2.60	2.78	16.70	1.51	.05	3.28	1.05	7.96
Indonesia[g]	1.56	2.08	.23	.46	.64	1.04	1.22	.29
Nepal[h]	.63	.27	.58	.15	—	—	.15	.22
Pakistan[i]	16.90	14.10	3.15	3.00	.02	.12	2.10	1.10
Philippines[j]	3.85	2.15	3.58	2.18	.19	1.35	1.19	.01
Thailand[k]	1.54	4.47	5.07	1.27	.05	.26	1.85	—
TOTALS	37.98	49.11	35.46	16.62	1.22	6.27	9.87	11.17
Project Total as Proportion of Regional Total				(per cent)				
	14.0	18.1	13.1	6.1	.5	2.3	3.7	4.1

Σ Col (1)/Σ Col (10), Σ Col (2)/Σ Col (10), etc.

(continued)

Source: Appendix II.
[a] For further explanation of the data in Table 23, see above, Table 7, footnote [a].
[b] (u), p. 218; and (a).
[c] See above, Table 15, footnote [c].
[d] See above, Table 11, footnote [d].
[e] (u), p. 227; (v), p. 232; (w), p. 139; and (x), p. 299. The figures shown represent both technical assistance ($15.0 million) and development assistance ($70.0 million). For an explanation of the development assistance category, see Chapter 6, section B.1. The sectoral breakdown of the proposed development assistance was: $6.0 million for agriculture; $20.0 million for industry; $6.0 million for transportation; $4.0 million for health; and $34.0 million for general and miscellaneous. The latter was largely for surplus agricultural commodities with the rupee proceeds to be used for internal development outlays under Section 402 of the Mutual Security Act of 1954, as amended. See above, Table 16, footnote [c].
[f] (w), p. 323. The $38.6 million shown for Indochina in column (10), the sum of col-

umns (1) through (9), includes both technical assistance and that part of so-called "defense support" designated for specific projects, and, in the case of column (9), for saleable commodity imports intended to generate local currency for specific projects. The $386.4 million shown in column (11) includes the remainder of "defense support," as well as $38.2 million of what was originally proposed as "direct forces support," but was later transferred to MAP and to Defense Department administration. Apart from the share allotted in the Administration's proposals for specific projects or sectors, the bulk of the assistance carrying the "defense support" label represented straight budgetary support for the Cambodian, Laotian, and Vietnamese government budgets. Since over 70 per cent of collective public expenditures in the three countries represented direct defense outlays, and an additional fraction represented outlays indirectly related to defense, for example, relief for refugees from North Viet Nam, all non-project "defense support" has been included

Table 23 (continued)

(9)	(10)	(11)	(12)	(13)	(14)
	Project Use			Country Total as Proportion of Regional Total	
General and Miscellaneous	Total Excluding Military Support	Military Support	President's Fund[1]	Excluding Military Support Col (10)/Σ Col (10)	Including Military Support Col (10) + Col (11) / Σ Col (10) + Σ Col (11)
(millions of dollars)				(per cent)	
–	2.00	–	–	.7	.3
–	–	–	–	–	–
34.25	85.00	–	–	31.4	12.3
2.67	38.60	386.40	–	14.2	61.8
.48	8.00	–	–	2.9	1.2
–	2.00	–	–	.7	.3
31.51	72.00	20.00	–	26.6	13.4
11.70	26.20	2.30	–	9.7	4.1
22.79	37.30	8.20	–	13.8	6.6
103.40	271.10	416.90	200.0	100.0	100.0
(per cent)					
38.1	100.0				

in "military support" (column [11]).

g (u), p. 270; and (a).

h (u), p. 236.

i (w), p. 246. The $72.0 million shown in column (10) includes both technical assistance ($9.0 million) and so-called "defense support" ($63.0 million). None of the $31.5 million shown as general and miscellaneous (column [9]) has been allotted to the military support category (column [11]) because, compared to Indochina (see above, footnote f), military outlays were a considerably smaller portion of total government expenditures in Pakistan, and also because, in practice, *none* of the sales proceeds generated by saleable commodity imports in Pakistan were withdrawn for military use. (See [e'], p. 8.) The $20.0 million shown for military support, column (11), was proposed as "direct forces support."

j (u), p. 304. Columns (1) through (10) include both technical assistance ($6.5 million) and so-called "defense support" ($19.7 million). None of the latter has been allotted to the military support category (column

[11]), for essentially the same reasons as mentioned in footnote i, above. As in the case of Pakistan, only the proposed "direct forces support," representing "common-use" items for the military, has been included in "military support" (column [11]).

k (w), p. 314. Columns (1) through (10) include both technical assistance ($5.5 million) and so-called "defense support" ($31.8 million). None of the latter has been allotted to the military support category, column (11), for essentially the same reasons mentioned in footnote i, above. As in Pakistan and the Philippines, only the "direct forces support," representing common-use items for the military, has been included in column (11).

1 President's Fund for Asian Economic Development. Japan, Korea, and Formosa were also eligible for assistance from the regional Fund, but the projects submitted by the Administration to illustrate possible uses of the proposed Fund were concentrated in Southern Asia. (See [w], pp. 346-348.)

Table 24

FUNDS OBLIGATED FOR UNITED STATES ECONOMIC AND TECHNICAL
ASSISTANCE AND MILITARY SUPPORT TO SOUTHERN ASIA,
FISCAL YEAR 1956[a]

(by country and project use)

	(1)	(2)	(3)	(4)	(5)	(6)	(7)	(8)
				Project Use				
Country	Agri-culture	Industry	Trans-porta-tion	Health	Labor	Public Admin-istra-tion	Edu-cation	Com-munity Devel-opment
				(millions of dollars)				
Afghanistan[b]	1.24	.14	14.80	.03	–	.64	1.02	.03
Burma[c]	–	–	–	–	–	–	–	–
Ceylon[d]	1.91	.03	1.88	.01	–	–	.58	–
India[e]	8.23	5.92	14.19	4.19	.37	.11	2.02	.26
Indochina[f]	3.70	1.08	18.14	2.11	.06	3.59	.80	8.69
Cambodia	(.95)	(.45)	(9.07)	(.62)	–	(.04)	(.33)	(.06)
Laos	(.78)	(.10)	(2.99)	(.35)	–	(.99)	(.14)	(.16)
Viet Nam	(1.97)	(.53)	(6.08)	(1.14)	(.06)	(2.56)	(.33)	(8.47)
Indonesia[g]	1.35	1.41	.25	3.66	.15	2.24	.94	.40
Nepal[h]	.12	.11	–	.49	–	–	.18	.22
Pakistan[i]	7.18	10.87	10.39	4.32	–	.14	2.06	1.72
Philippines[j]	4.15	1.60	3.20	2.52	.22	.71	.93	.32
Thailand[k]	1.78	.34	8.54	1.04	.04	.36	1.80	.01
TOTALS	29.66	21.50	71.39	18.37	.84	7.79	10.33	11.65
Project Total as Proportion of Regional Total				(per cent)				
	11.1	8.1	26.8	6.9	.3	2.9	3.9	4.4

Σ Col (1)/Σ Col (10), Σ Col (2)/Σ Col (10), etc.

(*continued*)

Source: Appendix II.

[a] See above, Chapter 4, Table 3, footnote a, for explanation of categories and terms used in this table. In 1956, unlike 1954 and 1955, what we have called "military support" obligations (column [11]) exclude software provided directly to the military forces of recipient countries. Responsibility for these so-called "common-use" items (direct forces support), was transferred to the Defense Department and consolidated with end-item (MAP) aid.

[b] (z), pp. 29, 34-35; and (a). The figures shown represent both technical assistance ($3.0 million) and development assistance ($15.3 million). Of the latter, $.5 million was for agriculture and $14.8 million for air transport. $5.0 million of the development assistance was provided as a long-term Mutual Security loan. *Report to Congress on the Mutual Security Program, June 30, 1956,* Washington, D.C., 1956, p. 8; and (g), p. 59.

[c] See above, Chapter 5, Table 16, footnote d.

[d] (z), pp. 29, 34-35; and (a). The figures

Table 24 (continued)

(9)	(10)	(11)	(12)	(13)	(14)
	Project Use			Country Total as Proportion of Regional Total	
General and Miscellaneous	Total Excluding Military Support	Military Support	President's Fund[l]	Excluding Military Support Col (10)/Σ Col (10)	Including Military Support Col (10) + Col (11) / Σ Col (10) + Σ Col (11)
(millions of dollars)				(per cent)	
.40	18.30	–	–	6.9	3.2
–	–	–	–	–	–
.59	5.00	–	–	1.9	.9
25.59	60.88	–	–	22.8	10.8
3.36	41.53	254.51	–	15.6	52.4
(.68)	(12.20)	(32.89)	–	(4.6)	(8.0)
(1.10)	(6.61)	(42.04)	–	(2.5)	(8.6)
(1.58)	(22.72)	(179.58)	–	(8.5)	(35.8)
.70	11.10	–	–	4.2	2.0
.84	1.96	–	–	.7	.3
30.00	66.68	40.88	–	25.0	19.1
12.93	26.58	2.50	–	10.0	5.2
20.55	34.46	–	–	12.9	6.1
94.96	266.49	297.89	.25	100.0	100.0
(per cent)					
35.6	100.0				

shown represent both technical assistance ($10 million) and development assistance ($4.0 million). Of the latter, $1.4 million was for agriculture; $1.9 million for transportation; $.2 million for education; and $.5 million for general and miscellaneous.

e (z), p. 29; and (a). The figures shown represent both technical assistance ($10.0 million) and development assistance ($50.9 million). Of the latter, $6.0 million was for agriculture; $3.0 million for industry; $14.0 million for transportation; $3.0 million for health; and $24.9 million for general and

miscellaneous, including $6.0 million in surplus agricultural commodities provided under Section 402 of the Mutual Security Act of 1954 as amended. See Table 16, above, footnote c. $37.5 million of the development assistance was provided as a long-term Mutual Security loan. See (i'), p. 72.

f (z), pp. 34-35; and (a). In 1956, for the first time, *all* obligations in the Associated States were made bilaterally by the United States in each individual state. Hence, the three totals can be disaggregated for Cam-

(Continued on following page)

[217]

ences between the two tables, namely those involving allocations for India and the Associated States of Indochina, are also among the easiest to explain.

If we again make the assumption that both the proposals and obligations data represented "optimal" allocations, from the standpoint of the Executive Branch and the Congress respectively; and if we ask what productivity and/or value judgments were necessary to validate the two sets of allocations, we can explain the altered absolute and relative allocation to India in the same terms previously used.[64] Nearly all of the $25 million reduction in the Indian aid, as originally proposed, represented a direct Congressional cut in the Administration's proposal for "development," as distinct from technical assistance to that country. Again, the reasons adduced for the cut were the same as those that had been advanced when Congress cut back the 1953 proposals for India: India's neutralism and its accompany-

[64] See Chapter 5, above, pp. 144-149, 164-170.

(Notes to Table 24 continued)

bodia, Laos, and Viet Nam individually. The obligations shown for the three corresponding rows in columns (1) through (10) represent both technical assistance and so-called "defense support." In dividing the latter between economic aid (columns [1] through [10]) and military support (column [11]), the procedure followed is the same as in 1955 and for the same reasons. (See Table 19, footnote ᵍ.) As in the latter case, it is probably the most reasonable procedure though nonetheless ambiguous. The military support shown in column (11) represents general budgetary support on a scale large relative to the budgets involved and for budgets in which military outlays predominated. As previously discussed, however, resource substitutability precludes the assertion that the military sector was the sole net beneficiary of the aid shown in (11).

Of the aid to Viet Nam, $25 million was provided as a long-term Mutual Security loan. See (i'), p. 72.

ᵍ (c'), pp. 34-35; and (a). The figures shown represent both technical assistance ($7.0 million) and development assistance ($4.1 million). Of the latter, $2.6 million was for health projects, and $1.5 million for public administration projects.

ʰ (c'), pp. 30, 34-35; and (a). The figures represent both technical assistance and development assistance, with the total (column

[10]) approximately equally divided between the two. Obligations for development assistance were for health ($.4 million), community development ($.1 million), and for saleable commodity imports ($.5 million).

ⁱ (c'), pp. 30, 34-35; and (a). The figures shown in columns (1) through (10) represent both technical assistance ($8.7 million) and *part* of "defense support," ($52.0 million). The figure in column (11) represents the part of "defense support" estimated to have contributed to increased defense outlays in Pakistan. Apart from the portion of so-called defense-support aid which was obligated for specific sectors, and is shown in columns (1) through (8), the split between "economic" aid and "military support" is arbitrary. Official records show $70.9 million for general and miscellaneous. In Table 24, this total has been divided between "economic" and "military" support as shown in columns (9) and (11). The division made in the table is based on the fact that military outlays in Pakistan rose by nearly $40 million, and public investment by nearly $30 million between fiscal year 1956 and fiscal year 1957, the figures used in columns (9) and (11), respectively. Interestingly enough, by the end of 1957, no Pakistani withdrawals from the counterpart account, into which the proceeds from general and miscellaneous

ing lack of appreciation for U.S. aid; and the dubious effectiveness of "development assistance" as such.[65]

In brief, the cut in the Indian proposals represented different judgments by the Congress concerning the (lower) productivity of "capital" as contrasted with technical aid, and the (lesser) value to the United States of stimulating development in "neutralist," as contrasted with "friendly," countries.[66] It is unnecessary to mention

[65] The second point was evidenced by the House Appropriations Committee's emphasis on the magnitude of unexpended balances from prior years' appropriations for "capital" assistance. The first point was evidenced by references in the House Committee to "Nehru's pro-communist attitude," and his failure to have "ever paid any compliments to the United States and our foreign policy directly." The quotations are from statements by the Chairman of the House Appropriations Subcommittee on Foreign Operations Appropriations. See *Mutual Security Appropriations for 1956,* Hearings before the House Committee on Appropriations, 84th Congress, 1st session, Washington, D.C., 1955, pp. 294, 310, et passim. It should be noted that the cuts in the Indian program were made in the appropriations legislation *after* the amount originally proposed had been authorized in full.

[66] See above, Chapter 5, pp. 139-149.

(*Notes to Table 24 continued*)

commodity exports were deposited, had been made for direct military purposes. (See [e'], p. 8.)

Of the total shown in column (10), $26.0 million was provided as a long-term Mutual Security loan, (see [i'], p. 72), and $13.7 million in the form of surplus agricultural commodities under Section 402 of the Mutual Security Act of 1954 as amended. (See above, Table 16, footnote c.)

[j] (c'), pp. 34-35; and (a). The figures shown in columns (1) through (10) represent both technical assistance, ($5.9 million) and all of "defense support," ($20.7 million), except for the $2.5 million shown as military support (column [11]). The latter is the amount by which internal military expenditures in the Philippines rose in fiscal 1956. (See *Economic Survey of Asia and the Far East 1956,* Bangkok, 1957, p. 190.) Of total aid, $10.0 million was provided as a long-term Mutual Security loan (i'), p. 72, and $18.36 million represented surplus agricultural commodities furnished under Section 402 of the Mutual Security Act of 1954 as amended. (See above, Table 16, footnote c.)

Besides Mutual Security aid, in March 1956, the Export-Import Bank authorized credits of $65 million to finance imports of U.S. equipment and services by public agencies and private corporations in the Philippines. Subsequently, $19 million of this total

was reauthorized for specific projects during fiscal year 1957. Export-Import Bank of Washington, *Report to the Congress,* Washington, D.C., January-June 1956, pp. 23, 64; and same title, July-December 1956, p. 24.

[k] The figures shown in columns (1) through (10) represent both technical assistance ($5.0 million) and defense support ($29.5 million). No defense support has been listed as military support in 1956 for two reasons: internal military outlays in Thailand actually *fell* slightly (by $1.6 million) in fiscal 1956 at the same time as total budgetary outlays were *rising* appreciably (by $45 million); (*Economic Survey,* 1956, *op.cit.,* p. 190); and counterpart withdrawals for military use in Thailand were negligible through fiscal 1957. For both reasons, it would seem more reasonable to attribute the resources made available through U.S. aid to non-military than to military uses. Consequently, all non-project defense support is shown in column (9), general and miscellaneous, and none under military support. Of the total aid, $10.0 million was provided as a long-term Mutual Security loan, (i'), p. 72.

[l] (i'), p. 25. Of the $100 million actually appropriated for the Fund, only the amount shown was obligated in 1956. See the discussion in the text, pp. 212-213; and p. 233, footnote [l].

[219]

again the inconsistency of these implicit judgments in 1956 with those arrived at on the same issues in 1954 and 1955.

In the case of Cambodia, Laos, and Viet Nam, the large reduction in military support obligations in 1956, compared both to the original 1956 proposals and to obligations in 1955,[67] cannot be explained this way. Actually, Congressional appropriations approximately equaled the amounts originally proposed for the Associated States. The explanation for the reduction in obligations involves two changes in circumstances that occurred during and after the enactment of MSP appropriations. The first was the transfer of administrative responsibility for so-called "direct forces support"[68] ("common-use items")— from ICA to the Defense Department, and the consolidation of this portion of the military support shown in Table 23 with MAP appropriations. Consequently, direct forces support does not appear in the 1956 obligations for non-end-item aid, shown in Table 24, but in Table 25, below. To this extent, of course, the "reduction" in aid to Cambodia, Laos, and Viet Nam is more apparent than real.[69]

There was, however, a "real" reduction in military support obligations, largely because the resource requirements in Viet Nam, both for internal military operations and for refugee relief, were less than had originally been estimated. President Diem's success in absorbing or eliminating the dissident sects, and in helping to make the half-million refugees from North Viet Nam self-supporting, lowered the requirements that had originally been anticipated for these purposes when the 1956 proposals were formulated.[70] In effect, the *marginal* productivity of aid for these purposes fell sooner and faster than originally foreseen, because the *total* productivity of a smaller amount of aid was higher than had been foreseen.

Some of the smaller changes in Tables 23 and 24 are harder to explain than those involving India and Indochina. Specifically, what accounts for the rise in the Afghanistan program (from $2 million proposed for 1956 and obligated in 1955, to $18.3 million obligated in 1956), the start of a program in Ceylon, and the rise in aid to Indonesia (from $8 million proposed for 1956 and $7.0 million obligated in 1955 to $11.1 million obligated in 1956)?

In these three cases, the program increases were made after, but

---

[67] See Table 19 above. [68] See above, Table 24, footnote a.
[69] See footnote 56 above.
[70] *Report to the Congress on the Mutual Security Program, December 31, 1955*, pp. 29-30; and *Report to the Congress on the Mutual Security Program, June 30, 1956*, pp. 23-24.

not directly because of, Congressional action. The increases represented Executive Branch action based on circumstances that had
either not yet arisen, or had not been taken into consideration, when
the 1956 proposals were made. If we again assume, for the sake of
the argument, that the Executive Branch action represented an
"optimal" adaptation to the altered circumstances, how can we account for these program changes?

One is hard pressed to find any economic reason for attributing the
program changes to the enhanced *productivity* of aid in the three
countries. The economic indicators for the three countries do not
suggest that the productivity of capital rose during 1956 in the three
countries, or that it had been inaccurately measured when the initial
1956 proposals were formulated.[71] Nor is there any reason for assuming a rise in "value" parameters for the three countries because of
participation in SEATO. All three countries, in fact, remained outside SEATO, and none signed a military assistance agreement with
the United States.

Only in the case of Indonesia is there some reason for possibly attributing the rise in aid to internal circumstances that might be
viewed as having enhanced the "value" to the United States of trying
to increase political stability. The circumstances, in brief, were
Indonesia's first national elections in September 1955, when the
Indonesian Communist Party received an unanticipatedly high 20
per cent of the popular vote. Even in Indonesia, one may question
the importance of the elections as an influence on U.S. aid compared,
for example, to such other factors as the relatively friendly and cooperative attitude of the interim Burhanuddin government, and
President Sukarno's acceptance of a Presidential invitation to visit
the United States. In any event, the effect of these, and perhaps other,
influences on the implicit Indonesian "value" parameter was considerable. Not only did MSP aid rise, as shown in Table 24. Surplus
commodity aid to Indonesia, amounting to $97.8 million under the
Agricultural Trade and Development Act (Public Law 480), was
also obligated in March 1956, the largest amount of such aid to any
Asian country up to that time.[72]

[71] Or, for that matter, had been measured *at all*, when the 1956 proposals were
formulated.

[72] See above, pp. 206-207. In August 1956, arrangements were concluded for
P.L. 480 sales to India of $360 million. See below, Table 27, footnote e. All P.L. 480
sales values are calculated at the pegged prices maintained for U.S. agricultural
commodities.

Explaining the implicit rise in the relative "value" parameters for Ceylon and Afghanistan is still more devious. Aid to Ceylon was not originally proposed for 1956 by the Executive Branch, because of the same Battle Act considerations which had led (in 1953) to the suspension of such aid barely after it had begun.[73] But, as Administration witnesses testified, and as the Congressional committees urged during the 1956 Hearings, the ban on aid to Ceylon was being reconsidered within the Executive Branch.[74] Nor is there much doubt as to the reason for this reconsideration. At the Afro-Asian Conference in Bandung in April 1955, Ceylon had shown strong and unexpected verbal support for the West, as well as unequivocal warnings to the other participants about the dangers of international communism in the Afro-Asian area.[75] In effect, Ceylon's public expression of pro-Western sentiments was responsible for an implicit rise in the "value" placed by the United States on aid to Ceylon, and hence for the resumption of such aid.

In the case of Afghanistan, too, the large increase in aid obligations (from $2 million proposed to $18 million obligated)[76] was due to altered international circumstances, rather than to differing value or productivity judgments applied to constant circumstances by the Congress. Though analyzing the causes of Executive Branch action is bound to be less than exact, it is hard to avoid the conclusion that the most prominent circumstantial change influencing U.S. aid to Afghanistan in 1956 was the Soviet loan commitment of $100 million to Afghanistan in January 1956.[77] Originally announced in December 1955, when Bulganin and Khrushchev were in Kabul, this evi-

[73] See Table 11, footnote d.

[74] See *Mutual Security Act of 1955*, House Committee Hearings, p. 163.

[75] See the testimony of Assistant Secretary of State Allen on the reasons for reconsidering aid to Ceylon, *ibid.*, pp. 136-138, and *Mutual Security Appropriations for 1956*, House Appropriations Hearings, pp. 290-291. For a fuller account of the statement at Bandung by Ceylon's Prime Minister, see George M. Kahin, *The Afro-Asian Conference*, New York, 1956, pp. 18-20.

Notwithstanding the Bandung statement, Ceylon continued its rubber shipments to China, the original reason for suspension of U.S. aid to Ceylon in 1953. Interestingly enough, the House Foreign Affairs Committee which had favored termination of aid to Ceylon two years previously because of the China trade, urged resumption of aid in 1956 because of the friendly sentiments expressed by Ceylon at Bandung.

One Congressman expressed the views of several, during the 1956 Hearings, as follows: "Would it be appropriate to think about taking [funds] . . . which we have earmarked (in the 1956 MSP proposals) for our not-so-certain friends, and transferring that to people like Ceylon, who have demonstrated their friendship?" *Mutual Security Act of 1955*, House Committee Hearings, p. 137.

[76] Tables 23 and 24.

[77] *Soviet Technical Assistance*, Senate Foreign Relations Committee, pp. 11-12.

dence of increased Soviet interest in its isolated southern neighbor apparently served to heighten U.S. interest. In effect, the proposed expansion of Soviet aid[78] seemed to raise the implicit "value" attached by the United States to Afghan aid, resulting in an eightfold increase over the prior year.[79]

If we consider Ceylon and Afghanistan together, they suggest the existence of somewhat different aid objectives from what we have previously characterized as promoting political stability. In the case of Ceylon, for example, it would seem that reward for, and hence promotion of, public pronouncements favorable to the West, became an objective influencing the allocation of economic and technical aid. In the case of Afghanistan, discouraging a recipient's further "orientation" toward the Soviet Bloc, in the sense of discouraging further requests to the Soviet Bloc for aid, seems to have become an objective influencing U.S. aid allocations. The inference is that an "uncommitted" recipient of United States aid would benefit by expressing pro-Western views publicly, or by requesting Soviet aid privately, or both. If this seems frivolous, it at least suggests an obvious, but important, point to which we shall return later: the improved allocation of aid necessarily depends on an improved formulation of the objectives to be sought with aid.

From the other allocations shown in Tables 23 and 24, it is clear that SEATO's effect on implicit "value" parameters remained as crucial in 1956 as in 1955.[80] Whatever the physical consequences (productivity) of aid, they tended, in 1956 as in 1955, to be more highly valued in those countries of the set that directly participated in SEATO. Pakistan's especially large share of the total 1956 obligations, shown in Table 24, can perhaps be attributed to its participation not only in SEATO, but, beginning in September 1955, in the Baghdad Pact as well. Quite apart from "military support," it is clear from Tables 23 and 24 that each of the three Asian participants in SEATO continued to fare relatively well in its share of total economic and technical aid to Southern Asia compared, for example, to its share in the pre-SEATO years.[81] The principle, as expressed by one Congressman, "that we should . . . take a more generous attitude

[78] Smaller Soviet aid credits to Afghanistan, totaling $6.6 million, had been extended in 1954, *ibid.*, p. 2.

[79] For suggestive, if not conclusive, evidence of this point, see *Mutual Security Act of 1956*, House Hearings, Washington, D.C., 1956, pp. 539-558; and *Report to the Congress on the Mutual Security Program, June 1956*, Washington, D.C., p. 8.

[80] See above, pp. 198-200.   [81] See, for example, Table 16, above.

toward . . . these countries which are . . . openly and avowedly our friends, like Pakistan, than [toward] those who maintain an attitude of neutralism, such as India," was not only verbally endorsed by the Administration during the 1956 Hearings,[82] but was directly implemented by non-military aid obligations to the SEATO countries.

5. Military Assistance

In addition, the SEATO countries continued to receive direct military aid. Together with Cambodia, Laos, and Viet Nam, which, though not members of SEATO, were technically included in the pact's "protected area," the SEATO countries remained the only recipients of MAP aid in Southern Asia. At the same time, the amount of newly appropriated MAP aid, for the Asian region as well as globally, further declined in 1956. Global MAP appropriations, together with estimated regional shares, are shown in Table 25, below.

It should be noted that the MAP data in Table 25 include "direct forces support" for the first time. For comparability with prior years, it is therefore necessary to subtract this component ($317 million)[83] from the total shown in the table. With this adjustment, the striking reduction in military aid in 1956 becomes evident. Compared with end-item appropriations of $1.2 billion in 1955,[84] new appropriations for end-items in 1956 were only $705 million.

In part, this deep global cut can be explained by the Administration's shift in emphasis to economic assistance in Asia. As the Senate Foreign Relations Committee stated:

"Since the United States embarked on major foreign assistance programs in 1948, the emphasis has shifted from economic assistance to Europe [1948-1950], to military assistance to Europe [1950-1952], and then to military assistance to Asia [1952-1954]. It is now shifting to economic assistance to Asia [1955].[85]

But *only* in part. The sharp reduction in global military aid in 1956 primarily reflected the priority accorded by the Congress and the Administration to over-all reduction in the aid budget, rather than to shifting "emphasis" among aid categories. It reflected, in other words, the implicit judgment that the resources previously

[82] The quotation is from *Mutual Security Act of 1955*, House Hearings, p. 99.
[83] Table 25, footnote ᵃ.
[84] See above, Table 21. MAP appropriations in 1955 were already sharply down from the $3.2 billion appropriated in 1954. See Table 17.
[85] *The Mutual Security Act of 1955*, Senate Foreign Relations Committee Report, p. 6. The bracketed dates are added.

Table 25
MILITARY ASSISTANCE APPROPRIATIONS,
FISCAL YEAR 1956

	Total Appropriations and Estimated Regional Allotments[a] (millions of dollars)	Proportion of Total[b] (per cent)
Europe	($ 481.4)	47.1
Near East and Africa[c]	(79.8)	7.8
Asia (Far East and Pacific)	(455.9)	44.6
American Republics	(5.1)	.5
TOTALS	$1,022.2	100.0

[a] As in 1955, funds for MAP in 1956 were appropriated on a global, rather than regional, basis. The estimated regional figures, shown in parentheses, represent the amounts "programmed" (that is, tentatively "reserved") for the indicated regions, *not* appropriations. They are included to permit rough comparison with the regional appropriations in prior years. In this case, the dollar amounts have been estimated from data showing the percentage shares for the four regions. (See footnote [b], below.)

The new *global* appropriations shown ($1,022.2 million), include funds appropriated for "direct forces support" ($317.2 million) as well as military end-items, infrastructure, and training. Compared to total MAP appropriations in 1956, the Administration's original proposals amounted to $1,717.2 million, of which $317.2 million was "direct forces support"—mainly intended for Korea, Indochina, Formosa, and Pakistan—and $1,400.0 million was for end-items, infrastructure, and related NATO requirements. See *The Mutual Security Act of 1955*, Report of the Committee on Foreign Relations, Washington, D.C., pp. 4, 8.

[b] The percentages are taken from a study by the Systems Analysis Corporation, published in *The Military Assistance Program of the United States*, Two Studies and a Report prepared for the Special Senate Committee to Study the Foreign Aid Program, 85th Congress, 1st session, Washington, D.C., March, 1957, p. 96. The regional distribution in the referenced study is captioned "military defense assistance program allocations," and includes, besides the four regions shown in Table 25, a share for "non-regional" allocations. Since most of this share was related to infrastructure, special weapons development, and other NATO uses, it is consolidated with the European share shown in Table 25.

[c] Under the Mutual Security Act of 1955, "South Asia" was removed from the "Near East, Africa, and South Asia" and included in the "Asia and Pacific" area. The latter was redesignated "Asia," the former, "Near East and Africa." See above, Table 21.

devoted to Mutual Security would be utilized to better advantage in other government programs or in the private sector of the economy.

Among the recipients of MAP in Southern Asia, the largest reductions were in the end-item program in Viet Nam. So large had been end-item deliveries in prior years, and so successful were the efforts of Vietnamese national forces in dealing with the remnant Viet Minh irregulars, as well as the dissident sects during 1956, that some previously delivered materiel was declared surplus to Vietnamese needs and made available for other parts of the Pacific Area.[86] Although the progress of internal security sharply reduced the attrition of materiel, the continued threat from North Viet Nam required large national ground forces in South Viet Nam. Maintenance of this capability, rather than a further buildup of materiel, became the primary goal of MAP and related military support to Viet Nam in 1956 and subsequent years.

In Pakistan, Thailand, and the Philippines, the military capabilities sought by MAP remained what they had been in prior years, and the end-item programs were not basically altered. Despite the reduction in new appropriations, end-item aid to Pakistan continued to rise. Moreover, the first deliveries of jet aircraft to the Pakistan Air Force in 1956 was further evidence that the program's aim was to create a capability directed toward meeting external attack.[87]

D. MUTUAL SECURITY IN 1957

Description of the Mutual Security program in Southern Asia during 1957 can be abbreviated for two reasons: first, because fewer data are available than in the earlier years; and second, because the circumstances and legislation affecting intercountry and interprogram aid allocations in fiscal 1957 were essentially similar to the two preceding years.

As in the two preceding years, coexistence meant flexible, and seemingly inconsistent, modes of Soviet behavior domestically and internationally. On the one hand, there was the dissolution of the Cominform (in April 1956), demobilization of over a million men in the Soviet Army (in May), qualified acceptance of the Eisenhower "open-skies" plan as part of the "new" Soviet disarmament proposals (in November), and a continuing rise in both economic aid offers and commitments to non-Bloc countries by the Soviet Bloc.[88] On the other hand, there was an increasing frequency of Soviet nuclear weapons tests (in March, April, August, September, and November of 1956),[89] ruthless suppression of the Hungarian revolt (in November), arms shipments to Egypt (early in 1956) and to Syria (toward the end of the calendar year), and, finally, the credible Soviet threat

[86] *Report to Congress on the Mutual Security Program, June 1956*, Washington, D.C., 1956, p. 23.

[87] *The Mutual Security Report, June 1956*, p. 24.

[88] For the specific Soviet aid agreements concluded with countries in Southern Asia during calendar year 1956, see below, Chapter 11.

[89] Richard P. Stebbins, *The United States in World Affairs, 1956*, New York, 1957, p. 400.

(in November) to send "volunteers" to Egypt, combined with the less credible threat to use nuclear weapons against Britain and France if they did not withdraw from Suez.

In presenting the Mutual Security Program for 1957 to Congress, the Program's principal coordinator, John Hollister, appropriately characterized this pattern of events as follows:

". . . We must recognize that the communist threat itself will continue to have many different aspects despite the Soviet tactics of shifting from time to time the emphasis from one form of offensive to another. In the period 1947-1953, the Soviets aroused well-founded fears of armed aggression through all the free world. Today, although their primary effort appears to be economic, there is no indication that war preparations have ceased."[90]

1. Changes in Mutual Security Legislation

The principal change in the Mutual Security Program itself in 1957, both as proposed by the Executive Branch and as enacted by Congress, was an increase in size: from $3.53 billion originally proposed and $2.70 billion actually appropriated for all categories of Mutual Security aid in 1956, to $4.86 billion proposed and $3.77 billion appropriated in 1957.[91] The Mutual Security Act of 1956—which authorized the 1957 program—also contained the first legislative answer to the recurring question of how long the MSP would continue: ". . . as long as international communism and the nations it controls continue by threat of military action, use of economic pressure, internal subversion or other means to attempt to bring under their domination peoples now free and independent. . . ."[92]

And, as if in response to the Soviet economic offensive in the "uncommitted" countries, Congress passed an amendment to the authorizing act which provided that:

"Assistance under this Act shall be administered so as to assist other peoples in their efforts to achieve self-government or independence under circumstances which will enable them to assume an

---

[90] *Mutual Security Act of 1956*, House Hearings, 84th Congress, 2nd session, Washington, D.C., 1956, p. 34.

[91] *Mutual Security Act of 1956*, Senate Hearings, 84th Congress, 2nd session, Washington, D.C., 1956, p. 78. Nearly all of the increase in 1957 appropriations was accounted for by increased military assistance, that is, end-item aid and direct forces support. See International Cooperation Administration, *Operations Report*, June 30, 1956, p. 3; and below, Table 27.

[92] *The Mutual Security Act of 1956*, Public Law 726, 84th Congress, 2nd session, July 18, 1956, Sec. 2.

equal station among the free nations of the world and to fulfill their responsibilities for self-government or independence."[93]

But in their basic content, both the legislation and the 1957 program authorized by it closely resembled those of the preceding year.[94] The broad objectives verbally attributed to the program remained what they had previously been: in the case of military aid, consisting of end-items and military support, to build or maintain the local forces necessary "to deter aggression and punish it should it occur";[95] and, in the case of non-military aid,[96] to help the underdeveloped countries "to strike at those conditions of poverty, disease, and low living standards which tend to create unrest . . . political instability . . . disorder or collapse."[97]

Given these familiar objectives, the allocation of the increased funds in the 1957 program followed a pattern in Southern Asia similar to that of the previous year. Obligations for 1957 in Southern Asia, and globally, other than those under the Military Assistance Program,[98] are shown in Table 26.

2. Economic Aid and Military Support in 1957

A comparison of Table 26 with Table 22 shows that the allocation of non-MAP aid in 1957 was broadly similar to that in 1956. The

[93] *Ibid.*

[94] Other innovations introduced by the amendments to the Mutual Security Act of 1954, which comprised the Act of 1956, were the authorization to obligate and spend funds appropriated as development assistance over a four-year period, and the requirement that 80 per cent of such funds be available on "terms of repayment." There were two exceptions provided in the Act to the loan requirement: development aid used either for *regional* (rather than national) projects or for financing sales of agricultural commodities. Moreover, since "soft" loans remained permissible, the new requirement was hardly more restrictive in practice than that of the President's Fund for Asian Development of the prior year. See above, Chapter 6, pp. 212-213, and *The Mutual Security Act of 1956*, Public Law 726, Sec. 6.

[95] The quotation is from testimony on the 1957 Mutual Security Program by Gordon Gray, then Assistant Secretary of Defense for International Security Affairs. See *The Mutual Security Act of 1956*, House Hearings, p. 100, and, in a similar vein, the testimony of Secretary of State Dulles, *The Mutual Security Act of 1956*, Senate Hearings, 84th Congress, 2nd session, Washington, D.C., 1956, p. 22ff.

[96] Mainly comprising technical assistance, development assistance, and, in principal at least, a portion of so-called "defense support" aid to countries also receiving military assistance.

[97] The quotation is from the testimony of John Hollister, Director of ICA on the 1957 Program. See *The Mutual Security Act of 1956*, House Hearings, p. 39. In a similar vein, see the mixed-metaphoric statement by Senator Morse—characterized by Secretary Dulles as "clearly our objective"—that "our intention is to try to help them build up their economic productive power so that they can stand firmly on their own political legs of self-government." *The Mutual Security Act of 1956*, Senate Hearings, p. 43.

[98] For MAP appropriations, and estimated obligations in 1957, see below, Table 28.

largest absolute and relative change in 1957 was in the increased economic and technical aid to Southern Asia (from $266.5 million obligated in 1956 to $341.2 million in 1957). Most of this increase (row 1 of Tables 26 and 22) is accounted for by the resumption of aid to Burma and by the increases in aid to Indonesia and Viet Nam.[99]

Table 26

UNITED STATES ECONOMIC AND TECHNICAL ASSISTANCE AND MILITARY SUPPORT TO SOUTHERN ASIA IN FISCAL YEAR 1957 COMPARED TO TOTAL ASIAN AND GLOBAL NON-MAP ASSISTANCE UNDER THE MUTUAL SECURITY ACT OF 1956[a]

	Obligations (millions of dollars)	As Proportion of:	
		Total Asian Aid	Global Aid
		(per cent)	
1. Economic and Technical Aid to Southern Asia	341.2	32.9	22.8
2. Military Support for Southern Asia	309.5	29.8	20.6
3. Total Non-MAP Aid to Southern Asia (1+2)	650.7	62.7	43.4
4. Non-MAP Aid to Formosa and Korea	387.3	37.3	25.8
5. Total Asian Non-MAP Aid (3+4)	1,038.0	100.0	69.2
6. Global Non-MAP Aid Under the Mutual Security Act of 1956	1,500.1	–	100.0

Sources: Table 27, below, and (i'), p. 57.

[a] As in 1956, obligations for "direct forces support" were consolidated with the MAP. Consequently, in 1957, non-MAP assistance refers to a somewhat smaller segment of the overall Mutual Security Program than in the fiscal years prior to 1956. See above, Table 22, footnote [a], and Table 20, footnote [a].

The detailed country and project obligations data, from which the obligations shown for Southern Asia in Table 26 are derived, are presented in Table 27, below. In contrast to previous years, a detailed comparison of Executive Branch proposals and subsequent obliga-

[99] Both the Burmese and Indonesian increments were accomplished through the technically non-obligating loan agreements mentioned in Table 27, footnotes [c] and [g], below. See also the discussion below, pp. 233, 235ff. Because the Burma and Indonesia loan commitments are *not* included in the official ICA record of global aid obligations, the Southern Asian share of economic and technical aid obligations in global non-MAP obligations (22.8 per cent) in Table 26 is somewhat larger than that shown in official records.

Table 27

FUNDS OBLIGATED FOR UNITED STATES ECONOMIC AND TECHNICAL
ASSISTANCE AND MILITARY SUPPORT TO SOUTHERN ASIA,
FISCAL YEAR 1957[a]

(by country and project use)

	(1)	(2)	(3)	(4)	(5)	(6)	(7)	(8)
				Project Use				
Country	Agri-culture	Indus-try	Trans-porta-tion	Health	Labor	Public Admin-istra-tion	Edu-cation	Com-munity Devel-opment
				(millions of dollars)				
Afghanistan[b]	2.76	1.87	4.81	–	–	.66	2.41	.15
Burma[c]	–	–	–	–	–	–	–	–
Ceylon[d]	1.56	.32	1.07	.22	–	.03	.43	–
India[e]	2.13	1.96	15.18	8.10	.06	.11	.75	2.23
Indochina[f]	5.64	9.39	29.57	5.26	–	8.38	2.61	.46
Cambodia	(.54)	(.12)	(8.46)	(.49)	–	(.11)	(.46)	(.06)
Laos	(.28)	(.39)	(2.31)	(.30)	–	(.96)	(.19)	(.40)
Viet Nam	(4.82)	(8.88)	(18.80)	(4.47)	–	(7.31)	(1.96)	–
Indonesia[g]	1.00	2.26	.28	2.86	.33	2.53	1.49	.09
Nepal[h]	.13	.35	1.96	.35	–	–	.32	.16
Pakistan[i]	1.57	19.84	9.97	1.09	–	.60	–	.44
Philippines[j]	3.36	.80	6.83	2.96	.12	.73	.90	.11
Thailand[k]	1.13	5.84	19.13	.82	.05	.34	1.19	.03
TOTALS	19.28	42.63	88.80	21.66	.56	13.38	10.10	3.67
Project Total as Proportion of Regional Total				(per cent)				
	5.6	12.5	26.0	6.3	.2	3.9	3.0	1.1

Σ Col (1)/Σ Col (10), Σ Col (2)/Σ Col (10), etc.

(continued)

Source: Appendix II.

[a] See above, Chapter 4, Table 3, footnote a, for explanation of categories and terms used in this table. In 1957, as in 1956, what we have called military support obligations (column [11]), exclude software provided directly to the military forces of recipient countries. Responsibility for these so-called "common-use" items (direct forces support), was transferred to the Defense Department and consolidated with end-item (MAP) aid. (See Table 25.)

[b] (i'), pp. 22, 24-25, 32-33, 72. The figures shown represent both technical assistance ($3.0 million) and development assistance ($11.4 million). Of the development assistance, $5.8 million was provided as a long-term Mutual Security loan.

[c] (i'), p. 72; and (a). In March 1957, the United States concluded a loan agreement with Burma that provided a credit line of $25 million for projects to be "mutually agreed upon . . . subject to the availability of funds." Initial plans called for utilizing

Table 27 (continued)

(9)	(10)	(11)	(12)	(13)	(14)
		Project Use		Country Total as Proportion of Regional Total	
General and Miscellaneous	Total Excluding Military Support	Military Support	President's Fund[1]	Excluding Military Support Col (10)/Σ Col (10)	Including Military Support Col (10) + Col (11) / Σ Col (10) + Σ Col (11)
(millions of dollars)				(per cent)	
1.73	14.39	–	–	4.2	2.2
25.00	25.00	–	–	7.3	3.8
2.45	6.08	–	–	1.8	.9
38.20	68.72	–	–	20.2	10.6
4.57	65.88	272.48	–	19.3	52.0
(.74)	(10.98)	(23.50)	–	(3.2)	(5.3)
(1.13)	(5.96)	(38.48)	–	(1.8)	(6.8)
(2.70)	(48.94)	(210.50)	–	(14.3)	(39.9)
15.88	26.72	–	–	7.8	4.1
1.08	4.35	–	–	1.3	.7
28.16	61.67	37.00	–	18.1	15.2
18.10	33.91	–	–	9.9	5.2
5.97	34.50	–	–	10.1	5.3
141.14	341.22	309.48	1.87	100.0	100.0
(per cent)					
41.4	100.0				

most of the credit for projects in agriculture, transportation, and other public services. However, none of the specific project content of the loan had been agreed upon by the end of the fiscal year, and the figures shown in Table 26 were technically *not* regarded as a legal obligation of 1957 funds, but as a *conditional* obligation against funds to be made available in the following year. The credit line is, nonetheless, shown on ICA records as a loan "authorized" in 1957. The occasion of the Burmese loan was the first

time that this procedure, that of "authorizing" a Mutual Security loan without simultaneously obligating funds to cover it, was applied in Southern Asia in the history of the Mutual Security program.

The dollar credit line shown in Table 27 was additional to an agreement for the sale to Burma of $22.7 million of surplus agricultural commodities, under Public Law 480, which was also concluded in March 1957. The bulk of the kyat proceeds (a sum
(Continued on following page)

tions cannot be made in 1957. Most of the original country proposals for so-called "defense support" aid, and some of the proposals for development assistance, were and are classified information. However, it is at least clear that Congressional reductions in non-MAP funds proposed for Southern Asia were minor. In fact, the only major reduction made by Congress in the Mutual Security Program proposals for 1957 was the billion dollar global reduction in MAP.[100] Apart from this, the Administration's original MSP proposals for 1957 were not significantly changed by Congressional action.

3. Country and Sectoral Allocations in Southern Asia

If we consider column (10) of Table 27, that is, aid obligations other than what we have estimated to be "military support," and if

[100] See above, p. 227 and below, Table 28, footnote a.

(Notes to Table 27 continued)

amounting to $17.3 million) from the sale was intended to be used for meeting internal development costs in Burma. See (e'), p. 29.

d (i'), pp. 22, 24-25, 32-33, 72. The figures shown represent both technical assistance ($1.1 million) and development assistance ($5.0 million). Of the latter, $2.5 million was provided as a long-term Mutual Security loan. Of the $2.45 million shown in column (9), $2.24 million represented surplus agricultural commodities furnished under Section 402 of the Mutual Security Act of 1954 as amended. See above, Chapter 5, Table 16, footnote b.

e (i'), pp. 22, 24-25, 32-33, 72, 76. The figures shown represent both technical assistance ($6.2 million) and development assistance ($62.5 million). Of the latter, $47.5 million was provided as a long-term Mutual Security loan. Of the $38.2 million shown under general and miscellaneous (column [9]), $31.05 million represented surplus agricultural commodities furnished under Section 402 of the Mutual Security Act of 1954 as amended. See above, Chapter 5, Table 16, footnote c.

The figures shown do not include the agreement of August 29, 1956, to sell India surplus agricultural commodities valued at $360.1 million over a three-year period under Public Law 480—the largest single transaction negotiated up to that time under the Agricultural Trade and Development Act. Under this agreement, the bulk of the rupee

sales proceeds (about $290 million) is intended to be used for meeting internal Indian development costs. (See [e'], p. 29.)

f (i'), pp. 22, 24-25, 32-33, 72. Though obligations for Indochina as such were discontinued in 1956 (see above, Table 24, footnote f), the separate data for Cambodia, Laos, and Viet Nam (shown in parentheses) have been cumulated to get the total obligations shown in Table 27 for purposes of comparison with prior years, when obligations were not so disaggregated.

The figures shown in columns (1) through (10) represent both technical assistance to the three countries ($7.9 million) and that part of so-called "defense support" which was obligated for specific sectors or project uses ($58.0 million). The remainder of defense support is included in column (11), military support, for the reasons and with the qualifications previously described. See Table 24, footnote f, and Table 19, footnote g.

Of the total for Viet Nam, $25.0 million was a long-term Mutual Security loan, and $11.8 million represented surplus agricultural commodities provided under Section 402 of the Mutual Security Act of 1954 as amended. See above, Table 16, footnote c.

g (i'), pp. 22, 24-25, 32-33, 72. The figures shown represent both technical assistance ($7.0 million) and development assistance ($19.7 million). Of the latter, $15.0 million was provided as a credit line under the same

we compare these obligations with the corresponding data for 1956,[101] a few not-too-surprising things can be said in explanation of the 1957 country allocations. The absolute amounts obligated in the individual countries remained close to the prior year, except in Burma, Indonesia, and Viet Nam. In each of these cases, the amounts of economic and technical aid shown in Table 27 represented appreciable increases over 1956: from zero to $25.0 million in Burma; from $11.1 million to $26.7 million in Indonesia; and from $22.7 million to $48.9 million in Viet Nam.

In Burma, the $25 million loan agreement, concluded in March 1957, represented a resumption of U.S. assistance after an interval of three years.[102] It was, moreover, additional to over $17 million of non-MSP aid provided in the form of surplus agricultural com-

---

[101] See above, Table 24.   [102] See above, Chapter 5, pp. 150-151.

(Notes to Table 27 continued)

procedure applied in Burma (see above, footnote c). By the end of fiscal 1957, less than $1 million of the total had technically been obligated, though the loan agreement for the full amount was signed in April 1957.

h (i'), pp. 22, 24-25, 32-33, 72. Of the total, $3.1 million is development assistance and $1.25 million technical assistance.

i (i'), pp. 22, 24-25, 32-33, 72. The figures shown in columns (1) through (10) represent both technical assistance ($6.0 million) and a part of so-called "defense support," ($55.7 million). The latter consists both of defense support obligations incurred for specific projects ($28.7 million) and "non-project" obligations equivalent to the amount by which internal public investment rose in 1957 (about $27.0 million). The remainder of the "defense support" obligations is included in column (11) and is approximately equal to the amount by which internal Pakistani defense outlays rose in 1957 ($37.0 million) over the preceding year. See Table 24, footnote i.

Of the totals shown in columns (10) and (11), $42.0 million was provided as a long-term Mutual Security loan.

j (i'), pp. 22, 24-25, 32-33, 72. The figures shown in columns (1) through (10) represent both technical assistance ($5.0 million) and all so-called "defense support" ($28.9 million). None of the latter has been attributed to military support, column (11), for

two reasons: internal military outlays in the Philippines were budgeted in fiscal 1957 for a reduction from the prior year by about $8 million, at the same time as total budgetary outlays were budgeted for a rise of $85 million; and there were no counterpart withdrawals for military use in the Philippines in 1957 ([e'], p. 9). (See *Economic Survey, op.cit.*, p. 190.) For both reasons it is more reasonable to attribute U.S. "non-project" aid (that is, column [9]) entirely to nonmilitary uses. See Table 24, footnote j.

Of the totals shown, $10 million was provided as a long-term Mutual Security loan, and $17 million as surplus agricultural commodities under Section 402 of the Mutual Security Act of 1954 as amended. See above, Table 16, footnote c.

k (i'), pp. 22, 24-25, 32-33, 72. The figures shown represent both technical assistance ($4.5 million) and all so-called "defense support" ($30.0 million). None of the latter has been attributed to military support for the same reasons noted in the Philippines (footnote j, above), and in Thailand in 1956. See Table 24, footnote k.

l (i'), p. 25. The obligations shown, for a Southeast Asian telecommunications survey, represent obligations incurred in 1957 from the original 1956 three-year appropriations. See the discussion in the text above, pp. 212-213.

modities under Public Law 480.[103] How can this resumption in aid be explained and how, at least as far as the relatively large MSP component is conceived, can it be justified as a preferred use of Mutual Security funds?

It is, of course, true that the Burmese government formally requested loan assistance from the United States in 1957, thereby, in effect, reestablishing Burma as a *possible* recipient of MSP funds.[104] In other words, what was not an available alternative in the three prior fiscal years became one in 1957. If this was a necessary condition for resuming aid to Burma in 1957, it was certainly not a sufficient condition. To establish the latter, we need to assume and defend the proposition that the productivity-and-value of U.S. aid in Burma combined to make it a preferable use of aid compared, for example, to alternative uses in Southern Asia. In other words, if the aid allocation to Burma in 1957 is to be considered "optimal," we need to consider not only the *feasibility* of resuming aid, but its *desirability* relative to available alternatives.

In these terms, a reasonable case can be made for the Burmese allocation in 1957. There were, for example, several reasons for expecting higher physical productivity from aid to Burma in 1957 than, say, in 1953. One reason was that Burma's foreign exchange position was considerably more stringent than in prior years. In contrast to the earlier period, when Burma's reserves were rising to a post-Korean war peak of $225 million at the end of calendar year 1953, Burma's reserves had declined by the first quarter of calendar 1957 to $135 million, largely as a result of a fall in rice prices. Consequently, the substitutability of aid for available, but idle, foreign exchange reserves was no longer a plausible discount on the net productivity of aid to Burma, as it might previously have been.

Moreover, the significant improvement in internal security conditions in Burma since 1953 tended to widen the opportunities for, and reduce the risks of, investment, and thereby to raise the productivity of aid. If the productivity of aid to Burma had been comparable to that in the other countries of the region during the 1951-53 period,[105] there were reasons for believing it had risen absolutely since the

[103] See above, this chapter, section 7. In fiscal 1957, $22.7 million of surplus agricultural commodities were shipped to Burma. Of the local currency proceeds, $17.3 million were to be loaned to Burma, subject to eventual repayment in local currency, for meeting internal development costs. See *Report to Congress on the Mutual Security Program, December 31, 1956*, Washington, D.C., 1957, pp. 3-4.

[104] *Ibid.*, pp. 4-5.   [105] See above, Chapter 4, pp. 93ff.

earlier period. Whether the absolute rise in productivity was also a rise relative to that in other countries of the set is, of course, not inferable from the points mentioned above. But it is at least a reasonable possibility, since there are no particular reasons for assuming any appreciable rise in the productivity of aid in most of the other countries of the set during the intervening period.

Inferring anything very specific about the value parameter implicit in the United States aid allocation to Burma in 1957 is no more conclusive than we have found it to be in a number of prior efforts. Nevertheless, there were reasons for assigning the value a relatively high rank within the set. On the political stability grounds, previously adduced as a major factor in U.S. judgments about value parameters, Burma remained a highly vulnerable—and hence relatively high-valued—aid claimant. The Burmese national elections of April 1956, in which the government coalition lost ground, and the communist Workers' and Peasants' Party gained, provided one obvious example of Burma's vulnerability.

Yet there is also the possibility that the value parameter implicit in the 1957 allocation to Burma owed relatively little to the political-stability objective of U.S. aid, and relatively more to quite different U.S. objectives. Having elicited offers of aid from the Soviet Bloc at the time of the Bulganin-Khrushchev visit to Rangoon in December 1955, Burma stood up staunchly against the Soviet Union in the United Nations debate on Hungary in December 1956. Burma was one of the two "neutralist" countries which voted with the free world to condemn the Soviet attack and call for withdrawal of Soviet forces. The Burmese delegate supported his vote with eloquent candor. "We do this," he noted, "to keep our self-respect. There but for the Grace of God, go we."

In effect, this sequence—probably quite unpremeditated in Burma's case—came fairly close to what would seem to be a promising strategy for a neutralist country bent on influencing the allocation of U.S. aid. The point is that a U.S. desire to reward pro-Western (or anti-communist) verbiage, and to counter Soviet aid offers (by outbidding them), may have influenced significantly the value parameters implicitly attached by the United States to alternative recipients of aid. The Burmese allocation in 1957 doesn't demonstrate the point. It is, however, consistent with it.

The substantial increase over 1956 in aid obligations in Indonesia in 1957 lends some further support to the point. In this case, neither

of the productivity reasons adduced in explanation of the aid allocation to Burma applied. Security conditions in Indonesia had not improved, nor had the balance of payments evidence of non-substituta-
bility of aid changed from the prior year when aid obligations were
$11 million.[106] It is hard for us to avoid the conclusion that what had
changed was Indonesia's negotiation of a $100 million loan agree-
ment with the Soviet Union in September 1956,[107] and that this led
to a rise in the relative value attached by the United States to aid to
Indonesia and to the $15 million increase in obligations shown for
1957 in Table 27.

The other large increase in obligations in 1957 was in Viet Nam,
where economic and technical aid rose by $26 million, military sup-
port by $31 million. It is reasonable in this case to adduce higher
physical productivity as the main explanation for the first of these
increases. In fiscal years 1955 and 1956, two internal problems had
restricted the productivity of economic and technical aid in Viet
Nam. One was the internal military insecurity created by dissident
politico-religious sects and remnant Viet Minh guerrilla units; the
other was the half-million refugees from North Viet Nam, whose
absorption previously had so strained South Viet Nam's administrative and technical resources as to limit sharply any developmental
uses of external aid.

By the summer of 1956, both problems had been substantially
solved, and the constraints they imposed on aid productivity eased.
As summarized by ICA: "The main emergency problems were largely
under control. The stage was set for the next major step—preparing
a longer-term program to . . . lay a foundation for a progressively
stronger economy."[108] Quite apart from implicit value parameters, it
is fair to contend that the relative productivity of economic and
technical aid in Viet Nam rose considerably by 1957. The doubling
of economic and technical aid obligations in Viet Nam in 1957 compared to 1956 can reasonably be explained in these terms.

The $31 million rise in estimated military support obligations in
Viet Nam for 1957 (from $179.6 million in 1956 to $210.5 million in
1957) can also be understood in these terms. The assumption we
have used for estimating the military support component of total
aid to Viet Nam in prior years—namely, that all *non-project* aid can

[106] See above, Table 24.   [107] See Chapter 11, below.
[108] *Report to Congress on the Mutual Security Program, June 30, 1957*, Washington, D.C., 1957, pp. 24ff.

be construed as military support in Viet Nam because 70 to 80 per cent of public expenditure represented defense outlays[109]—is no longer valid in 1957. In *calendar* year 1956, defense expenditures in Viet Nam fell absolutely and relatively: from 11.4 billion piastres ($326 million) or 73 per cent of total budgetary outlays in 1955, to 7.6 billion piastres ($217 million) or 56 per cent of the total in 1956. Over the same period, administrative and equipment expenses for economic development and social services rose from about 800 million piastres ($23 million) or 5 per cent of the total, to 2.1 billion ($60 million) or 15 per cent of the total.[110] Consequently, "non-project" aid from the United States, that is, saleable commodity imports to generate local currency (for financing more than half of total Vietnamese budgetary outlays), probably represented, in fiscal 1957, an increasing net contribution to developmental, rather than military, outlays. The rise in military support obligations in 1957, shown in column (11) of Table 27, is thus misleading. Actually, because of the substantially altered composition of Viet Nam's budget, some of what is shown as "military support" ought, in 1957, more properly to be regarded as economic and technical aid, and explained on the same grounds already used to account for the increase in such aid (that is, column [10]).

As Table 27 shows, allocations to the three SEATO countries (Pakistan, the Philippines, and Thailand) in 1957 remained about what they were in 1956.[111] SEATO continued to be a factor affecting the implicit allocative value parameters, or, stated differently, maintenance of the alliance by favoring members seems to have remained an aid objective implicit in the allocation data. At the same time, the *share* received by the SEATO countries of total non-MAP aid (both inclusive and exclusive of military support) declined somewhat in 1957.[112] This decline in aid shares suggests, at least, that other factors affecting the implicit value parameters—such as the factors we have alluded to in the Burmese and Indonesian cases—acquired relatively greater importance as objectives of U.S. aid in 1957.

Before leaving Table 27, it is interesting to note that the shift in sectoral allocations, in favor of the longer-term industrial and transport projects, and away from agricultural and health projects, con-

[109] See above, Table 19, footnote g.
[110] *Economic Survey for Asia and the Far East, 1956*, pp. 173, 190.
[111] See Table 24, above.
[112] See Tables 24 and 27, columns (13) and (14), for Pakistan, the Philippines, and Thailand.

tinued in 1957, as in the three years since 1954. In 1957, for example, industry and transport allocations comprised over 38 per cent of total economic and technical aid, compared to 35 per cent in 1956 and 26 per cent in 1955. At the same time, the general-and-miscellaneous obligations (column [9]) continued to grow, absolutely and relatively, quite probably for the same reasons previously mentioned in discussing sectoral obligations in 1955.[113]

4. Military End-Item Appropriations

Turning to military assistance in 1957, the salient unclassified data concerning MAP appropriations are summarized in Table 28 below.

Not much can or need be said in amplification of the MAP data in Table 28. Available qualitative (as well as quantitative) information on the program's composition is more limited than in prior years;[114] and the main capabilities, construed in terms of country force goals, which were sought by MAP in Southern Asia in earlier years, remained unchanged in 1957.

The billion dollar increase in the global 1957 MAP, over the preceding fiscal year when MAP appropriations were $1.0 billion,[115] reflected a general view in the Administration that progress toward the established force goals in the several regions required a rapid replenishing of the end-item pipeline. In the two preceding fiscal years, the sharp drop in military aid appropriations had not resulted in a commensurate fall in end-item deliveries. Instead, the pipeline of MAP end-items had been depleted by allowing expenditures (deliveries), from previous appropriations, to run substantially ahead of the 1955 and 1956 appropriations. To maintain deliveries at the current rate, it was therefore necessary to increase new appropriations.[116]

Besides the fiscal argument, there were other factors which explained the increased emphasis on military aid in the 1957 Mutual

[113] Above, p. 201.
[114] Since the inception of MDAP in fiscal 1950, the availability of public information on annual military assistance has steadily decreased. Compare, for example, the five-page account of MAP for 1957 (*Mutual Security Report, June 30, 1957*, pp. 5-10) with the earlier fifty- to one hundred-page semi-annual reports to Congress in the first two years of MDAP (for example, *Third Semi-Annual Report to Congress on the MDAP*, October 6, 1950, to March 31, 1951, and *Fourth Semi-Annual Report to Congress on the MDAP*, April 1, 1951, to October 9, 1951), Washington, D.C., 1952.
[115] See Table 25, above.
[116] For elaboration of the fiscal argument for increase MAP appropriations in 1957, see the testimony of Gordon Gray, then Assistant Secretary of Defense for International Security Affairs, *Mutual Security Act of 1956*, House Hearings, p. 99.

Security Program. For example, MAP in 1957 included a substantial provision for "advanced weapons." Consisting largely of missiles for European defense, the advanced-weapons program was hopefully intended to compensate for the less-than-adequate buildup of conventional forces in the NATO countries.[117]

Table 28
MILITARY ASSISTANCE APPROPRIATIONS
FISCAL YEAR 1957

	Total Appropriations and Estimated Regional Allotments[a] (millions of dollars)	Proportion of Total[b] (per cent)
Europe	($ 891.7)	44.2
Near East and Africa	(316.8)	15.7
Asia (Far East and Pacific)	(784.8)	38.9
Latin America	(24.2)	1.2
TOTALS	$2,017.5	100.0

[a] In 1957, MAP funds were again appropriated on a global, rather than a regional basis. The dollar figures in parentheses are estimates based on the assumption that the regional shares of the actual appropriations can be considered the same as the regional shares in the Administration's original proposals. (See footnote [b], below.)

Compared to total MAP appropriations for 1957, the Administration's original proposals amounted to $3.0 billion, a tripling of appropriations in the prior year and an increase of over 75 per cent above the prior year's MAP proposals. See Table 25, above.

[b] The percentages are the regional shares in the Administration's original MAP proposals for 1957. See *The Mutual Security Program—Fiscal Year 1957—A Summary Presentation*, Department of State, Department of Defense, International Cooperation Administration, Washington, D.C., April 1956, pp. 74-75. The cited source includes so-called "non-regional programs," representing nearly 19 per cent of the total. Since most of these programs (for example, infrastructure, "new weapons" and "mutual weapons development") related to NATO defense goals, they have been included in the European regional share shown in Table 28.

In the Middle East, the substantial increase in military aid shown in Table 28 over 1956 was intended to provide support for the Baghdad pact, and to permit more rapid progress toward previously planned force goals in the member countries or an increase in the goals themselves.[118] Implicitly, the pact itself seemed to raise either the productivity of incremental end-item aid in the pact countries, or the utility to the United States of deterring hostilities in which pact members might be involved.

[117] *Ibid.*, pp. 96-97, and *Mutual Security Report, June 30, 1957*, pp. 6-7.
[118] *Mutual Security Act of 1956*, House Hearings, p. 98.

In Asia, the rise in MAP over the prior year (from $455.9 million to $784.8 million)[119] had little effect on the countries of Southern Asia, concentrating instead on Korea, Japan, and Formosa. In Southern Asia, the capabilities and forces sought by MAP remained what they had previously been: in Viet Nam, replacement of obsolescent conventional equipment to maintain defensive national forces large enough to meet the continued threat from North Viet Nam; in Pakistan and Thailand, modernizing and expanding air and ground forces to provide both an internal security and an external defense capability; and in the Philippines, nearly exclusive attention to the internal security capability.

5. Objectives and Allocations: Some Hard Questions

In some ways more significant than the billion dollar rise in MAP appropriations for 1957 over the 1956 level was the approximately equal cut made by Congress in the Administration's original MAP proposals, the largest Congressional cut made in military assistance since 1953.[120] Unlike Congressional cuts in various parts of the Mutual Security Program in prior years, the reduction in MAP in 1957 was accompanied neither by choler nor criticism. Implicitly, in 1957 as in prior years, MAP cuts were equivalent to a differing Congressional judgment concerning the relative returns to be derived from this form of aid, on the one hand, and both alternative forms of aid and non-aid uses of U.S. resources, on the other hand. But in 1957 the implicit Congressional judgment was accompanied by a mood of uncertainty and questioning which was not typical of prior years.

If one looks through the Congressional hearings on the 1957 program—which is the best evidence for this generalization—the unusual number of references, both by Congressmen and Administration witnesses, to the need for "study," "rethinking," and a "new look" in the foreign aid field, is apparent.[121] Nor is the reason for this enquiring approach hard to find. The increased flexibility of Soviet Bloc foreign policy in general, and the acceleration of its economic offensive in the uncommitted areas of the world in particular, provided the stimulus for reassessing the premises, purposes, and possi-

[119] See Tables 25 and 28.
[120] See above, Table 28, footnote ᵃ; and Chapter 5, pp. 153-154.
[121] See, for example, *The Mutual Security Act of 1956*, Senate Hearings, pp. 35, 46-49, 52-55; and the House Hearings on the same Act, pp. 12, 983, 987-992.

bilities of U.S. foreign aid.[122] In the era of competitive coexistence, the Soviet Union had, in Secretary Dulles' words, seen "the advantage of having 'a mutual security program' of its own."[123]

The result was to focus attention, both in Congress and the Executive Branch, on a number of serious questions concerning the U.S. program that had been around and unanswered for a number of years: how, for example, to evaluate the relative emphasis that should be placed on "military" and "economic" aid;[124] how to evaluate the relative gains to the United States from comparable types of aid to its allies and to the "neutralist" countries; how to determine whether the United States should try to outmatch Soviet Bloc aid offers or should, in Senator Knowland's words, "more or less call their bluff";[125] how to measure the accomplishments both of economic and military aid;[126] and how to formulate criteria that would make possible more effective use of MSP appropriations, or, from the Congressional standpoint, that would permit "due consideration (to be given) to each item that we appropriate from year to year."[127]

[122] The prominence accorded the Soviet aid offensive in the hearings on the 1957 program is spread throughout the transcript. See, especially, *Mutual Security Act of 1956*, Senate Hearings, pp. 24-25, 31, 40ff.; and House Hearings, pp. 11, 34, 983ff.

[123] House Hearings, p. 982.

[124] See, for example, Senator Fulbright's question of Secretary Dulles: "Is there a formula, or what is the procedure by which you arrive at the distribution of funds as between the military and non-military in this program?" Senate Hearings, p. 51ff.

[125] *Ibid.*, pp. 40-41.

[126] *Ibid.*, pp. 45, 55ff.

[127] The quotation is from Senator George's statement concerning the proposal for a Senate study of the entire Mutual Security Program. In accordance with the George proposal, the Senate in July 1956 created a Special Committee to Study the Foreign Aid Program, instructing it:

". . . to make exhaustive studies of the extent to which foreign assistance by the United States Government serves, can be made to serve, or does not serve the national interest, to the end that such studies and recommendations based thereon may be available to the Senate in considering foreign aid policies for the future."

See *Foreign Aid*, Report of the Special Committee to Study the Foreign Aid Program, Washington, D.C., 1957, p. 1. Besides the referenced report, the Special Committee's "exhaustive studies" comprised twenty-one separate reports on various aspects of the MSP prepared for it by private contractors, and extensive hearings conducted between March 20 and April 15, 1957. For a complete list of the separate reports, see *ibid.*, pp. 33-35. For the transcript of the Committee Hearings, see *The Foreign Aid Program*, Hearings Before the Special Committee to Study the Foreign Aid Program, U.S. Senate, 85th Congress, 1st session, Washington, D.C., 1957.

The House Foreign Affairs Committee produced a companion study under the direction of its then Chairman, Congressman James Richards. *Foreign Policy and Mutual Security*, Draft Report Submitted to the Committee on Foreign Affairs, Washington, D.C., 1956.

In addition to the Congressional studies, the Executive Branch produced two

All were really different versions of the same question. Could the *objectives* of the Mutual Security Program be defined and related to the different parts of the program with sufficient precision to help in making decisions about how to use the program to better advantage? The question was not new. It had existed before "coexistence," during the "cold war." And it had been given one of its clearest expressions by President Truman, during the warm Korean war:

". . . Certain choices have to be made—hard choices based on the best judgment we can bring to bear—as to how we shall allocate our great but not unlimited resources between use at home and use abroad, between use in various areas of the world, and between various types of programs designed primarily to strengthen our defenses, strengthen the free-world economies, or strengthen the political and social forces that are working generally for the preservation and extension of freedom.

". . . The questions that arise concern mainly the relationship of the Mutual Security Program to our over-all political, military and economic policies; the magnitude of the Program; the proper balance between military, economic and technical assistance; the proper emphasis of effort by geographic area; and the choices involved between the relatively short-term results and the relatively long-term results that we are seeking."[128]

Competitive coexistence has not basically changed these issues. It has certainly not made it any easier to reach better decisions about them. But, by confronting the United States with a Soviet adversary more flexible and more ready to take advantage of opportunities that become available, coexistence has made it imperative that we look for ways to make better decisions about the use of foreign aid.

---

reports of its own during fiscal year 1957, in preparation for the 1958 program: *Report to the President by the President's Citizens Advisers on The Mutual Security Program* (Fairless Report), Washington, D.C., 1957; and *A New Emphasis on Economic Development Abroad: A Report to the President of the United States on Ways, Means and Reasons for U.S. Assistance to International Economic Development* (Johnston Report), Washington, D.C., 1957.

Not since the Harriman, Herter, Krug, and Nourse Reports, preceding the European Recovery Program of 1947, had foreign aid been as thoroughly studied and reported upon as it was in 1957. For a suggestive review of the reports and of the issues on which they agreed and disagreed, see Thomas C. Schelling, "American Aid and Economic Development," in *International Stability and Progress: United States Interests and Instruments*, The American Assembly, New York, 1957, pp. 121-167.

[128] *Third Report to Congress on the Mutual Security Program, December 31, 1952*, Washington, D.C., 1953, pp. x-xi.

E. SUMMARY

"Competitive coexistence" is an ambiguous euphemism. Rather than signifying the compatibility of conflicting systems, it has signified the compatibility of political *détente* and military threats. It has, for example, by no means meant that the probabilities of all local war contingencies have diminished. The implications of coexistence with respect to the improved allocation of foreign aid are, consequently, as ambiguous as the term itself.

In fiscal 1955, the glossary of foreign aid was redefined to include both military end-item aid (the Military Assistance Program), "direct forces support," and "defense support." "Development assistance" was established as an explicit category of aid. As before, transferability of funds among the several aid categories implied that, at a "higher" objectives level, the categories were parts of a *single* system of allocation.

Mutual Security aid allocations in 1955 reflected the increasing prominence of the Asian area, already apparent in 1954. Within Southern Asia, the largest increases in non-MAP aid allocations were in Pakistan, Thailand, and the Philippines. At the same time, there seemed to be no reason for believing that the physical productivity of incremental aid rose in these three countries over 1954. To validate the relative and absolute increases that they received requires assuming that their adherence to SEATO in itself resulted in a higher policy "value" attributed to them by the United States.

Within the Military Assistance Program, SEATO members were similarly favored and without any apparent justification in terms of enhanced military aid productivity. In terms of the local war contingencies facing Pakistan and Thailand, for example, there seem to be strong reasons for doubting the "optimality" of the reallocations that were made.

Sectoral allocations of economic and technical aid to the later-maturing and longer-yielding sectors in 1955 were larger than to the quicker-yielding sectors, though by a smaller margin than in 1954. But the more impressive change in allocations was in the general-and-miscellaneous category, whose share of the total rose substantially. The growing need to use dollar aid to meet the local costs, no less directly than the foreign exchange costs, of investment projects is one explanation for this change.

In 1956, emphasis on allocation for Asia continued to grow. Moreover, as a result of an increasing verbal concern by the United States for contributing to political stability and cohesion in recipient countries, a larger amount and share of non-MAP aid went to economic and technical assistance in Southern Asia than in the preceding year. One indication of this concern was the new Asian Economic Development Fund, although the Fund's lack of explicit allocation criteria and multi-year authorization limited the use made of it in 1956 (and 1957).

However, country allocations of economic and technical aid in Southern Asia were not entirely consistent with announced U.S. policy. Economic and technical aid to India, for example, was reduced, in comparison with 1955. While economic and technical aid to Ceylon was resumed, and that to Afghanistan and Indonesia increased, relatively minor considerations (like Ceylon's voicing of anti-communist sentiments at the Bandung Conference, and Afghanistan's receipt of a Soviet loan commitment) may have had a significant influence on these reallocations.

Direct military assistance was cut in 1956 below the 1955 level. In part, the cut was due to the shift of MSP emphasis to non-military aid; in part, too, it was due to the over-all Congressional reduction in MSP, and to the implicit Congressional judgment that resources previously devoted to the Program would be used to better advantage in other government programs or in the private sector of the U.S. economy.

This over-all judgment was changed in the 1957 program when total MSP appropriations rose nearly 40 per cent, with most of the increase concentrated on MAP. At the same time, economic and technical aid in Southern Asia increased substantially above the preceding year, mainly as a result of a resumption of aid to Burma, and a doubling of these categories of aid to Indonesia and Viet Nam. The size, if not the resumption, of aid obligations in Burma seems to have been affected by the unpremeditated, but nonetheless effective, sequence of Burma's having both received Soviet aid offers and having voiced anti-Soviet sentiments (the latter, in the UN debate on Hungary). Increased aid to Indonesia would also seem to have been affected by the first of these considerations. On the other hand, the increased allocation to Viet Nam in 1957 is explainable in terms of the heightened productivity of non-military aid in that country, as a result of improvement in internal security conditions.

Though appropriations for MAP rose again in 1957, the increases had little effect on military aid in Southern Asia. The capabilities sought by MAP in Southern Asia remained what they had been since the end of the Indochina war.

In many respects, the attitude accompanying Congressional consideration of the 1957 Mutual Security Program was more significant than the actual appropriations. In large measure as a response to the expanded economic offensive of the Soviet Bloc, both Congressional and Executive Branch attention began to focus on a number of hard questions concerning the objectives and the uses of Mutual Security aid. The questions had been around and largely unanswered for many years. In the coexistence era, the need to find better answers appeared to be especially imperative.

PART III

THE OBJECTIVES OF FOREIGN AID

CHAPTER 7

THE OBJECTIVES OF UNITED STATES
ASSISTANCE PROGRAMS IN SOUTHERN ASIA

A. Some General Considerations

IT IS A TRUISM that the objectives of United States foreign aid should also be objectives of United States foreign policy. It is a truism in the same sense that the objectives of foreign trade policy should be objectives of foreign policy, or that the objectives of Army or Air Force policy should be objectives of national defense policy. Yet it does not follow that *all* foreign policy objectives should be objectives of foreign aid. Some objectives of foreign policy have little or nothing to do with foreign aid; for example, the reunification of Germany and Korea, the evacuation of Soviet armed forces from Eastern Europe, the non-admission of Communist China to the United Nations. Clearly, if U.S. aid does not contribute to these ends, they cannot rationally be its objectives.

Foreign policy consists of many types of actions and programs, of which the public transfer of a portion of the U.S. national product is an important, but not the only, one. Diplomacy, the positioning and composition of the armed forces, public information and cultural relations, commercial and trade policy are some other foreign policy instruments. In part, the objectives of these different instruments overlap. For example, non-discriminatory access by private American capital to foreign resources is an objective both of U.S. diplomacy and of commercial and trade policy. But the fit is not exact. Some objectives of particular foreign policy instruments are not common to all. Hence, the objectives of foreign policy include, but are not confined to, the objectives of any single foreign policy instrument. The objectives of foreign aid are part of, but not identical with, the objectives of foreign policy.

1. Objectives "Levels" and the Inevitability of One More "Why"

It is convenient and customary to define objectives as the ends toward which action (or intentional inaction) is directed. But the question that can always be asked of an end is "why?" And the answer—other than "why not?"—must be in terms of some other end.

If we contend, for example, that the United States provides external aid in order to increase investment and accelerate economic growth in recipient countries, or in order to increase the size and strength of their military forces, the question can be asked *why* should the United States desire these objectives? And if we answer by saying that the United States desires these objectives because they contribute, respectively, to political stability in recipient countries, and to their ability and will to resist military aggression, the original question can be repeated again. In turn, its answer can be that these "higher-level" objectives are valued because they contribute to the prosperity or the security of the United States, or both. Even this doesn't necessarily end the matter. If we pursue the process further, the familiar "ultimate" objectives of national security and prosperity can, in turn, be justified by recourse to still higher-level aims. As an Assistant Secretary of State expressed these aims to the Colombo Plan Consultative Committee:

"We give aid . . . to the Asian people because their objectives of peace, freedom, and human dignity are our objectives. . . . We give aid since the cause of freedom, independence, and human dignity anywhere in the world is our cause as well."[1]

The point is that there is no logical end to this sequence. There is always one more "why" that can be asked of any objective. The only end to a question of ends is an assumption.

Foreign aid and foreign policy are, in this respect, no different from domestic public programs. In both cases, these are differing levels to which the assessment of their corresponding objectives can be pursued. What are objectives at one level and for one problem are means toward other objectives in "higher-level" problems. Analytically, the objectives level that is appropriate depends on the problem concerned.

In principle, it would be nice to use "high-level" objectives in trying to solve any particular problem. But usually it isn't possible to do so. The higher we ascend in the hierarchy of objectives, the less useful the objectives are for determining preferred solutions to specific decision-making problems. To assert that international peace and freedom, or national security, for example, are objectives of U.S. foreign aid, does not help at all in determining how to use foreign

[1] The quotation is from Assistant Secretary Walter Robertson's statement before the ministerial meeting of the Colombo Plan Consultative Committee in December 1956. *State Department Bulletin*, December 17, 1956, p. 958.

aid efficiently. It is true that these are the broad objectives toward which foreign aid is directed. But we simply know too little about how to measure progress toward objectives that are as broad as these. We know too little about how (or whether) we can precisely relate the use of foreign aid to these higher-level objectives, to permit us to apply them as guides to choosing preferred uses of aid.

Instead, for this problem, we need to descend the hierarchy of objectives. We need to formulate objectives more narrowly so that they are more precisely—that is, more measurably—connected to the aid inputs whose efficient use we are concerned with. From the standpoint of the higher-level objectives, the narrower—and more useful— ones are "proximate" objectives that are associated with the higher-level objectives in a general, but usually imprecise, way. From the standpoint of the higher-level problems of peace, freedom, and security, the problem of efficient use of foreign aid is a "sub-problem" and its solution, at best, a "suboptimization."[2]

2. Proximate Objectives and the
Danger of Inconsistency

To quantify aid objectives is at once a useful, deceptive, and difficult task. It is useful insofar as it can help in clarifying objectives and in assessing the effectiveness of alternative allocations of aid. It is deceptive because superficially it seems so natural and easy to do. Indeed, public policy statements concerning the Mutual Security Program frequently, if not consistently, express aid accomplishments and, inferentially, aid objectives in quantitative terms. Consider, for example, Secretary Dulles' statement, referring to MAP, and to what we have called military support:

"With these programs, we are enabled to spend *far less* on our own military programs—and to achieve *far greater security*—than would otherwise be the case."[3]

[2] For a fuller discussion of these terms and some of the general points discussed here, see Roland N. McKean, *Efficiency in Government Through Systems Analysis*, New York, 1958, pp. 25-49.

[3] *Mutual Security Act of 1957*, Senate Hearings, 85th Congress, 1st session, Washington, D.C., 1957, p. 2. (Italics added.) The same point was also expressed in May 1956, by Secretary Dulles: "I would say that if we did not have this mutual security budget of some $4 billion, we would probably have to increase our national defense budget by considerably more than $4 billion. . . . Taking the things as a whole, it [the Mutual Security Program] is the most economical way to get the defense that we want." From testimony before the House Appropriations Committee, cited in *The Military Assistance Program of the United States*, Special Senate Committee to Study the Foreign Aid Program, p. 155.

Or, consider Eisenhower's message to Congress presenting the Administration's Mutual Security Program for 1959:

"Our expenditures for mutual security are fully as important to our national defense as expenditures for our own forces, and *dollar for dollar buy us more in security.*"[4]

In the same vein is the following account of Defense Secretary McElroy's testimony before the Senate Appropriations Committee on the 1959 Program:

"Senator Johnson . . . asked Mr. McElroy whether Congress could guarantee this country more security by adding funds to the President's defense budget or by restoring to the foreign aid program the $597 million requested by the President (but eliminated by the House Appropriations Committee).

"If a choice had to be, Mr. McElroy replied, funds for more B-52's than the President had requested . . . would be 'secondary to our very urgent requirement' for the full foreign aid program. General Twining concurred.

"Senator Johnson said . . . he wanted to be able to tell the electorate that 'the Secretary of Defense tells me . . . we can get more security for our dollar' from the Mutual Security Program than from the defense budget, 'and that the Chairman of the Joint Chiefs of Staff . . . concurred.' "[5]

On closer scrutiny, however, the quantification of aid objectives becomes an extremely difficult task. The most obvious reason is that in an important sense, aid objectives are *qualitative*, notwithstanding the cited quotations. The same problem arises whether we think of higher-level objectives like "human freedom" and free-world "security," or lower-level objectives like deterring aggression, strengthening political stability in recently independent countries, and building "morale" and a "psychological will" to resist aggression. In large part, aid objectives involve *qualities* or *characteristics* which we have difficulty in conceiving in quantitative terms. It can be said, and

---

[4] *The Mutual Security Program Fiscal Year 1959*, Department of State, Department of Defense, International Cooperation Administration, Washington, D.C., p. 1. (Italics added.) To infer from the statement that transfers of government expenditures from other government "security" programs to MSP would increase total returns is tempting, but not necessarily valid. *Average* returns (in "security" terms), which are referred to in the quotation, tell us nothing about *marginal* returns. Nevertheless, it is at least interesting that, for the superficial inference *not* to be valid, the shape of the implied functions relating "security" gains to expenditures would have to be significantly different for MSP and "other" major security programs, namely, the defense budget.

[5] The *New York Times*, Friday, July 25, 1958.

with some justification, that the term *"qualitative"* is another way of referring to what we do not know enough about to refer to quantitatively. To repeat a point previously mentioned, we simply know too little about the broader objectives we seek from foreign aid to express them directly in numerical terms.

In principle, an approach to solving this problem is to try to formulate proximate objectives, which *can* be quantified, as substitutes for the higher-level objectives which cannot. But the principle is easier to assert than to apply. The formulation of suitable, proximate objectives requires not only ingenuity, but caution. For some objectives, try as we may, quantitative measures just cannot be devised that satisfactorily reflect the objectives really sought. Strengthening the "morale" of military forces, and hence their "will" to resist aggression, is a case in point. Promoting "friendship" and cooperative association with the United States may be another case. In these cases, to adopt quantitative, proximate objectives may be quite misleading. Quantitative measures for these objectives may simply be spurious measures. Analytically, we will probably do better to exclude the objectives entirely from an allocation model, and to assert explicitly that the model's solution must be adjusted by the exercise of responsible intuition (judgment) which tries to take them into account.

Even when we are able to formulate quantitative, proximate objectives that are appropriate in certain circumstances, they may be quite inconsistent with higher-level objectives in other circumstances. Additional military forces in recipient countries may be useful as a quantitative aid objective because they generally contribute to U.S. security by helping to deter or to meet aggression. But if the forces are—or are likely to be—infiltrated by communist organizers, or if the political reliability of the government commanding them is questionable, or if geographical conditions make external aggression extremely unlikely, force additions may be quite inconsistent with higher-level U.S. objectives.

The risk of inconsistency between quantitative, proximate aid objectives and qualitative, higher-level objectives is clear. Awareness of the risk is probably the only way of providing partial insurance against it. We simply have to re-examine, from time to time, the consistency of the proximate, quantitative objectives with the higher-level, qualitative objectives that we are really after. Efficiency should not be entirely separated from philosophy.

3. *The Multiplicity of Aid Objectives*

There is yet another difficulty confronting efforts to quantify aid objectives. As we have seen in the preceding review of the Mutual Security Program, and as we will discuss more fully below, aid objectives are emphatically plural. The difficulty here is not that there are different *levels* to which the appraisal of objectives can be carried; namely, that A is a proximate objective because it is a means to B, which in turn is valued because it is a means to C, and so on. The difficulty is that, at any *given* level, foreign aid has multiple objectives, that these objectives are frequently competitive with one another, and that they are likely to be expressed in incommensurable units.

We have seen, from our discussion of the Mutual Security Program in Southern Asia, how diverse have been the objectives affecting the allocation of foreign aid: in the case of military aid, for example, adding to local forces, maintaining the SEATO alliance, and securing military bases for U.S. forces; in the case of non-military aid, enhancing political stability through economic development, stimulating internal resource use in recipient countries, encouraging "friendly" behavior toward the United States, and countering Soviet aid offers. The problem posed by multiple aid objectives is not their quantifiability, but the incommensurability of the quantities in which they are expressed. Objective A_1 may be expressed in squadrons or battalions, A_2 in acres of real estate for U.S. bases, A_3 in dollars, A_4 in national (or UN) votes. In principle, a solution to the problem is to estimate what the United States would be willing to pay for a given (unit) change in each objective's scale through alternative, that is, non-aid, expenditures; in effect, to establish commensurability among diverse objectives by establishing dollar exchange rates among them.[6]

For some groups of objectives this can be done readily. The dollar "worth" of specified U.S. overseas bases or specified local ground forces might be compared by determining the alternative costs which the United States is already incurring to procure equivalent capabilities through additional domestic defense outlays; for example,

[6] Where similar returns are in fact already being purchased by the use of non-aid resources, the exchange rates are the ratios between the aid costs and the corresponding alternative costs. Where no corresponding purchases are being made, the exchange rate will depend on what the United States would have, *and would be willing*, to pay for similar objectives. See below, pp. 289-290.

through outlays on additional tankers for refueling, in the one case, and on additional U.S. mobile ground forces, in the other. But in other instances a dollar exchange rate cannot be so readily determined. If, for example, units of A_1 and A_2 (for example, external economic growth, and "friendly" statements by a recipient government, respectively) are not being purchased with other U.S. resources, and if it cannot be determined what it would cost to do so, then alternative costs will not help establish commensurability. In this case, the analytical problem is, first, to arrange the multiple objectives in reasonably homogeneous groups;[7] second, to try to express each of the objectives quantitatively as a function of aid inputs;[8] and third, to determine *policy* exchange rates among competing objectives, that is, to focus responsible policy judgment on the need to determine how much of A_1, under given circumstances and at a given time, is to be "traded" for a unit of A_2 in allocating aid among alternative uses.

The role of analysis in the process is that of quantifying and grouping the multiple objectives, not choosing among them. "Policy" exchange rates depend, finally, on judgment, not analysis. But it is likely that the clearer the formulation of the multiple objectives, the more accurately will the policy rates actually reflect the judgment of those responsible for making them.

4. The Criterion Problem

The purpose of clarifying and quantifying aid objectives, and trying to determine exchange rates among them, is to attempt to increase the efficiency of foreign aid use. To increase efficiency—that is, to obtain higher returns from the resources available, or to get constant returns with fewer resources—we need to know how to calculate returns. As Paul Nitze, in a nice understatement of the point, has observed: "If one is not clear as to the validity and importance of the purposes of a program, it is difficult to find criteria on which to base judgments as to amounts or methods."[9]

On the other hand, if one can be "clear as to the . . . purposes of a program,"—clear enough to formulate relevant (proximate) ob-

[7] See section B, this chapter.

[8] It does not, of course, follow that the objectives have to be expressed in the same (dollar) units as the inputs.

[9] Paul H. Nitze, "The Policy Background for Military Assistance," in *International Stability and Progress: United States Interests and Instruments*, The American Assembly, New York, 1957, p. 100.

jectives quantitatively and to establish exchange rates among them—then the general test, or criterion, for choosing a preferred aid program from the available alternatives is evident: to maximize the gains (or returns or effectiveness) obtainable from given resources; or, what is logically equivalent, to minimize the budget required for attaining specified gains.[10]

In practice, the determination of a suitable criterion is likely to be considerably more complex. In actual decision-making problems, especially in a field as complex and fluid as foreign aid, some objectives cannot be quantified at all. Of those that can, commensurability may be possible only for some. Even where commensurability is possible under conditions of certainty, the uncertainty accompanying some outcomes may make it difficult to evaluate them all in comparable terms. (Is the small chance of a relatively large return to be preferred to the large chance of a relatively small return?) We shall have more to say later about these matters in connection with military aid criteria and allocation.[11] But it should be clear that, in practice, criterion selection requires careful adaptation of the general criterion in order to meet these difficulties.

B. Categories of Foreign Aid Objectives

In our review of aid allocations in Part II, we have repeatedly commented on the number and changeability of labels applied to foreign aid. In seven years, no less than nine different labels were used to refer to various portions of the Mutual Security Program: the Mutual Defense Assistance Program (MDAP); special technical and economic aid; technical assistance; special economic aid; development aid; defense support; direct forces support; Fund for Asian Economic Development; the Military Assistance Program (MAP).[12] In general, we have criticized these labels because they

---

[10] *Not* to obtain "maximum benefit to the receiving countries, with minimum costs to the United States," as one report to the Senate has expressed it. Lewis W. Jones, *South Asia—Report on United Foreign Assistance Programs*, prepared at the request of the Special Senate Committee to Study the Foreign Aid Program, Washington, D.C., 1957, p. 10. Even if we knew how to measure "maximum benefit," we could not obtain it at "minimum costs." "Minimum cost" means *no* aid, and "*maximum* benefit" requires a lot more aid than there is any likelihood of providing. No way has yet been found to have the cake and eat it.

[11] See below, Chapter 10. For a fuller treatment of criterion problems, see McKean, *op.cit.*, Chapter 2, "The Criterion Problem," pp. 25-49.

[12] The list could be expanded by including other categories which were not discussed in Part II: for example, the President's annual "contingency fund," and multilateral (United Nations) technical assistance.

have as frequently obscured as reflected the objectives sought by the corresponding programs and, consequently, have confused rather than clarified the problem of aid allocation.

But there is a point behind the diversity of aid labels which is relevant and useful for our analysis. "Foreign aid" is not sufficiently homogeneous to be dealt with as a single category of allocation. The multiple objectives of foreign aid are simply too varied to be considered simultaneously. As with all big problems, foreign aid allocation must be broken down into smaller ones to be analyzed effectively. To this end, we need to group the multiple objectives of foreign aid into more homogeneous subcategories within which the previously mentioned problems, of quantifying objectives and considering rates of exchange among them, may be more manageable.

For this reason, we will discuss specific objectives in terms of those relating to "military" aid, and to "non-military" aid. For the sake of convention and non-hyphenation, we will sometimes call the latter "economic aid." The assumption underlying the distinction is that some (that is, "military") aid objectives can be considered as substitutable for some objectives of U.S. domestic defense outlays;[13] while other (that is, "economic") aid objectives can be considered as *proximately* measured by certain more or less standard economic and social indicators in recipient countries.[14] The distinction assumes that *within* each category there is sufficient homogeneity of objectives to permit comparison among them, at least to permit it to a greater extent than *between* categories. Overseas bases and facilities, for example, can more reasonably be compared with incremental local forces than either can be compared with higher internal investment in recipient countries. As we shall see, the distinction is not without drawbacks. Some "non-military" aid objectives (for instance, "friendship" and "influence") cannot be considered "economic," in the sense indicated above, by any stretch of imagination or semantics. Even among the objectives of military aid, one major objective—namely, internal security forces—cannot be considered as substitutable for *any* capabilities purchased through

[13] And hence, in principle, dollars spent for these aid objectives can be evaluated in relation to the alternative costs of buying comparable benefits through domestic defense expenditures.

[14] And hence, in principle, dollars spent for these objectives can be evaluated as a problem in investment allocation.

U.S. domestic defense expenditures.[15] Two allocation subcategories may, in other words, just not be enough.[16]

But, despite its shortcomings, the military-economic distinction is a reasonably useful way of arranging the multiple aid objectives into more or less homogeneous groups. It corresponds to terms that have become familiar in the foreign aid history, and it provides an analytically convenient way of approaching some of the major allocation choices that arise.

It should be clear that the military-economic objectives distinction rests on the intended *objectives*, not the *form*, of aid. The choice of form—the commodity content of aid—is frequently less a problem of aid allocation than of public relations.[17] From a public relations standpoint, for example, it might be preferable to extend aid, though earmarked for the agreed purpose of increasing internal military outlays, in the form of "civilian" consumer or producer goods rather than in the form of military end-items. (Military aid to a "neutralist" country like India—perhaps an unlikely, but not an inconceivable contingency—might be an illustration.) At the same time, there might be circumstances where aid, though primarily intended to accelerate internal economic growth, might preferably be extended in the form of military end-items. (A portion of the "economic" aid to a SEATO member might be an example.) But in either case, the aid allocation involved should be considered in relation to the allocation category in which the primary aid objectives fall.

[15] See below, pp. 292-293.

[16] Analytically, such irreducibly heterogeneous objectives can be dealt with in three ways: by applying them as "constraints" in the criterion used for selecting a preferred allocation within a given subcategory; by creating "other" allocation subcategories to take account of these objectives (what is currently referred to in the Mutual Security Program as "special assistance" essentially consists of such "other" subcategories—including requirements for meeting unforeseen contingencies); or by assuming that allocation "solutions" arrived at in both the "economic" and "military" subcategories must be adjusted by explicit policy judgments that try to take into account the excluded objectives. In the simplified mathematical models to be discussed later, we will adopt the last of these procedures. See below, Chapter 10.

[17] Assuming that the objectives of donor and recipient coincide. If they do not, there may, under certain circumstances, be good reasons for confining aid to commodities that are closely connected with the end-use intended by the donor. In such circumstances, intended objectives are more likely to be advanced if aid commodities are tangibly related to the intended objectives. The leaders of a recipient country may, for example, be far from unanimous in their views as to the desirability of increasing local military forces. Aid extended in the form of military hardware may suffice to decide the issue because of the inconvenience that would be involved for the recipient in diverting the aid resources to other uses.

For a discussion of the substitutability of resources and its bearing on the form of aid, see Appendix I; Chapter 5, pp. 159-162; and Chapter 6, pp. 187-189.

This is not to say that public relations are not important, but only that they are not part of the analytical problem we are concerned with here, namely, how aid objectives can be formulated to help in making better decisions on allocation—specifically, intercountry allocation decisions—*within* the United States government.[18]

C. The Objectives of Non-Military Assistance

In discussing the objectives of non-military aid, we shall be mainly concerned with what these objectives *are*, and what they *have been* since the beginning of U.S. assistance in Southern Asia. If we regard these objectives as a list of goals, the list has not changed fundamentally during the period covered by the historical review of Part II.[19] What have changed have been the relative "priorities," or what we have referred to as the rates of exchange, among aid objectives. These changes, in turn, occurred in response to changes in international circumstances, and also as a result of changing (and

[18] The emphasis on *"intra"*-governmental decisions has another implication that perhaps should be made explicit. While it is patently necessary for decision-makers to be clear about the objectives actually sought with military or economic aid in order for aid allocation to be improved, clarity doesn't necessarily imply publicity.

One of the confusing controversies that often arises in discussing aid objectives, for example, is that between advocates of "positive" as against "negative" objectives, or "attainment" as against "containment"; more specifically, the building of "successful" governments or institutions in recipient countries as against "anti-Communism." (For some of these formulations, see Harlan Cleveland, *The Theory and Practice of Foreign Aid*—A Paper Prepared for the Special Studies Project of The Rockefeller Brothers Fund, Syracuse, 1956, especially pp. 27-31; Max F. Millikan and Walt W. Rostow, *A Proposal—Key to an Effective Foreign Policy*, New York, 1957, especially pp. 19-25; Lewis W. Jones, *South Asia—Report on U.S. Foreign Assistance Programs*, Special Senate Committee to Study the Foreign Aid Program, Washington, D.C., 1957, p. 4ff.; and Paul H. Nitze, "Aims and Methods of United States Foreign Policy," in *Bulletin of the Atomic Scientists*, October 1957, p. 293.)

In large part, the controversy involves "professed" rather than "actual" objectives. Whether U.S. objectives are expressed in "positive," rather than "negative," terms may have important psychological effects, especially in an area as sensitive to verbal slogans as Southern Asia. But if the terms refer essentially to the same set of desired consequences—the one expressed in terms of what is sought, the other what is sought to be avoided—the actual objectives are no different, gains and losses are both counted in the same coin, and the allocation problem is essentially unchanged.

[19] In the testimony on the Mutual Security Program for 1956, the following exchange between Secretary Dulles and Congressman Bentley is of interest:

Mr. Bentley: . . . Would you say . . . that the program is not basically . . . changed from when it was initiated . . . ?

Secretary Dulles: The purposes behind the program have remained pretty constant. As the program has accomplished results in one area, the emphasis has been shifted to another. But, basically, the spirit and the purpose is much the same.

Mutual Security Act of 1955, House Hearings, Washington, D.C., 1955, p. 23.

sometimes inconsistent) judgments applied to essentially unchanged circumstances.[20]

Besides describing what the specific objectives of economic aid have been, we shall comment on their usefulness and relevance for dealing with the problem of aid allocation. To be useful for this problem, objectives should be susceptible of formulation, at least proximately, in quantitative terms. To be relevant, they should bear an identifiable relationship to aid, or to other variables which aid can affect.

The multiple objectives which have justified and influenced the use of non-military aid in Southern Asia can be conveniently arranged in a familiar trinity: political objectives; economic objectives; and humanitarian objectives.[21] Of these, the most important, historically and currently, as well as the most difficult to formulate in a relevant and useful way, are the political objectives.

1. Political Objectives of Non-Military Aid

a. *Political Stability and Vulnerability.* At the risk of making the simple seem complex, the "political" objectives of aid can be defined as those which entail certain relationships—between the government and the people of a recipient country (or influential segments of "the people"),[22] or between the recipient government or people and the governments of other countries (including the United States)— that are both valued by the United States and are believed to be affected by aid. What are the "relationships" that comprise the political objectives of non-military aid?

First and foremost among these objectives is *internal political strength and stability.* We have seen its prominence in our historical review of the Mutual Security Program. In the up-dated China "lesson" set forth by the Griffin Mission before the Korean war, in the conclusions of the Gray and Rockefeller Reports during the Korean war, and in testimony and legislation on the Mutual Security Program from 1952 to 1957, building internal political strength and stability in recipient countries has been a ubiquitous objective of U.S. non-military aid in Southern Asia.[23] In his message to the Con-

---

[20] See Chapter 4, pp. 75-77, and Chapter 5, pp. 164-166.

[21] For a similar formulation, see the perceptive discussion by Edward S. Mason, *Promoting Economic Development: The United States and Southern Asia,* Claremont, 1955, especially pp. 12-19, 28-32.

[22] See below, pp. 263-264.

[23] See, for example, the quotations previously cited. Chapter 4, pp. 82-83; Chapter 5, pp. 112-113, 118, 136-137, 163-164; and Chapter 6, pp. 211-212, 227-228.

gress on the Mutual Security Program for fiscal year 1958, President Eisenhower expressed the main objective of non-military aid as follows:

"This part of the [Mutual Security] programs helps less developed countries make the social and political progress needed to preserve their independence. Unless these peoples can hope for reasonable economic advance, the danger will be acute that their governments will be subverted by communism.

"To millions of people close to the Soviet and Chinese Communist borders, political freedom is still new. To many it must still prove its worth. To survive it must show the way to . . . freedom from the poverty and hopelessness in which these peoples have lived for centuries. With their new freedom, their desire . . . to develop their economies [is] intense. They are fixed upon raising their standards of living. Yet they lack sufficient resources. Their need for help is desperate—both for technical know-how and capital.

"Lacking outside help, these new nations cannot advance economically as they must to maintain their independence. Their moderate leaders must be able to obtain sufficient help from the free world to offer convincing hope of progress. Otherwise their people will surely turn elsewhere. Extremist elements would then seize power, whip up national hatreds and incite civil dissension and strife. The danger would be grave that these free governments would disappear. Instability and threats to peace would result. . . .

"The help toward economic development that we provide these countries is a means to forestall such crises. Our assistance is thus insurance against rising tensions and increased dangers of war. . . ."[24] Testifying in support of the 1958 program, Secretary Dulles reiterated the same view of the main political objective of economic aid:

"For generations these people [of the underdeveloped countries] have fatalistically accepted stagnation. But now their mood is different. Two intense emotions grip . . . [them]. The first is a desire to maintain and strengthen their newly won political freedom. The second is a determination to raise their pitifully low standards of living and get started quickly on the inevitably long road to economic betterment.

"But the obstacles to growth are substantial. There is a shortage . . .

[24] *The Mutual Security Program, Fiscal Year 1958*, Department of State, Department of Defense, International Cooperation Administration, Washington, D.C., 1957, p. 4.

of technicians. The governments are inexperienced . . . very little can be saved and invested. Without outside help, the prospects of economic growth are indeed very slim.

"These people are determined to move forward. If they do not succeed, there will be increasing discontent which may sweep away their moderate leaders of today and bring to power extremist leaders who will resort to extremist measures fostered by international communism.

"Today millions of people in these countries seek the answer to this simple question: Do political independence and freedom mean economic growth? If these peoples do not feel that in freedom they get growth, then freedom will be on its way out in much of the world.

"It is in our interest to demonstrate that freedom and growth go hand in hand."[25]

Implicit in these statements, as in the many similar statements previously cited, is a particular hypothesis: the vulnerability of poor, newly independent nations to internal political extremism depends on a relationship between public aspirations for economic improvement in these nations, and public confidence in existing and prospective opportunities for achieving economic improvement. If the hypothesis is accepted, and with it the further assumption that external aid can increase the opportunity for economic improvement in recipient countries, the political stability objective of non-military aid follows.[26] The objective of aid is, then, to reduce political vul-

[25] *Mutual Security Act of 1957*, Senate Hearings, 85th Congress, 1st session, Washington, D.C., 1957, pp. 4-5.

[26] Follows, that is, if it be assumed that it is in the interest of the United States to strengthen political stability in recipient countries. If the question is asked why indeed political stability *is* in the U.S. interest, the answer requires an ascent in the "objectives" hierarchy (see above, pp. 4-5). In the era of nominal "coexistence" there is, as we have seen, a wide range of strategies available to the Sino-Soviet Bloc which poses a correspondingly wide range of threats to the security of the United States. Besides central nuclear war, or limited "local" war, one prominent possibility is that of communist acquisition of local power peacefully through the electoral process, supplemented by internal subversion, if necessary.

As we have previously noted (see above, Chapter 6, pp. 208-209), this may be a real possibility in a number of countries in Southern Asia, given time and internal malperformance by the governments of these countries. That it is in the U.S. interest to prevent such a contingency is, at a higher objectives level, a matter of U.S. national security. A peaceful "nibbling away" of foreign areas could make the U.S. defense position more difficult—ultimately by making the United States itself relatively less able to recover from all-out war than an ever-expanding communist world, and hence diminishing the U.S. ability to deter such a war. Even beyond the effect on our defense position, it is not too hard to envision that, in a largely communist

nerability by increasing the opportunities for and the pace of economic development in recipient countries.

The same hypothesis can also be formulated more affirmatively. The chances of survival and consolidation of free political systems in the Asian area—free in the sense that they are based to a considerable extent on consent rather than coercion—depend on these systems' conducing to "successful" economies—"successful" in the sense that the level of output, its rate of growth and its distribution are considered sufficient, in relation to accepted norms, to evoke consent.

A variant of this hypothesis involves the consent, not of the masses, but of the Asian elites who determine public opinion, as well as the public support, or lack of it, enjoyed by government. If the hypothesis previously described can be referred to as one concerning "mass" behavior, this variant can be referred to as a "class" hypothesis. It views the process by which economic development promotes political stability in terms of enlisting the energies, and thereby the loyalties, of elites through their participation in development programs. If it is assumed that the degree of elitist enlistment is a function of the rate of development, the two versions of the vulnerability hypothesis are likely to yield similar predictive results. If, on the other hand, elitist enlistment depends on other factors—for example, on rising national prestige, or a growth of heavy industry, or the number of nuclear reactors—the two versions of the vulnerability hypothesis are likely to yield quite different predictive (and policy) conclusions.[27]

Though its dominant role among the objectives of non-military aid is evident, the "political vulnerability" hypothesis is complex and tricky. As an analytical hypothesis, which purports to describe certain relationships between economic variables and political behavior, it suffers, for example, from a risk of tautology. The "success" of particular societies, or the "sufficiency" of their economic growth, may only be determinable from their survival. If they survive, their

---

world, the kind of society the United States would itself become would make what we have to defend seem much less valuable.

[27] For a statement of the "class" variant, see *The Objectives of U.S. Economic Assistance Programs*, A Study Prepared at the Request of the Special Senate Committee to Study the Foreign Aid Program by the Center for International Studies, Massachusetts Institute of Technology, Washington, D.C., 1957, pp. 21-22; and Max F. Millikan and Walt W. Rostow, *A Proposal*, New York, 1957, pp. 28-29.

economic growth was "sufficient." If they do not, then their growth was insufficient, and their "success" too limited.

The point is simply that, for the hypothesis to be testable, it is necessary to have some way of measuring the "sufficiency" and "success" of a country's economic growth that is independent of its survival. Without an independent measure of the sufficiency of a country's economic growth, the hypothesis lacks meaning because it cannot be refuted.

Besides the risk of tautology, the political vulnerability hypothesis presents other difficulties. Though the hypothesis suggests a relationship between economic variables and political behavior, both concepts are extremely diffuse. What are the relevant economic variables and what are the relevant indicators of political behavior? And what, moreover, is the precise functional relationship between them which the hypothesis implies? We need at least rudimentary answers to these questions before the hypothesis can be formulated with sufficient clarity to be at all relevant and useful for the problem of aid allocation. Both because of the historical prominence of the political vulnerability hypothesis as an articulated objective of non-military aid, and because of the analytical complexities which it presents, the next two chapters will be concerned with an attempt to formulate the hypothesis in a testable form for use as an analytical tool in the allocation of economic aid.

b. Friendship and Influence. Another political objective of economic aid can be variously described as the acquisition (or maintenance) of "friendship," influence, good-will and cooperation. Whereas the objective of political stability implied an *internal* relationship between the recipient government and its domestic constituency, promoting cooperation or friendship implies an external relationship between donor and recipient, or between donor and particular groups or individuals in the recipient country.

In our historical review of Mutual Security in Southern Asia, we have seen occasional evidence that this has indeed been an objective of aid. Promoting friendship toward the United States has been an aid objective in the direct sense that it has affected the allocation of aid. If the allocation of a resource is affected by a given preference, then the preference is likely to reflect an objective, that is, a "value," which the resource is trying to "produce." If, for example, additional aid is intentionally allocated to recipients whose relationship to the United States is friendly and cooperative, it is reasonable to infer that encouraging or perpetuating this relationship is one of the aims of aid. The aid allocations to the Philippines in 1951,[28] to the SEATO members in 1955-1957,[29] and to Ceylon in 1956[30] are cases in point.

Besides the question of whether friendship and influence *has been* an aid objective, there is the question of whether it is an *appropriate* objective. In our review of the Mutual Security Program, we have referred to the view that friendship and cooperation with the United States ought to be an objective of aid and hence affect its allocation.[31] In March 1957, the President's Advisory Committee (Fairless Committee) on the Mutual Security Program endorsed this view, observing that: "In foreign assistance programs a higher priority should be given to those countries which have joined in the collective security system."[32]

On the other hand, the view has been as vociferously opposed as it has been advocated. Testifying on the proposed Development Loan Fund for 1958, for example, Secretary Dulles observed:

"Not for one minute do I think the purpose . . . is to make friends. The purpose . . . is to look out for the interests of the United States. Whether we make friends, I do not care. . . . We are doing these things because it will serve the interests of the United States."[33]

But quite apart from whether friendship and cooperation ought to be objectives of economic aid is an antecedent question: whether,

[28] Chapter 4, pp. 95-96.

[29] Chapter 6, pp. 199-200, 223-224. It should be noted that we are referring here to allocations of "economic," that is, non-military, aid. To the extent that allocations to the SEATO countries reflected the costs in hardware or software of "purchasing" additional (or stronger) local forces which were substitutable, in principle at least, for additional U.S. defense outlays—to this extent the allocations should properly be regarded as military aid validated by "military" objectives. However, as indicated in the citations of Chapter 6, much of the additional aid allocations to the SEATO countries neither produced nor were intended to produce such military returns. Instead, the additional allocations seemed to depend on the anticipated strengthening of cooperative and friendly associations between the SEATO countries and the United States.

[30] Chapter 6, p. 222.

[31] See, for example, the Congressional argument for reducing the Administration's aid proposals for India (Chapter 5, pp. 144ff.), and, in this connection, the assertion "that we should . . . take a more generous attitude toward . . . our friends, like Pakistan, then [toward] those who maintain an attitude of neutralism," Chapter 6, pp. 223-224; and p. 222, footnote 75.

[32] *Report to the President*, by the President's Citizen Advisers on the Mutual Security Program, Washington, D.C., 1957, p. 11.

[33] *Mutual Security Appropriations for 1958*, Hearings Before the House Appropriations Committee, 85th Congress, 1st session, Washington, D.C., 1957, p. 120. The contrast in the two cited quotations is based on the tacit premise that "friends" are more likely to join the U.S. collective security system, and hence that "making friends" should be an objective of aid (the first view), or should not be (the second view).

logically, they *can* be. From the standpoint of aid allocation, an objective that is rationally acceptable must be related in an appreciable and predictable way to the aid inputs to be allocated.[34] Without such a relation, the "objective" cannot be an "output" of aid and hence, plainly, cannot be an objective of aid.

Moreover, the relation must be *continuous* rather than discrete if the objective is to be useful in aid allocation. If, for example, friendship, influence and cooperation depend on giving *some* aid, but their extent is not affected by the *amount* of aid given, they should, clearly, not affect the allocation of aid. They would be relevant in deciding whether to give aid, but not how much to give.

The point of these comments is to suggest, without proving, that friendship, cooperation and influence are too unpredictable as consequences of aid to be acceptable objectives of aid. For illustrations of this unpredictability, one thinks both of hostile changes in behavior toward the United States by countries which were favored recipients of aid, and of friendly changes in behavior by countries receiving little or no aid. Egypt (that, prior to the summer of 1956, had received substantially more aid from the United States than any other Arab country), and, to some extent, India as well, are examples of the first sort, at least through 1957. The countries of Latin America, always minor recipients of Mutual Security assistance, as well as Burma and Ceylon during the period that neither received any assistance from the United States, are examples of the second sort.[35]

Of course, there may be particular instances in which additional aid to a recipient will yield an anticipated return in terms of influence and negotiable good-will advantageous to the United States. In such cases, if the judgment of the responsible decision-makers is sufficiently acute to discern them, an appropriate adjustment in aid allocations should be made. But, in general, friendship, influence, and cooperation are too unreliably related to aid to have a justifiable effect on its use.

Yet it can be argued that friendship and influence are no *less*

[34] "Predictable" does not mean that the objective must be related to the aid input with certainty, but rather that the probability distribution of the relationship is known or can be subjectively estimated. "Appreciable'" implies that the mean of the distribution is greater than zero by enough to be interesting.

[35] To state the point baldly, if we could think of some quantitative measure of friendship and cooperation—for instance, UN voting record, government statements favorable to the West, etc.—a frequency distribution of the change in this measure per unit change in annual aid allocations might well have a zero mean.

reliably, nor *more* discretely, related to aid than is political stability. And the argument perhaps deserves special consideration inasmuch as it is probably fair to characterize Soviet foreign aid as "influence-maximizing," rather than "stability-maximizing."[36]

However, it is the contention of the next two chapters that at least some aspects of the political stability-economic aid connection can be generalized, while the same cannot be said concerning the connection between "influence" and aid. The point is not that friendship and influence are irrelevant to the use of aid, but rather that such relevance as they have can only be discerned by *ad hoc* judgments concerning particular personalities in particular circumstances. General analytical methods can be of little help in a situation of this kind.

Yet we ought not to make this judgment too assuredly nor too soon. Perhaps it is possible to make and test some useful generalizations concerning the political relationships between donor and recipient that are "produced" by aid. One might begin, for example, by distinguishing "friendship" (or "good-will"), from "influence" (or "cooperation"). If friendship is not a reliable, nor even necessarily desirable, result of aid, perhaps influence is. Moreover, perhaps it is possible to think in terms of more or less precise "payoffs" associated with U.S. influence. We might, for example, identify influence with a *bargaining power* to alter specific external political conditions in directions we deem favorable: to prevail upon India and Pakistan to forswear the use of force in Kashmir, or to induce Asian neutralists to propose UN-policed elections in divided Viet Nam, or to widen membership in SEATO (if indeed the latter is desired). If, besides, we could relate variations in aid inputs to changes in our power to bargain for such political adjustments, we might have a basis for treating influence as a valid and useful objective of non-military aid.

Although skepticism concerning such analytical possibilities may be warranted, they should at least be carefully considered. In any event, another important qualification needs to be added to our observations about both friendship and influence as objectives of aid. As previously noted, the objectives of foreign aid are part of, but not identical with, the objectives of foreign policy. Even granted that it may not be admissible to consider friendship, influence, and cooperation as objectives of foreign *aid*, because they are neither

[36] See Chapter 11, pp. 390-391.

predictably nor continuously related to aid, it may be quite admissible to consider them as objectives of foreign *policy*. Under this circumstance, friendship considerations might affect aid allocations, not as *objectives* presumed to vary in magnitude with the amounts of aid allocated to different uses (countries), but as foreign policy *parameters*, applied to evaluating the objectives that *do* vary with the amounts of aid allocated.

If, for example, political stability is an objective of aid, and is thought to vary with the amount of aid allocated, it can be argued that enhanced political stability is simply more important to the United States in "cooperative," than in "neutral," countries. Even if cooperative behavior is not "produced" by aid, it may nevertheless be a parameter (or weight) applied to evaluating the effects that *are* produced by aid.

Two points should be noted in reply. The first is that, if allocations *are* to be affected by cooperation-influence-friendship considerations, the generally parametric character of these considerations should be recognized more explicitly than perhaps has been true in the history of Mutual Security allocations. The second point is that judgments concerning the relative cooperativeness of potential recipients, at any particular time, are perhaps especially hazardous among the countries of Southern Asia—those "allied" with the United States no less than those which are most assertively neutral. In contemplating judgments about friendship parameters, the likelihood that such judgments may be inacccurate—in Sir William Gilbert's words, that skim milk may masquerade as cream—may be sufficient grounds for not attempting them in the first place.

c. Countering Soviet Bloc Economic Aid. A third political objective frequently associated with economic aid is that of using aid to counter aid offers or commitments by the Soviet Bloc. As Soviet economic aid has become an increasingly prominent feature of the "coexistence" era, efforts to counter it have become an increasingly prominent objective of U.S. aid. We have, for example, previously noted its influence on U.S. aid allocations in Afghanistan and Indonesia.[37] The United States offer—subsequently withdrawn—in 1956 to help Egypt construct the Aswan Dam was another among many notable examples outside Southern Asia.

It has never been entirely clear exactly what aims underlie Soviet economic assistance to non-Bloc countries. Subversion and "ideolog-

[37] See Chapter 6, pp. 222, 235-236.

ical penetration," encouraging neutralism, disrupting the U.S. alliance system, increasing the "respectability" and the influence of the Soviet Union and of internal communist parties in recipient countries, to mention a few, have been advanced as possible Soviet aims.[38] Yet despite our uncertainty about the aims of Soviet aid, the need for U.S. action to meet this "challenge" has been widely stressed. The counteractions urged have included additional U.S. economic aid, relatively lower interest rates on U.S. development loans, and "new methods and techniques" in the extension of U.S. aid.[39] In effect, the reasoning has been that Soviet Bloc aid must entail some prospective political advantage for the donor, and hence denial or diminution of this gain should be an aim (objective) of U.S. aid.

This reasoning can be disputed. It can be contended, for example, that the primary objective of U.S. economic aid is the enhanced political stability consequent to economic development in recipient countries. If Soviet aid contributes to this result it may well abet United States aims. Hence, Soviet aid to a particular recipient, rather than requiring offsetting U.S. aid, might even warrant some reduction in U.S. aid. *If* U.S. aid were optimally allocated *before* Soviet aid to a particular country, the advent or increase of Soviet aid might lower the returns from marginal U.S. aid, warranting its reallocation to a higher-yielding use.[40]

We will discuss Soviet Bloc aid in more detail in Part IV, and will leave this issue until then.[41] Here, however, we must at least express skepticism about the suitability of "countering" Soviet Bloc aid as an objective of U.S. aid for reasons similar to those advanced in commenting on the objective of friendship and cooperation. Not

---

[38] See, for example, *The Foreign Aid Program*, Hearings Before the Special Senate Committee to Study the Foreign Aid Program, Washington, D.C., 1957, pp. 38-39; *Foreign Assistance Activities of the Communist Bloc and Their Implications for the United States*, a Study Prepared at the Request of the Special Senate Committee to Study the Foreign Aid Program, by the Council for Economic and Industry Research, Washington, D.C., 1957, pp. xv, 33-34; *Foreign Policy and Mutual Security*, Draft, Report (the Richards Report) Submitted to the House Committee on Foreign Affairs, Washington, D.C., 1956, pp. 16R-18R.

[39] *Ibid.*, p. 21R.

[40] As one observer, the Chairman of the U.S. Chamber of Commerce, has stated: "Because our aid program is based upon . . . previously appraised total need, it would appear that each and every gift . . . from Communist . . . or any other sources, if it contributed to meeting this over-all need, . . . should make possible a corresponding reduction in the total U.S. aid." Clement Johnson, *Southeast Asia: Report on U.S. Foreign Assistance Program*, Prepared at the Request of the Special Senate Committee to Study the Foreign Aid Program, Washington, D.C., 1957, pp. 8-9.

[41] See Chapter 11.

only is it not clear that Soviet Bloc aid is invariably inimical to U.S. interests. In addition, it is not at all clear that, within a reasonable range, reallocation of U.S. aid can reliably counter whatever benefits the Soviet Bloc derives from aid extended outside the Bloc. It is questionable, for instance, whether U.S. counter offers can, in fact, prevent a recipient from taking advantage of Soviet aid offers. Typically, recipients can and do accept both. And if the United States were to make its aid conditional on non-acceptance of Soviet aid, it is not clear that "higher-level" U.S. foreign policy objectives would be served. "Countering" Soviet aid may be an inappropriate objective of U.S. economic aid because it is an infeasible objective; that is, an objective to which varying allocations of U.S. aid cannot contribute much.

2. Economic Objectives of Non-Military Aid

The economic objectives of non-military aid, like the economic objectives of foreign policy more generally, are those which contribute to increasing the national product or its rate of growth, and which are (at a higher objectives level) validated by this contribution. Reducing barriers to international trade, for example, is an economic objective of U.S. commercial policy. It is justified, insofar as it is a strictly economic objective, by its contribution to expanding the national product. Similarly, obtaining non-discriminatory treatment for American investors abroad is another economic objective of commercial and trade policy. By enabling American investors to choose among a wider range of alternatives, non-discrimination tends to raise expected returns from foreign investment, and hence, to increase real national product.

Economic objectives have played a role, though not a primary one, among the objectives of non-military aid to Southern Asia since the program's inception.[42] These objectives have been broadly stated by the President as follows:

"We . . . have an economic interest in promoting the development

[42] For both Administration and Congressional references to the broad economic objectives of non-military aid to Asia, see, *Report to the President on Foreign Economic Policies* (Gray Report), Washington, D.C., 1950, Chapter 5 above, pp. 112-113; *The Mutual Security Program*, House Hearings, Washington, D.C., 1951, pp. 159, 177-179; *Mutual Security Act Extension*, House Hearings, Washington, D.C., 1952, pp. 8, 850; *Resources for Freedom: A Report to the President by the President's Materials Policy Commission* (Paley Commission), Washington, D.C., 1952, especially the Summary of Volume I, pp. 61-65; and *Mutual Security Act of 1955*, House Hearings, Washington, D.C., 1955, pp. 58-64.

of the free world. In the years to come, the increased economic strength of less developed countries should prove mutually beneficial in providing growing markets for exports, added opportunities for investment and more of the basic materials we need from abroad.[48]

There are three principal ways of viewing the economic objectives of U.S. non-military aid to the underdeveloped countries globally, and to Southern Asia in particular. They may be referred to as the "gains-from-trade" objective, the "strategic-materials" objective, and the "investment-income" objective.[44]

a. Gains from Trade. International trade is one of a select group of activities from which all participants benefit. The reason all countries typically benefit is that their relative costs of producing similar commodities differ. And the principal reason their relative production costs differ is that they are endowed with, and acquire, productive factors—rainfall and monazite no less than people and machinery—in differing proportions. Because relative production costs differ among countries, trade is an efficient way of "producing" those commodities in which a country's costs of production are relatively high. It is "efficient" because the country concerned can acquire more of the commodities for which its production costs are relatively high, by importing them in exchange for exports of commodities in which its costs are relatively low, than by directly producing the imports at home instead of the (foregone) exports. Variety is, in other words, the spur to trade no less than it is the spice of life.

The diversity of relative costs and conditions of production, then, explains *why* countries gain from trade. The relative *amount* a

---

[48] *The President's Message to Congress on the Mutual Security Program for 1959,* the *New York Times,* February 20, 1958. For a similar formulation of the economic objectives of U.S. aid, see Lincoln Gordon, *Economic Aid and Trade Policy as an Instrument of National Strategy,* Prepared for the Special Studies Project, Rockefeller Brothers Funds, New York, 1956, p. 39.

[44] A fourth objective, which may be called the "domestic employment" objective, is sometimes attributed to U.S. aid by Asian recipients. Their underlying notion is that aid is intended to stimulate domestic employment in the United States by promoting an export surplus. There are two reasons why the notion is erroneous and why, consequently, it has not entered into the U.S. discussion of economic objectives of aid: (1) During most of the period of sustained U.S. foreign economic aid (since 1948), the domestic U.S. economy has been bothered by inflation and substantially full employment. Pumps that are drawing at capacity do not need to be primed. (2) In periods of slack in the U.S. economy, for example, 1953-54 and 1957-58, there are cheaper, faster, and politically more palatable ways of stimulating domestic employment than external aid.

country gains depends on the volume of trade and the terms of trade.[45] For a given volume of trade, gains tend to increase as export prices rise relative to import prices. For given terms of trade, gains tend to increase as the volume of trade rises.

If this homily is a familiar one, its connection with the economic objectives of non-military aid may be obscure. The connection arises from the fact that increased gains from trade, presumed consequent to economic growth in the underdeveloped areas, have frequently been advanced as an objective, albeit a secondary one, of U.S. economic aid to these areas.[46] To appraise this objective, we need to

[45] Assuming competitive markets and a balanced trade account, changes in the gains from trade, expressed as a relative varying around zero, can be defined as:

$$Qx_t \cdot \frac{Px_t}{Pm_t} - 100$$

where Qx_t is the index of export volume, Px_t the index of export prices, and Pm_t the index of import prices—calculated at a time t, based on a prior period $t-n$. $\frac{Px_t}{Pm_t}$ represents the net barter terms of trade, $Qx_t \cdot \frac{Px_t}{Pm_t}$ the income terms of trade. Changes in gains from trade, as defined in the above expression, are thus synonymous with changes in capacity to import. See Charles P. Kindleberger, *The Terms of Trade: A European Case Study*, New York, 1956, pp. 288-289.

This definition is adapted from that used in Kindleberger's computations,

$$Qx_t \left(\frac{Px_t}{Pm_t} - 1 \right).$$

Using Qx_t as the subtrahend, as Kindleberger's formula implies, rather than Qx_{t-n} ($=100$), creates one problem. With no changes in the net barter *terms of trade*,

$$\left(\text{that is, } \frac{Px_t}{Pm_t} = 1 \right)$$

but with a rise in trade *volume*, ($Qx_t > Qx_{t-n}$), the Kindleberger formula would record *no* increase in gains from trade.

[46] As stated by the Special Senate Committee on Foreign Aid, for example: "A second national interest . . . is the long-range economic well-being of the United States. The future growth of this nation . . . requires an expanding world commerce as well as expanding sources of raw materials. This dual expansion depends to a considerable extent on the economic development of other countries . . . especially the so-called less-developed nations." *Foreign Aid*, Report of the Special Senate Committee, 1957, p. 9.

For similar views, see the statement by President Eisenhower (above, p. 270, as well as the other references cited on p. 271, footnote 43), and *The Role of Foreign Aid in the Development of Other Countries*, A Study Prepared at the Request of the Special Senate Committee to Study the Foreign Aid Program by the Research Center in Economic Development and Cultural Change of the University of Chicago, Washington, D.C., 1957, p. 73. See also the references and quotations cited in Chapter 3, section F.2.

consider the variables influencing gains from trade—both the terms and the volume of trade—and how and whether they are likely to be affected by economic development.

(1) Terms of Trade. It is reasonable to contend that, as economic growth occurs in underdeveloped areas, their factor endowments may become more like those of the developed countries.[47] As an illustration, the stock of capital is likely to increase in relation to other factors. As, or if, factor endowments become more similar, divergences in relative production costs between developed and developing countries may decline, and with such a decline may come an improvement in the terms of trade of the developing countries.

If, for example, before its development accelerated, a country could itself produce one pound of coffee or five pounds of steel for the same factor cost, it would be clearly advantaged to trade coffee for steel on any terms more favorable to it than 1:5. But if, with internal economic development, the *relative* domestic cost of producing the capital-intensive good, steel, falls by, say, 20 per cent, it will no longer trade coffee on any terms less favorable to it than 1:6. Its terms of trade will thus tend to improve, while those of the developed steel producers will tend to decline. In effect, a rise in its *domestic* supply schedule for steel tends to improve the terms of trade of the importing country.

The possible effect of development on the price elasticity of export supply is another reason why economic development may affect the terms of trade of more advanced countries adversely. Consider, for example, an underdeveloped country which we will call "Neutralia." Assume that its economy is divided into two sectors: a backward subsistence sector, producing food for domestic consumption; and a "modern" sector producing primary agricultural products—such as rubber, copra, and jute—for export. Assume, further, that, in the short run, the export sector's output depends mainly on the amount of labor employed, and that there is considerable unemployed and underemployed labor concentrated in the backward sector, but available for use by the modern sector.[48]

[47] For an example of this contention, see Karl-Erik Hanssen, "A General Theory of the System of International Trade," *American Economic Review*, March 1952, pp. 59-68.

[48] The supply of labor for the modern export sector is, in other words, highly elastic at the current wage rate. The current wage may, nevertheless, be an "equilibrium" wage if lower wages would have the effect of lowering the productivity

Under these conditions, let us assume that export demand rises. Neutralia can readily increase output in the export sector by employing more labor. It can, moreover, do so at relatively small cost because wage rates do not have to be raised appreciably. Consequently, output will rise in response to relatively little price inducement. The supply of exports is, thus, likely to be relatively elastic with respect to price increases above the current price.

Now assume that economic development gets underway in Neutralia. New sectors appear which, for simplicity, we will identify as "domestic industry." Domestic industry absorbs underemployed and unemployed labor from the subsistence sector. Wage rates between domestic industry and the export sector tend toward equality, and the supply of labor in the export sector is likely to be less elastic than it was.

Again, let export demand rise. Output in the export sector also rises. But now, hiring more labor will mean higher wage rates because labor must be attracted away from domestic industry. As labor moves toward the export sector, wage rates tend to rise in domestic industry because reduced industrial employment raises the marginal productivity of industrial labor. Increased output in the export sector therefore encounters increasing wage costs. The rise in export supply for a given increase in price will thus be less than before development occurred. Neutralia's customers will now have to pay a higher price to induce a desired increase in export supply. From their point of view, the terms of trade are less favorable because the supply of Neutralia's exports is *less* elastic with respect to price increases than before development got underway. More generally, the point is that the elasticity of export supply will tend to decrease to the extent that the supply elasticity of labor (or other factors) decreases as a result of economic development.

How is this reasoning related to the economic objectives of non-military aid? The inference we have drawn is that the terms of trade of developed countries may well decline with accelerated growth in the underdeveloped countries.[49] It therefore becomes

of previously employed labor. See Harvey Leibenstein, "The Theory of Underemployment in Backward Economies," *Journal of Political Economy*, April 1957, pp. 94-102.

[49] Kindleberger's recent study of Europe's terms of trade since 1872 provides some support for this inference: ". . . There are forces which tend to make the terms of trade bad for underdeveloped countries, good for rapidly developing countries, and somewhat worse again for countries which have passed their most rapid rate of development," Kindleberger, *op.cit.*, pp. 307-308.

dubious that U.S. aid, ostensibly directed toward maximizing growth in the underdeveloped countries, can, at the same time, be considered validly as contributing to an improvement in future U.S. terms of trade.

(2) *Volume of Trade.* Of course, this is not the whole story. Gains from trade depend, as we have already noted, on the volume of trade as well as the terms. Though economic growth may conceivably impair United States terms of trade, this gain-reducing effect may be more than offset by a rising volume of trade. How, then, is rising income in the underdeveloped areas likely to affect prospective U.S. trade volume?

On a *global* basis, it seems to be generally true that the absolute amount of a country's trade increases as its output and income increase. Income elasticities of export supply and import demand are greater than zero. More precisely, there is a statistically significant correlation between national income and imports, and between national income and exports, for the world's principal trading countries. As shown in Table 29, the rank correlation coefficients for these paired variables in 1955 are .679 and .796 respectively. For 1956, the corresponding coefficients are .825 and .816, respectively.

Table 29

RANK CORRELATION COEFFICIENTS AND SIGNIFICANCE LEVELS—
MERCHANDISE TRADE, AND INCOMES OF PRINCIPAL
WORLD TRADING COUNTRIES, 1955

Correlated Variables[a] (N = 15)	Rank Correlation Coefficient[b]	Significance Level[c]
Imports and National Income of Principal Importing Countries	.679	< .01
Exports and National Income of Principal Exporting Countries	.796	< .01
Per Capita Imports and Per Capita Income of Principal Import Countries	.689	< .01
Per Capita Exports and Per Capita Income of Principal Export Countries	.396	> .05

[a] For the data used in the correlation, see Appendix III, Table 1.

[b] According to:

$$\rho = 1 - \frac{6 \, \Sigma \, (d^2)}{N \, (N^2 - 1)}$$

[c] The significance test used was that of E. G. Olds, "The 5% Significance Levels for Sums of Squares of Rank Differences and a Correction," *Annals of Mathematical Statistics*, Vol. 20, 1949, pp. 117-118, cited in Wilfred J. Dixon and Frank J. Massey, *Introduction to Statistical Analysis*, New York, 1951, p. 261.

For both years, the null hypothesis, that the paired variables are independent, can be rejected at a significance level of less than 1 per cent. Consistent with, though not necessary for, these correlations, is the frequently observed fact "that the economically advanced countries are each others' best customers."[50]

But we must be wary of the fallacy of division: what applies to the whole does not necessarily apply to its parts. More particularly, when we look at U.S. trade with its principal trading partners in 1955, we find quite a different pattern from that prevailing globally. Among the principal trading partners of the United States, the correlation between U.S. imports and the national incomes of principal countries of destination, is *not* statistically significant. As shown in Table 30, the lack of significance applies whether each of the paired variables is expressed on a total or a per capita basis.[51] Moreover, the results do not appear to be unique for 1955. Essentially similar results are obtained with 1956 data.[52]

The results summarized in Table 30 suggest that, among the principal U.S. trading partners, there is apparently no marked connection between higher income and increased trade with the United States. To be sure, this is not the same as saying that increased income in

[50] Ragnar Nurske, *International Trade and Development Policy*, Roundtable of the International Economic Association, Rio de Janeiro, August 1957, p. 8. As Nurkse points out, of total world exports in 1955, 40 per cent were exports by twenty advanced industrial countries to each other and only 25 per cent were exports by these advanced countries to all less-developed countries outside the Communist Bloc.

Logically, the income-trade correlations, cited in the text, could exist even if there were no trade among the advanced countries. If, for example, there were a relatively small number of rich countries, and a relatively large number of poor countries, and if trade between rich countries and poor countries was large relative to trade *among* poor countries, the income-trade correlations could occur in the absence of trade among the rich countries.

[51] From the data on which Table 30 is based, it can be conjectured that U.S. imports, rather than depending on the relative income of trading partners, depend to a greater extent on such factors as geographical proximity and transportation costs (for example, Canada and Mexico), preferential tariff and quota arrangements (for example, Cuba and the Philippines), and resource complementarities and specific U.S. raw materials requirements (for example, Malaya, India, and Venezuela). These factors, in turn, strongly influence the quantity and direction of U.S. exports through their effect on the distribution of international dollar earnings.

[52] Using trade data for 1956, together with the income data for 1955 shown in Appendix III, Table 2, results in a correlation coefficient for U.S. imports and the national incomes of principal countries of import origin of .509, and for U.S. exports and national incomes of principal countries of export destination of .419. The latter calculation involved fifteen countries, the former only eleven countries, because the twelfth largest U.S. import source in 1956 was the Netherlands Antilles, for which no national income figures are available. Neither coefficient is significant at the 5 per cent significance level.

Southern Asia will have *no* effect on U.S. trade. Increased income in Southern Asia may increase that region's trade with "third" countries and these, in turn, may increase their trade with the United States. But since there appears to be no significant connection between income and trade for the major U.S. trading partners, we must at least be skeptical about whether the multilateral rise in trade will necessarily include a rise in U.S. trade as well. And we must be

Table 30

RANK CORRELATION COEFFICIENTS AND SIGNIFICANCE LEVELS—
U.S. MERCHANDISE TRADE, AND INCOME OF PRINCIPAL
U.S. TRADING PARTNERS, 1955

Variables[a] Correlated	Rank Correlation Coefficient[b]	Significance Level[c]
U.S. Imports from and National Income of Principal Countries of U.S. Import Origin ($N = 13$)[d]	.220	> .05
U.S. Exports to and National Income of Principal Countries of U.S. Export Destination ($N = 15$)	.407	> .05
U.S. Imports Per Capita and Income Per Capita of Principal Countries of Import Origin ($N = 13$)[d]	.463	> .05
U.S. Exports Per Capita and Income Per Capita of Principal Countries of Export Destination ($N = 15$)	.328	> .05

[a] For the data used in the correlations, see Appendix III, Table 2.
[b] According to:

$$\rho = 1 - \frac{6 \Sigma (d^2)}{N (N^2 - 1)}$$

[c] The significance test used was that of Olds, cited in Dixon and Massey, *op.cit.*, p. 261.
[d] The sample was limited to thirteen for countries of import origin, because no national income figures were available for the fourteenth largest U.S. import source, the Netherlands Antilles.

skeptical, too, about accepting the familiar argument that since *some* of the largest U.S. trading partners are high-income countries and since *some* of the smallest U.S. trading partners are low-income countries, raising income in the lower-income countries will tend to increase U.S. trade.[53] This may be so, but it is not suggested by the data.

[53] The argument has been frequently advanced in the course of Congressional presentations of the Mutual Security Program. See, for example, *Mutual Security Act of 1955*, House Hearings, pp. 63ff.

Consequently, U.S. economic aid, to the extent it is directed explicitly toward maximizing Asian income and output, can hardly include increased U.S. trade as a realistic objective. As we have previously noted, to be a realistic objective of any resource allocation, a desired consequence should be related, predictably and appreciably, to the inputs that are to be allocated.

b. Strategic Materials. The "strategic materials" objective of economic aid is a special case of the "gains from trade" objective. It is based on several propositions. First, U.S. requirements for imports of certain basic materials will rise substantially over the next few decades. Second, economic development of the underdeveloped countries, which are major sources of these materials, will increase exportable supplies. And finally, the United States should, therefore, provide assistance to spur economic development because of the anticipated increase in international materials supplies.

Quantitatively, the principal basis for the first proposition is the 1952 Report of the President's Materials Policy Commission.[54] For example, the Paley Commission estimated that, assuming constant *relative* prices between 1950 and 1975, U.S. demand for tin would rise by 23 per cent; iron, copper, lead, and zinc, by 40 to 60 per cent; petroleum and rubber, by 100 per cent; and bauxite, by 400 per cent. Over the same period, U.S. reliance on imports of these materials was estimated to rise: for iron ore, from 6 per cent of consumption in 1950 to 35 per cent in 1975; for copper, from 25 per cent to 40 per cent; for zinc, from 33 per cent to 50 per cent; for petroleum, from 8 per cent to 20 per cent.[55]

The weakness in the materials argument is the second proposition. It is one thing to assume that economic development, by raising productivity generally, will tend to increase the supply of strategic materials; that is, that the income elasticity of supply of such materials is greater than zero. It is quite something else to infer that more of these materials will be exported to the United States, assuming constant relative prices. An alternative, and perhaps more likely, inference is that consumption of basic materials by the pro-

[54] *Resources for Freedom: Report of the President's Materials Policy Commission,* Washington, D.C., 1952, 5 vols. See above, Chapter 5, p. 113.

[55] *Ibid.,* Vol. II, "The Outlook for Key Commodities," Chapters 2, 5, 6, 7, 8, 20. Import requirements for tin were estimated as likely to fall because of greater use of domestic scrap (*ibid.,* p. 50). Import requirements for lead in 1975 were estimated as remaining at about 47 per cent of increased total U.S. consumption. No estimates of import requirements for bauxite or natural rubber in 1975 are given in the Paley Report.

ducing countries themselves, as well as by other developing countries, may rise still more than the increased supply. In other words, if the income elasticity of demand in the developing countries, is sufficiently greater than the income elasticity of supply, exportable supplies to the developed countries, at constant relative prices, will fall.[56]

Nor is the point purely theoretical. Recent estimates of the materials requirements that are likely to be associated with various growth rates in the underdeveloped countries, suggest that income elasticities of demand may be high relative to supply elasticities for some of the major strategic materials. Harrison Brown, for example, takes it as a fair assumption that India's industrialization program will double her consumption of metals every ten years, an annual rate of increase of 7 per cent.[57] Extrapolating from current production levels, he then estimates that Indian pig iron production will reach 15 million tons by 1975 and 80 million tons by 2000, by which time total cumulative production will be 2 billion tons (*sic*). By 2000, India's annual consumption of copper will have risen to 1.5 million tons and of tin to 150 thousand tons. He concludes:

"This means that India will be forced to import . . . and will as a result become a competitor for a number of raw materials on the world market. . . . As time goes by, she will become a heavy competitor for (to mention a few shortages) copper and zinc, petroleum and sulphur."

The issue is, of course, not one of "absolute" shortages of foreign supplies—like the lack of a horse for which Richard was prepared to trade his kingdom. It is an issue of cost. If the rising materials demand, generated by economic growth within the underdeveloped countries, raises export prices, the United States will draw on domestic sources and synthetic substitutes to an increasing extent.

It cannot therefore be presumed that aid directed toward economic development in a group of underdeveloped countries, like

[56] More precisely, it can be shown that exportable supplies will fall if the income elasticity of demand exceeds the income elasticity of supply by more than

$$e_d \left(1 - \frac{D}{S} \right),$$ where e_d is the income elasticity of demand, and D and S are,

respectively, initial demand and supply within the underdeveloped exporting country. See Charles Wolf, Jr., "Gains From Trade, Materials Supplies, and Economic Development," P-1583, The RAND Corporation, Santa Monica, 1959, p. 17.

[57] Harrison Brown, James Bonner, John Weir, *The Next Hundred Years*, New York, 1957, pp. 40-42ff.

those of Southern Asia, will, on balance, contribute significantly to increased exports of strategic materials by these countries.[58] The strategic materials objective would therefore seem to have limited relevance or usefulness for the task of allocating development aid. Indeed, it is plausible that development which is general in character, rather than specifically related to materials projects, may reduce exportable supplies of these materials. Hence, for the strategic materials objective to become relevant to the allocation of economic aid, it would be necessary (a) to consider allocation alternatives not as countries, but as projects directly affecting the supply of certain specified strategic materials; and (b) to allocate economic aid among the alternative projects so as to maximize the estimated present value of the resulting materials output, given certain assumptions about relative materials prices, that is, to choose the projects whose internal rate of return, in terms of these materials and prices, is highest. In principle, this was the intent of the Basic Materials Development Fund, which was included in the Mutual Security Program for 1953 as a regional fund for allocation among projects in certain specified materials fields.[59]

c. Investment Income. Besides strategic materials and gains from trade, a third economic objective may be referred to as the "investment-income" objective. Economic aid can be used to raise the yield on private capital in underdeveloped countries by creating a variety of external economies, from a more literate labor force to the more familiar "social overhead" facilities. To the extent that aid has this effect, that is, that such external economies predominate over the tendency toward diminishing returns, it will raise income from U.S. private investment abroad, and hence U.S. real national product.

The investment-income objective was a more evident part of the original "Point Four" technical assistance program than it has been in most other economic assistance under the Mutual Security Program. More recently, it has become a more prominent, though still minor, verbal objective of the Development Loan Fund included in the 1958 Mutual Security Program.[60] Nevertheless, it is not clear

[58] It can, however, be argued that economic development will increase the likelihood of U.S. access to strategic materials supplies by contributing to political stability in the underdeveloped countries. To this extent, the strategic materials objective might be identified more appropriately with the political stability objective of aid. See section C.1(a).

[59] For further discussion of the short-lived Basic Materials Development Fund, see above, Table 10, footnote a.

[60] See, for example, the statement by the then-Deputy Undersecretary of State

how the investment-income objective could be expressed in a form that would be useful for allocating economic aid. There is no apparent reason for assuming, for example, that "maximum economic growth" would also yield maximum income to present and potential U.S. investors in underdeveloped countries. It would also seem that any attempt to express investment-income as a useful objective would require the allocation of aid on a project, rather than country basis. Actually, increasing the income from U.S. external investments may be more reasonable as a hope, than an objective, of U.S. economic aid.

To summarize our main discussion of economic objectives, we have argued that both anticipated gains from trade and increases in strategic materials supplies probably ought not to be objectives of economic aid because they are not closely related to such aid. We have suggested that these should not be aid objectives because, in effect, they *can't* be.

As a matter of fact, in the history of United States aid to Southern Asia, economic objectives have not been particularly important in the sense of directly affecting the allocation and use of aid. But the reason has been different from the one we have advanced. The reason has been that, in the context of both "cold war" and "competitive coexistence," political objectives in Southern Asia were considered of such overwhelming priority that they became the determining guides to aid needs and uses. Nor is this surprising. Economic aid is an instrument of foreign policy. As such, whatever the alternative *possible* objectives of aid, the objectives that should actually govern its use must depend on the higher-level choices of U.S. foreign policy.

3. Humanitarian Objectives of Non-Military Aid

The humanitarian objective identifies the purpose of aid in terms of neighborliness, brotherhood, and the Golden Rule. It implicitly suggests that U.S. aid should be given in order to reduce per capita income disparities between developed and underdeveloped countries, and, by extension, among the underdeveloped countries themselves; or between per capita incomes in the underdeveloped countries and some specified minimum standard. At a higher level, the humanitarian objective follows from a moral view that, within certain limits, human beings are equivalent "values"; that, within these

for Economic Affairs, Douglas Dillon, "Foreign Investment and Economic Development," *Department of State Bulletin,* January 27, 1958, pp. 141-142.

limits, there is a single "utility" function with respect to income for every individual, *and* that the function increases at a constantly decreasing rate. It follows that an additional aid dollar will provide more benefit if given to an individual (or country) with a lower, rather than a higher, income.

Essentially, the humanitarian objective considers that U.S. aid to the poorer countries must, at least in part, be considered "an act of simple justice," in Chester Bowles' words.[61] It is not our purpose here to disturb the dust that has settled over the argument between "realism" and "idealism" in American foreign policy. But it is appropriate to cite some sober comments on the facts, rather than the proprieties, in the matter:

". . . Humanitarianism can hardly be described as a national interest or as an important objective of public policy . . . governments simply do not act on the basis of such unadulterated considerations."[62]

It should, nevertheless, be noted that there have been occasional instances when humanitarian considerations have directly affected foreign aid decisions. The initiation and continuation of the Point Four Program is the most obvious example.[63] On some occasions, too, humanitarian considerations have influenced specific country aid allocations in Southern Asia, notably during the Indian and Pakistan famines of 1951 and 1952. But such cases have, in large measure, involved special circumstances and have been dealt with through special legislative authorizations outside the established Mutual Security Program. Only rarely, and then only when the requirements were very limited, have humanitarian objectives affected Mutual Security allocations directly.[64]

With these exceptions, it is probably accurate to say that humanitarian objectives have played only a confirmatory, and hence superfluous, role in government aid decisions affecting intercountry and interprogram allocations. Where strong political or, less frequently, economic objectives were believed to be served by a particular

[61] See his "The U.S. and Asia" in *A Guide to Politics*, ed. Quincy Howe and Arthur M. Schlesinger, Jr., cited in Mason, *op.cit.*, p. 15.

[62] Mason, *op.cit.*, p. 13.

[63] See, especially, above, Chapter 3, section F.2. Also, *Act for International Development*, Senate Hearings, Washington, D.C., 1950, pp. 41, 62, 99ff.; and nearly any volume of the annual Congressional Hearings on the Mutual Security Program dealing with technical assistance, for example, *Mutual Security Act Extension*, House Hearings, Washington, D.C., 1952, p. 957; *Mutual Security Act of 1954*, House Hearings, Washington, D.C., 1954, pp. 509, 524.

[64] For example, the surplus wheat ($1.15 million) provided to Afghanistan in 1954 for famine relief. See Table 16, footnote c.

allocation, humanitarian objectives have sometimes also been invoked in support of the allocation.

Certainly, one should not casually depreciate humanitarian objectives. Not only is it invidious to do so, but advocacy of such objectives is both conceptually and methodologically defensible. Humanitarian objectives might, for example, be formulated rigorously in terms of the following criterion for allocating a given amount of aid among a specified set of countries: allocate so as to minimize the differences in average per capita incomes among the set countries; or, alternatively, allocate so as to minimize the differences between average per capita income and some specified *standard* per capita income (such as a "subsistence" minimum for all countries in the set, or the average per capita income over some prior, say, five-year, period in each country of the set). Under certain simplified assumptions, this could mean that all aid would be allocated to the poorest country in the set. If, on the other hand, all countries were at approximately the same per capita income level, aid would be allocated in proportion to population.

Nevertheless, even though humanitarian objectives *can* be defended on methodological grounds, we should be clear as to whether they really have been effective, operational objectives of foreign aid. In this connection, it is worth noting the following statement on the objectives of the Mutual Security Program by President Eisenhower in a speech to the Conference on Foreign Aspects of U.S. National Security early in 1958:

"If anyone wants to judge the entire program only on a what's-in-it-for-me basis, he can find all the justification he needs. But beyond this, if others want to add another element, do unto others as you would have them do unto you, I see no reason to apologize . . . for this kind of motive.

"I can see no great evidence of intelligence in sneering at "do-gooders" if their "do-gooding" helps America at the same time it helps our friends."[65]

But there is a difference between "sneering," and trying to understand whether particular objectives are effective or adventitious. The effective test of a particular objective's influence on decision-making is simply whether a different decision would be made in the absence of the objective. In terms of this test, humanitarian objectives are

[65] The *New York Times*, February 26, 1958.

not, nor do they appear likely to be, prominent among the continuing objectives of U.S. foreign aid.

D. The Objectives of Military Assistance

As we have previously stressed, "competitive coexistence" is characterized by flexible Soviet Bloc foreign policy, and a resulting diversity of threats to the United States and the free world. This diversity extends all the way from the possibility of nuclear war against the United States, to the possibility of more or less free choices in favor of "national" communism by electoral majorities or pluralities in certain countries of the free world. Fortunately, the former contingency seems to decrease in likelihood as prospective retaliation increases in severity; unfortunately, the latter contingency may increase in likelihood if national communism becomes more moderate and the political alternatives to it become discredited.

Between these extremes is a wide interval encompassing what we have previously described as local or limited war, ranging in possible geographical scope, and in the types and numbers of military forces and weapons employed.[66] The purposes and intended consequences of military aid in the Asian area are largely related to contingencies in this interval. More specifically, the objectives of military assistance in Asia mainly involve creating capabilities, and signifying intentions, to meet various contingencies within the spectrum of possible local wars.

In this context, "capability" can be defined as any means of inflicting losses (costs) on a potential aggressor. "Intentions" represent the potential aggressor's estimate of the likelihood that particular capabilities will be used against him in the event of possible aggressive acts. If we attribute "rationality" to the potential aggressor, it can be presumed that he will be deterred from any particular aggressive act when his estimate of defensive capabilities and intentions entails higher costs (losses) than he believes the aggression to be worth. If his belief concerning the gain to be had from aggression remains unchanged, then any measures that raise the capabilities (costs) confronting him, or that reinforce intentions to invoke these capabilities, will tend to deter aggression.

[66] See above, Chapter 4, pp. 104-105.

1. Capabilities, Intentions, and Deterrence

"Deterrence," then, depends on *both* capabilities and accredited intentions. For a given defensive capability, an aggressor will be the more deterred the higher he estimates the intention (likelihood) that the capability will be used against him. For a given estimate of intentions, he will be more deterred by the existence of a greater capability to inflict losses on him. A U.S. nuclear capability, that may effectively deter central war, cannot be relied on to deter local war because the intention to use it in a limited war may simply not be believed by a potential aggressor.

Consequently, the lack or diminution of *either* capabilities, or intentions to use them, degrades deterrence and increases the likelihood of local war. The Korean war and its prelude was an instance of the insufficient deterrence provided by strong military capabilities without accredited intentions to use them.[67] By contrast, it can be argued that currently the SEATO alliance represents an affirmation of intention to oppose local aggression in Southeast Asia without accompanying capabilities to do so.

If, in the military-aid context, it is assumed that the intentions estimated by a potential aggressor are not affected by aid allocations, or that the estimated intentions depend *uniformly* on defensive capabilities, then, clearly, the distinction between intentions and capabilities has no significance for allocations. Under either of these circumstances, the objectives of military aid must be formulated exclusively in terms of defensive capabilities. There is still another circumstance in which the distinction between intentions and capabilities loses meaning, and military capabilities alone are relevant as aid objectives. It can be argued that the "rationality" assumption, on which the capabilities-intentions distinction is based, has restricted applicability in the real world. Limited war in Southern Asia, for example, may depend more on chance than calculation.[68] In this case, "deterrence," and with it the "intentions" attributed by an aggressor to the defender, cease to have relevance as military aid objectives. The sole relevant objectives become the defensive capabilities necessary to meet various local war contingencies whose occurrence is presumed to be randomly determined.

However, if it is assumed that the intentions—more particularly,

---

[67] See Chapter 3, section D.
[68] See the discussion of a "random" war between India and Pakistan, above, Chapter 6, pp. 204-205.

the intentions accredited to the United States—are a separate variable which can be influenced by military aid allocation, then the distinction between capabilities and intentions has relevance. In this case, an issue arises concerning the relative costs and gains to the United States from using aid to affect capabilities, on the one hand, or accredited intentions to respond to local aggression, on the other.

2. Multiple Military Aid Objectives

In discussing specific military aid objectives, we shall have occasion to refer again to the distinction between capabilities and intentions, though our stress will be on capabilities. As was the case in examining the objectives of non-military aid, we shall find that the objectives sought through military aid are quite diverse. But there is an important difference between the multiplicity of objectives in the two cases. In principle, at least, most of the objectives of military aid—unlike those of economic aid—can be made commensurable by estimating the dollar costs of similar returns actually purchased, or purchasable, with appropriations in the regular U.S. defense budget.[69] For example, local defense forces in the SEATO countries, which are bought or strengthened through military assistance (MDAP), might be evaluated in terms of the delivered dollar costs of U.S. tactical units for which the local forces are believed substitutable. In principle, the "value" of a particular capability obtained through military assistance can be regarded as the cost of providing a comparable (substitutable) capability through the domestic defense budget. In the allocation of military aid funds among alternative recipients and uses, this cost should be an upper limit on the cost of providing such a capability through military aid.

It should be clear that the dollar costing of military aid returns has implications with respect *both* to allocating military aid among different uses, and to allocating U.S. military appropriations *between* domestic defense and foreign military assistance. Thus, in allocating given MDAP funds among capabilities $F_1, F_2, \ldots, F_n$, whose alternative marginal "values"—in terms of the domestic U.S. defense costs of obtaining increments in equivalent capabilities—are, respectively, $v_1, v_2, \ldots, v_n$, a necessary optimality condition is that the marginal MDAP costs of the capabilities that receive allocations be

[69] For a suggestive discussion of the conceptual as well as empirical difficulties involved in this approach to evaluating returns, see Malcolm W. Hoag, "Economic Problems of Alliance," *Journal of Political Economy*, December 1957, pp. 524-525ff.

proportional to the alternative cost (value) parameters.[70] And in allocating total U.S. military appropriations between domestic defense and foreign military assistance programs, a necessary condition for optimality is that marginal costs of comparable (substitutable) capabilities be equal in both programs.

It is hardly necessary to note that these implications are more than a little bit easier to state than they are to apply. Nevertheless, they at least suggest an approach to the problem of improved military aid allocation which is analytically interesting and may also be useful in practice.[71]

With these preliminary observations, what, then, are the objectives of military assistance? Stated broadly, military aid objectives have been, and are, typically described in terms of enhancing U.S. security by increasing the defensive strength of the free world and cementing the U.S. alliance system.[72] Valid as these broad objectives are—both as description, and as goals of United States policy—they are not of much help in making military aid decisions, other than the decision that to have a program is better than not to have one. They do not help much in arriving at decisions concerning how much military aid is needed, or how best to use whatever aid becomes available. To analyze such questions, we need to look at the lower-level objectives toward which military aid is directed.

The lower-level objectives of military aid can be formulated in terms of local military forces, U.S. overseas bases, and local support facilities, or "infrastructure," for possible use by U.S. as well as indigenous forces. Analyzing these objectives, we shall be principally concerned with how, or indeed whether, the value of increments to each objective can be assessed.

However, there is one category of objective which we shall not

---

[70] Let M represent the total military aid to be allocated, with M_1, M_2, . . . , M_n, the optimal allocations to capabilities F_1, F_2, . . . , F_n respectively. Then:

$$M_1 = M - M_2 - \ldots, - M_n, \tag{1}$$

and

$$v_1 \cdot \left(\frac{\Delta F_1}{\Delta M_1} \right) = v_2 \cdot \left(\frac{\Delta F_2}{\Delta M_2} \right) = \ldots, = v_n \cdot \left(\frac{\Delta F_n}{\Delta M_n} \right), \tag{2}$$

where v_1, v_2, . . . , v_n, are the alternative cost parameters described in the text.
[71] See below, Chapter 10, section C, for further discussion of this approach.
[72] See, for example, the President's Message to Congress, *The Mutual Security Program for 1958, A Summary Presentation*, p. 2; *The Military Assistance Program*, Special Senate Committee to Study the Foreign Aid Program, pp. 26-28; *Foreign Aid*, Report of the Special Senate Committee, pp. 3-4, 8.

attempt to assess: the use of military aid to gain influence, friendship, or a formal or informal commitment of a recipient's political support. Providing modern weapons in order to accede to a recipient's desire for the prestige which they confer, apart from the relevance of the military capabilities produced by the aid, is a case in point. The reason for neglecting this objective here is that our previous comments concerning friendship and influence as objectives of economic aid are equally applicable to military aid.[73] In fact, the main distinction between military and economic aid that is provided with this objective in view is simply the military rather than civilian character of the group whose support is sought in the two cases. As in the case of economic aid, there are grounds for skepticism concerning the appropriateness of this objective in the case of military aid, because of the general unpredictability of the relation between the amount of military aid and the degree of loyalty of those receiving it. Of course, there may be instances in which such a relationship holds, and in which a consequent change in the allocation of military aid may be warranted. But these instances will probably depend on particular people in special circumstances. Again, as in the case of economic aid, ad hoc judgments rather than general analytical methods must be relied on to discern such instances.

3. Local Military Forces

a. External Defense Forces. Consider, first, local war contingencies involving direct attack or indirect support by the Communist Bloc. In Southern Asia, there is only a limited number of such contingencies with probabilities sufficiently high to be of concern from the standpoint of U.S. military aid;[74] for example, a North Vietnamese attack against South Viet Nam, North Vietnamese or Chinese support for an attack by the Pathet-Lao against Laos or by the "Free Thai" against Thailand, a Chinese attack against Burma, Soviet

[73] See above, section C.1(b).

[74] It is easier and more defensible to divide possible local wars into those which are so unlikely that they can be neglected and those which are sufficiently likely that they need to be given serious consideration, than it is to try to estimate the relative probabilities within either category. See Henry A. Kissinger, *Nuclear Weapons and Foreign Policy*, New York, 1957, p. 277. "For a power with limited resources, the wisest course is to define the most likely dangers and concentrate on meeting them." With two modifications, this statement makes good sense: (1) *all* powers have limited resources; (2) it may be wiser to concentrate on a less likely danger if its potential "disutility" is greater than that of the "most likely" dangers.

occupation of Afghanistan.[75] One major purpose of U.S. military aid in Southern Asia has been to provide local military capabilities to deter such contingencies, or to meet them if they arise.[76]

In principle, as previously suggested, the "value" of a particular local military capability to the United States is the cost that we would have to incur to obtain a substitutable capability by other means.[77] If a substitutable capability is *already* provided for in the domestic U.S. defense budget, alternative cost evaluation is relatively tractable. The "value" of a particular local military capability can then be considered the cost of the substitutable U.S. capability; for example, a tactical air squadron, a mobile army battle group (appropriately based in the region), or an amphibious Marine battalion in the Seventh Fleet. This is not to say the evaluation is *easy*. Obviously, vast problems (of data collection, of allocating "joint" costs, of effectiveness and reliability discounts, etc.) remain. But there is at least some reason for contending that they are likely to be manage-

[75] As a background for this list of higher-likelihood local wars, the following statement by Admiral Felix B. Stump, then Commander in Chief of the U.S. Pacific Command, and regional coordinator of all military aid in Asia, is pertinent:

"United States [military] assistance . . . is directly related to the security of the free world against further Communist aggression in this critical [Asian] area. . . . Communist ground forces in Asia facing my command area consist of over 2,500,000 Chinese Communists and 300,000 Viet Minh, totaling about 3 million. These ground forces have support by a relatively young but modern Chinese Communist air force composed of over 2,000 aircraft, with a large percentage of modern jets. Furthermore, the Chinese Communist navy is rapidly expanding with its main units, destroyers and submarines. These forces could be quickly utilized to launch an attack against the offshore islands and South Asia. . . . Finally, scattered throughout . . . southeast Asian countries are less obvious subversive elements, which the Communists are so adept at using, conducting operations designed to weaken the internal security of these presently independent countries."

Mutual Security Appropriations for 1957, Hearings before the House Committee on Appropriations, 84th Congress, 2nd session, Washington, D.C., 1956, p. 86.

[76] For references to this objective, see Chapter 5, pp. 156, 178, and Chapter 6, pp. 203-205, 226, 239. In this context, "meeting" contingencies simply means creating local capabilities adequate to repel a small-scale aggression, or to "buy" time, for example, for U.S. reinforcement, in case of a larger-scale aggression.

[77] Note Admiral Stump's further testimony (footnote 75):

"Although the military capability of our Southeast Asian and nationalist Chinese allies . . . is not adequate without United States participation to defend indefinitely against even a localized but substained offensive, we must appreciate the progress that has been made possible by mutual defense assistance. *Only by continued military assistance can the United States avoid costly additional deployment of United States forces in the Pacific.* . . .

"The contribution of Southeast Asian countries and of Taiwan to collective defense of the area will continue to be directly proportionate to the amount of mutual defense assistance provided them."

Mutual Security Appropriations for 1957, House Appropriations Committee Hearings, p. 86. (Italics added.)

able. Similar problems, both analytical and empirical, have been met and frequently resolved in other systems analysis.

If no readily substitutable capability is already provided for in the U.S. defense budget, evaluation then requires both an estimate of the alternative costs of providing such a capability, and a conjecture as to whether the United States would be willing to incur them in the absence of the corresponding local capability. For, if the United States were not willing to pay the costs of a substitutable capability, these costs would clearly overstate the "value" of the local military force provided by military assistance. In this case, the question of the latter's "value" becomes a question of judging (within the U.S. government) what, in fact, the United States *would* be willing to pay for a substitutable capability. Though such a judgment is bound to be hazardous and debatable, we would reassert a prejudice that has been mentioned before: judgments are apt to be more reliable if they are made explicitly.

An important criticism which can be raised against this approach is that, though it may be a necessary part of assessing the value of local forces, it is not sufficient. We can argue, for example, that this approach actually overlooks the main value of such forces in Southern Asia, namely their value as a symbolic deterrent to aggression, and their value as a legitimizer of rapid U.S. intervention should aggression occur.[78] As we have already noted, deterrence depends not only on capabilities, but on accredited intentions to use them. The value of local forces supported by military aid in Southern Asia may (and probably, for most of the contingencies previously mentioned, does) lie less in their combat strength than in the fact that they symbolize a U.S. intention to invoke more potent capabilities in the event of local war.

Without denying the validity of the point, we can question its bearing on the allocation of military aid. Though the symbolic deterrence represented by local forces receiving U.S. military aid may be substantial, it is not clear that *larger* forces (obtained with more aid) means *more* deterrence. The relation between military aid and symbolic deterrence may, in other words, be discrete rather than continuous.

Nor is this surprising. It is to be expected that a potential aggressor's estimate of U.S. intentions to defend a particular country

---

[78] The following discussion concentrates on the symbolic deterrence of local military forces supported by military aid. *Mutatis mutandis*, it applies equally to their symbolic value as a legitimizer of U.S. intervention in the event of aggression.

will depend in large part on the existence of close and continuing relationships between that country and the United States. To maintain such a relationship, small-scale military assistance, for example, as well as the more traditional methods of diplomacy—and even, for that matter, economic rather than military assistance—may be quite as effective as larger-scale military aid. Communist China, for example, may have as much reason for anticipating U.S. intervention in response to an attack on Burma or India as it has for anticipating U.S. intervention in the event of an attack on Thailand.

It can be contended, then, that the symbolic deterrent value represented by local military forces can be obtained in other, and substantially cheaper, ways than military aid. Consequently, from the standpoint of assessing the value to the United States of military aid, symbolic deterrence can perhaps be left aside. That is, we can assume, at least in Southern Asia, that deterrence could be preserved whatever the intercountry allocations or, within limits, the total amount of regional military aid.

b. Internal Security Forces. Our discussion of force objectives has so far dealt with *external defense forces* related to specific, foreseeable local war contingencies. But as we have previously seen, *internal security forces* have also been prominent as objectives of military aid at various times and in various countries of Southern Asia.[79] In fact, a strong case can be made for the view that the most "valuable" military assistance in Southern Asia is that which contributes to internal order rather than to external defense.[80] Not only do such forces reduce the danger of internal subversion; but, in circumstances that are not unusual in Southern Asia, internal security forces may sometimes be a self-liquidating economic investment. Over the past several years, the substantial losses in national output as a result of internal dissidence and dacoity in Burma, Viet Nam, and Indonesia are well known.[81] It may even be true that these losses occasionally exceeded the costs of the additional security forces that would have been necessary to maintain internal order.[82]

[79] Cf. Chapter 4, p. 103; Chapter 5, pp. 132, 155; Chapter 6, pp. 225-226, 240.

[80] See, for example, *The Military Assistance Program—Two Studies and A Report*, Special Senate Committee to Study the Foreign Aid Program, 1957, pp. 119, 157-158; and Clement Johnson, *Southeast Asia*, Special Senate Committee, 1957, pp. 9-10. See also, Chapter 5, section C.11.

[81] For a discussion of the economic effects of internal disorder in Indonesia, for example, see Benjamin Higgins, *Indonesia's Economic Stabilization and Development*, New York, 1957, pp. 109-110.

[82] In certain circumstances, the case for loan financing of military aid (for internal security purposes) might even be stronger than that for some categories of "economic" aid.

Yet the argument can be pressed too far. Improving internal order through additional security forces soon results in diminishing returns. The China "lesson," while the most notable example in the Asian area, is not the only one. Britain's protracted effort to establish order in Malaya, prior to the Federation's independence, is another. Moreover, there is, perhaps, a point at which aid to strengthen internal security might actually contribute more if used for economic development than for local security forces. Though the problem is, analytically, not a particularly tractable one, it at least suggests that there are distinct limits to the amount of military aid that can be effectively used to improve and maintain internal security. The limits will, of course, vary from country to country, depending notably on geography and topography,[83] on the degree of cultural and legal cohesion, and on the extent of organized internal subversion. But the limits should be roughly discernible on the basis of technical military considerations, and responsible military and political judgment.

There are also reasons for believing that these limits will be fairly low relative even to the modest scale of U.S. military aid in Southern Asia in recent years. In the absence of Chinese or Soviet military support to internal dissidence, small and highly mobile constabulary forces are likely to be quite adequate to maintain internal order. And for such forces, equipment requirements are small and operations relatively inexpensive. If, on the other hand, external communist support is extended to internal dissidence, then a larger-scale local war impends, comparable to some of the specific contingencies already mentioned. In this case, the "value" of additional military aid can be dealt with reasonably through the alternative costing of external defense forces, in the manner previously outlined.

However, if the question is asked how a commensurable value can be assigned to internal security forces, as an objective of military aid, the plain answer is that it cannot be. It is fair to say that *no* U.S. defense expenditure can be construed as buying a product that is, in any reasonable sense, equivalent to an improvement in internal order in Indonesia or the Philippines or Viet Nam. Probably, the only category of U.S. government expenditure whose effects can be considered even partly commensurable with the effects of aid to

[83] Pakistan's bifurcation is, perhaps, the most striking example of the impact of geography on force requirements for internal security.

internal security forces is economic aid, insofar as it contributes to political strength and stability.

A paradoxical conclusion results. One of the most important objectives of "military" aid—internal security forces—cannot be evaluated in military terms at all. Fortunately, from the standpoint of military aid allocation, the paradox can be resolved by an expedient. If we recall that the forces that can be effectively used for internal security are likely to be small and inexpensive, and if we simply assume that military aid to such forces has a substantial, if incommensurable, "value," we can then incorporate these specific aid requirements as a constraint in comparing alternative allocations within a given region. Aid required in each country for genuine internal security forces would become a "not-less-than" condition for any acceptable allocation of military aid among countries.[84]

4. Bases and Infrastructure

As objectives of military aid, bases and infrastructure have been of minor importance in Southern Asia in contrast to their major importance in Western Europe and, initially at least, in North Africa. U.S. base rights were an acknowledged aim of initial military assistance to the Philippines just after independence, but this was the only such instance in Southern Asia.[85] Though infrastructure has occasionally been discussed as an objective of so-called "defense support" aid, it has not exercised any appreciable influence on the allocation of aid in Southern Asia. Nevertheless, as important objectives of military aid in other areas, and as possible objectives in Southern Asia, both bases and infrastructure warrant consideration.

In common, bases and infrastructure both represent facilities intended to increase the effectiveness of possible U.S. operations in the event of particular contingencies:[86] infrastructure, mainly in the event of the higher-likelihood local war contingencies previously

---

[84] See below, Chapter 10, p. 371.

[85] See above, Chapter 2, section B.4. Pending the start of military assistance to Pakistan, it was reported, but not confirmed, that bases, "to be operated only in case of war," were to be constructed as part of the program. James W. Spain, "Military Assistance to Pakistan," *American Political Science Review*, September 1954, p. 748.

[86] In Europe, of course, infrastructure has been justified by its contribution to the effective operation of NATO, rather than U.S., forces. In the SEATO area, regional alliance forces are absent. Consequently, any appreciable expansion of road, harbor, and airfield facilities, using MDAP funds, should be thought of in terms of its possible contribution to the effectiveness of U.S., as well as indigenous, forces in local operations.

listed; bases perhaps mainly in the event of a central war with the Soviet Union and Communist China.

In principle, the "value" to the United States of additional base rights, or of additional infrastructure, can be approximated by applying the alternative-cost approach previously described. Thus, for a central war contingency, the "value" of a possible base in Southern Asia can be considered to be the cost the United States would have to incur to obtain equal payload delivery on specified enemy targets by other means (that is, using the least-cost combination of bases located elsewhere) and other delivery systems. For tactical, rather than strategic, use, the same yardstick, with a different target system, would be applicable. For comparison, of course, it would also be necessary to estimate the costs of obtaining use of the base under consideration: both the costs of construction and operation, and the "bargaining price" required to obtain the base-right in the first place.[87]

Similarly, the value to the United States of a particular local facility can be roughly approximated by estimating the adjusted costs which the United States would have to incur to permit equally effective military operations without the facility, in the event of the higher-likelihood local wars. It should, for example, be possible to estimate the cost to the United States of meeting an attack, of a specified scale, by North Viet Nam and China against Laos or Thailand, with and without roads through northeast Thailand, or a larger harbor at Bangkok, or a longer landing strip at Don Muang airport. The reason for adjusting the alternative costs in this case arises from the uncertainty that the infrastructures would be available for use by the United States even if local war occurred. There is, of course, always uncertainty about whether the United States would be "invited in" by the attacked country. But there is also another source of uncertainty. After all, besides facilitating U.S. military operations, good roads can also ease the path of an invader, and harbors and airstrips are relatively vulnerable targets.[88] After we make reasonable guesses to allow for these uncertainties, it might then be possible to

---

[87] In Southern Asia, there are obvious political reasons why the bargaining price is likely to be relatively high; in most cases, perhaps, higher than the "value" of the base itself. Thus, in countries where the U.S. already has one or more bases, the military value of an additional base would probably be low; while in countries where the U.S. does not have base rights, the bargaining price of obtaining them would probably be high.

[88] Clement Johnson, *Southeast Asia*, Report to the Special Senate Committee, *op.cit.*, p. 30.

estimate the net value of particular infrastructures in Southern Asia.

Despite the analytical difficulties involved, it would seem highly desirable to take the value of infrastructures and bases into explicit account in considering the gains from different allocations of military aid. We shall attempt to do this in discussing analytical approaches to improved allocation decisions.[89] However, before doing so, we must consider in detail some of the basic questions concerning political stability as an objective of economic aid, which were previously raised, but not answered. Systematic conjectures, if not answers, are needed before we can consider the problem of allocation directly.

[89] See below, Chapter 10.

CHAPTER 8

ECONOMIC CHANGE AND POLITICAL BEHAVIOR:
AN EXPERIMENTAL APPROACH IN THE ASIAN SETTING

A. A NOTE ON METHOD

OUR AIM IN THIS CHAPTER is to set forth a somewhat novel and experimental method for analyzing an extremely complex subject. In a sense, method is like fashion: the need to explain arises only if one appears to be out of step. The method used here is derived partly from the factual context of Southern Asia, partly from personal judgment as to which of the facts are relevant to the problem at hand, and partly from reasoning about the relevant facts. To permit the approach to be tested, if only in a preliminary way, we will translate it into a mathematical model. The model, like all models, simplifies the phenomena it is concerned with. It aggregates complex interactions into a few variables. It suppresses other variables, either because they are considered of secondary importance, or because using them would make the model untestable for lack of data. It frequently assumes other-things-equal conditions, even when we know that in the real world which the model is trying to simulate the "other things" may not be equal.

There is nothing new about such simplifications. They are the very core of analytical method. What is new is the attempt to apply them to as complex a socio-economic problem as the relationship between economic change and political behavior. Since this is our intention, it is fair to raise the question of whether we are not trying to mix oil and water. How appropriate is quantitative method for the kind of problem we are considering? What purpose can the method serve in view of the qualifications and limitations already noted?

In part, the answer is that our purpose is to stimulate further research and future refinement of the approach we are suggesting. We want to see how and to what extent this problem *can* be treated systematically. Our aim is to begin, not to exhaust, consideration of a problem which, from an analytical standpoint, has been relatively neglected. As noted in the preceding chapter, promoting political health, strength, and stability has been (and is) one of the most prominent objectives of U.S. aid in the underdeveloped areas generally, and Southern Asia particularly. Underlying this objective is a presumed relationship between economic aid (or, what is the same thing, between variables which aid can affect), and political behavior. In stating this relationship as a formal, quantitative hypothesis, our purpose is to enable it to be tested statistically. Our purpose is, further, to develop an analytical tool that, in the light of the test results, can perhaps be helpful in improving the allocation and use of U.S. foreign aid.

We have said that the method used is derived from the factual context of Southern Asia. In the immediately following section, the essential components of this context will be briefly summarized. As we move from factual context to analytical model, questions arise concerning the method of selecting and combining variables. The procedure followed is to state a general behavioral principle that underlies a particular function in the model. In part, credibility of the cited principles is based on the initial contextual description. Selection and combination of the variables in each function is then discussed in the light of the cited principle. In each case, the principle delimits, but does not precisely define, the form and content of the function actually used in the experimental model. The functions are consistent with, but not uniquely determined by, the general principles. Within the limits set by the principles, definition of the functions is admittedly arbitrary.

However, we have tried to follow a counsel of simplicity and convenience in constructing the model. Consistent with the principles, variables have been selected on the basis of current or prospective convenience in securing the corresponding data; and consistent with the principles and variables, the forms of the functions have been chosen for reasons of computational simplicity in handling the data. This procedure does not eliminate the arbitrary element, but should help the reader to see more clearly where it enters in. Some may disagree with the principles underlying the functions, some with the variables selected, and others with the forms of the functions. But the procedure followed will, we hope, make the point of disagreement easier to locate and the general approach easier to follow.

B. SOUTHERN ASIA: A BACKGROUND SUMMARY

The so-called "arc of free Asia" is a region both vast and varied. It comprises thirteen independent countries with a population of over 675 million people and a land area of 3.2 million square miles, slightly larger than the United States.[1] Its cultural variety is suggested by the fact, among others, that more than 300 different languages are spoken in the area, while its religions cover the world's gamut: Hinduism in India; Islam in Pakistan and Indonesia; Buddhism in Burma, Thailand, Cambodia, Laos, and Viet Nam; and Christianity in the Philippines, as well as various unique syntheses and variants like the Cao Dai and Hoa Hao of Viet Nam. In the midst of this diversity, there is, nonetheless, a reasonable degree of homogeneity among the countries of the region. Several of the common characteristics, shared by the countries of Southern Asia, significantly influence the setting for the problem which concerns us.

1. The Acceleration of Social Change

In the period since World War II, Southern Asia has been the scene of an explosive acceleration of social, political, and economic change which has, not inaccurately, been referred to as "the revolt of Asia." This acceleration can be usefully thought of as an attempt at telescoping into a relatively brief period changes which, in Western history, extended over several centuries. Asia's post-war revolt is thus a complex mixture of changes associated in the West with the Industrial Revolution and the Enlightenment of the 18th century, the intense political nationalism of the 19th century, and the massive social and technological innovations of the 20th century.

Perhaps the main factor in this process of accelerated social change has been the altered content and importance of human aspirations, both individual and collective. Until very recently, norms and goals of life in Asia were fixed by tradition. The established practices and experiences of village and family life determined the limits of what was desirable and possible for the individual and the group. Traditional behavior patterns were considered best, at least in part because alternatives were thought impossible. Sustained by tradition, social and economic conditions tended to be accepted as inevitable. The idea of purposive social and economic change was dismissed or discounted as fanciful. In effect, aspiration, based as it is on a belief in the possibility of change, was irrelevant, to the extent that tradition encouraged belief in the impossibility of change, and irreverent, to the extent that tradition made change appear undesirable.

[1] Malaya is included in this background summary as well as the twelve countries previously enumerated. See above, Chapter 1, p. 4.

Clearly, this interpretation needs qualification. For one thing, Asian traditions are neither as simple nor as uniform as these comments imply. Brahman tradition in India, for example, instilled markedly different attitudes toward change and norms in different castes; and these in turn differed from attitudes instilled by the traditions of Burmese culture. Nor is the image we are suggesting one that was valid at a given period and then suddenly disappeared. A loosening of the hold of tradition on Asian society has been under way for many decades. At the same time, the attitudes we have described as undergoing pervasive change still persist currently, in varying degrees. But there has been a decisive change during the course of Asia's recent and continuing revolt. Goals once dismissed as irrelevant because unattainable are now increasingly regarded—and perhaps overoptimistically so, in some cases—as both feasible and necessary. Aspirations have been and are being stimulated and have acquired an importance for the individual and the group which, in degree if not in kind, is a distinctly recent change in the Asian scene.

The stimuli behind the quickened tempo and heightened importance of new aspirations are not hard to find. One stimulus in the past generation has been the rapid and remarkable diffusion of information—by mass media, education, and the development of communications facilities—about the dramatic realization of aspirations in other countries—the United States, the Soviet Union, and Japan, especially. World War II strongly reinforced this stimulus in Asia. Japan's wartime occupation of parts of Southern Asia carried with it an effective demonstration that Western technology could be mastered successfully by an Asian country, even to the point of challenging the West in military conflict. Moreover, by abruptly removing the established colonial rulers and providing a wider opportunity for nationalist leaders to exercise authority, especially in Burma and Indonesia, the Japanese occupation, even where it was most oppressive, further weakened the hold of tradition on personal and national motivations.

2. Aspirations and Reality

It is not our purpose here to do more than summarize in an abbreviated way themes and interpretations that have been fully dealt with elsewhere.[2] But it is important to stress the relationship between

[2] Among the general references are Cora Du Bois, *Social Forces in Southeast Asia*,

what we have been saying and the analysis which follows. For the loosening of traditional bonds in Southern Asia is not only a condition of human growth; it is also a far-reaching source of current and potential political instability. With a new belief in the possibility of change and improvement, aspirations have become an extremely important factor in shaping human motivations and reactions. Where aspirations are thus accredited, failures or delays in their realization evoke resentment, frustration, and opposition. In Southern Asia there is a particular likelihood that realization may be delayed and inadequate because, while aspirations have been and are being continually heightened, the immediately available capacity for realizing them is limited. That these are conditions on which internal and international communism thrives is a generalization as valid as it is familiar. This is not to deny that other conditions may contribute to the expansion of a movement uniquely alert to the existence of openings and opportunities. Local military weakness, real or presumed, is a case in point, as the Korean experience suggests. What we are suggesting is that where the gap between aspirations and reality is wide, where, in other words, the realization of aspirations is seriously retarded, communism can exercise an appeal that makes the use of force unnecessary for its expansion.

The relationship between aspirations and reality is central to the following analysis of economic change and political behavior, and we will return to it at greater length. First, however, we need to consider two other aspects of the factual context in Southern Asia that significantly influence the character and content of aspirations in the region.

The primary goal of Asian aspirations has been political independence. Excepting Afghanistan and Thailand, all of the countries in the region have become independent nations since 1946. Except for Viet Nam, all are now members of the United Nations. With the independence of Malaya in August 1957, European colonial rule in Southern Asia has largely become a thing of the past. With a few

---

Minneapolis, 1949; Philipps Talbot (ed.), *South Asia in the World Today*, Chicago, 1950; K. H. Landon, *Southeast Asia—Crossroad of Religions*, Chicago, 1949; Philip W. Thayer (ed.), *Southeast Asia in the Coming World*, Baltimore, 1953; E. H. Jacoby, *Agrarian Unrest in Southeast Asia*, New York, 1949; Brian Harrison, *Southeast Asia—A Short History*, London, 1954; W. H. Elsbree, *Japan's Role in Southeast Asia's Nationalist Movements*, Cambridge, 1953.

exceptions,[3] it is fair to say that the major immediate objectives of nationalist aspirations in Southern Asia have been attained. While the force of nationalist aspirations has thus been somewhat attenuated since the early postwar period, the pride, prejudice, and sensitivity of nationalism remain active influences in domestic and international affairs throughout the region.

3. *The Economic Component of Asian Aspirations*

The second most prominent goal of aspirations is the desire for rapid economic development. To an unusual extent, and for reasons that are historical rather than logical, the anticipation of rapid economic development was and is intimately connected with the political force of nationalism in the particular region we are concerned with. Historically, in the "plural" societies of colonial Asia, there was a direct correspondence between political and economic status. Europeans were in a commanding position politically, as well as economically, while the indigenous Asian community tended to be limited no less in its economic than its political status, and the Chinese community generally occupied an intermediate position in both hierarchies. Under these circumstances, it was easy and perhaps natural for Asian nationalists to proceed from observed correlation to attributed causation. A widespread conviction grew among nationalist leaders and followers that political independence, by changing political stratifications, would somehow bring about economic improvement as well. As a result, emergent Asian nationalist movements acquired a distinct and enduring economic orientation. In effect, nationalism in Asia tended to direct individual and group aspirations toward the goal of economic improvement to an unusual extent. This is an important and pervasive fact in current Asian politics. It is a fact whose impact extends across the political and geographic boundaries between SEATO and neutralist countries in Southern Asia. It is also a fact that bears directly on the analytical approach we will develop later.

Given the importance we are ascribing to economic aspirations, what can be said of their content? One way of approaching the question is to consider the major economic characteristics that the

[3] The remaining European possessions in Southern Asia are Singapore, British Borneo, Portuguese Goa, Portuguese Timor, and the western part of New Guinea held by the Netherlands and claimed by Indonesia.

countries of the region have in common. These characteristics are at least suggestive of the types of goals toward which economic aspirations are directed, and of the starting points from which change and improvement are taking place.

At the grossest level, average annual per capita income is about $100, typically lower in rural areas.[4] As in other underdeveloped economies, the rural agricultural sector occupies a dominant position. From 50 to 70 per cent of national product originates in the agricultural sector, and between 65 and 80 per cent of the working population is engaged in rural agriculture. Unemployment and underemployment are high, together comprising perhaps 15 to 20 per cent of the labor force, while the capital stock is relatively small, methods of production tend to be labor-intensive, and both skilled manpower and training facilities are scarce. Labor productivity is consequently low—usually lower in agriculture than in other sectors of the economy—and the average level of annual factory wages is around $200 per employed urban worker. Agricultural tenancy is relatively high, though there are important exceptions. In areas like South Viet Nam, Central Luzon, and the Sind in West Pakistan, for example, about 50 per cent of cultivated acreage is farmed by tenants, while in most of Indonesia and such states as Uttar Pradesh and Madhya Pradesh in India, a large majority of cultivators own their land.

Currently in most of the countries of the region, and in all of them until very recently, the rate of growth in real national income has barely equaled population growth. Net annual domestic capital formation has typically been below 7 per cent of national income and the annual rate of population growth around 1.5 per cent. The tendency toward unchanging per capita income (and consumption) has thus been at relatively low rates of growth in both aggregate

[4] For additional background data, see *Economic Survey of Asia and the Far East,* Vols. i-viii, Economic Commission for Asia and the Far East, Bangkok and New York, 1951-1958; *Commonwealth Consultative Committee on Economic Development in South and Southeast Asia*—(Colombo Plan)—*Annual Reports,* London, 1952-1957; *Statistics of National Income and Expenditure,* United Nations, New York, 1957; *Demographic Yearbook,* United Nations, New York, 1956; *United Nations Statistical Yearbook 1957,* New York, 1957.

The per capita income figure, like the others cited here, is less significant as a precise magnitude than as a general indicator of the degree of poverty prevalent in Southern Asia. Since we are interested only in broad characteristics common to the economies of the region, problems that arise from international price differences, varying degrees of inclusiveness and reliability of national income statistics—indeed, all the technical problems that make any attempt at precise comparisons of international income levels dubious—need not concern us here.

population and income. Low rates of growth in population have, however, occurred at relatively high birth and death rates. Potential population growth is therefore high. With an anticipated lowering of death rates, the additional capital and income required to maintain, let alone increase, real per capita income, will be substantial.

Throughout the region, welfare indicators show a similar pattern. Per capita adult food consumption is generally below 2,000 calories per day. Life expectancy at birth is about 35 years. The incidence of disease is uniformly high. Literacy is confined to about 25 per cent of the population, except in the Philippines. (Even in the Philippines, there is some question whether the rate is actually higher or the term merely more loosely defined.) Education has been typically restricted to the few, and for the masses is both a new and a valued experience.

C. The Vulnerability Function

In this setting, how can the relationship between economic change and political behavior be approached? What theoretical framework can we use for exploring this relationship? Difficulties come to mind more readily than answers. Each of these phenomena is extremely complex in itself, and their relationship is still more obscure. There is, moreover, not one relationship but many; while there is interaction between them, there are also exogenous influences affecting both. Admitting these difficulties, we may nevertheless hypothesize that, within the regional context we are interested in, a definite and measurable relationship exists between economic change and political behavior and, given a large number of cases, this relationship will be a significant one.

In pursuing this premise, we may restrict our inquiry to particular aspects of the relationship. We need not consider all the political manifestations that may be associated with economic change. From the standpoint of United States foreign policy, and foreign aid allocation more specifically, there are many possible political manifestations in sovereign countries that—if related to economic change at all—are of little or no concern to U.S. policy planning. The structure of parliamentary institutions, the federal or unitary character of a state, the centralized or decentralized administration of economic development programs, and the blending of statutory and customary law, are examples of political manifestations that, though they may be related to economic change, usually have no bearing on U.S. foreign policy decisions. Consequently, we shall be concerned with a particular class of political manifestations that *does* bear on U.S. policy, namely, what may be termed "political extremism"—especially committed support for internal and international communism. There are, of course, other forms of political extremism than communism; in Southern Asia, for example, communalism and militarism. The following discussion will, however, stress communist extremism, both because it is, in fact, the most active and effective extremist movement in Southern Asia, and because U.S. foreign policy is directly concerned with combatting it, rather than "other" forms of extremism.

Given this focus on *extremist* political behavior, one condition for an acceptable formulation of the hypothesized relationship follows. On the one hand, an adequate formulation must take into account the common sense notion that extremist political behavior tends to be associated with poverty.[5] On the other hand, it confronts the fact that in too many cases to be considered exceptions, poverty has been accompanied by political passiveness, while extremism has been associated instead with the alleviation of poverty.[6] Consequently, one condition for an acceptable formulation of the relationship we have hypothesized is that it should reconcile these two conflicting facts—assuming, of course, that both are valid. Stated another way, an acceptable formulation should show that these apparently conflicting facts are simply special cases of a more general relationship between economic change and political behavior.

[5] See, for example, the discussion of this notion in connection with research on the psychology of leftist voting, in S. M. Lipset, P. F. Lazarsfeld, A. H. Barton, J. Linz, "The Psychology of Voting: An Analysis of Political Behavior," *Handbook of Social Psychology*, Vol. II, Cambridge, 1954, pp. 1134ff.

[6] De Tocqueville's relevant comments on the French Revolution, though of untested accuracy, are probably the first and best-known example. Thus, he observed that "in no one of the periods which have followed the Revolution of 1789 has the national prosperity of France augmented more rapidly than it did in the twenty years preceding that event"; and concludes with the suggestion that, apparently, "The French found their position more intolerable the better it became." (See A. de Tocqueville, *On the State of Society in France before the Revolution of 1789*, London, 1888, pp. 149, 152).

Eric Hoffer extends de Tocqueville's point in his perceptive analysis of the appeals of revolutionary movements in general, *The True Believer*, New York, 1951, particularly pp. 25-32. Another observer has suggested that there was a positive correlation between income and communist voting in Sweden's 1952 elections: W. Phillips Davison, "A Review of Sven Rydenfelt's Communism in Sweden," P-570, The RAND Corporation, 1954, pp. 27-29.

1. The Economic Index of Political Vulnerability

To describe the relationship, let us begin with a concept we shall call an economic index of political vulnerability, denoted by Pe. To refer to the average value of the index in a set (say, a region or country), we shall use the symbol $\overline{Pe}$, and in a specific subset (country or province, respectively) within the set, we shall use Pe_i. The vulnerability index encompasses two meanings relevant to our problem: susceptibility to the socio-economic appeals of internal communist political parties and organizations, and susceptibility to influence by Soviet and Chinese foreign policies. The second meaning does not exclude the possibility that countries with relatively low vulnerability indexes may be *targets* of communist foreign policy, for instance, as recipients of Soviet economic aid, while more vulnerable countries may not be. The statement refers to the opportunities and potential consequences of communist foreign policy, not its selection of targets.

It should be noted that while our emphasis here is deliberately on vulnerability to *communist* extremism, the index is intended to refer to vulnerability to extremist political changes more generally.[7] In principle, a higher index implies a greater vulnerability to extremist movements collectively, rather than to communism alone. But it is plausible to assume that vulnerability to particular forms of extremism (and especially to the most relentless and irrevocable form, communism) usually varies directly with vulnerability to extremism as a whole. Consequently, for analytical purposes, the distinction between communism and other extremist movements can initially be neglected.

In formulating the relationship between political vulnerability and economic change, we shall be guided by a general behavioral principle that is implied but not specified in the preceding remarks. The principle is that the basic motivation toward the kind of extremist political behavior or sympathy symbolized by Pe derives in large

---

[7] Including, for example, such changes as the establishment of military rule in Pakistan and Burma in 1958. One could conceivably even extend the concept of vulnerability to the single "committed" communist country in Southern Asia, North Viet Nam, if, for example, vulnerability were construed as susceptibility to violent overthrow of internal communism, or to divisive influence exerted by the foreign policies of the free world. The behavioral implications of the index in this case would be problematic. Before there would be any serious manifestations of "deviations" or dissidence, the index of vulnerability presumably would have to reach explosive dimensions.

part from the human proclivity for comparing realities or performance with aspirations or norms concerning what is desirable. Where a sharp disparity between aspirations and reality is experienced by the individual or the group, susceptibility to extremist political solutions or appeals tends to increase.[8] Although we have termed the principle "general," its generality is likely to be confined to poorer areas. In richer countries, for example, we would not expect the same behavioral consequences of a given disparity between aspirations and realities. In this case, the risk of a greater loss from an extreme political upheaval would probably attenuate the extremist consequences of the initial disparity. Vested interests in preserving the status quo are, in other words, likely to be more pervasive in rich, than in poor, countries. Hence, vulnerability to extremist appeals is likely to be less pronounced for a *given* aspirations-realities disparity.

To develop the aspirations-realities principle, we shall define both aspirations and realities largely in terms of economic variables. Our reasons for doing so are twofold. The first derives from the particular regional context we are concerned with. As previously indicated, aspirations have not only acquired a new significance and immediacy in Southern Asia; they have also been heavily endowed with economic content. As a result, economic aspirations and economic progress toward fulfilling them increasingly and rapidly, play an unusually powerful political role in Southern Asia currently.[9]

[8] To explore in detail the evidence and reasoning behind this principle would carry us too far afield. For a general discussion of the role and importance of comparisons between aspirations and realities in human motivation, see J. McV. Hunt (ed.), *Personality and the Behavior Disorders*, New York, 1944, Vol. 1, Chapter 10, and the other references contained therein, especially those to the work of K. Lewin and W. A. Lurie. For some applications to economics, see R. Centers and H. Cantril, "Income Satisfaction and Income Aspiration," *Journal of Abnormal and Social Psychology*, Vol. 41, 1946, and G. Katona, *Psychological Analysis of Economic Behavior*, New York, 1951, pp. 91-93. A point of view similar to the one we are suggesting is contained in Hoffer's discussion of the historical appeal of political mass movements, Hoffer, *op.cit.*, pp. 25-28, 30, and in numerous other references to the current political urgency of realizing economic aspirations in underdeveloped areas, for example, W. Arthur Lewis, *The Theory of Economic Growth*, London, 1955, p. 434; Max F. Millikan, testimony in *Hearings before the Subcommittee on Foreign Economic Policy of the Joint Committee on the Economic Report*, 84th Congress, Washington, D.C., 1955, pp. 17-18; and Committee for Economic Development, *Economic Development Abroad and the Role of American Foreign Investment*, Washington, D.C., 1956, pp. 2-7.

[9] See the following statement from *The Eastern Economist* in its discussion of the appeals of communism in Asia: "Communism has been making its strongest appeal, in those areas of the world which are uncommitted wholeheartedly to a democratic way of life, through its promise of a high rate of economic progress. . . ," "India and

The second reason for defining aspirations and realities largely in economic terms is methodological. Our aim at this point is not to analyze all the factors affecting or reflecting political vulnerability, but to focus on one group of factors and try to handle this group systematically. We shall focus on the economic factors because they are the ones most directly influenced, or capable of being influenced, by U.S. non-military aid programs. In so doing, we are not implying that vulnerability depends *only* on economic factors. Rather we are implying that, to the extent that vulnerability does depend on economic factors, the dependence is determined by a relation between what people want and what they have, expressed largely in economic terms. This is why we refer to Pe as an *economic* index. In excluding a number of political, cultural, and military factors from our consideration of vulnerability, we are admittedly limiting the general import of Pe. In the real world, these "other things" will not be equal, and in individual cases the inequalities may have a decisive influence on political behavior. However, given a large enough number of cases, the hypothesis we are advancing contends that in Southern Asia the influence of economic factors on political behavior is likely to be pervasive and significant. This contention underlies the analytical model we shall elaborate in the remainder of this chapter, and the preliminary test of the model which is presented in the next chapter.

In applying the principle, we shall say that Pe is a function of three variables: economic aspirations, the level of living, and economic expectations. For general reference, we shall denote the variables by A, E, and Ex, respectively. For reference to the average value of the variables in a set (a region or country), we shall use $\overline{A}$, $\overline{E}$, and $\overline{Ex}$, and for reference to the value in a specific subset (a country or province), we shall use A_i, E_i, and Ex_i. (As other variables are introduced into the discussion, the same notations for average and

the Communist World in 1955," Vol. xxv, No. 26, New Delhi, December 30, 1955, p. 993. See also this statement by Assistant Secretary of State Walter S. Roberston: "There are many factors affecting political stability in the underdeveloped countries besides the economic. However, over a period of years . . . the popular test of the success of national leadership may well be the adequacy of the rate of economic progress. If conservative or middle-of-the-road leadership does not produce the popularly desired result, the peoples of these countries may be expected to listen attentively to the flowing, if illusory, promises of the extreme left . . . ," Statement before the Senate Committee on Foreign Relations, March 28, 1958, in *Department of State Bulletin*, April 28, 1958, p. 701.

subset values will be used.) *A* represents the prevailing[10] economic standards (or goals) that are accepted or believed in by the people of an area. It is the norm for judging how economic conditions *ought* to be, and determines reactions (satisfaction, acceptance, resentment) to what is actually experienced or expected. *E* represents the current level of living, conceived in social welfare terms that will be made explicit later. *Ex* represents the prevailing estimates (reasoned or "felt") of how things *will* be in the future. It is an estimate of the time-shape of *E* over a short-term future period. In contrast to *A*, which is an imperative, *Ex* is a future-indicative.[11]

E and *Ex* together comprise what we previously called "reality" or "performance." In other words, it is assumed that the appraisal of reality can be divided into a present and a future component. Outcomes expected in the future have a present value which, in principle, should permit them to be compared or "traded" with outcomes already realized—provided we know something about the degree of confidence with which they are expected, and the accepted time discount.

2. *Characteristics of the Vulnerability Function*

Certain characteristics of the function can be inferred from our general principle and from the preceding remarks about the regional context. If we identify extremist political susceptibility with the disparity between aspirations and reality, then vulnerability (*Pe*) will rise as aspirations (*A*) rise, and as expectations (*Ex*) and the level of living (*E*) fall. Conversely, *Pe* can be presumed to fall as *A* falls, and as *Ex* and *E* rise.

The three variables are admittedly not completely independent of each other. For example, there may be some tendency for expectations to be affected by aspirations. And it is likely that the actual level of living will affect the standards or norms that prevail in the community. Success in attaining or moving toward given aspirations tends to raise the level of aspirations. In other words, the variables are interrelated rather than independent.

[10] For the present, we assume that the distribution (of aspirations, expectations and levels of living) is normal in the subset population. Consequently, the "prevailing," or modal, value is also the mean.

[11] Because the two terms, aspirations and expectations, are frequently used loosely and interchangeably, the distinction intended here should be stressed. For an example of their confusing interchange, see William Y. Elliott (and associates), *The Political Economy of American Foreign Policy*, New York, 1955, pp. 50-51, 154.

Actually, interrelationships among variables presumed for analytical purposes to be independent characterize *many* economic and social problems. In economic growth theory, for example, we speak of output as a function of capital stock, technology, and other resources, assuming full employment of each. Yet, strictly speaking, the first two variables are interrelated rather than independent. At any given time, technology depends to a considerable extent on the size and composition of the capital stock, and vice versa. Considered over a period of time, changes in technology lead to changes in kind and amount of capital, while changes in the stock of capital usually stimulate particular types of innovations in technology. Or, to take an example from quite a different field, it is sometimes said that the international power position of a country depends on its economic base and its military strength, although here again the independent variables are related to each other.

While in these, as in other examples that might be cited, the independent variables are thus partly interrelated, each is, at the same time, affected by dissimilar factors to an extent sufficient to make the assumption of independence feasible and useful. The point applies as well to the variables in the vulnerability function. While E may be expected to affect A, there will be sufficient influences on each that will not affect the other, to warrant treating them, and thinking about them, as analytically independent variables.

Using symbols, we can summarize the characteristics of the vulnerability function as follows:[12]

$$Pe_i = \phi\ (A_i,\ E_i,\ Ex_i). \tag{1}$$

$$\frac{\partial \phi}{\partial A_i} > 0;\ \ \frac{\partial \phi}{\partial E_i} < 0;\ \ \frac{\partial \phi}{\partial Ex_i} < 0. \tag{2}$$

We will consider later the question of a specific form for the vulnerability function (1), consistent with the conditions stated in (2). In any event, it is clear that quantitative significance can be attached to the concept of political vulnerability only if we can measure aspirations (A), the level of living (E), and expectations (Ex). The objection may be raised that these variables are essentially "subjective," and that they depend on feelings and attitudes to such an extent that their measurement by "objective" economic data is dubious. Economic data generally measure what happens and what

---

[12] Those who are bothered by mathematical notations can skip them. The text states verbally what we intend the notations to summarize.

is, not how people feel. Granting that the variables we are interested in concern feelings and attitudes, and assuming that the same economic phenomena may be accompanied by quite varying feelings and attitudes, how are these variables to be measured?

One answer is to measure aspirations, expectations, and attitudes toward the level of living, by direct sample surveys. We could, presumably, formulate questions to find out what economic norms people profess, how they estimate the short-term economic future and what they estimate it to be, and what they consider the major components of their "welfare." Though the tools of survey research would, in this case, involve some subtle methodological problems, such as inferring "actual" aspirations from expressed responses, they would nevertheless be relevant and useful for helping to measure the variables with which we are dealing.

One very practical difficulty with this approach is that such survey data do not now exist, and the operating problems involved in getting them, in Southern Asia especially, would be considerable and expensive. Recognizing the experimental nature of our inquiry, we therefore shall propose a different approach to give some initial quantitative content to A, E, and Ex, and hence to the vulnerability function. A, E, and Ex are extremely complex functions in themselves. But if we consider each in turn, we will find that there are good grounds for using certain variables—data for which are frequently accessible—as indirect measures of the functions we seek, given the regional context of Southern Asia and assuming that we are thinking of large numbers of cases rather than exceptions. With such measures for approximating A, E, and Ex, we may then be able to formulate and test the vulnerability function in tentative but quantitative terms.

It should be emphasized that some of the variables used to determine the aspirations, level of living, and expectations functions are likely to be applicable uniquely to Southern Asia, for reasons we shall indicate. In other areas, somewhat different indicators for these functions would be needed. The point is that while the vulnerability function itself has fairly general validity, the specific approach we will develop for measuring A, E, and Ex has more limited applicability in the particular regional context we are interested in. We turn now to a consideration of the determinants of economic aspirations, the level of living, and expectations.

D. The Aspirations Function

In developing the aspirations function, we shall start with the principle that the level of economic aspirations depends on the amount and kind of information that a region or country is exposed to. When information is widely diffused, economic aspirations are presumed to rise. In fact, the relationships involved are considerably more complex. Some types of information, for example, will have no effect on economic aspirations, while others may even attenuate aspirations. But in societies like those of Southern Asia, which are not only economically underdeveloped, but which have been recently freed from the restraints imposed by tradition on the *desire* for development, the principle has considerable validity. In this context, aspirations are especially sensitized to new experience and information. And much of the information and experience conveyed by modern communications media is likely to stimulate imaginations, and to evoke that heightened sense of the possible and the desirable on which aspirations depend.

It should be stressed that the principle we are asserting is not universal, but rather is distinctly bound in place and time. In other places, and in Southern Asia at other times, the diffusion of information is perhaps as likely to allay as to arouse economic aspirations. However, given these limitations, the principle is useful.

In applying it, three variables will be used as indirect measures of the level of economic aspirations: (1) per capita operating expenditures on education and educational services; (2) literacy; and (3) contact and comparison by members of a subset with levels of living different from their own. The first two variables constitute rough measures of the *amount* of information to which the area is exposed. While other indicators might be used as well,[18] the data for the two variables chosen have the advantage of greater accessibility. The third variable refers to a particular *kind* of information, namely that arising from intergroup comparisons of living levels within the larger region or set of which the particular area or subset is a part. In the remainder of this section, we shall consider the variables in the aspirations function in detail.

[18] For example, newspaper circulation, size of the radio audience, and the urban-rural distribution of the population.

1. *Educational Expenditures*

Let us denote per capita expenditures on education and educational services by D. If we think of total educational outlays as divided between investment and consumption outlays, or overhead and operating outlays, D measures the consumption or operating segment, public and private. The assumption behind this choice is that through active contact and interaction among students, teachers, and teaching materials—in effect, through the learning process rather than the formation of educational capital—new information and experience are conveyed and aspirations stimulated. As an approximation, the extent of this stimulus can be considered to depend on the magnitude of the *operating* segment of total educational outlays, that is, salaries of teachers and educational administrators, purchases of books and other teaching materials, and other variable costs.[14]

By contrast, the investment segment of educational outlays (for example, outlays for new schools, libraries, dormitories, etc.) will raise expectations—that is, estimates of future consumption—without appreciably affecting aspirations. It is only as the social capital created by such investment is used and the stream of consumer benefits from educational capital actually starts to flow, that new wants will be awakened and aspirations raised. The construction of a school, for example, creates visible evidence of benefits to be realized in the future. It carries with it, and in Asia with the particular force of the unfamiliar, the promise of a rosier future. In our terminology, it raises expectations. As we have suggested, it is the actual operation of the school which will raise aspirations. D, therefore, represents only the consumption or operating segment of total educational outlays.

Whether we are comparing variations over time or variations among several subsets at a given time, it should be clear that we are interested in real resources devoted to education. In intertem-

[14] Further refinements in the measurement of D might be introduced. For example, within operating costs a distinction might be made between outlays on primary education and on secondary or higher education, and between technical and general education, on the grounds that the latter of each of these pairs is likely to have a more direct impact on aspirations per unit of outlay. Hence, D might measure only this "aspirations-oriented" portion of total operating costs, or, alternatively, give greater weight to it relative to other operating costs. In the model and data we use, this refinement is omitted.

poral comparisons, the D_i's, denoting the subset values of D, must, therefore, be in terms of constant prices. In interregional comparisons, the D_i's must be adjusted for differing rates of exchange to assure constant unit values.[15]

In principle, D should include an allowance for depreciation of educational plant and durable equipment. In practice, we will neglect this allowance, partly because of data limitations, and partly because the useful life of most educational capital is long and the necessary allowance small relative to direct operating outlays.

However, time enters into the measurement of D in another way which cannot be neglected. What we want to measure with D is not a single, annual level of operating outlays on education, but a continued flow over time. If, as we have suggested, the learning process affects aspirations, and if we use educational operating expenses to measure the extent of this process in a given subset, then D is a cumulative function of time, within certain limits. As between two areas with the same *annual* operating educational expenses, we should expect higher aspirations to prevail in the one which has maintained (or exceeded) the annual rate over a longer period. In an area that has maintained the annual rate for, say, five years, we should expect higher aspirations than in a subset that has only just attained this rate, both because the learning process will have permeated more thoroughly in the first case, and because, with the passage of time, more of the beneficiaries will attain an age when their aspirations *directly* affect political vulnerability.

Yet there will probably be limits to the time period relevant for calculating D. Perhaps especially in the fluid social context of Asia, education tends to be a rapidly contagious influence. It is thus not clear that the "aspirations-effect" of a given rate of operating outlays will be less marked if maintained over, say, twenty years than thirty years. D will thus be a discontinuous function of time, but precisely where one expects the discontinuity to occur is probably more a matter of intuition than analysis. As a reasonable guess, we would suggest that, in the region we are focusing on, the discontinuity is likely to appear at somewhere around fifteen years.

[15] To avoid repetition, it should be assumed that the need for constant unit values applies to all other variables that are expressed originally in monetary terms. Because some of the variables in the model are not in monetary units, as well as for other reasons discussed later, subsequently we will convert all the subset variables to index numbers based on the set mean, see below pp. 342-343.

Thus, if t is the year we are concerned with, we can say that

$$D_t = D_{t_t} + D_{t_{t-1}} + D_{t_{t-2}} \ldots + D_{t_{t-n}}$$

or

$$D_t = \sum_{a=0}^{n} D_{t_{t-a}} \tag{3}$$

with n perhaps between ten and twenty years.

Besides the technical problems of measuring D, several important conceptual issues connected with its use in the aspirations function warrant consideration. Essentially what we have suggested is that, from the standpoint of its broad political impact, education is a special and perhaps unique kind of consumption in the current Asian context. Like other forms of consumption, education provides "welfare," and meets "felt" needs. It thus contributes to the level of living, E, and to expectations, Ex, which we will discuss later. But unlike other kinds of consumption, or at least to a greater extent, the educational experience vitally affects aspirations, as well. These effects admittedly will be subtle and varying. If the content of education is traditionalist, for example, aspirations may tend to be stifled. And beyond a certain point, whether traditionalist or "modernist," education may either diminish aspirations or redirect them in ways that will not affect political vulnerability or may actually reduce it. How, then, does the approach we are adopting meet these objections?

In using D as a measure of economic aspirations, we are contending that, while the relationship between educational outlays and aspirations is, in general, complex and varying, in Southern Asia it currently has the characteristic that increased outlays lead to heightened aspirations. Coming to most people as an essentially new experience, in the wake of the tradition-shattering impacts of World War II and the post-war decade, education seems likely in the short-run to give content and stimulus to awakening aspirations. Stated formally, the contention is that, *within a certain range*, aspirations are an increasing function of education. Beyond this range, the function may be decreasing, but this need not presently concern us. In the context under consideration here, we are likely to be within the range.

There is another implication of the argument that should also be faced. If education raises aspirations, and higher aspirations raise the vulnerability index, the conclusion seems to follow that economic development—and, by extension, foreign economic aid—should seek to minimize the growth of educational services in the Asian countries. On strict *ceteris paribus* grounds, and given the assumption that vulnerability minimization is the only objective, the conclusion follows from the logic of our argument. In practice, when decisions have to be made, other objectives will affect them. Moreover, the excluded factors will not be equal and, frequently, may dominate the aspirations effect of *D*. For example, an expansion of educational services may be a commitment already explicitly made and publicized by a politically perceptive government in response to popular demands. It may thus be a constraint, rather than a variable, in development planning. Burma, and the prominent place it has already assigned to mass education in its development plan, is a case in point.

Moreover, regardless of its short-term effect on aspirations, a substantial expansion of educational services in Asia is essential for technological innovation, for higher labor productivity—in fact, for any sustained economic development and for any appreciable rise in levels of living in the long run. We have already indicated, too, that education is itself a part of the level of living and that new educational capital exerts an important influence on expectations. From the standpoint of programming economic development and foreign aid, these long-run considerations may compensate for the short-run risks involved in raising aspirations through increased educational outlays.[16] Without laboring the point, it should be clear that we are dealing here with extremely complex interactions, and that applying this conceptual framework requires particular care to avoid reaching premature policy conclusions.

2. *Literacy*

The second variable we use in the aspirations function, literacy, can be denoted by *L*, the fraction of an area's total population able to read and write. In general, the influence of literacy on aspirations, and the reasoning behind its use in the function, follows

[16] For references to the long-run productivity of educational outlays, see Gerald M. Meier and Robert E. Baldwin, *Economic Development: Theory, History and Policy*, New York, 1957, p. 368. For a discussion of the ambivalent effects of education in underdeveloped areas (on political instability on the one hand, and economic growth on the other), see Gunnar Myrdal, *An International Economy*, New York, 1956, pp. 186-188.

the discussion of D fairly closely. We impute to both L and D a measurement of exposure to information and perceptions extending beyond what is directly experienced in a group's physical environment, and thereby tending to stimulate a new and higher sense of the desirable and the possible. As in the case of D, and by similar reasoning, we may assume that, among different geographic or temporal subsets, higher literacy implies greater exposure and hence higher aspirations. Inasmuch as L and D relate to a basically similar influence on aspirations, we use their arithmetic average, $\left(\dfrac{D+L}{2} \right)$, in measuring aspirations.

One may argue that L is only a gross measure of what we are interested in, and that it might be preferable, for example, to look at the fraction of the total subset population with a secondary school or higher education. This is the group which, in Asia as in other underdeveloped areas, usually articulates and leads the aspirations of the population. Consequently, differences in the relative size of this group might be a better indicator of enhanced aspirations than differences in rates of literacy. Nevertheless, we will continue to use the literacy measure, rather than the "educational standards" indicator, on the grounds that the two are likely to be closely correlated, and the relatively greater accessibility of data on L makes its use more convenient. However, future work on the model might profit from use of the educational standards indicator in the aspirations function in place of, or in addition to, L.

From the standpoint of data accessibility, there is some reason to rely on L, rather than D. Educational operating outlays in any single year may represent a significant change from previous years whose impact on aspirations will be felt subsequently, and then only if the outlays are maintained. Hence, we need a time series to arrive at D. By contrast, we can safely assume that changes in literacy are much more gradual and that, in any subset, the figure for a single (recent) year can be considered to represent the cumulative influence on aspirations that we are seeking. On the other hand, from the standpoint of data reliability, L may be inferior to D. The definition of literacy in Asian censuses tends to be vague, and the precise meaning and comparability of the data dubious. Using both L and D may reduce the inadequacy of each alone as an indicator of aspirations.

3. *The Demonstration Effect*

The third indicator of aspirations relates to the effect of contact and comparison by members of a subset with levels of living different from their own. As literacy and education provide new mental experiences, direct contact provides new visual experiences of what is desirable and possible. Consider a number of groups or subsets within a more or less homogenous context or set. The argument is that contact among the groups leads to comparisons of levels of living. The comparisons, in turn, yield a kind of information that is of particular relevance to the generation of aspirations. Keeping up with the Joneses is a more recent phenomenon in Asia than elsewhere, but not a fundamentally different one.

As one among many relevant observations that might be cited from Asian sources on the effect of contact with higher levels of living, a recent comment by the Indonesian representative to the United Nations Economic and Social Council is interesting:

"Through modern means of communication, they [the people in the underdeveloped countries] have become increasingly aware of the divergencies between their incomes and that of the people of the more industrialized areas of the world. Hence, there is a growing impatience when their desires remain unfulfilled, desires which are material as well as spiritual in character. This situation prevails in all underdeveloped countries but perhaps it is strongest in the areas where the people have recently won their freedom and independence."[17]

Essentially, we are dealing here with the same type of phenomenon which Duesenberry calls, in a different context, the "demonstration effect."[18] He suggests that the consumption function in the United States (the functional relation between consumption and income), depends not on the absolute level of income, but—to a significant extent—on interpersonal comparisons: that is to say, on the frequency

[17] *Report on Indonesia*, Embassy of Indonesia, Washington, D.C., November 1955, p. 14.

[18] J. S. Duesenberry, *Income, Saving and the Theory of Consumer Behavior*, Cambridge, 1949, pp. 1-5, 25-32. Duesenberry uses the demonstration effect to reconcile data from family budget studies in the United States, which show that at any time the average propensity to consume tends to be lower for higher personal income classes, with aggregative time series data, which show a tendency for secular stability in the propensity to consume with rising levels of national income.

Nurkse's extension of the demonstration effect to the international economy is also relevant. Ragnar Nurkse, *Problems of Capital Formation in Underdeveloped Countries*, Oxford, 1953, pp. 61-75.

with which individuals come in contact with consumption levels superior to their own. If all incomes rise, such contact will become more frequent. Hence, consumption by a given income class at different times, during a period of rising incomes, will tend to be higher at the later time, even though the ratio of consumption to income at any single time will be lower the higher we go in the income scale.[19]

In the present case, we suggest that aspirations depend in part on intergroup contact and on the resulting comparison of observed levels of living. But even if one accepts a functional relationship of this sort, the problem of defining it more precisely remains. Duesenberry's approach is to consider the frequency distribution of various income classes and to assume that the probability of contact with superior incomes depends on position in the distribution.[20] The same position on the distribution over time indicates the same frequency of contact with higher incomes. Hence, in Duesenberry's model, the same ratio between consumption and income persists for the economy as a whole, despite changes in the absolute level of income.

There are several difficulties in applying this approach to the aspirations function. For one thing, frequency of contact presumably will be affected by a number of factors apart from a subset's position on the frequency distribution of levels of living in the entire set. It would, for example, be desirable to consider what might be termed a "geographic factor" in estimating contact frequencies within the set. Thus, the members of two subsets, both at the same position on the frequency distribution, might contact other levels of living more or less often, depending on their respective geographical and topographical situations, on transportation and communications facilities, and on the rural-urban composition of the subset populations. The incidence and influence of such communications barriers on contact frequencies—and hence on aspirations—is likely to be much greater in Asia than in the United States, for instance, and hence the desirability of including the geographic component should be correspondingly greater in our present model.

Similarly, frequency of contact with higher levels of living will be affected by the extent to which the subset is an "open" or "closed" economy. Trade, foreign investment, tourism, and other economic

[19] Duesenberry, op.cit., pp. 47-58.
[20] Ibid., pp. 50-54.

relations with areas outside the set will tend to affect frequency of contact. We would also expect such open-economy indicators to have a greater influence on aspirations in Asia than in the United States, because in the former case we can safely assume that contact with the international economy generally will be contact with substantially different (higher) levels of living.

Moreover, it seems questionable whether the aspirations effect of contact with different levels of living is accurately reflected by the frequency of such contact alone. In an established feudal context, for example, contact may be frequent and yet not affect aspirations. By contrast, in the dynamic social situation in Southern Asia currently, the effect of contact may depend as much on the size of the difference between the individual or group levels of living involved, as on the frequency of contact.

There is yet another difficulty in applying this variable to the aspirations function. It is fairly evident that contact with *superior* levels of living will raise aspirations, but it is less clear what the effect will be of contact with inferior levels of living. How, for example, will contact affect the aspirations of a group that is already enjoying a relatively higher level of living than the group contacted?

The preliminary approach we adopt takes these difficulties only partly into account. It is based on the premise that within a reasonably homogeneous set, the average level of living represents a rough standard of comparison in the determination of aspirations. It can also be considered the most typical (frequent) level of living that the members of a subset will encounter in their contact with the rest of the set. The effect of intersubset contact and comparison will then depend on the difference between the average level of living in the entire set, $(\bar{E})$, and the level in a subset, (E_i). As this difference, $(\bar{E} - E_i)$ increases, aspirations are presumed to rise, and conversely. We thus assume the aspirations function is also effected by negative values of $(\bar{E} - E_i)$. If the level of living in a subset exceeds the average in the set [that is, $(\bar{E} - E_i) < O$], we expect contact outside the subset to attenuate aspirations. Larger negative values for $(\bar{E} - E_i)$ imply more frequent contact with lower levels of living, and, according to our reasoning, a lowering of what otherwise would be the accepted standards or aspirations.

Whether this type of influence actually occurs is by no means clear. We might, instead, take the position that the contact phenomenon only influences aspirations when $(\bar{E} - E_i) > O$. For the present, however, we assume that aspirations are a continuous function of intraset contact, and hence that aspirations are affected by negative, as well as positive, values of $(\bar{E} - E_i)$. Our grounds for doing so are that, even if frequent contact with lower living levels, *acting alone*, is not as likely to lower aspirations as contact with higher living levels is to raise aspirations, frequent contact with lower levels is at least likely to counter the stimulating effects of other influences —for example, literacy and education—on aspirations. Inasmuch as these influences will normally be acting jointly, the continuity assumption is a convenient one to make.

With the symbols used in this section, we can summarize the discussion of aspirations as follows:

$$A_i = f\,[D_i, L_i, (\bar{E} - E_i)]\tag{4}$$

$$\frac{\partial f}{\partial D_i} > 0;\ \frac{\partial f}{\partial L_i} > 0;\ \frac{\partial f}{\partial(\bar{E} - E_i)} > 0,\ \text{or}\ \frac{\partial f}{\partial \bar{E}} - \frac{\partial f}{\partial E_i} > 0.\ ^{21}\tag{5}$$

E. THE LEVEL-OF-LIVING FUNCTION

The level of living is a more common, but no more precise, term than economic aspirations.[22] In relating it to the vulnerability model, we proceed from the following principle: as the measure of what we have referred to as present economic conditions, or "realities," the level of living, E, can be considered to depend on two different components of welfare, a "consumption" component and a "status" component.

The consumption component—the net current use of goods and services by consumers—is clear enough. Neglecting savings, it involves the simple and convenient assumption that "it is only consumption which contributes directly to current welfare."[23] As specific measures of the consumption component in the level-of-living function, we use per capita consumption (C), urban wage rates (W), and unemployment expressed as a fraction of a subset's total labor force (U).

[21] Since $\dfrac{\partial f}{\partial \bar{E}} > 0$ and $\dfrac{\partial f}{\partial E_i} < 0$,

$$\frac{\partial f}{\partial \bar{E}} - \frac{\partial f}{\partial E_i} > 0.$$

[22] See *Report on International Definition and Measurement of Standards and Levels of Living*, United Nations, New York, 1954, especially pp. 1-6 and 26ff.

[23] J. R. Hicks, "The Valuation of Social Income," *Economica*, Vol. 7, 1940, p. 123.

By "status" component, we mean that different feelings of satisfaction or well-being are associated with any given income, depending on the "status" or "prestige" concomitants of that income. To the extent—and it is a significant one—that status, prestige, and self-respect are affected by the economic environment, we want to allow for them in quantifying the level of living. We use a single indicator for the status component: ownership of land by agricultural cultivators, defined as the ratio of land owners to total cultivators, and denoted by O.

The status and consumption components of the level of living are independent of each other. A change in one may be accompanied by a rise, fall, or stability of the other. There will be a rate of substitution between the two components at any given level of living. We will return to this later in discussing O. Let us first examine in more detail the consumption components of E.

1. Consumption Components of the Level of Living

The first measure, per capita consumption (C), refers either to family budget data on consumer outlays, supplemented by data on output of current services by government, or to aggregate expenditure data showing the consumption share of total outlays—both expressed on a per capita basis. It may be suggested that we err in excluding savings and that we should use per capita income, rather than consumption alone, as a measure of the level of living. Certainly it is reasonable to argue that *voluntary* savings do contribute directly to current welfare, for example, by providing insurance and security for the future. However, we cannot impute the same recognized benefits to involuntary, as to voluntary, savings. Moreover, in Southern Asia, voluntary personal savings are relatively small, while involuntary savings, notably by and through government, are a relatively large share of total savings. Since we intend E to refer to benefits or welfare realized currently, and since it is difficult to separate the small voluntary savings from the relatively larger involuntary portion, it seems preferable to use per capita consumption, rather than per capita income, as the relevant measure.

In using per capita consumption, we are faced with the problem of the distribution of consumption benefits. Average per capita consumption may be equal in two subsets, although the fraction of the population at or near the average may be very different in the two cases. If the frequency distributions for consumption are normal, the variance in each subset may be quite different. If the distributions are not normal, extreme values may account for the mean in one case, while the mean itself may be typical in the other. Given our interest in political vulnerability in the particular context of Southern Asia, the proposition may be suggested that the level-of-living equivalence of a given C_i, denoting average per capita consumption in a subset, should be considered higher the less is the degree of inequality in actual per capita consumption levels. The proposition involves a judgment that individual welfare functions, in the area and in the politically oriented terms we are using, are characterized by diminishing marginal utility. Hence, the level of living in a subset, to the extent that it affects political vulnerability, will be raised if consumption extremes are reduced.

It is clear that this hypothesis, forsaking Pareto for Marshall, assumes interpersonal comparability and equality of "utility" functions. At the same time, it may be argued that there is perhaps more justification for this assumption in terms of our particular problem orientation, than there otherwise would be. In the underdeveloped Asian countries, it seems likely that consumption and income inequalities have been and are greater than in the developed countries of the West.[24] Moreover, with the onset of rapid social change, economic egalitarianism has acquired special political force. Consequently, within certain limits, it is reasonable to contend that for a given level of consumption, C_i, the "felt" level of living tends to be higher, in this particular regional context, where the variance in consumption is less. However, since we do not know the operative limits, and since data on the variance in the distribution of consumption within the subset are not available, it will not be incorporated in the level of living function.[25]

[24] See Simon Kuznets, "International Differences in Capital Formation and Financing," in *Capital Formation and Economic Growth*, Princeton, 1955, pp. 48-49, and the same author's "Economic Growth and Income Inequality," *American Economic Review*, March 1955, pp. 20-26. Also W. Paul Strassman, "Economic Growth and Income Distribution," *Quarterly Journal of Economics*, August 1956, pp. 432-436ff.

[25] An attempt to do so might, for example, involve adjusting per capita consumption to allow for the degree of inequality in distribution. If $\sigma^2_{C_i}$ is the variance, and C_i is average per capita consumption in a subset, we can indicate adjusted per capita consumption, C'_i, by the expression:

$$C'_i = C_i - \lambda \sigma^2_{C_i}$$

The second consumption component is urban wage rates, (W). W represents average wages per urban worker per specified work period. For a subset with a higher W_i, consumption and the level of living tend to be higher. In intersubset comparisons, we need not worry about adjusting W_i for variance. In this case, given a reasonably well-organized urban labor market, we can assume more of a tendency for real wages to cluster closely around the average than we can for average per capita consumption. The question may be raised why we include wage rates among the consumption components at all if we already propose using per capita consumption. In general, in the region we are concerned with, per capita consumption and wage rates will be closely correlated. They may differ only in that they measure the level of living from two different standpoints: expenditure and income. To the extent that they diverge, for example, if wages prove to be more rigid than employment (and consumption), per capita consumption may be a better, because more inclusive, indicator of the level of living.

In part, the answer is that the two measures can be used as a cross-check, since there is reason to expect incompleteness in both types of data, but no reason to expect systematic bias in either. There is, however, additional justification for using wage rates in the present model. In Southern Asia, somewhere between 65 and 80 per cent of the population derive their livelihood from rural agriculture. Aggregate consumption figures, which are usually the only data available, will therefore tend to reflect per capita consumption in the dominant rural agricultural sector more accurately than in the smaller urban sectors. To measure per capita consumption in areas where nonagricultural sectors (commerce, construc-

---

The value of the constant, λ, will depend on the shape of the utility function in the subset.

An alternative approach to the problem of distributive inequalities would be to adjust the aspirations function, rather than the level-of-living function, to allow for the variance in C_i (or E_i). This would follow logically from the discussion of intersubset contact and comparison as a factor affecting aspirations (see above, pp. 317-320). The argument would be that for any level of living in a subset, interpersonal comparisons within the subset will tend to raise aspirations depending on the dispersion about the average level of living. On this basis, the aspirations effect of *intersubset* comparisons of levels of living might be adjusted to allow for the effect of *interpersonal* comparisons *within* a subset. The allowance would correct the intersubset indicator, $(\overline{E}\text{-}E_i)$, for the variance in E_i. Thus, adjusted aspirations, A'_i, as a function of intersubset *and* interpersonal level-of-living comparisons, might be expressed as:

$$A'_i = a[(\overline{E} - E_i) + \lambda \sigma^2_{E_i}]$$

tion, public utilities, and manufacturing) are concentrated, urban wage rates are a more reliable guide. While the segment of the population deriving its support from the urban sectors is relatively small, its importance in articulateness, influence, and political activity is disproportionately great. In most of Asia, it is from this segment that the leadership and active membership of political parties and organized interest groups are derived. And it is in this segment that the formation and expression of public opinion tends to be concentrated.

Though the point is important and valid in the context we are concerned with, it can as readily be overstated as ignored. To strike the proper balance requires a nice exercise of judgment in this case, no less than in the design of abstract models of real-world processes, generally. In an effort to approach this balance, we will give urban wage rates a weight equal to per capita consumption in the measurement of level of living.[26]

The third indicator of the level of living is, unemployment (U), measured as a fraction of the labor force. In general, we can assume that increased unemployment implies lowered output and hence lower per capita consumption. In principle, we should include underemployment, as well as unemployment, in the level-of-living function. If underemployment is defined as labor which, though not classified as unemployed, could be withdrawn from its present employment without lowering output, then it becomes directly relevant to measuring the level of living. In general, we would expect income and consumption to be higher the lower are unemployment *and* underemployment.

Moreover, it is a commonplace that underemployment in Southern Asia is widespread. In varying degrees and in various ways, working habits and social institutions have been progressively—or retrogressively—adapted to stretch out the limited job opportunities that are available in the economies of the region, especially in rural agriculture.[27] As would be expected under these circumstances, unemployment statistics that exclude underemployment are likely to be misleading and inaccurate. For example, in India's most populous

[26] Thus, we will assume that: $\dfrac{\partial E_i}{\partial C_i} = \dfrac{\partial E_i}{\partial W_i}$

[27] Harvesting rice, by cutting each stalk separately with a knife instead of using a sickle, is one example. See Karl Pelzer, *Pioneer Settlement in the Asiatic Tropics*, New York, 1945, p. 202.

state, Uttar Pradesh, unemployment in 1951 officially was reported as only .1 per cent of the estimated active labor force of nearly 27 million persons. For the entire country, only 700,000 people were reported as "applicants for work" at the end of 1955.[28] In principle, therefore, it is important to include underemployment in level-of-living comparisons between subsets.

The difficulty with underemployment, however, is not the principle, but its measurement. While unemployment data alone are likely to be misleading, comprehensive underemployment data for Southern Asia are likely to be non-existent. Although some of the conceptual and statistical problems of measuring underemployment are being studied,[29] prospects for solving them are not too bright. In including an underemployment measure in our present model, we therefore do so for heuristic, rather than practical, reasons. In fact, data limitations preclude use of *both* the underemployment and unemployment measures in the model's test.[30]

If, however, we use U_i^o to denote officially-reported unemployment in a subset, U_i^* to denote underemployment, and F_i to denote the total labor force, we can express the adjusted unemployment measure as:

$$U_i = \frac{U_i^o + U_i^*}{F_i} \qquad (6)$$

2. The Status Component of the Level of Living

Besides being a consumption indicator, U_i is also relevant to the status component of the level of living. If, for example, per capita consumption is equal in two cases, but unemployment differs (due, for example, to differences in labor productivity, we may expect that the sense of status will be higher where there is less unemployment, and consequently, the level of living—in our terms—will be higher. Unemployment itself will, in other words, tend to diminish the status value associated with any given level of per capita consumption.

However, the status effects of unemployment probably will be more limited in Asia than in Western societies. Where, as in the

[28] See *United Nations Monthly Bulletin of Statistics*, May 1956, p. 19.

[29] See, for example, a recent study of techniques for obtaining underemployment data in India, N. A. Majumdar, "Some Aspects of Underemployment," *Indian Economic Journal*, July 1957, pp. 8-18.

[30] See below, p. 335.

rural sector of the Asian economies, unemployment is *shared* through the kind of work stretch-outs we have referred to, it tends to be a socially accepted fact of economic life. To the extent that U_t is a measure of *under*employment, it will therefore not give rise to the same status and prestige repercussions in Asia that we would expect in urban, industrialized economies.[81]

In the region we are concerned with, a more inclusive and reliable measure of status is ownership of agricultural land. Needless to say, the measurement of differential status is a difficult and hazardous venture. Sociologists usually approach it by devising occupational prestige scales in which the ranking of occupations is determined by interviewing a sample of the population. Among the industrialized countries, considerable similarity has been found in the resulting prestige scales.[82] While the data available on the underdeveloped countries are less adequate, it is probably accurate to say that in Southern Asia agricultural cultivators owning land enjoy uniformly higher prestige and status than non-owners.[83] If we think of the agricultural population as divisible into three occupational classes—owners, tenants, and wage laborers—we can say that where the incidence of ownership, expressed as the ratio of owners to total agricultural population, is higher, the status value of any given income or consumption level will tend to be higher. If we let O signify this ratio, the level of living will vary directly with O.[84]

It follows that there is some marginal rate of substitution between the status component, O, and consumption, C. At a constant level

[81] But within the urban, westernized sector, accurate measures of unemployment, expressed as a fraction of the urban labor force, may be a useful status indicator.

[82] A. Inkeles and P. H. Rossi, "National Comparisons of Occupational Prestige," *The American Journal of Sociology*, January 1956, p. 332.

[83] According to a recent sample of occupational prestige rankings in the Philippines, for example, the occupation of "farmer" was ranked eleventh; "farm tenant," twenty-first; and "plantation worker," twenty-second. Edward A. Tiryakian, "The Prestige Evaluation of Occupations in an Underdeveloped Country: The Philippines," *The American Journal of Sociology*, January 1958, p. 394. Also compare the prestige rankings in a small Thai village. Lauriston Sharp and Associates, *Siamese Rice Village: A Preliminary Study of Bang Chan 1948-1949*, Cornell Research Center, Bangkok, 1953, pp. 105-107.

[84] The Census of India (1951) divides the agricultural population, inclusive of dependents, into four classes: (1) cultivators of land wholly or mainly owned; (2) cultivators of land wholly or mainly unowned; (3) cultivating laborers; and (4) non-cultivating owners. Typically, (4) is small relative to the others. In all of the Indian states, it is under 3 per cent of the total. In the classification we are using, O includes both (1) and (4). If T denotes the fraction of the agricultural population comprising tenants and wage laborers, then $O = 1 - T$. See *Census of India*, Vol. II, Part II-B, Allahabad, 1952, pp. 4-15, for a discussion of the classification system used in the Indian census.

of living, a rise in C implies a fall in O, other things equal. We cannot say, a priori, precisely what the rate of substitution will be. For the moment we assume that if both are expressed as index numbers, a given rise in C is equivalent to a commensurate fall in O.

Admittedly, land ownership is only a partial status indicator. In some cases, quite a different type of measure might be more appropriate. In India, caste would be an example, though by no means a simple one to work with, either conceptually or statistically.[85] Moreover, O does not reflect the status implications of urban occupations. Nevertheless, in areas like Southern Asia, where the bulk of the population is agricultural and rural, it can be safely presumed that O is a more inclusive status measure than it would be in more industrialized and urbanized areas.

We may summarize our discussion of the level-of-living function, E_i, as follows:

$$E_i = g\left(C_i, W_i, U_i, O_i\right) \tag{7}$$

$$\frac{\partial g}{\partial C_i} > O; \frac{\partial g}{\partial W_i} > O; \frac{\partial g}{\partial U_i} < O; \frac{\partial g}{\partial O_i} > O. \tag{8}$$

F. The Expectations Function

As already suggested, we regard economic expectations, Ex, essentially as a forecast of the time-shape of the level of living, E. In the Asian context, granting the impatience for economic improvement to which we have previously alluded, it can be presumed that the relevant time period will be fairly short, say, between five and ten years. Beyond this limit, improvements in the level of living are not likely to be considered in the formation of current expectations.

It is clear that the factors influencing economic expectations are numerous, varying among cases, and, to a considerable extent, qualitative. The problem concerns not only whether people formulate their expectations "rationally," but—if they do—how they combine and weigh such heterogeneous factors as current and previous economic indicators, confidence in government and government

[85] Low caste is perhaps less significant than intercaste rivalries and distinctions among the higher castes. One commentator, for example, considers intercaste rivalries to be the dominant influence on certain political events in India. See S. S. Harrison's paper on "Caste and the Andhra Communists," *American Political Science Review*, June 1956, pp. 378-404.

plans, the ability and integrity of public leaders, and the designs or whims of nature. In the light of the assumptions he makes concerning such factors, even the rational forecaster will confront a large number of alternative possibilities. He will also arrive at some subjective estimate of the varying probabilities associated with these alternatives in making the judgments we have referred to as economic expectations. Moreover, it is by no means clear whether forecasts should (or do) proceed by expected-value calculations; by choosing the minimum (in the pessimist's case), or the maximum (in the optimist's case), among the possible outcomes at each period; or by a unique "best guess" concerning the expected outcome for each period. In a field where either normative or descriptive generalizations are hazardous, we shall nevertheless try to simplify the problem by suggesting two principles which seem reasonable and relevant for the measurement of Ex.

The first is that expectations are strongly affected by experience. More precisely, judgments about the future time-shape of E are, to a significant extent, arrived at by projection of the rate of change in E in the recent past.[36] The hypothesis may be presumed to have particular relevance in the regional context we are concerned with. Where a widespread emphasis on rapid economic improvement has been stimulated by national independence, it is likely that people will be disposed to judge what they can expect in the future from governments, development programs, and leaders, by what they have actually experienced in the recent past, rather than by non-economic evidence of possible future improvements. We will therefore assume that economic expectations depend on the experienced time-rate of change in both the consumption and status components of the level of living. As between two subsets, we hypothesize that expectations will vary directly with the time rate of change in the level of living.

The second principle is that expectations-formation is related to capital formation. In part, people base their estimates of the future time-shape of E on tangible evidence of economic growth *other* than what has already resulted in direct consumer benefits. One important and general evidence of this kind is the creation of productive capital to which the expectation of future benefits is attached. The uninstructed, and illiterate, Asian frequently tends to

---

[36] Compare Hicks' notion of the effect of changes in current prices on expectations concerning future prices. J. R. Hicks, *Value and Capital*, London, 1939, pp. 204-205.

adopt—though he certainly does not know—the classical theory of capital in arriving at judgments about expected future economic outcomes: he tends to view visible capital as "stored-consumption" that will yield a flow of benefits in the future. He will, to some extent, attribute to the construction of a school or a hospital in the present, the availability of services and benefits to him in the future. Where he sees evidence of the drilling of irrigation wells or the digging of drainage canals on his property or in his village, he will expect higher productivity, income, and consumption in the future—at least he will if the activities of the agricultural extension service have been successful.

Economic expectations will be affected by the kinds of capital as well as by the amounts. We must assume that it is the tangible evidence of capital, rather than a general theory of capital, which has the expectations-effect we are suggesting. If the Asian confirms Böhm-Bawerk to some extent, he certainly reads him to no extent. If new capital takes forms he does not see (such as foreign assets), or does not understand (such as inventories), it presumably will not affect his expectations.

For this reason, it is preferable to use, as the investment measure of expectations, a combination of the investment figures for certain specific sectors rather than aggregate investment for the economy as a whole. The sectors chosen should be those in which capital formation is likely to be generally visible and intelligible to people who, though perceptive, are not inclined to think in terms of inter-industry-flows and roundabout-methods-of-production. While the choice will be somewhat arbitrary, we suggest that the investment measure of expectations can be expressed as the sum of current net per capita investment in electric power, transportation facilities, agriculture (specifically, irrigation, drainage, and flood control), and social services (specifically, health and education). If we call the resulting per capita investment measure in a subset I_i, then Ex_i will vary directly with I_i.

Combining the two hypotheses, we can summarize our discussion of economic expectations as follows:

$$Ex_i = h \left[\frac{dE_i}{dt}, I_i \right]. \qquad (9)$$

$$\frac{\partial h}{\partial \left[\dfrac{dE_i}{dt} \right]} > O; \frac{\partial h}{\partial I_i} > O. \tag{10}$$

G. A SUMMARY OF THE MODEL

The model we have outlined can be summarized by recapitulating the functions and the partial derivative conditions of the preceding sections, using the following terms:

Pe = index of political vulnerability
A = economic aspirations
E = level of living[37]
Ex = economic expectations
D = educational operating outlays per capita
L = literacy
C = per capita consumption
W = industrial wage rates
U^o = unemployment
U^* = estimated underemployment
F = total labor force
U = unemployment, adjusted for underemployment, expressed as fraction of total labor force
O = land-owning cultivators as fraction of total agricultural population
$\dfrac{dE}{dt}$ = time rate of change in level of living
I = per capita investment,

and with the subscript, i, denoting a subset or group within the set.

For the vulnerability function and its derivative conditions, we then have:

$$Pe_i = \phi \, (A_i, E_i, Ex_i) \tag{1}$$

with $\dfrac{\partial \phi}{\partial A_i} > O; \dfrac{\partial \phi}{\partial E_i} < O; \dfrac{\partial \phi}{\partial Ex_i} < O.$ (2)

The aspirations function is:

$$A_i = f \, [D_i, L_i \, (\bar{E} - E_i)] \tag{4}$$

where $D_i = \sum_{a=o}^{n} D_{i_{t-a}}$, (3)

[37] $\bar{E}$ refers to the mean level of living in the set as a whole.

[330]

and $\dfrac{\partial f}{\partial D_i} > O; \dfrac{\partial f}{\partial L_i} > O;$ and $\dfrac{\partial f}{\partial (\overline{E} - E_i)} > O.$ \hfill (5)

The level of living function is:

$$E_i = g\,(C_i, W_i, U_i, O_i) \tag{7}$$

where $U_i = \dfrac{U_i^o + U_i^*}{F_i}$, \hfill (6)

and $\dfrac{\partial g}{\partial C_i} > O; \dfrac{\partial g}{\partial W_i} > O; \dfrac{\partial g}{\partial U_i} < O;$ and $\dfrac{\partial g}{\partial O_i} > O.$ \hfill (8)

And the expectations function is:

$$Ex_i = h\left[\dfrac{dE_i}{dt}, I_i\right] \tag{9}$$

with $\dfrac{\partial h}{\partial\left[\dfrac{dE_i}{dt}\right]} > O; \dfrac{\partial h}{\partial I_i} > O.$ \hfill (10)

The derivative conditions ([2], [5], [8], and [10]) constrain, but do not define the functions in the model. Consistent with these conditions, the specific forms we use for the functions are frankly experimental. For the vulnerability function (1), we might, for example, use a sum or a quotient. Either one, with appropriate signs, would be consistent with the given conditions. Tentatively, we reject the sum on the grounds that it would not allow for differences in the absolute size of the independent variables among the subsets.[38] The form of the vulnerability function which we use instead is:

[38] If the variables are in the first degree, as we presently assume, and the function were in the form of a sum, a given change in one variable would have the same effect on vulnerability in any subset regardless of the absolute value of the variable: that is, the partial derivatives would be constants. If

$$\phi\,(A_i, E_i, Ex_i) = A_i - (a\,E_i + Ex_i) = Pe_i,$$

then

$$\dfrac{\partial Pe_i}{\partial A_i} = 1$$

$$\dfrac{\partial Pe_i}{\partial E_i} = -a$$

$$\dfrac{\partial Pe_i}{\partial Ex_i} = -1.$$

In contrast, from the standpoint of the aspirations-realities principle discussed in the text above, (pp. 305-307), we would expect a given change in one of the variables

$$\phi\,(A_i,\,E_i,\,Ex_i) = K\,A_i\,(aE_i + Ex_i)^{-1} = Pe_i, \tag{1a}$$

where K and a are weights fitted according to the procedure described below.[39]

For the aspirations, level-of-living, and expectations functions, we assume that, within the range and the region we are interested in, the functions are linear and the independent variables in each function have unit coefficients, except for D_i and L_i where the arithmetic mean is used. On these assumptions:

$$f\,[D_i,\,L_i,\,(\bar{E}-E_i)] = \frac{D_i + L_i}{2} + (\bar{E}-E_i) = A_i, \tag{4a}$$

$$g\,(C_i,\,W_i,\,U_i,\,O_i) = C_i + W_i - U_i + O_i = E_i, \tag{7a}$$

and $\quad h\,\left[\dfrac{dE_i}{dt},\,I_i\right] = \dfrac{dE_i}{dt} + I_i \qquad\qquad = Ex_i \tag{9a}$

The assumptions about weighting and linearity are in considerable part a counsel of expediency. As more work is done with the model, and we get a better idea of relative weights and possible non-linearities, the simplifying assumptions can be modified and the experimental model adjusted accordingly.

---

to have a greater effect (negative or positive) on vulnerability for lower absolute values of the variable. More specifically, a given rise in per capita consumption is likely to have a greater negative effect on vulnerability if the rise is from an initially low level than from a higher level. The aspirations-realities comparison, underlying the vulnerability function, suggests proportionality.

[39] See Chapter 9, pp. 344-348.

[40] Since D_i and L_i measure the same, or a closely similar, influence on aspirations, we use their arithmetic average in the function. See above, pp. 315-316.

CHAPTER 9

ECONOMIC CHANGE AND POLITICAL BEHAVIOR:
A PRELIMINARY TEST
OF THE VULNERABILITY MODEL[1]

A. The Test Design

WE HAVE USED the concept of political vulnerability in presenting an experimental model of the complex relationships between economic change and political behavior in the real world, or, more accurately, in a particular part of the real world. Yet neither the concept nor the model exactly corresponds to any directly observable reality. They are abstractions from reality. Like concepts and models generally, their purpose is to facilitate description, explanation, and, hopefully, prediction about the real world, rather than to reproduce it. To test the model, we need to find out whether, and to what extent, conclusions that can be inferred from it correspond to behavior that can be observed and measured independently.

The test we use is based on several premises. The first is that the vulnerability index measures actual or potential extremist political behavior. The second is that one independent measure of extremist political behavior is the voting strength of communist and directly-allied political parties in elections where these parties are organized and legal in the sense that their electoral activity is permitted. If the two premises are valid, we would expect the vulnerability index, Pe_i, to be closely related to communist voting strength. We will denote the latter, expressed as a percentage of the total vote in a given subset, as V_i.

To apply the test, we use Indian data because they are more readily available and generally more reliable than comparable data for other countries in Southern Asia, and because the Indian Communist Party and its affiliated organizations have been, for the most part, overtly active throughout the country. Consequently, electoral data can be considered a valid and independent measure of political extremism. The subsets in the test are the six geographic regions

[1] I am indebted to my RAND colleague, Andrew W. Marshall, for assistance in preparing this chapter. Besides providing general advice, he has written the first part of the chapter appendix: *"The Statistical Model."*

into which India has been divided for the National Sample Survey. For each subset we calculate the share of the total vote received by the Communist Party of India and directly allied parties in the Parliamentary elections of 1951-1952; that is, we derive $V_1, V_2, \ldots, V_n$. We then calculate vulnerability indices for the same subsets: Pe_1, $Pe_2, \ldots, Pe_n$, according to the model. The test consists of fitting a regression of the V_i's on the Pe_i's and calculating the correlation coefficient for the two series. The regression and the correlation coefficient are then tested for significance as described below.

We turn now to a summary of the data in Sections B and C. The statistical model used for the test, and the computations and numerical results, are described in an appendix to this chapter. Some brief comments on the results are presented in Section D.

B. The Electoral Data

India's first national Parliamentary elections were held between the end of October 1951 and the end of February 1952.[2] Over 100 million valid votes were cast by nearly 50 per cent of the eligible electorate. Among all parties participating, the Communist Party received the fourth largest number of votes and won the second largest number of Parliamentary seats, though in both respects it ran far behind the dominant Congress Party.

To calculate the communist and allied radical vote, the official election returns for each state were grouped into the six National Sample Survey regions. There are a few exceptions to the general adequacy of the available data. In Travancore-Cochin, the Communist Party was banned, and Party candidates ran as "independents." In Bombay State, communist candidates ran on a "Joint Front" ticket, and the votes received by the smaller allied radical parties were not fully reported in the available data. In these two cases, it was necessary to estimate communist voting strength. These results were checked to assure consistency with press reports and with votes received by other parties. The figures summarized in Table 31 can be accepted as reliable. The V_i's appear, appropriately, in the fifth column from the left opposite the rows marked A-F. Table 31 also shows the returns from the State Assembly elections

[2] India's second national elections took place in February and March 1957. However, a retest of the vulnerability model against the later electoral data must await availability of the necessary economic data for the 1956-57 period from the relevant rounds of India's National Sample Survey.

for comparison with the Parliamentary figures. They indicate, as would be expected, a pattern closely similar to the Parliamentary data, though only the latter are correlated with the vulnerability indices in the test.

C. DATA FOR THE VULNERABILITY MODEL

Calculation of the vulnerability indices is based on the model summarized in Section G of the preceding chapter. In several respects, application of the model necessitated further simplification to accord with limitations of data and time.

As already noted, for the vulnerability function we use equation (1a), (above, p. 332):

$$Pe_i = KA_i \, (a \, E_i + Ex_i)^{-1}$$

K and a are obtained from a regression equation which is discussed in the appendix to this chapter.

For the aspirations function, we use equation (4a), (above, p. 332). In applying (4a) to the data, D_i (per capita outlays on education) presents some difficulties, which we shall return to later.[8] For this reason we shall also try an alternative form of the aspirations function A'_i, *without* D_i. Excluding D_i, we have:

$$A'_i = L_i + (\bar{E} - E_i) \tag{4b}$$

The separate use of A'_i requires an additional set of calculations for the various parts of the test.

The data we have been able to obtain on unemployment and underemployment are too fragmentary and unreliable to permit us to use U_i in the model. Consequently, for our present experimental purposes, we reduce the level-of-living function to:

$$E_i = C_i + W_i + O_i \tag{7b}$$

As previously noted, there is reason to believe that unemployment and underemployment, which are excluded from (7b), are closely correlated with C_i, which remains part of the level-of-living function.

Data limitations require a similar modification in the expectations function. Regional investment figures for the individual sectors required for I_i are not available. However, there is some reason to believe that, if we had investment data for the Indian regions, they

[8] Below, pp. 339 and 342-343.

[335]

Table 31

RESULTS OF INDIA'S NATIONAL ELECTIONS, 1951-1952

PARLIAMENTARY ELECTIONS

Regions and States	Vote Polled by C.P.I. (1)	Vote Polled by Other Radical Parties[a] (2)	Total Vote Polled by Radical Parties (3)	Total Valid Votes Cast (4)	Percentage Vote Received by Radical Parties V_t = Col (3)/Col (4) (5)
A. North India					
1. Uttar Pradesh	59,669	85,456	145,125	17,074,957	.850
B. East India	1,080,525	693,964	1,774,489	24,176,742	7.340
2. Assam				2,647,127	
3. Bihar	39,272	133,320	172,592	9,901,452	1.743
4. Manipur	13,178		13,178	151,467	8.700
5. Orissa	211,303		211,303	3,705,393	5.703
6. Tripura	96,468		96,468	157,371	61.300
7. West Bengal	720,304	560,644	1,280,948	7,613,932	16.824
C. South India	1,853,623	1,207,515	3,061,138	26,307,225	11.636
8. Coorg				63,813	
9. Madras	1,780,301	350,257	2,130,558	19,928,519	10.691
10. Mysore	73,322		73,322	2,824,427	2.596
11. Travancore-Cochin		857,258[b]	857,258	3,490,466	24.560
D. West India	111,138	129,332	240,470	12,410,577	1.938
12. Bombay	111,138[c]	129,332[d]	240,470	11,528,291	2.086
13. Kutch				119,580	
14. Saurashtra				762,706	
E. Central India	1,421,542	34,137	1,455,679	14,876,314	9.785
15. Bhopal				169,457	
16. Hyderabad	1,367,404[e]		1,367,404	4,854,862	28.166
17. Madhya Barat	24,716		24,716	1,953,571	1.265
18. Madhya Pradesh	29,422	34,137	63,559	7,192,591	.884
19. Vindhya Pradesh				705,833	
F. Northwest India[f]	292,241	202,801	495,042	11,051,503	4.479
20. Ajmer	25,128		25,128	178,999	14.038
21. Delhi				655,900	
22. Himachal Pradesh				223,189	
23. PEPSU		85,522	85,522	1,475,112	5.798
24. Punjab	261,623	117,279	378,902	4,992,339	7.590
25. Rajasthan	5,490		5,490	3,525,964	.156
TOTALS	4,818,738	2,353,205	7,171,943	105,897,318	6.773

(*continued*)

TESTING THE MODEL

Table 31 (*continued*)

RESULTS OF INDIA'S NATIONAL ELECTIONS, 1951-1952

STATE ASSEMBLY ELECTIONS

Regions and States	Vote Polled by C.P.I. (6)	Vote Polled by Other Radical Parties[a] (7)	Total Vote Polled by Radical Parties (8)	Total Valid Votes Cast (9)	Percentage Vote Received by Radical Parties Col (8)/Col (9) (10)
A. North India					
1. Uttar Pradesh	155,869	142,623	298,492	16,791,139	1.778
B. East India	1,246,633	830,810	2,077,443	23,374,015	8.888
2. Assam	69,431	10,133	79,564	2,448,890	3.249
3. Bihar	108,671	117,277	225,948	9,544,439	2.367
4. Manipur	5,298		5,298	139,332	3.802
5. Orissa	206,939	82,828[g]	289,759	3,670,275	7.895
6. Tripura	55,333	2,775	58,108	128,382	45.262
7. West Bengal	800,961	617,797	1,418,758	7,442,697	19.062
C. South India	2,618,425	1,066,013	3,684,438	26,206,360	14.059
8. Coorg	1,386		1,386	87,871	1.577
9. Madras	2,591,923	155,840	2,747,763	19,974,801	13.756
10. Mysore	25,116		25,116	2,745,515	.915
11. Travancore-Cochin		910,173[b]	910,173	3,398,173	26.784
D. West India	137,854	100,137	237,991	12,192,567	1.952
12. Bombay	130,063[c]	98,516[d]	228,579	11,123,388	2.055
13. Kutch				115,414	
14. Saurashtra	7,791	1,621	9,412	953,765	.987
E. Central India	1,150,595	87,291	1,237,886	15,096,451	8.200
15. Bhopal	424		424	226,190	.187
16. Hyderabad	1,086,111[e]		1,086,111	5,202,142	20.878
17. Madhya Barat	39,600		39,600	1,987,622	1.992
18. Madhya Pradesh	24,460	87,291	111,751	6,997,489	1.597
19. Vindhya Pradesh				683,008	
F. Northwest India[f]	307,623	295,666	603,289	10,523,748	5.733
20. Ajmer	3,494		3,494	234,788	1.488
21. Delhi	2,591	810	3,401	521,776	.652
22. Himachal Pradesh				179,475	
23. PEPSU	63,238	82,656	145,894	1,354,835	10.768
24. Punjab	221,119	210,869	431,988	4,974,234	8.685
25. Rajasthan	17,181	1,331	18,512	3,258,640	.568
TOTALS	5,616,999	2,522,540	8,139,539	104,184,280	7.813

would be closely correlated with the rate of change in the level of living *for the time period we are concerned with*.[4] Hence, exclusion of I_t will probably affect the results less than if the current investment and level-of-living series were independent.

[4] In 1951, before the effective launching of the First Five-Year Plan, no sharp change, from the pattern of previous years, appears to have occurred in *relative* rates of investment as among the various Indian regions. If the time rate of change in a subset's level of living at a given period (t) is considered to be a function of investment in an earlier period, $(t\text{-}n)$, and if relative real investment among the subsets has not changed from the earlier period, then the current rate of change in level of living can also be expressed as a function of current investment.

$$\text{If } \frac{dE}{dt} = f(I_{t\text{-}n}),$$

$$\text{and if } I_{t\text{-}n} = k\,I_t,$$

$$\text{then } \frac{dE}{dt} = f(k\,I_t).$$

Under these circumstances, which seem applicable to the data we are using, we do not need I_t, except as a check on $\dfrac{dE_t}{dt}$, to derive the expectations estimate, Ex_t.

Notes to Table 31

Sources: Indian Press Digests, Berkeley, 1952, Vol. IV, No. I, Tables IV, V; M. R. Masani, *The Communist Party of India*, New York, 1954, pp. 158ff.; Press Information Bureau election statistics, Government of India, New Delhi, 1952.

[a] Radical parties are regarded as those firmly allied with or dominated by the C.P.I. in 1951, or explicitly committed to violent measures in their party program. The following parties are included: Forward Bloc (Marxist), Forward Bloc (Subhasist), Kerala Socialist Party, Kisan Kamgar Paksha, Revolutionary Socialist Party of India, Revolutionary Socialist Party of Uttar Pradesh, United Front of Leftists (including C.P.I. "independents" as well as Kerala Socialist Party and Revolutionary Socialist Party in Travancore-Cochin only), Lal Communist Party, Revolutionary Communist Party of India, Bolshevik Party, and Independent People's Party. Radical right-wing parties have been deliberately neglected because, apart from the problem of accurate identification, their voting strength in 1951-52 was too small to affect the results summarized in Table 31.

[b] Because the Party was banned in Travancore-Cochin, communist candidates ran as "Independents" in a "United Front of Leftists." Votes received by the United Front were not shown separately in the data consulted. The figures were estimated by assuming the same ratio between seats won and votes received for the United Front and the Congress Party. Nationally, as well as in Travancore-Cochin, both Congress and communist candidates actually received a higher proportion of Parliamentary seats than of votes.

[c] Includes votes received by the Joint Front.

[d] Voting regulations required that candidates polling less than 12.5 per cent of the votes cast had to forfeit their candidacy deposit. The figures for Bombay were estimated by multiplying the number of radical-party candidates who lost the election but did not forfeit by 12.5 per cent of the votes cast for the seats which they contested.

[e] The C.P.I. was banned in Hyderabad and communist candidates ran as the "People's Democratic Front." The figure is the vote received by the Front.

[f] Excluding Bilaspur where no elections were held.

[g] Estimated from the same assumption stated in footnote [b] above.

In our preliminary test of the model, we define the expectations function in terms of the rate of change in the level of living only:

$$Ex_i = \frac{dE_i}{dt} \qquad (9b)$$

From (7b), it follows that:

$$\frac{dE_i}{dt} = \frac{dC_i}{dt} + \frac{dW_i}{dt} + \frac{dO_i}{dt}$$

We lack a time series for land ownership (O_i), and hence cannot derive $\frac{dO_i}{dt}$. However, it is likely that in the period with which we are concerned (1950-51), changes in land ownership were negligible.[5] Assuming that $\frac{dO_i}{dt} = O$, we can therefore say, as an approximation, that:

$$\frac{dE_i}{dt} = \frac{dC_i}{dt} + \frac{dW_i}{dt} = Ex_i, \qquad (9c)$$

which is the form of the expectations function used in calculating the vulnerability indices.

The data and sources used in the model are summarized in Table 32, below.

The data on literacy (column [1]), and land ownership (column [5]), are from the 1951 Census of India, and those on factory wages (column [4]), are from official statistics of the Labor Ministry. They are believed to be reliable. For these three series, the regional figures are derived from data for the major states within the regions using total population, agricultural population, and employment, respectively, as weights to get the regional estimates. The other data, from the first three rounds of the Indian National Sample Survey, are more difficult to evaluate. Standard errors for the survey rounds have not been published. However, the results seem to check with rough qualitative information (for example, on relative consumption levels

[5] The effects on ownership of the *Bhoodan*, or land gift, movement, and of land reform measures in the States probably were not significant until two or three years later. See S. Thirumalai, *Post-War Agricultural Problems and Policies in India*, New York, 1954, pp. 132-144.

Table 32

SELECTED ECONOMIC AND SOCIAL DATA FOR STATES AND
REGIONS OF INDIA

Regions and States	Literacy, 1951 (Per cent of Total Population)[a]	Per Capita Consumer Expenditure on Education, 1951 (Annual Rate in Rupees)[b]	Per Capita Consumer Expenditure in Rural Areas, Apr.-Nov. 1951 (Annual Rate, 1949-1950 Rupees)[c]
	(1)	(2)	(3)
North India	10.8	1.08	264.16
Uttar Pradesh	10.8	1.08	264.16
East India	16.7	1.32	242.98
Assam	18.1		
Bihar	11.9		
Manipur	–		
Orissa	15.8		
Tripura	–		
W. Bengal	24.5		
South India	22.7	1.56	224.28
Coorg	–		
Madras	19.3		
Mysore	20.6		
Travancore-Cochin	45.8		
West India	23.5	1.32	269.20
Bombay	24.1		
Kutch	–		
Saurashtra	–		
Central India	11.5	1.56	244.53
Bhopal	–		
Hyderabad	9.2		
Madhya Barat	–		
Madhya Pradesh	13.5		
Vindhya Pradesh	–		
Northwest India	12.5	1.80	332.39
Ajmer	–		
Delhi	30.4		
Himachal Pradesh	–		
PEPSU	7.0		
Punjab	16.5		
Rajasthan	8.4		
ALL-INDIA AVERAGE	16.7	1.40	254.66

(*continued*)

Table 32 (*continued*)

SELECTED ECONOMIC AND SOCIAL DATA FOR STATES AND
REGIONS OF INDIA

Regions and States	Average Annual Wages of Factory Workers, 1951 (Rupees)d	Land Ownership, 1951 (Per cent of Agricultural Population Owning Land)e	Rate of Change in Per Capita Consumer Expenditure in Rural Areas, July 1949-Nov. 1951 (Rupees per month)f	Rate of Change in Factory Wages, 1950-51, (Rupees per month)g
	(4)	(5)	(6)	(7)
North India	960.4	85.4	3.11	2.25
Uttar Pradesh	960.4	85.4	3.11	2.25
East India	1006.1	69.1	1.71	7.02
Assam	1017.9	80.2		0
Bihar	1241.5	–		15.20
Manipur	–	–		–
Orissa	762.4	77.0		3.86
Tripura	–	–		–
W. Bengal	942.3	57.5		5.40
South India	664.9	59.7	1.13	6.14
Coorg	–	63.8		–
Madras	664.9	56.9		6.14
Mysore	–	63.6		–
Travancore-Cochin	632.1	50.1		–
West India	1270.5	69.5	.85	8.33
Bombay	1270.5	69.5		8.33
Kutch	–	–		–
Saurashtra	–	–		–
Central India	862.0	65.8	2.46	−6.23
Bhopal	–	–		–
Hyderabad	–	64.0		–
Madhya Barat	–	–		–
Madhya Pradesh	862.0	67.2		−6.23
Vindhya Pradesh	–	–		–
Northwest India	962.4	66.2	.97	7.58
Ajmer	694.	86.7		2.85
Delhi	1292.6	73.0		19.21
Himachal Pradesh	–	91.8		–
PEPSU	–	70.0		–
Punjab	756.	63.4		−1.27
Rajasthan	–	63.5		–
ALL-INDIA AVERAGE	1035.6	69.8	1.84	5.73

in different parts of India), and the sample design shows considerable sophistication.[6] In any event, they are the best data of this type currently available for India or for any other country in Southern Asia.

Among the Sample Survey data, consumer expenditure on education (column [2], Table 32) warrants special comment. It will be recalled that we defined operating expenditures on education and

[6] The National Sample Survey, Number 5, *Technical Paper on Some Aspects of the Development of the Sample Design*, pp. 1-54, Department of Economic Affairs, Ministry of Finance, Government of India, New Delhi, 1955.

Notes to Table 32

Sources: *National Sample Survey*, Numbers 1-3, New Delhi, 1953-54; *Census of India, 1951*, Vols. II-IV, VI-X, XIII.

[a] The regional figures are calculated from National Census data for the major states. Regional and all-India figures are calculated by using state populations as weights. *Census of India, 1951*, Vol. VI, Part I-A, pp. 133-135; Vol. VIII, Part I-B, pp. 130-131; Vol. X, Part II-A, p. 170; and Vol. IV, Part II-B, p. 400 (collective figures for Bombay, Saurashtra, and Kutch).

[b] The series is from the Third Round of the National Sample Survey (Aug.-Nov. 1951), except for North India which is from the Second Round (Apr.-June 1951). Inspection of the data suggests that the Third Round figure for North India is substantially in error. *National Sample Survey*, Number 2, Delhi, 1953, pp. 15, 18-24; and Number 3, 1954, pp. 27-34.

[c] Rupee figures have been deflated by the Indian wholesale price index for 1951, in order that the rate of change in consumer expenditure (column 6) will be in real terms. Expenditures for the period Apr.-Nov. 1951 represent the mean of consumer expenditures in the Second Round (Apr.-June 1951), and Third Round (Aug.-Nov. 1951). *National Sample Survey*, Number 2, pp. 18-24; and Number 3, pp. 26-34.

[d] Regional and all-India figures are calculated from wage data for the major states, using factory employment in 1951 as weights. In Central India, only the data for Madhya Pradesh were available. However, most factory employment in Central India is in that state. No factory employment data were available for Travancore-Cochin. *Indian-Labour Gazette* (cited in *The Eastern Economist*, October 14, 1955, p. 612), and *India—A Reference Annual*, Delhi, 1955, pp. 432, 440.

[e] Calculated from National Census data for occupational classes I (cultivators of land wholly or mainly owned) and IV (non-cultivating owners), including dependents, in the major states. The available data did not include Bihar. *Census of India, 1951*, Vol. II, Part II-B, pp. 31-43; Vol. VIII, Part I-B, p. 21; Vol. X, Part I-A, pp. 106-108; Vol. III, Part I, pp. 38-41; Vol. VI, Part I-A, p. 344; Vol. IX, Part II-A, pp. 214-215; Vol. XIII, Part I, p. 6; Vol. IV, Part II-B, pp. 25-60; Vol. VII, Part II-B, pp. 2-25. Regional and all-India figures are calculated using agricultural population as weights.

[f] Per capita consumer expenditure in the period July 1949-June 1950 is from the First Round of the Sample Survey. *National Sample Survey*, General Report Number 1, Delhi, December 1953, pp. vi-xiii. If C_0 and C_1 represent consumer expenditures in rupees of constant value in periods t_0 (July 1949-June 1950), and t_1 (April-November 1951), then the average monthly rate of change in consumer expenditure is given by: $\dfrac{C_1 - C_0}{t_1 - t_0}$.

[g] Wages for 1950 are from the same sources mentioned in footnote [d], above. State employment figures for 1951 are used as weights in calculating rates of change for the six Indian regions and for the country as a whole.

educational services, D_t, as the sum of expenditures over a period of n years, with perhaps $10 < n < 20$. (Equation [3]).[7] However, the Sample Survey data cover only 1951, so that, in effect, we are obliged to set $n = 1$. In the present case, the results are probably not materially affected by this procedure. In 1951 the pattern of educational outlays in the Indian regions was not significantly different from earlier years. It is only after 1951, under the influence of the Five-Year Plan, that this pattern altered. Consequently, the relative expenditure figures for 1951 can be considered a reasonably good approximation of the pattern in previous years.

However, D_t raises some other difficulties. The Survey data cover only the direct consumer-outlay component of educational expenditures, such as school and teacher fees, purchases of books, stationery, etc. While these outlays may comprise a relatively higher share of total operating outlays than in countries with more extensive systems of public education, it is clear that omission of the states' operating outlays, which do not enter into the consumer budget studies of the Survey, limits the validity of the results for our present purposes. We, therefore, make a separate calculation of Pe_t, based on the other variables in the aspirations function besides D_t, as shown in equation (4b), above.

The data used in the vulnerability model present a general problem of differing units and orders of magnitude. Not only are some of the variables expressed in rupees and others in percentages, but even among those expressed in the same terms, there are wide differences in orders of magnitude. Mean values for some of the variables, for instance, differ by factors of several hundred. Given the linear form of the aspirations, level-of-living, and expectations functions, this presents difficulties because we are interested in according equal weight to the independent variables in the sense of an x per cent change in any independent variable implying a y per cent change in the dependent variable. With respect to the level-of-living function, for example, we want a given percentage change in per capita consumption to have an equivalent effect on the function as would the same percentage change in wage rates.

To meet the problem, we treat the independent variables in the model as index numbers based on the India-wide mean as 100. In the actual computation of the vulnerability indices, the variates

[7] Above, p. 314.

shown in Table 32 are replaced by the corresponding relatives, that is, a variate, x_i, becomes instead $\dfrac{x_i}{\bar{x}} . 100$, where $\bar{x}$ is the mean of the series.[8] The resulting indices for the independent variables are shown in Table 33 and for the aspirations, level-of-living, and expectations functions in Table 34. Because of the use of index numbers for the independent variables, comparisons among vulnerability indices in different sets can only be made by reference to the original means on which the relatives are based.

D. Evaluation of the Test Results

A technical appendix to this chapter describes the statistical model used in testing the explanatory power of the vulnerability index, *Pe*. The appendix also summarizes the computations and the numerical results of the preliminary tests. In brief, the results provide some support for the hypothesis that the vulnerability index has explanatory power with respect to the voting data. However, it should be evident from what has already been said that the methods used and the results obtained are primarily of experimental interest and cannot be treated as conclusive. The character of some of the available data, as well as the unavailability of other data and the limitations of the statistical tests themselves, preclude conclusiveness. However, at this stage, our aim is not to be conclusive, but rather to demonstrate how the proposed conceptual framework, relating economic change to political behavior, can be applied using fairly familiar data; and to suggest that the results obtained are of sufficient experimental interest to warrant further testing in other cases.

When the necessary Indian economic data become available for the 1956-57 period, it should be possible to retest the model against voting data from India's second national elections in 1957. In principle, other tests might also be made, using, for example, electoral data from the national elections in Indonesia in 1955, or Burma in 1956. Actually, the paucity of time series data on economic con-

---

[8] For the "demonstration" variable, $(\bar{E}\text{-}E_i)$, in the aspirations index, $\bar{E}$ represents the sum of the means in the level-of-living index for the set, and E_i represents the sum of the separate index numbers for each subset. With three component series in the level-of-living index,
$$\bar{E} = 300,$$
$$\text{and } E_i = 100 \ (C_i/ \, \bar{C} + W_i/ \, \bar{W} + O_i/ \, \bar{O}).$$

Table 33

INDEX NUMBERS OF SELECTED DATA FOR REGIONS OF INDIA

Regions	Literacy, 1951 (L) (1)	Per Capita Consumer Expenditure on Education, 1951 (D) (2)	Difference Between All-India and Regional Level-of-Living Indices ($\bar{E}-E_i$)[a] (3)	Per Capita Consumer Expenditure in Rural Areas, April-Nov. 1951 (C) (4)	Average Annual Wages of Factory Workers, 1951 (W) (5)	Land Owner-ship, 1951 (O) (6)	Rate of Change in Per Capita Consumer Expenditure, July 1949-Nov. 1951 (dC/dt) (7)	Rate of Change in Factory Wages, 1950-51 (dW/dt) (8)
North India	65	77	−19	104	93	122	169	39
East India	100	94	9	95	97	99	93	123
South India	136	112	62	88	64	86	61	107
West India	141	94	−29	106	123	100	46	145
Central India	69	112	27	96	83	94	134	−109
Northwest India	75	129	−19	131	93	95	53	132
All-India	100	100	0	100	100	100	100	100

Sources: See references for the corresponding series in Table 32. Table 34, column (2), where $\bar{E}$ represents the all-India relative
[a] ($\bar{E}-E_i$) is derived from the level of living indices shown in ($=300$), and E_i is the corresponding relative for the regional subset.

Table 34

INDEX NUMBERS OF COMPONENT FUNCTIONS IN THE
VULNERABILITY MODEL

Regions	Index of Economic Aspirations (A)[a] (1)	Level-of-Living Index (E)[b] (2)	Index of Economic Expectations (Ex)[c] (3)	Alternate Index of Economic Aspirations (A')[d] (4)
North India	52	319	208	46
East India	106	291	216	109
South India	186	238	168	198
West India	88	329	191	112
Central India	117	273	25	186
Northwest India	83	319	185	158
All-India	100	300	200	100

Sources: Tables 32 and 33.

[a] $A_i = \dfrac{L_i + D_i}{2} + (\overline{E} - E_i)$

[c] $Ex_i = \dfrac{dC_i}{dt} + \dfrac{dW_i}{dt}$

[b] $E_i = C_i + W_i + O_i$

[d] $A_i' = L_i + (\overline{E} - E_i)$

ditions in different sections of these countries probably makes it more appropriate to anticipate retests of the model on future, rather than past, elections in Indonesia and Burma. It might be recorded here that rough inspection of the regional distribution of communist voting strength in Indonesia's 1955 elections,[9] together with the author's qualitative impressions concerning regional variation in economic and social conditions within Indonesia, suggests that the Indonesian case may be consistent with the earlier Indian results.

In any event, the results obtained so far appear to be of sufficient interest to warrant consideration of the vulnerability model's relevance to the problem of U.S. aid allocation in Southern Asia. We turn to this problem in the next chapter.

APPENDIX TO CHAPTER 9

1. The Statistical Model

In this section we describe the statistical model used in analyzing the voting data and the vulnerability indices. As in many applied

[9] See Herbert Feith, *The Indonesian Elections of 1955*, Ithaca, 1957, pp. 66-85.

statistical problems, one is reduced to plausible and reasonable expedients in formulating and testing the model.

The statistical model applied is:

$$V_i = Pe_i\,(a, K) + u_i \qquad (i = 1, 2, \ldots, n)$$

$$= \frac{KA_i}{aE_i + Ex_i} + u_i.$$

The random disturbances, the u_i's, are assumed to have mean zero, standard deviation σ, and to be uncorrelated. To test the explanatory power of the index, Pe, we assume that the u_i's are normally and independently distributed.

In analyzing the data, our method is to take the regression of the V_i's on the $Pe_i\,(a, K)$'s, using a least-squares procedure to estimate the best values of the parameters a and K. Because the true least-squares equations are difficult to solve, we have adopted the procedure of obtaining a least-squares fit subject to the constraint that the means of the V_i's and Pe_i's are equal, that is, $\bar{V} = \overline{Pe}$. The computing procedure was as follows: for a set of a's, ranging over the interval in which the minimum sum of squares was considered likely to be found, the values of the $Pe_i\,(a, K)$'s were computed for each a, with each K chosen as a function of a so that $\overline{Pe}\,(a, K) = \bar{V}$. Then the sum of squares

$$\theta\,(a) = \sum_{i=1}^{n} [V_i - Pe_i\,(a, K)]^2$$

was computed and graphed as a function of a. From this graph the minimizing value of a, and therefore of K, was estimated.

The hypothesis we wish to test is that the vulnerability index, Pe, has some explanatory power vis-à-vis the voting data. A test statistic that is plausible in this case is the following:

$$F_{n-1,\,n-2} = \frac{\dfrac{1}{n-1} \sum\limits_{i=1}^{n} (V_i - \bar{V})^2}{\dfrac{1}{n-2} \sum\limits_{i=1}^{n} [V_i - Pe_i\,(a, K)]^2}.$$

Under the null hypothesis of no explanatory power of the index Pe, this statistic should be distributed nearly as F with $n-1$ and $n-2$

degrees of freedom. The $n - 2$ degrees of freedom assigned to the denominator reflect an allowance that should be roughly correct of the loss of one degree of freedom for the fitting of a. On the other hand, if the index does explain much of the variation in the V_i's, the numerator will be larger than the denominator, and large values of F will result. Thus, we should choose as our region of rejection for the null hypothesis the set where $F_{n-1,\ n-2} > F_o$. The F_o therefore defines the significance level of this test. For levels of significance of 10 per cent, 5 per cent, and 1 per cent, we have for F_o (with $n - 1 = 5$ and $n - 2 = 4$), the values 4.05, 6.26, and 15.5, respectively.

While this is probably the best test we can use for the vulnerability index, the sample correlation coefficient, r, of Pe_i and V_i, is also calculated and tested for significance, and a confidence interval for this correlation coefficient is constructed. An adjustment of the loss of one degree of freedom for the fitting of a is again made in this case. To be valid, the correlation analysis requires additional assumptions. In contrast to the assumptions required in the regression analysis, namely that the u_i's be normally distributed and independent, the use of the sample correlation coefficient as a test statistic, or in the construction of a confidence interval, requires that the V_i's and Pe_i's be normally distributed and independent pair by pair. Since the latter assumptions are less credible than those underlying the regression, the correlation coefficient is probably a less suitable test statistic. Nevertheless, the correlation coefficient has descriptive value because its square represents the proportion of the variation in the V_i's attributable to the Pe_i's. For this reason, and also because it is generally familiar, we include it in the test.

2. Computations and Results of the Preliminary Tests

From the component functions in Table 34, vulnerability indices for the six regions were computed according to the regression procedure described in the preceding section. For reasons already indicated, two sets of indices were computed: one, including per capita educational expenditures in the aspirations function (A_i), and the other excluding it (A'_i). Table 35 shows the vulnerability indices for the fitted values of a and K.[10]

[10] The indices computed with the other values of a are used in a sensitivity test which we will return to below, footnote 12.

Table 35

ECONOMIC INDICES OF POLITICAL VULNERABILITY

$Pe\ (a, K)$[a]

	Trial I ($a = 1.33, K = 29.52$)	Trial II ($a = .5, K = 15.98$)
North India	24	20
East India	52	48
South India	113	110
West India	41	50
Central India	89	95
Northwest India	40	37
All-India	49	46

Source: See Table 34, above.

[a] Trial I is computed from $Pe_i = K A_i\ (a\ E_i + Ex_i)^{-1}$, and Trial II, by substituting A'_i for A_i.

The hypothesis we wish to test is that vulnerability indices computed according to the model (the Pe_i's in Table 35), are of value in explaining communist voting in India in 1951-52 (the V_i's in Table 31). As noted in the preceding description of the statistical model, the main test is based on the regression of the V_i's on the Pe_i's. A secondary test is made using the correlation coefficient. Results of the tests are shown in Table 36.

On the basis of Table 36, the null hypothesis, that the regression, Pe_i, has no explanatory value for estimating communist voting, is rejected at the 6 per cent and 10 per cent levels of significance, depending on whether the Pe_i's are calculated with or without D_i (Trials I and II, respectively). Viewed from the correlation standpoint, the null hypothesis asserts that the population coefficient, ρ, is zero. On the basis of Table 36, the $\rho = 0$ hypothesis is rejected at the 2 per cent and 4 per cent significance levels, again depending on whether D_i is included or excluded. Table 36 also shows that the 90 per cent confidence interval for the population correlation coefficient is between .5227 and .9940 where A_i is used in the model, and between .3004 and .9899 where A'_i is used instead.

It is clear from Table 36 that exclusion of educational outlays (D_i) from the model lowers the significance level in both tests. The reason is that D_i is more closely correlated with the V_i's than is the literacy series (L_i) for the six regions. Consequently, eliminating

[349]

Table 36

VULNERABILITY INDICES AND VOTING PATTERNS—SIGNIFICANCE LEVELS, CORRELATION COEFFICIENTS, AND CONFIDENCE INTERVALS

	Significance Level of the Regression $\sum_{i=1}^{6} [V_i - Pe_i(K,\alpha)]^2$ †	Sample Correlation Coefficient	Significance Level of Sample Correlation Coefficient ‡	Confidence Interval for Population Correlation Coefficient § (p = .10)
Pe_i (Trial I, with A_i, and $\alpha = 1.33$)	.06	.9403	.02	.5227 < ρ < .9940
Pe_i (Trial II, with A'_i, and $\alpha = .5$)	.10	.9005	.04	.3004 < ρ < .9899

† Calculated from distribution of F, where

$$F'_{n-1, n'-2} = \frac{\dfrac{1}{n'-1} \sum_{i=1}^{6} (V_i - \bar{V})^2}{\dfrac{1}{n'-2} \sum_{i=1}^{6} [V_i - Pe_i(K,\alpha)]^2},$$

and $n' = 6$.

‡ Calculated from distribution of t, where

$$t = \frac{r}{\sqrt{1-r^2}} \cdot n'-3, \text{ and } n = n'-3.$$

§ Interval for population correlation coefficient, ρ, calculated from Fisher's z-transformation, see R. A. Fisher, *Statistical Methods for Research Workers*, London, 1946, pp. 197-201.

(N.B.: Each of the footnoted calculations makes an allowance of the loss of one degree of freedom for the fitting of α).

D_i from the aspirations function weakens the regression's predictive value with the data we are using.[11]

Finally, a partial test was made of the sensitivity of the results shown in Table 36 to changes in a, by computing vulnerability indices using values for a other than the minimizing value. The test indicates the results are not significantly affected by changes in a over a relatively wide range.[12]

[11] In this connection, it is interesting to consider the relation between each of the separate variables in the model and the voting series. For this purpose, rank correlation coefficients, as well as product moment coefficients, for the V_i's and each of the series in Table 33 were computed. The results were insignificant for six of the series in Table 33, and significant for only two, land ownership (O_i), and the intersubset, or "demonstration," variable ($\overline{E} - E_i$).

[12] $\theta(a)$ was graphed against a, on a logarithmic scale, where

$$\theta(a) = \sum_{i=1}^{6} [V_i - Pe_i(a, K)]^2.$$

The resulting curve was nearly horizontal within the range $1 < a < 10$, when Pe_i included D_i, and within the range $\cdot 3 < a < 2$, when Pe_i excluded D_i. A similar result is obtained if the correlation coefficient, r, is plotted against a.

PART IV

FOREIGN AID AND FOREIGN POLICY

CHAPTER 10

AN ANALYTICAL APPROACH
TO THE ALLOCATION OF ECONOMIC
AND MILITARY AID

A. INTRODUCTION

IN THE FOLLOWING DISCUSSION we shall consider abstractly three problems that have been referred to repeatedly in the previous review of the Mutual Security record in Southern Asia: the allocation of economic aid among countries of a particular regional set; the corresponding intercountry allocation of military aid; and the allocation of a given total of mutual security assistance in a particular region between economic and military programs. It would be nice if we were able to say that the discussion provides conclusive answers to these problems. It would be gratifying if we were able to say that the discussion provides even tentative answers. Unfortunately, neither is the case. Instead, the methods and models discussed are intended as analytical tools to help in arriving at answers.

There are, of course, obvious limitations to the applicability of rigorous analytical methods to decision problems as complex, as fluid, and as imperfectly understood as the allocation of foreign assistance. Indeed, in attempting to solve such problems, it is all too likely that analytical rigor may be purchased at a price of operational relevance. The cautions offered in the discussion of aid objectives in Chapter 7 are pertinent here as well. A few additional comments on method may also be appropriate.

1. The Operational and Heuristic Uses of Models

In their application to problems of decision-making, analytical methods can be used in two different ways. First, they can be used *operationally*, to *make* decisions and to *solve* problems, or parts of problems. Analytical methods can be so used when the problems concerned are "well-structured": that is, when they can be adequately described in terms of numerical variables, when the objectives sought can be stated in the form of a precise objective function (for example, minimizing cost or maximizing profit), and when computational methods exist that permit the calculation of a preferred choice

[355]

or solution.[1] In their operational use to solve well-structured problems, analytical methods can replace judgment entirely, and can yield improved solutions by so doing.

Second, analytical methods can be used *heuristically*: to clarify a problem—or a portion of it—and to facilitate its exposition, its understanding, and its further investigation. Indeed, the heuristic use is the only reasonable use of analytical methods in problems that are "ill-structured": that is, in problems in which one or more important variables are conceptually unmeasurable, or, if conceptually measurable, are unmeasured in the sense that the requisite data are unavailable or unreliable.[2] When decisions or choices have to be made in these problems, analytical methods cannot serve as substitutes for judgment. But they can be of assistance in *focusing* judgment where it is most needed. By locating more precisely the points at which analysis stops and judgment needs to be exercised, analytical methods can help even in ill-structured problems. They can, specifically, lead to more explicit judgments by those organizationally responsible for making them. In practice, a particular decision about the amount of aid to be given to a country frequently depends significantly on objectives—such as influence, friendship, or symbolic deterrence—which are not especially tractable to analytical methods. Even here analysis can help; for instance, by uncovering the *costs* involved in such a decision,[3] and thereby pro-

---

[1] See Kenneth J. Arrow, "Decision Theory and Operations Research," *Operations Research*, December 1957, pp. 765ff., and Herbert A. Simon and Allen Newell, "Heuristic Problem Solving: The Next Advance in Operations Research," *Operations Research*, January-February 1958, pp. 4-5.

[2] The data problem is an especially troublesome one in the models we will describe. As with the data required for the vulnerability model discussed in Chapters 8 and 9, the unavailability of complete data, and the unreliability of the available data needed for the models to be discussed in this chapter, make it especially necessary to be cautious about expecting too much from them. Nevertheless, there are two points to remember concerning the data limitations inherent in the models we will discuss. The first point is that developing improved data in the future depends to a considerable extent on establishing persuasively in the present the sorts of data that intelligent decision-making requires. This, in turn, requires formulating the best models and analytical techniques we can. The second point is that whether the available data are good or bad, decisions—in this case allocations—must somehow be made. It is at least preferable to make the best use we can of the available data as an aid to judgment, than to rely on judgment which is unaided by the use of data. For a similar view, see Russell L. Ackoff, "Operations Research and National Planning," *Operations Research*, August 1957, p. 466.

[3] "Costs" in the special sense of the divergence between the proposed allocation and that which would result in the absence of the untractable objectives. Use of the term "costs" implies that, while the analytically untractable objectives may be significant in some cases, the tractable ones will be significant in *most* cases.

viding some of the data required for the exercise of responsible judgment. As Charles Hitch has put it:

"It will always be necessary to use judgment and good sense in interpreting and applying the results of operations research, but we must try to . . . place a less overwhelming burden upon these qualities."[4]

It should be clear from the methodological comments we have made earlier that aid allocation, like most problems of public policy, is so complex and fluid that analytical methods must be used heuristically rather than operationally.[5] This is so not only because some objectives, such as those just mentioned, are unavoidably qualitative, and because objective functions may change rapidly. It is also the case because relationships among the relevant variables—quantitative no less than qualitative—are frequently embedded in a complex chain of intercountry bargaining sequences. As a result, the aid costs of obtaining various military force increments, for example, may depend on assumptions about a recipient country's fiscal intentions, which in turn may depend on its assumptions about the availability of U.S. aid, which in turn may depend, . . . and so on. In such problems, resolving uncertainty requires judging the personalities and circumstances that are involved, not estimating a hypothetical probability distribution. In such problems, analytical methods and models may be helpful adjuncts to the exercise of judgment. They cannot be substitutes for it.[6]

What do these comments mean from the standpoint of the problem we are concerned with here? They mean that the sorts of analytical models we shall describe in this chapter must inevitably exclude a number of considerations that are generally relevant, and in particular cases may be decisive, in arriving at decisions on allocations. Consequently, as we have previously stressed,[7] the allocation "results" yielded by the models would, in practice, have to be

[4] Charles J. Hitch, "Economics and Military Operations Research," *Review of Economics and Statistics*, August 1958, p. 205.

[5] Of course, the distinction between heuristic and operational uses of analytical models is a distinction of degree. Judgment is involved even in the operational use of models; for example, in specifying the appropriate objectives that make a problem well-structured. But distinctions of degree are important. After all, the difference between boiling and freezing is a matter of degree.

[6] For further discussion of the pitfalls of model-building in solving "ill-structured" problems, see Jan Tinbergen, "The Relevance of Theoretical Criteria in the Selection of Investment Plans," in *Investment and Economic Growth*, Center for International Studies, Massachusetts Institute of Technology, Cambridge, 1954, pp. 7-13.

[7] See Chapter 7, pp. 253ff., and p. 258, footnote 16.

adjusted by the exercise of judgment that tries to take into account the considerations the models do not.

It is important to recognize and to emphasize the limitations involved in using analytical methods for dealing with problems of foreign aid allocation as, in fact, for dealing with any other "big" problem. For such problems, analytical methods must be used heuristically, rather than operationally. Yet we should not depreciate this heuristic role in the process of arriving at decisions. In the Mutual Security context, for instance, U.S. decisions such as furnishing military aid to Pakistan, forming SEATO, or responding to Soviet aid offers outside the communist bloc, might well have been different decisions if a more extensive use of analytical methods had been possible.

2. Formal Assumptions of the Models

A few final words should be added concerning the formal assumptions underlying our approach to the three allocation problems mentioned at the beginning of this chapter. We assume, initially, a given regional total of Mutual Security aid, B, consisting of a specified amount of economic aid, G, and a specified amount of military aid, M, available for allocation among the countries of a particular, reasonably homogeneous region, namely Southern Asia.[8] By definition,

$$B = M + G. \tag{1}$$

The first problem we deal with, in Section B, is the allocation of a given G among n countries of the regional set. The second problem, discussed in Section C, is the allocation of a given M among m countries of the regional set. Finally, in Section D, the assumption of fixed G and M is relaxed, and we consider the allocation of a specified B between the economic and military components.

An important difference between the analytical approaches used in the next two sections should be noted. In Section B, the inter-country allocation of economic aid, G, is approached directly in terms of the relative returns attached to alternative country alloca-

[8] For clarification of the "economic" and "military" distinction, see Chapter 7, section B. As emphasized there, the distinction relates to the objectives underlying the aid categories, not to the form in which aid is provided.

For clarification of what is meant by a "reasonably homogeneous region," see p. 298, and the succeeding discussion of "common characteristics" shared by the countries of Southern Asia.

tions. Specific project or sectoral allocations within each country are *not* explicitly considered in arriving at country allocations. Aggregate, country-wide parameters are used in the allocation model, rather than parameters pertaining to the detailed project composition of country aid programs. By making appropriate changes in the parameters used, the allocation model could be applied on a project or sectoral basis.[9] In Section C, however, the intercountry allocation of military aid is approached indirectly in terms of the relative returns attached to alternative local military capabilities (that is, military "projects" or "sectors") within each country. A particular country's allocation of military aid is treated as the sum of the allocations for specific capabilities in that country.[10]

The reason for this difference of approach is primarily an assumption about the differing degree of resource substitutability in the cases of military and economic aid. We can assume that, in general, the "project" or "capability" content of military aid is likely to reflect the real impact on a recipient country more accurately than is the project content of economic aid. In the case of economic aid, opportunities for internal resource substitutions may frequently make the ostensible project content of aid a less accurate indicator of the real impact on the recipient country.[11] Because of this difference, the specific project content of *economic* aid is perhaps less essential for arriving at intercountry allocations of economic aid, than is the project (that is, "capability") content of military aid for arriving at intercountry allocations of military aid.

Admittedly, there is a note of unrealism and a measure of incompleteness in considering country allocations of military and economic aid within a fixed regional total, B. In the real Mutual

---

[9] In principle, therefore, the model could be adapted to programming the Mutual Security Program's current Development Loan Fund, whose allocation is conceived on a project, rather than country, basis.

[10] The allocation of a regional amount of economic aid, G, among n countries can thus be expressed as:

$$G = \sum_{i=1}^{n} G_i .\qquad (2)$$

The allocation of a regional amount of military aid, M, among l capabilities in m countries, can be represented by:

$$M = \sum_{i=1}^{l} \sum_{j=1}^{m} M_{ij} .\qquad (3)$$

[11] See the general discussion of substitutability in Appendix I.

Security budget process, the regional total has usually been built up from the individual country allocations or "requirements," rather than the other way around. But the reality is deceptive. Whether the process is viewed from the bottom up (that is, from the country allocations to the regional total), or from the top down (from a given regional total to the individual country allocations), inter-country comparisons are involved. In the first procedure, they are implicit: the resulting country allocations are simply assumed to be optimal, and the possibility of gains from marginal transfers is precluded by assumption. In the second procedure, intercountry comparisons become explicit; marginal optimizing is, in fact, the heart of the process. This second procedure is adopted in the discussion that follows. Adopting it means that we start—and end—with a regional total that is determined exogenously. The analysis presented does not deal with the larger question of how much foreign aid should be extended to a particular region, nor, indeed, the question of how large a global Mutual Security Program is desirable. We shall comment on these questions in the conclusions of Chapter 12.

B. The Allocation of Economic Aid

1. A "Production-Function" for Economic Aid

The heuristic model we use is an elaboration of that already summarized in interpreting the allocation record of economic aid in Southern Asia.[12] In their essentials, the two models are identical.

We assume that the United States, as donor, has an amount of economic aid, G, which it wishes to allocate for a particular time period, among n countries, comprising a reasonably homogeneous set in the sense already described. It is assumed that each country has a "production function," with respect to aid,

$$O_i = a_i G_i^a \quad (i = 1, 2, \ldots, n) \tag{4}$$

showing the relationship between additions to the country's national output, O_i, that are induced by economic aid, and the amount of aid provided, G_i. For reasons typically referred to as "limitations on capacity to absorb external capital," or, more simply, for the

[12] See Chapter 4, pp. 92-93, footnote 38.

usual "other-fixed-inputs" reasons identified with diminishing marginal returns, the exponent a is assumed positive and less than unity.[18]

We can assume in the model that the productivity of aid in a recipient country is, in part, reflected by the productivity of increments in the country's domestic capital stock. The parameter, a_i, is intended to measure the aggregate contribution to national product of a unit of net domestic capital formation in a country of the set. Hence, a_i may be thought of as measuring the aggregate-growth-contribution of investment.[14] For simplicity—perhaps oversimplicity—a_i is assumed to be invariant with respect to the amount of aid, G_i. Within the relevant range, G_i is likely to be fairly small compared to a country's domestic investment. Consequently, the marginal productivity of domestic investment may be considered independent of G_i.[15]

[18] To satisfy the two familiar conditions that marginal productivity be positive and diminishing

$$\left(\text{that } \frac{\partial O}{\partial G_i} > 0, \text{ and } \frac{\partial^2 O}{\partial G_i^2} < 0\right),$$

it is necessary that: $1 > a > 0$.

The assumption that a is a constant for all countries, rather than a parameter varying among countries, means that the marginal productivity of the same aid allocation to different countries is proportional to the productivity parameters, a_i.

[14] See Otto Eckstein, "Investment Criteria for Economic Development and the Theory of Intertemporal Welfare Economics," *Quarterly Journal of Economics*, February 1957, pp. 67-69ff. For a general review of the literature on investment choice in underdeveloped economies, see A. K. Sen, "Some Notes on the Choice of Capital-Intensity in Development Planning," *Quarterly Journal of Economics*, November 1957, pp. 561-571.

[15] Even though a_i is assumed independent of G_i, the form of the aid production function (equation (4), p. 360 above) implies that for a given a, the marginal productivity of G_i exceeds a_i when G_i is small (more precisely, when $G_i < (a)^{\frac{1}{1-a}}$). For larger values of G_i,

$$\frac{\partial O_i}{\partial G_i} < a_i.$$

The *deus ex machina* is, of course, a which is assumed positive, but less than unity. The reasoning behind this contrivance is that initial doses of aid may provide certain "key" resources (for example, technical services, innovational equipment, etc.) that a recipient country is unlikely to provide from domestic savings. Hence, the productivity of these initial doses may be extremely high. (This is the "catalytic effect" of aid, which we have previously noted. See above, Chapter 4, pp. 82-83.) As more aid is provided, however, its productivity may diminish—among other reasons, because of resource substitutability. (See Appendix I.) Aid may then begin to substitute for internal savings, and hence its *net* productivity may decline substantially. It does not follow that the marginal productivity of *new domestic* investment has also fallen. Instead, the marginal productivity of aid may fall below the marginal productivity of domestic investment.

2. Aggregate Productivity: The Net
Rate-of-Turnover Component

The concept of capital productivity that is relevant to the inter-country allocation of growth-directed aid has two components. The first is the increase in annual net output generated by an increment in the stock of capital. We shall call this component the net turnover coefficient, and denote it by β. The second component is the fraction of increases in annual net output that is saved and reinvested. We shall refer to it as the reinvestment coefficient, and denote it by γ.

To clarify β and facilitate its measurement, two concepts should be distinguished: the expansion of output that can be imputed to the increased capital input *alone* (the social marginal productivity of capital or *SMP*); and the expansion of output generated by creating new productive capacity (β), but typically utilizing other resources as well.[16] In both cases, annual capital consumption must be deducted from the increase in gross output to arrive at the net increase (ΔO). However, *SMP* differs from the capacity or rate-of-turnover, concept in that it requires, as well, the deduction of *other* factor costs incurred in the expansion of net output. Social marginal productivity is thus defined:

$$SMP = \frac{\Delta O - \Delta c}{I}, \qquad (4.1)$$

where ΔO is the increase in annual output net of capital consumption, Δc represents the increased annual costs of other factors, and I represents the rate of change in the stock of capital, that is, annual net investment. [17]

[16] For further discussion of the distinction between *SMP* and β, see Francis M. Bator, "On Capital Productivity, Input Allocation and Growth," *Quarterly Journal of Economics*, February 1957, pp. 89-90; and Charles Wolf, Jr., "Factor Productivity and Economic Growth," *Proceedings of the Western Economic Association*, 1957, p. 86.

[17] As defined in (4.1), *SMP* implies that the stipulated increment in the annual flow of output will be maintained in perpetuity. The implication is reasonable *if* all costs are subtracted from the increase in gross annual output in calculating *SMP*. Deducting capital costs would, for example, permit perpetual rejuvenation of an obsolescing producer good to maintain the initial addition to annual output.

If we assume instead that the economic life of an investment is finite, even after cost deductions, and that the annual increment in output varies over the investment's life, *SMP* can be computed by:

(a) Calculating the present value, λ, of the investment over the T years of its life, according to

On the other hand, measurement of the total increase in output does not involve deduction of non-capital costs. The net turnover coefficient is thus defined:

$$\beta = \frac{\Delta O}{I}, \qquad (4.2)$$

which is the reciprocal of the incremental capital-output ratio.

Theoretically, the two concepts should yield a similar answer, *from the standpoint of the economy as a whole*. If we assume competitive equilibrium in factor markets, factors of production that are employed as a result of the new investment would be paid approximately what they were previously earning. Total non-capital costs for the economy as a whole would therefore not change appreciably. Hence, Δc in equation (4.1) would be negligible, and SMP and β would be approximately equal.

The same conclusion results even if it is assumed that some of the factors that are employed by the new capital were previously underemployed or unemployed. Since the social costs of employing previously idle resources are zero, Δc should also be zero, and SMP should again be equal to β. If this were indeed the case, we should expect interest rates to be similar to β. It is interesting, in this connection, that a recent study of interest rates in underdeveloped countries seems to provide limited support for this hypothesis.[18]

$$\lambda = \sum_{t=1}^{T} \frac{(\Delta O_t - \Delta c_t)}{(1 + r)^t},$$

where r is the interest rate, and the output and cost increments, ΔO_t and Δc_t, are incremental with respect to the period preceding the initial investment.

(b) Converting λ into a constant annual addition to net output that is maintained in perpetuity ($\Delta O - \Delta c$), and expressing the latter as the annual yield on the initial investment (the social marginal productivity of capital):

$$\frac{\lambda \cdot r}{I} = \frac{\Delta O - \Delta c}{I} = SMP.$$

[18] U Tun Wai, "Interest Rates in the Money Markets of Underdeveloped Countries," and "Interest Rates Outside the Organized Money Markets of Underdeveloped Countries," *International Monetary Fund Staff Papers*, August 1956, pp. 249-278, and November 1957, pp. 80-142, respectively. The study deals with both "organized" and "unorganized" money markets in underdeveloped countries. After a detailed survey of institutional and non-institutional interest rates in the unorganized money markets of most of the underdeveloped countries, the author concludes that "the weighted average rate of interest . . . is usually between 24 and 36 per cent per annum" (*ibid.*, second cited article, p. 102). By comparison, the incremental capital-

In general, however, this is unlikely to be the case. Trade unions, minimum wage laws, governmental monetary policy, and other institutional circumstances are likely to make interest rates depart from their equilibrium level. Interest rates in Southern Asia, particularly those in the "unorganized" money market, should be a useful complement to, but not a substitute for, the investment and output data used in measuring β. In practice, β is likely to exceed interest-rate measures of SMP largely because of overvaluation of the costs of newly employed factors of production.

The reason for using β rather than SMP in the model is that, from the standpoint of the growth of an economy as a whole, and hence from the standpoint of growth-directed aid, mobilization of underemployed and unemployed factors is essential for the effective use of capital, even if costs of these factors are overvalued. To the extent that there is divergence between β and SMP, the incremental capital and output data underlying β are likely to be a more appropriate indicator of the productivity of capital for the economy as a whole.

It should be added, however, that what is appropriate for the economy as a whole is emphatically *not* appropriate for particular sectors or projects within the economy. The use of β for measuring the productivity of capital in particular projects would generally be quite inappropriate. A high β would *not* necessarily imply high capital productivity because it would not allow for the costs of diverting factors from—and consequently lowering output in—other sectors. By contrast, for the economy as a whole, the loss of output due to shifting factors from their previous employment would be allowed for directly in the measurement of ΔO.

Of course, even granted the theoretical usefulness of β, major data problems—concerning both availability and reliability of investment and output data—remain. They are an illustration of a general point we have noted before: the difficulty and limitations of quantitative analysis where statistical imperfections are as great as they are in Southern Asia. At the same time, we should recall another previous comment: developing *better* data depends, to a considerable extent, on showing what they are needed for and how

output ratio most frequently cited in development planning is 3, with a range from 2 to 5. See Harvey Leibenstein, *Economic Backwardness and Economic Growth*, New York, 1957, p. 247.

they can be used.[19] In the present case, we assume that it should be possible to arrive at useful estimates for the countries of the set we are concerned with by assembling data both on interest rates and on incremental capital-output ratios. We assume, further, that the exercise itself would be likely to lead to more reliable data in the future.

3. Aggregate Productivity: The Reinvestment Component

The second component of aggregate productivity is the *marginal reinvestment coefficient*, γ, representing the fraction of increases in net output that is saved and invested.[20] For the economy as a whole, γ is simply the marginal propensity to save,[21]

$$\gamma = \frac{\Delta S}{\Delta O}. \tag{4.3}$$

The aggregate productivity of an increment in investment depends not only on the initial increase in output that is generated, but also on the portion of the increase in output that is reinvested. For a unit of annual investment, the direct, first-round addition to annual output is β. The indirect, second-round addition will be the product of the first addition, the reinvestment coefficient, γ, and β, or $\beta^2 \gamma$. The third-round addition is $\beta^3 \gamma^2$, and so on. Since γ cannot be greater than unity and β will be less than unity,[22] for the economy as a whole the productivity parameter, in the ith country, becomes

$$a_i = \frac{\beta_i}{1 - \beta_i \gamma_i}. \tag{5}$$

Equation (5) assumes that the additions to output, which result from the initial investment, occur immediately. If, instead, we as-

[19] See p. 356, footnote 2.
[20] Walter Galenson and Harvey Leibenstein ("Investment Criteria, Productivity, and Economic Development," *Quarterly Journal of Economics*, August 1955, pp. 351-352) are responsible for the term and for stressing its importance in economic growth. Recognition of its practical importance preceded its recognition and discussion in the growth literature. In the foreign aid context, for example, the Griffin mission's emphasis in 1950 on "a maximum . . . effort at self-help as a condition of aid" carried with it the notion that "self-help" meant that recipient countries should reinvest as much as they could of income increases generated by U.S. economic and technical aid.
[21] For the particular projects or sectors, γ depends on the distribution of income from the project, and on the marginal savings propensities of the income recipients.
[22] See p. 363, footnote 18.

sume that the successive additions occur in successive years, a time discount needs to be included in the equation. Denoting the time discount by r, the discounted addition to annual output at the end of the first year is $\beta/1 + r$; at the end of the second year, $\beta^2 \gamma/(1 + r)^2$; at the end of the third year $\beta^3 \gamma^2/(1 + r)^3$, and so on. Summing this series, the discounted productivity parameter, a'_i, becomes:

$$a'_i = \frac{\beta_i}{1 + r_i - \beta_i \gamma_i}. \tag{5.1}$$

4. An Objectives Function for Economic Aid

In formulating an objectives function for economic aid, we assume that the *returns* derived by the United States from aid depend not only on the aid production function,[23] but also on certain *value* parameters representing the political or policy "prices" attached by the United States to accelerating economic growth and contributing to political strength in the countries of the set. In other words, we assume that the United States is interested in maximizing the "political" returns it can obtain from aid. Given its foreign policy objectives, the United States is (and *should* be, if its allocation actions are to be consistent with its objectives) prepared to allocate aid to a less, rather than more, productive country, if the lesser *economic* productivity has a (sufficiently) higher *political* value.[24] The value measures we use are, Pe_i, representing the political vulnerability parameter discussed in Chapter 8, $1/P_i$, representing the reciprocal of population, and a size or scale parameter, S_i.

The inclusion of Pe_i in the model is based on the central importance we have accorded it in the discussion of economic aid objectives, and on the view, implicit in Chapters 8 and 9, that political vulnerability, though a complex and multidimensional phenomenon, can be reduced by development-oriented aid.[25] Although Pe_i is thus

---

[23] Equation (4), above.

[24] See Schelling, *op.cit.*, pp. 137-138. "There is nothing but intellectual laziness to favor the [allocation] criterion of maximum economic impact. If we put all of the aid money into the countries that can most effectively use it, . . . we have not necessarily maximized our achievement of any important objective. There is no reason to suppose that the countries that happen to have the resources for a rapid rise in income are those where economic development is most urgently needed from the point of view of world peace or United States foreign policy."

[25] Unless, of course, changes in other variables intervene in an opposing direction. If, for example, norms or aspirations rise independently, "development" may have

conceived as a decreasing function of economic aid (or, more precisely, of the aid production function $O_i = a_i G_i^a$), Pe_i is treated as a parameter rather than a variable in the model. In so doing, we assume that, *for countries of equal population*, a unit increase in O_i will generally have the same tendency to reduce political vulnerability in any country of the set, but that the policy *value* to the United States of this tendency varies directly with the size of the initial Pe_i. To reduce vulnerability is assumed to be more pressing in a country with a high, than with a low, initial vulnerability level.

Of course, country populations are *not* equal. Inclusion of the population reciprocal $(1/P_i)$ is based on the premise that a unit increase in O_i will have less effect on vulnerability if the increase must be spread over a large, than a small, population. If we think of the value parameters as ways of assessing the relative value to the United States of the "outputs" of the aid production functions, then $1/P_i$ implies that a unit increment in O_i is less "valuable" in a densely, than in a sparsely, populated country.

On the other hand, the United States is likely to accord a higher policy "value" to accelerating development and reducing political vulnerability in a "large," than in a "small," country. We assume that the large country is simply more important because of its size. Nevertheless, the appropriate units for measuring the scale parameter, S_i, are debatable. In different contexts and from different points of view, a case might be made, for example, for using national income, foreign trade, oil or uranium reserves, or some average of several such measures, as the relevant indicator of scale. Population itself might be one of the more appropriate indicators to use. Human beings are certainly not the least significant stake in the international coexistence contest. However, for the moment, we use S_i to denote a scale parameter whose specific character is undefined. As in the case of the other parameters in the model, the S_i's, however defined, are to be expressed as pure numbers, that is, as relatives based on the mean of the set.

---

no apparent effect on vulnerability. Moreover, development itself *may* conduce to a rise or fall in vulnerability depending on the form the development takes; more particularly, depending on whether the aspirations variables increase relatively more or less than the level-of-living and expectations variables, as a result of development. (See Chapter 8, section C.) The simplifying assumption of the allocation model is that the aspirations variables are independently determined, and that U.S. economic aid is so allocated *within* each recipient country that its effect is on what we have called the "performance," rather than aspirations, variables.

Given the production function, O_i, and the value parameters, Pe_i, $1/P_i$, and S_i, the "returns" or objectives function, R_i, for United States economic aid in each country of the set might be written:

$$R_i = (a_i G_i^a) Pe_i P_i^{-1} S_i, \qquad (i = 1, 2, \ldots, n) \qquad (6)$$

where R_i = returns to the United States from aid to country i,[26]

a_i = aggregate productivity (equation 5, above)

G_i = economic aid allocated to country i,

Pe_i = political vulnerability,

P_i = population,

S_i = size or scale,

and it is assumed the exponent, a, is positive and less than unity for reasons previously noted.

5. A Solution to the Allocation Model

The allocation problem, then, is to maximize total regional returns in n countries of the set,

$$R = (a_1 G_1^a) Pe_1 P_1^{-1} S_1 + (a_2 G_2^a) Pe_2 P_2^{-1} S_2$$
$$+ \ldots + (a_n G_n^a) Pe_n P_n^{-1} S_n, \qquad (7)$$

subject to the condition that total aid allocated equals the total available:

$$G = G_1 + G_2 + \ldots + G_n. \qquad (8)$$

From our convenient, but plausible, assumption that the production functions for aid are subject to diminishing marginal returns, it follows that maximizing (7) requires equalizing marginal returns in each country that receives aid,[27]

$$\frac{\partial R_1}{\partial G_1} = \frac{\partial R_2}{\partial G_2} = \ldots = \frac{\partial R_n}{\partial G_n}. \qquad (9)$$

[26] R_i will be expressed in dollars because G_i is in dollars, and the parameters are pure numbers based on the set mean of each series. The R_i dollars should be interpreted as imputed or "accounting" dollars, rather than "real" dollars.

[27] Actually, there is no reason to assume that every country in the set will receive aid. If the marginal returns from aid in a particular country, for the first unit of G, were less than the marginal returns in other countries, from the first unit through relatively large amounts of G, the particular country would receive no aid. There would then be one less equation from (9) and a corresponding reduction in the number of unknown, positive G_i's.

Differentiating (6) with respect to G, gives:

$$\left(\frac{a_1}{G_1^{1-a}}\right) Pe_1\, P_1^{-1}\, S_1 = \left(\frac{a_2}{G_2^{1-a}}\right) Pe_2\, P_2^{-1}\, S_2$$

$$= \ldots = \left(\frac{a_n}{G_n^{1-a}}\right) Pe_n\, P_n^{-1}\, S_n, \qquad (10)$$

and

$$\frac{G_1}{G_2} = \left(\frac{a_1\, Pe_1\, P_1^{-1}\, S_1}{a_2\, Pe_2\, P_2^{-1}\, S_2}\right)^{\frac{1}{1-a}} =$$

$$\ldots = \left(\frac{a_{n-1}\, Pe_{n-1}\, P_{n-1}^{-1}\, S_{n-1}}{a_n\, Pe_n\, P_n^{-1}\, S_n}\right)^{\frac{1}{1-a}} = \frac{G_{n-1}}{G_n}. \qquad (11)$$

Given equation (8), and $(n-1)$ equations from (11), the optimal G_i's can be readily solved.

6. Some Conclusions and Qualifications

If we make the simplifying assumption that the scale parameter is measured in terms of population, then the S_i's and the P_i's cancel out of (11). If we can assume, further, that a is likely to be small,[28] we may infer, as an approximation from (11), that *optimal allocation of economic aid in the region requires country allocations proportional to the product of the vulnerability parameter, Pe_i, and the productivity parameter, a_i.*

It should be clear from our previous remarks that this conclusion is one whose usefulness is heuristic rather than operational. In practice, the results of this model, as of many, would require adjustment by the exercise of responsible judgment that tries to take into account considerations the model neglects or oversimplifies.

Consider, for instance, the model's assumption that a is constant and small. Though perhaps a plausible assumption, it is not an entirely comfortable one. It would clearly be preferable to convert a into a parameter, varying among the countries, if we could. One way

---

[28] The assumption implies that the marginal productivity of aid diminishes rapidly, see above, pp. 360-362, and footnote 15, p. 361.

of approaching this problem might be to try to judge the relative capacities of the countries in the set to absorb aid. Countries with relatively well-developed administrative and distribution facilities, larger numbers of trained personnel and higher literacy, for example, might be presumed able to absorb more capital without immediately incurring diminishing marginal aid productivity than countries with lower absorptive capacity. In the former countries, a would be presumed closer to unity than in the latter, and the marginal productivity of aid (from equation [4]) would be more closely approximated by the parameter, a_4. Even if quantification of a is precluded, this consideration would help focus judgment on one sort of adjustment required in the model's results.

Moreover, there may even be cases in which the marginal productivity of aid *increases*, rather than diminishes. In one or more recipient countries, a may, in other words, exceed unity. To initiate self-sustaining economic growth, for example, a "big push" may sometimes be necessary: to create "social overhead" facilities; to enable income increases to gain a substantial lead over population increases; to change savings habits; to alter economic and social institutions. Cumulative "little pushes" may not be effective. They may instead be caught and wasted in the familiar Malthusian trap.

Conceivably, aid may provide the difference between the ineffective little pushes and an effective big one. If the budget level for foreign aid were large enough to permit a recipient country to realize increasing returns,[29] concentration, rather than division, of aid might be warranted. Equalizing the marginal returns from aid would then be inconsistent with maximizing total returns. In this case, there could conceivably be only a single non-zero aid allocation in a region. If, however, the budget were still larger, diminishing marginal aid productivity would presumably reappear. The type of allocation model previously described would again become relevant.

In practice, we can probably regard a diminishing returns model as the generally applicable one. Where it does not apply, we shall have to rely on that always scarce factor, informed judgment, to perceive the special circumstances, and adjust the aid allocations accordingly. To be satisfied with the final allocations, we must be convinced that no *net* gains would result from large, as well as from small, reallocations.

[29] See above, Chapter 3, pp. 64-66.

There are other considerations, as well, whose neglect by the model would require adjustment of its allocation results. We have referred before to several such considerations; for example, to objectives such as influence and closer cooperation with the United States—which the value parameters of the model neglect, but which may be important in particular cases; to the bargaining dimension of the relationship between donor and recipient which may warrant altered aid allocations if the result is judged likely to affect the expectations and actions (for instance, concerning domestic resource mobilization) of a recipient country.[30] As we have previously stressed, the model's purpose is to focus and direct judgment and to make it more explicit, not to substitute for it.

C. The Allocation of Military Aid

In analyzing the problem of military aid allocation, we assume that the United States, as donor, has a specified amount of military aid, M, to be allocated among l capabilities in m countries of a specified region for a particular time period.[31] The allocation problem is to maximize returns from $(M - M^o)$, where M^o denotes aid required for internal security in the region. In keeping with our earlier discussion, we assume that M^o will be small, and can be regarded as technically given. We treat M^o as a first claimant on M because, as previously noted, adequate internal security forces, in the area we are concerned with, constitute a high priority objective that is not strictly commensurable with the other objectives of military aid.[32] How can we calculate the returns we wish to maximize with $(M - M^o)$?

1. Higher-Likelihood Local Wars

In answering the question, we assume that, in the region we are considering: (1) there is only a limited number of local war con-

---

[30] See above, this chapter, pp. 357-358.

[31] As previously noted, "military" here refers to the objectives, not to the form, of aid. Translated into the current (1960) Mutual Security terminology, this means that both components of the Mutual Defense Assistance Program—the hardware component represented by the Military Assistance Program (MAP), and the software component represented by Defense Support—are treated as part of a single system of allocation. See above, Chapter 7, pp. 256-259. The meaning of "capabilities," as used in the text, is that discussed in Chapter 7, pp. 284-285ff.

[32] Chapter 7, pp. 291-293.

tingencies whose probabilities are sufficiently high to be of concern from the standpoint of U.S. military aid; and (2) a list of these higher-likelihood local wars can be drawn up, including reasonably reliable order-of-battle estimates of the scale of attack involved in each contingency.[33] As previously noted, such a listing is simply intended to distinguish the *more*-likely from the *un*-likely local wars; to provide ordinal, not numerical, probabilities.

Clearly, the formulation of a reliable list of higher-likelihood local wars requires a nice combination of political and military judgment: military judgment to arrive at likelihood estimates by considering where an aggressor might achieve the biggest military gains for a given commitment of military resources; political judgment to arrive at likelihood estimates by considering the prominent political motives for, and restraints on, various possible local wars.[34] Admittedly, the process is bound to be an inexact one. But from at least some experience with it, in local-war gaming, the process would seem to be sufficiently feasible to make our initial assumption tenable.

The next step proceeds from the assumption that, given the higher-likelihood local wars, it should be possible to formulate an array of local military capabilities for the countries of the region which would have relevance to the specified local war contingencies. ("Relevance" here means that additions to the "relevant" capabilities will inflict additional costs [losses] on a potential aggressor in the specific higher-likelihood local war contingencies already defined.[35] The amount of these incremental aggressor-costs need not concern us yet; they will enter into the determination of relative "worth" parameters for the various military capabilities.)

Measurement of the relevant capabilities would be in differing units corresponding to the several military aid objectives previously described: local defense forces (varying by service and function); infrastructures; bases.[36]

[33] For an illustrative list of higher-likelihood local wars in Southern Asia see Chapter 7, pp. 288-289.

[34] In practice, the required combination of political-military judgment would depend on a further combination of "field" and Washington judgment: the former exercised by the appropriate embassies, including the Military Assistance Advisory Groups, and the regional military commander; the latter exercised by the Joint Chiefs of Staff, the State Department, and the National Security Council.

[35] See above, Chapter 7, pp. 284-286. In line with our earlier discussion of military aid objectives, it should be recalled that our stress on the military *capabilities* facing a potential aggressor, and our neglect of his estimate of the defender's *intentions* to use them, carries this implication: that the intentions accredited by the enemy either depend *uniformly* on, or are independent of, defensive capabilities.

[36] See above, Chapter 7, section D.4.

2. *The Capability-Cost Function*

Each of the relevant local military capabilities is presumed, further, to have a corresponding military-aid *cost* function, showing the estimated relationship between allocations (inputs) of MDAP dollars, M—covering both MAP and Defense Support aid—and the resulting size of the corresponding local capabilities in each country of the region. Denoting the ith capability in the jth country as F_{ij}, the capability-cost function for each of the l capabilities in m countries of the set can be written:

$$F_{ij} = f_{ij}(M_{ij}), \quad \begin{matrix} (i = 1, 2, \ldots, l) \\ (j = 1, 2, \ldots, m) \end{matrix} \qquad (13)$$

The resulting capability-cost matrix can be designated F.

This notation is intended only as a convenient simplification. In practice we should not find, and should not expect, continuous cost functions for the f_{ij}'s. Small additions to existing capabilities may be purchased at relatively small and constant marginal MDAP costs. Larger increases will probably entail sharply increasing MDAP costs initially, before a new range of possibly constant costs is reached. With MDAP costs on the abscissa and a specified military capability on the ordinate, we might expect a capability-cost function of the following shape:

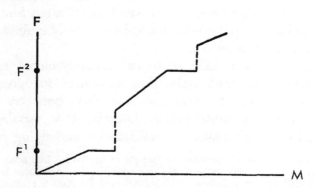

Discontinuities are indicated by the dotted lines at the F^1 and F^2 steps. Discontinuities arise because costs that can be regarded as fixed for relatively small additional capabilities become variable costs if larger additions are considered. Existing barracks and warehousing can be used more intensively, at a negligible increase in cost, if only one or two battalions are to be added to a country's ground forces; an additional division requires a substantial increase in such overhead facilities.

Consequently, in practice, we probably should not find a single, continuous function for each f_{ij}, but, rather, several different functions depending on the scale of the contemplated capability increments.[37] For simplicity, however, we will continue to assume that the capability-cost data fit into an agreeably continuous function.

3. The Capability-Worth Parameters

Associated with the capability-cost matrix, F, is a *capability-worth* matrix, V. Corresponding to each f_{ij} is a worth parameter, V_{ij}, indicating the estimated dollar worth to the United States of a unit addition to the ith capability in the jth country. V is an *incremental* capability-worth matrix.

Derivation of the V_{ij}'s would be according to the alternative-cost technique described in Chapter 7.[38] If a military capability substitutable for a particular F_{ij} is provided for in the U.S. *domestic* defense budget, the worth of an increment in F_{ij} would be the incremental cost of the substitutable domestic capability. If *no* substitutable domestic capability is provided for in the defense budget, the worth of F_{ij} would be either the alternative costs that the United States would *have* to incur to provide a substitutable, tactical capability of its own, or the alternative costs which the United States would be *willing* to incur to provide such a substitutable capability, whichever of the two is lower.

It should be clear that such an alternative-cost estimation of capability-worth must make due allowance for possible differences, in both effectiveness and reliability, between the local capabilities and the substitutable domestic U.S. capability. For example, possible differences in malfunction and flying rates, and

[37] Each cell of the F matrix can thus be thought of as divided into several sub-cells, each referring to a particular range of F_{ij}, for example, 1-5 battalions; 1-2 divisions; etc., with sub-cell entries specifying the MDAP cost function for capability levels within the indicated range.

Of course, it is one thing to resolve the problem of discontinuity conceptually, and quite another to find appropriate data for the matrix.

Procedurally, the primary source of the data inputs for the capability-cost matrix would probably be the U.S. Military Assistance Advisory Groups in each MDAP country. Given the established list of higher-likelihood local war contingencies, the MAAG's would be responsible for judging the "relevant" local military capabilities, and costing them in terms of MDAP aid requirements.

[38] See above, Chapter 7, pp. 286-287.

inevitable differences in the degree of U.S. control over deployment and use, are likely to make the marginal rate of substitution between Pakistani squadrons of F-100's and U.S. squadrons of F-100's considerably greater than unity. If the appropriate allowance for effectiveness and, especially, for reliability differences is bound to be uncertain, we assume estimates will be the better for being explicit.

4. An Objectives Function for Military Aid

The two matrices, F and V, are the basic analytical tools needed for a formal solution of the military aid allocation problem. Together, they permit us to formulate an objectives function, Z, representing the returns from military aid. In the notation we have been using, Z can be written:[89]

$$Z = \sum_{i=1}^{l} \sum_{j=1}^{m} V_{ij} F_{ij}. \tag{14}$$

The optimal allocation of military aid requires maximizing Z subject to the constraint that

$$\sum_{i=1}^{l} \sum_{j=1}^{m} M_{ij} = M - M^{o}, \tag{15}$$

where M_{ij} denotes the military aid allocation to the ith capability in the jth country, M is the total amount of military aid available for the region, and M^{o} is the sum of the military aid allocations for internal security forces in the countries of the region.

Maximizing (14), subject to (15), proceeds along the familiar lines of equalizing marginal returns for all M_{ij}'s. Given the capability-cost functions according to equation (13), an optimum allocation of M requires that:

$$V_{11} f'_{11} = V_{12} f'_{12} = \ldots = V_{lm} f'_{lm}. \tag{16}$$

With the $(lm - 1)$ equations from (16), together with equation (15), the lm unknowns, that is, the (M_{ij})'s, are soluble.

[89] Z is expressed in imputed dollars. Thus,

$$V_{ij} F_{ij} = \frac{\text{dollars}}{\substack{\text{unit of military capability } i \\ \text{in } j^{th} \text{ country}}} \cdot \substack{\text{units of military capability } i \\ \text{in } j^{th} \text{ country}}$$

$$= \text{dollars}.$$

Actually, it is quite unlikely that each of the l capabilities in each of the m countries will receive military aid. As in the case of economic aid,[40] it is not even necessary that each country receive a positive allocation of military aid. If the aid costs of some capabilities are sufficiently high for initial allocations of aid, these capabilities will receive no allocations. If all of the l capabilities in a particular country have sufficiently high incremental aid costs, the country itself will not receive any aid. In this case, both the number of equations in (16) and the number of positive military aid allocations (M_{ij}) will be correspondingly reduced. Equalizing the marginal returns from military aid allocations may, in other words, mean zero allocations for some capabilities and some countries.

5. Some Qualifications to the Model

An important qualification concerning the multiple use of forces should be added to the model. Essentially, the capability-worth parameter, V_{ij}, has been defined as the answer to the question: what would the United States *have*, or be *willing*, to pay for a U.S. tactical capability substitutable for an increment in F_{ij}? Implicit in the case for military aid is the presumption that $V_{ij} \geq f'_{ij}$.[41] As long as this presumption is warranted, the United States would appear to be in a better position to meet the higher-likelihood local wars if it uses additional MDAP dollars to enhance local capabilities in the countries of the region, rather than, say, using MDAP dollars to "buy" additional U.S. capabilities.

In practice, this apparent advantage may be illusory. The substitutable U.S. local war capability may have a higher cost than the F_{ij} for which it can substitute, but it may also have *multiple local war uses*, while the F_{ij} may not. A mobile U.S. tactical division may, for example, cost six times as much as each comparable local division in seven MDAP countries. But if the U.S. division has a potential usefulness in seven local war contingencies, while each comparable MDAP division would be limited to use in a *single* local war, MDAP dollars would be better spent on U.S., rather than on local, divisions.[42] If the comparison were made between tactical air, rather than

[40] See above, footnote 27.

[41] As already noted, within the U.S. budget an optimal allocation of total military appropriations between MDAP and domestic defense would require, in principle, that $V_{ij} = f'_{ij}$. See above, pp. 286-287.

[42] Assuming that the probability of simultaneous occurrence of two or more of the higher-likelihood local wars is low enough to be overlooked.

ground forces, the initial difference in the cost of the U.S. and the local tactical forces would probably be less because of the relatively larger share of equipment costs in total costs for air units. Hence, the dominance of the multiple-use U.S. force might tend to be still greater in the case of air than of ground forces.

The paradoxical conclusion results that it may sometimes be militarily advantageous to buy a seemingly higher-cost, mobile U.S. tactical capability rather than an apparently cheaper local capability. Despite the more familiar argument to the contrary, MDAP dollars may sometimes be more profitably spent on building up conventional local war capabilities in the U.S. armed forces, than on building them abroad.

The question of aggregation that is involved here requires us to impose a further condition on our solution to the military aid allocation problem already outlined. Besides the marginal equalization condition of equation (16), an optimal set of country and capability allocations (the M_{ij}'s), requires that there be no *group* of capabilities within the F_{ij}'s, whose aggregate cost exceeds that of a U.S. domestic capability able to substitute for the group as a whole. The point is an illustration of the general qualification discussed in connection with the economic aid model. To be really satisfied with the final allocations, we must be convinced that no net gains would result from either large or small reallocations.[43]

To this formal qualification to our model should be added an informal one. I writing the objectives function, Z (equation 14), we have neglected two possibly important types of military-aid "values": the symbolic deterrent value of the MDAP relationship between donor and recipient; and the value of MDAP as a legitimizer of U.S. intervention in the event aggression occurs.[44] The reason for neglecting these possible values is partly that there is no convenient way to take them into quantitative account. But expediency is not the only reason. As we have suggested before, the alternative, *non-MDAP* costs of maintaining deterrence and of legitimizing possible U.S. intervention—for example, through the traditional techniques of diplomacy, and even through economic rather than military assistance—may be quite low, at least in *some* of the MDAP countries of Southern Asia. Consequently, neither value need be taken into account in arriving at an optimal regional allocation of military aid funds.

[43] See above, p. 370.   [44] See above, pp. 290-291.

Whether this reasoning is valid in practice will depend on many circumstances—not excluding the imagination and flexibility of U.S. foreign policy itself. If it is not valid, clearly, the results that would be obtained by allocating according to the model would require correction to allow for the objectives overlooked by the model. Here, again, the model is intended to be a technique for focusing, not supplanting, judgment.

D. The Allocation of Regional Aid Between Economic and Military Programs

We now ask the question how, given an amount, B, of Mutual Security aid for a region, a preferred allocation between military programs, M, and economic programs, G, can be analyzed?

Before suggesting an approach to the question, another question needs to be asked, namely, why *try* to consider G and M in terms of a fixed regional B? Is the interprogram allocation of a fixed B the most appropriate way to approach G and M?

1. The Comparison of Incommensurables

It is always tempting to evade a difficult question by asking a question about it. But in this case, there is more to the counter question than evasion. First, recall our repeated assertion that the basic distinction between G and M lies in the objectives and the intended uses, not the form, of the two types of aid.[45] Next, accept the assumption that resource substitutability in the recipient countries does not nullify the intended uses and objectives of G and M. Putting the last point another way, assume that different consequences *do*, in fact, result from aid intended for military uses than from aid intended for economic-developmental uses—either because of convergent donor-recipient interests or because, if interests diverge, the amount of military (economic) aid is large relative to the domestic resources which a recipient might shift from military (developmental) uses in an effort to nullify the donor's intended effect.[46]

Once these considerations are accepted, the reason for questioning

[45] See above, Chapter 7, section B.
[46] See the discussion of resource substitutability in Appendix I. It is quite possible that the different effects of "economic" and "military" aid may frequently be due to convergent donor-recipient interests in the former case, and to the relatively large amount (and inflexible type) of aid involved in the latter case.

the question with which we started is simply this: the effects, and hence the "returns," attributable to M and G are quite incommensurable. The level at which the objectives of economic and military aid merge is so high and general (for instance, promoting the freedom and strength of the free world), as to preclude any useful, quantitative comparisons between them. It is one thing to try to compare the returns from economic *or* from military aid as among different countries of a region, as we have done in discussing the *intercountry* allocation of a given G and a given M. It is quite another to try to compare the returns from economic aid with those from military aid in arriving at a preferred *interprogram* allocation of regional Mutual Security aid.

The point is an illustration of quite a general limitation of attempts to apply analytical techniques to budget optimizing on too grand a scale. One can proceed, for example, with some confidence to try to allocate funds between "forest-fire control" and "forest management" programs *within* the Department of Interior's Forest Service budget.[47] But one stands on much shakier ground in trying to allocate funds between the Forest Service itself and, say, the Federal Bureau of Investigation, the National Institutes of Health, or even the Agricultural Extension Service. Where the returns from different programs cannot be measured in the same coin, analytical optimizing techniques are not likely to be of much use.

Inasmuch as the returns from military, M, and economic, G, programs are hardly comparable, it can be argued that the question of how to allocate a fixed regional total, B, between M and G is not the appropriate question to ask. It might, for example, be more appropriate to approach an "optimal" M by considering it as an alternative to appropriations for increasing local war capabilities within the *domestic* U.S. defense budget, rather than as an alternative to additional regional economic aid, G. This may yet be the result of the Mutual Security legislation of 1959, which authorized military end-item aid (MAP) as part of the Defense Department's regular appropriation beginning in fiscal year 1960.

However, defense support remains part of the Mutual Security authorizing and appropriations legislation. Implicitly, anyhow,

[47] For this illustration, as well as more general comments on the pros and cons of applying operations research techniques to "performance" or "program" budgeting in the Federal Government, see McKean, *op.cit.*, Chapter 13, "Analysis for Performance Budgeting," pp. 247-278.

regional economic and at least defense support aid are still parts of the same system of allocation by virtue of the provision in the enabling legislation permitting transfers of funds between aid categories.[48] This is one important reason for asking the question with which we began this section, and to which we will return in a moment.

There is another reason, as well. If we look broadly at the many aspects of "competitive coexistence" in Southern Asia, it is useful to distinguish between an *internal* and an *external* aspect: the former centering around the problem of internal cohesion, political stability, and economic growth; the latter, involving the latent threat of limited external aggression. In different countries of the region at a given time, and in the region as a whole at different times, the relative priority of the two aspects will differ. To decide on a specific G and M is to make an *implicit* judgment about prevailing priorities. One of the disturbing dilemmas of competitive coexistence is that the threat of limited external aggression may recede if the prospect of internal disintegration rises. The surest way to prevent aggression may be to allow internal disintegration to proceed. If communism has an increasing chance of coming to power peacefully, through free electoral choice, the gains to be realized from communist military adventurism decline. Conversely, the more successful are efforts to strengthen internal cohesion and reduce political vulnerability in Southern Asia, the higher may be the likelihood of limited local wars. The point underscores the need for consciously and continually reassessing the relative priority of the internal and external dimensions of the problem in foreign aid planning.

Perhaps the best reason for directly considering the question of interprogram aid allocations is to focus judgment *explicitly* on the prevailing or anticipated balance between internal and external threats, and the desirable balance between economic and military aid. Even if the returns from M and G remain technically incommensurable, it is perhaps helpful in establishing judgmental commensurability to formulate them as precisely as we can.

2. An Approach to Interprogram Allocations

Essentially, this is all our approach to the problem of interprogram allocation amounts to. The approach we use is to apply the models

[48] See p. 186, footnote 10.

already described in Sections B and C, for allocating economic and military aid, to the intercountry allocation of different *pairs* of M and G. The trial pairs are chosen arbitrarily, subject to the condition that each pair equals total Mutual Security aid, B, available for the region.[49] Incommensurability of returns remains. But the purpose of the exercise is to permit responsible decision-makers to judge explicitly the desirability of alternative G and M allocations by considering: (1) what the optimal country allocations of various (G, M) pairs would be; (2) what would be sacrificed by marginal transfers from M to G;[50] and (3) how the economic aid allocations to particular countries would be reduced by marginal transfers from G to M.[51]

The procedural steps can be briefly summarized. First, we arbitrarily assume that a limited number of (G, M) trial pairs—say, five—will be sufficient to cover the interesting alternatives. To simplify the process, though not necessarily its arbitrariness, we can use the currently prevailing G and M levels, say (M^1, G^1), as a basis for deriving the other pairs. The alternative trial values of M might then be set by making additions to and reductions in M^1, in fairly large steps. For example:

$$M^2 = M^1 + .2G^1 ,$$
$$M^3 = M^1 + .4G^1 ,$$
$$M^4 = M^1 - .2G^1 ,$$
$$M^5 = M^1 - .4G^1 .$$

For each trial value of M, the corresponding trial value of G is $(B - M^i)$, in this case with $(i = 1, 2, .., 5)$.

Next, for each (G, M) pair, the heuristic models previously described can be applied to arrive at intercountry allocations. For each of the five pairs, a set of n country allocations of economic aid, and a set of lm country-capability allocations of military aid, results. For visual clarity, the results can be summarized in several simple charts. For each (G, M) pair, the indicated country allocations can be shown as a series of points (labeled by country) located in terms of an abscissa representing economic aid (G_i), and an

---

[49] See above, equation (1), p. 358.

[50] In terms of the imputed dollar value of various local war capabilities in particular countries.

[51] The increase in regional real income that is foregone by transfers from G to M could also be estimated from the resulting change in the country allocations of economic aid, (G_i), and from the corresponding aid production functions.

ordinate representing military aid, (M_j). Countries *not* receiving military aid thus will appear as points on the G axis. Countries not receiving economic aid will appear as points on the M axis. Countries receiving *neither* military nor economic aid will be located at the origin. Similarly, the amounts of specific military capabilities purchased in the region with different levels of military aid can be visually represented by a series of l graphs, each representing amounts of a particular capability plotted in terms of the five trial values of M.

As previously noted, this procedure still leaves us with incommensurables. An imputed "rate of exchange" between the returns from economic and military aid remains to be determined by *judgment*, not on technical grounds. But to repeat what we have already said, our goal here is not that of establishing commensurability, but simply that of assisting responsible decision-makers to do so, by showing the allocation results of various arbitrarily assumed combinations of military and economic aid.

CHAPTER 11

SOVIET ECONOMIC AID IN SOUTHERN ASIA*

A. INTRODUCTION

LET US SHIFT OUR ATTENTION from the abstract analysis of the several preceding chapters to the concrete issue of Soviet economic aid in Southern Asia. What, if any, implications does the analysis have concerning Soviet aid, and, more particularly, its bearing on U.S. Mutual Security aid in Southern Asia and on U.S. foreign policy more generally? Is Soviet aid in Southern Asia a clear threat to U.S. interests? Does it warrant reallocation of U.S. economic aid? Stated another way, should offers of aid by the Soviet Bloc be responded to by U.S. counter-offers of more aid on more favorable terms? And what can be said about the effect on our SEATO allies of Soviet aid to "neutralist" countries?

B. THE MAGNITUDE AND CHARACTER OF SOVIET BLOC AID

Before looking for answers to these questions in terms of the preceding discussion, let us define more precisely the character and size of Soviet Bloc economic aid in Southern Asia.[1]

Beginning early in 1954, but largely concentrated in the period since early 1956, Soviet diplomacy in Asia has included an active effort to extend economic aid to countries who qualify as non-allied with the United States, or, in some sense of the convenient if overworked term, as "neutralists." By the middle of fiscal year 1958, the Soviet Bloc had made aid commitments in Southern Asia of nearly $600 million in India, Afghanistan, Indonesia, Burma, Cambodia, Ceylon, and Nepal. Table 37 shows the amounts and project composition of these commitments.

These figures represent "commitments," not deliveries or expenditures. Over the 1954-58 period, deliveries under the Soviet Bloc aid agreements, were, of course, substantially below the total commit-

---

* An earlier version of the material contained in this chapter appeared in *World Politics*, Vol. X, No. 1, October 1957.
[1] Soviet *military* credits are deliberately excluded from the following discussion. Although most Soviet military aid outside the Bloc has been concentrated in the Middle East, military credits of about $25 million have also been extended to Afghanistan and an undisclosed amount to Indonesia. It is notable that Soviet military, no less than economic, aid has been typically provided as credits rather than grants.

ments shown in the table. The relative magnitudes of U.S. and Soviet Bloc aid can be indicated by comparing the figures shown in Table 37 with U.S. economic aid *obligations* in the same countries for the fiscal years 1955 through 1957. The comparison is made in Table 38, below. Although the Soviet Bloc commitments cover a four-year period, 95 per cent of these commitments were made in the same three years covered by the U.S. obligations shown in Table 38.

In comparing the Soviet Bloc and United States aid data, it should be noted that a far larger share of U.S. obligations represents grants rather than loans for the indicated period. Thus, 76 per cent of the U.S. obligations were grants, compared with only 9 per cent of the Soviet Bloc commitments. Moreover, although the interest rates on the loan portion of U.S. aid are typically higher than those shown in Table 37 for Soviet credits, U.S. terms of repayment have been "softer," involving either longer periods, local currency repayment options, or both.

Even allowing for the minor discrepancies between the coverage of the U.S. and Soviet data, it is evident that the Soviet Bloc economic "offensive" represents an effort of considerable size. Between 1954 and 1958, Soviet Bloc aid commitments to countries of Southern Asia with a neutralist orientation, amounted to about $172 million less than U.S. obligations ($593 million and $765 million, respectively). Virtually all of this difference was accounted for in India and Indonesia. In the other countries, Soviet commitments either approximately equalled, or exceeded U.S. economic aid obligations.

What significance does a Soviet Bloc effort of this scope have for U.S. assistance programs and U.S. foreign policy?

C. "Instrumental" and "Influential" Views of Economic Aid

1. The Contrasting Views

In our discussion of aid objectives and political vulnerability in Part III, and in the heuristic model of economic aid allocation described in Chapter 10, we have elaborated and applied a particular view of economic aid. Essentially, this view has been that the returns to the United States from economic aid depend mainly on the economic effects of such aid. Aid supplements the resources otherwise available to recipients for increasing investment and consumption, spreading technical knowledge and providing various institutional requirements for growth. And it is on these kinds of effects that the returns from aid depend.

This is emphatically *not* to say that the returns are not "political" returns, but rather that the economic changes realizable through aid are a necessary instrument for achieving political returns. In most of Southern Asia, as we stressed in Part III, the disparity between widely held aspirations and economic conditions—currently experienced or actively expected—is one major source of political instability. If the economic changes induced by aid can be reasonably expected to contribute to lessening this disparity, aid can be said to yield political returns. In terms of the vulnerability model of Chapter 8, the political returns that are realized will depend on the extent to which aid affects the indicators of economic performance, rather than of economic aspiration.[2] This view can be referred to as an "instrumental" view of economic aid.

By contrast, it can be argued that the returns from aid are rather to be found in holding, winning and influencing friends.[3] In this view, the bilateral discussions and negotiations involved in the programming of economic aid comprise a continuing relationship between donor and recipient. Through and from this relationship the donor can exercise influence on the recipient and can induce him to behave in a manner more congenial to the donor. In this view, the returns from aid depend on the procedures and relationships accompanying the provision of aid rather than on the economic changes that it produces. For convenient reference, this can be referred to as an "influential" view of economic aid.

To some extent the two views are merely different, rather than conflicting. Aid may contribute to sound economic growth as well as make recipients more amicably disposed toward the donor. And if there is a conflict between the two views that is resolved by considering one of the objectives as primary, we at least implicitly constrain rather than exclude the other objective. Clearly, the economic growth of an aid recipient is hardly of interest to a donor if the recipient is likely to become an unswerving ally of the donor's adversary.

However, quite different policy conclusions result from adopting one view rather than the other. For example, adherents of the in-

[2] See pp. 305-310 and 366-367, footnote 25.
[3] See Chapter 7, section C.1(b).

Table 37

SOVIET BLOC ECONOMIC AID COMMITMENTS TO NON-BLOC COUNTRIES IN
SOUTHERN ASIA, JANUARY 1954–DECEMBER 1957: AMOUNT (millions of dollars),
PURPOSE, REPAYMENT TERMS, AND DATE OF AID AGREEMENT[a]

Recipient Donor	Afghanistan	Burma	Cambodia	Ceylon
CHINA		$4.2; textile mill; 12 yrs. at 2½ per cent; December 1956.	$22.4; (grant) textile mill; cement, paper, and plywood plants; roads and bridges; June 1956.	$16.0; commodity grant for rubber rehabilitation; September 1957.
CZECHOSLOVAKIA	$5.0; cement plants; textile mill; leather-proc- essing plant; road-building equipment; 8 yrs. at 3 per cent; August 1954.			$3.4; sugar factory; (terms not available); August 1957.
EAST GERMANY				
USSR	$3.5; grain elevators; 8 yrs. at 3 per cent; January 1954	$30.0; technological institute; hospital; sports stadium; hotel; theatre; (repayment in rice over 20 yrs., no interest specified); April 1956.		

(continued)

Table 37 (*continued*)

SOVIET BLOC ECONOMIC AID COMMITMENTS TO NON-BLOC COUNTRIES IN
SOUTHERN ASIA, JANUARY 1954–DECEMBER 1957: AMOUNT (millions of dollars),
PURPOSE, REPAYMENT TERMS, AND DATE OF AID AGREEMENT[a]

Donor \ Recipient	India	Indonesia	Nepal	Donor Total
CHINA			$12.6; commodity and currency grant; October 1956.	$ 55.2
CZECHOSLOVAKIA		$1.6; tire and rubber factory; 5 yrs. at 4 per cent; May 1956.		$ 10.0
EAST GERMANY		$9.2; sugar mill and trucks; 6 yrs., interest rate not specified; February 1955.		$ 9.2
USSR	$1.5 (gift); farm machinery; December 1955. – – – – – $132.3; steel plant; 12 yrs. at 2½ per cent; March-May 1956.	$100.0; coal-mining and metallurgical equipment; power plants; building materials; 12 yrs. at 2½ per cent; September 1956.		$518.2

(*continued*)

Table 37 (*continued*)

SOVIET BLOC ECONOMIC AID COMMITMENTS TO NON-BLOC COUNTRIES IN
SOUTHERN ASIA, JANUARY 1954–DECEMBER 1957: AMOUNT (millions of dollars),
PURPOSE, REPAYMENT TERMS, AND DATE OF AID AGREEMENT[a]

Donor	Recipient	Afghanistan	Burma	Cambodia	Ceylon
USSR (*continued*)		$3.2; oil storage tanks; road-building equipment; (terms not available); August 1954. – – – – $2.1; asphalt factory; Kabul road-paving; concrete-mixing plant (terms not available); May 1955. – – – – $100.0; hydroelectric stations; irrigation works; auto repair shops; and other enterprises; 30 yrs. at 2 per cent; January 1956.	$4.2; irrigation works; 12 yrs. at 2½ per cent; December 1954. – – – – $3.1; agricultural implements factory; 5 yrs. at 2½ per cent; December 1957.		
Recipient Total:		$113.8	$ 41.5	$ 22.4	$ 19.4

Sources: *Foreign Assistance Activities of the Communist Bloc and Their Implications for the United States,* A Study Prepared at the Request of the Special Senate Committee to Study the Foreign Aid Program by the Council for Economic and Industry Research, Washington, D.C., 1957, pp. 80-81, 88, 103-109, 110-111, 119; *The Sino-Soviet Bloc Economic Offensive in the Far East,* Department of State Intelligence Report No. 7670, February 28, 1958, pp. 12-16; "Resume of Soviet Aid Projects in Underdeveloped Lands," The *New York Times,* January 15, 1958; *The Sino-Soviet Economic Offensive in the Less-Developed Countries,* Department of State Publication 6632, Washington, D.C., 1958.

a Aid figures are in millions of U.S. dollars. In some cases, the original agreement is stated in dollars; in others, in rubles; and in

(continued)

Table 37 (*continued*)

SOVIET BLOC ECONOMIC AID COMMITMENTS TO NON-BLOC COUNTRIES IN
SOUTHERN ASIA, JANUARY 1954–DECEMBER 1957: AMOUNT (millions of dollars),
PURPOSE, REPAYMENT TERMS, AND DATE OF AID AGREEMENT[a]

Recipient Donor	India	Indonesia	Nepal	Donor Total
USSR (*continued*)	$12.3; petroleum drilling rigs; diamond mining equipment; (terms not available); May-June 1956. - - - - - $126.0; fertilizer plant; oil refinery; coal-mining equipment; 12 yrs. at 2½ per cent; November 1956.			($518.2)
Recipient Total:	$272.1	$110.8	$ 12.6	$592.6

others, in the currency of the recipient country. In all dollar conversions, official exchange rates were used. The real values of the dollar figures are, however, quite ambiguous. To make them more precise, it would be necessary to determine the dollar prices imputed to the particular commodities and services provided by the Soviet Bloc donor countries. In cases providing for repayment in commodities, for example, rice repayment by Burma, the implicit barter terms of trade would need examination to arrive at precise estimates of the real values of Bloc credits. A preliminary and quite incomplete inspection suggests that the credit agreements do not seem to involve terms of trade that are unfavorable to the recipient countries.

Table 38

U.S. AND SOVIET BLOC ECONOMIC AID OBLIGATIONS
TO SELECTED COUNTRIES OF SOUTHERN ASIA

(millions of dollars)

	(1) U.S. Obligations (Fiscal Years, 1955–57)	(2) Soviet Bloc Commitments (Jan. 1954–Dec. 1957)
Afghanistan	34.7	113.8
Burma	42.3	41.5
Cambodia	25.9	22.4
Ceylon	11.1	19.4
India	504.0	272.1
Indonesia	142.6	110.8
Nepal	4.4	12.6
TOTAL	$765.0	$592.6

Sources: For Column (1), Chapter 6, above, Tables 19, 24, and 27; for Column (2), Table 37. The U.S. figures include, besides economic aid under the Mutual Security Program, surplus commodity assistance under Public Law 480 to India, Indonesia, and Burma, amounting to about $405 million over the 1955-57 period, valued at U.S. support prices. See footnotes c and e, Table 27, for the Indian and Burmese references, and Chapter 6, p. 221, for the Indonesian reference.

fluential view tend to see the sometimes less-than-friendly behavior of neutralists, such as India and Indonesia, as an indication that U.S. aid programs in these countries are not achieving their purpose, and hence as justification for reducing or eliminating them. Since the instrumental view regards the economic effects produced by aid as the link between aid and the political returns sought, it tends to be more concerned with productivity than friendship as a criterion for allocating aid. The prominent role we have accorded the aid production function and the productivity parameter, a_4, in the allocation model of Chapter 10, reflects this aspect of the instrumental view.[4]

The two views also contrast in their evaluation of Soviet Bloc aid in Southern Asia and other non-communist areas. The influential view regards Soviet aid as intended and likely to evoke obligation and goodwill toward the Soviet Bloc, and hence as a threat to American interests in the recipient countries. (In this connection, it is quite likely that the Soviet Bloc's aid in Southern Asia reflects the Soviet Union's own acceptance of the "influential" view.)

[4] See Chapter 10, section B.3,4.

The instrumental view tends to look at Soviet—and American—aid in terms of whether and how much such aid contributes to reducing the gap between prevailing economic conditions and aspirations in recipient countries. In this view, if Soviet aid contributes to this end, it represents a positive score for the United States. If this is admittedly only one entry in an extremely complex foreign-policy-accounting ledger, it is at least one that is both important and often overlooked.

2. Some Comments on the Instrumental View

It should be clear that the instrumental view of aid has underlain much of the analysis of the last several chapters. As we have previously noted in discussing aid objectives, there are two principal reasons for avoiding the influential view in an analytical discussion of aid allocation. The first reason is that, in general, aid is too unreliable a means of winning friends and influencing countries for this to be its objective. Economic aid may be a necessary condition for holding on to friends we already have, for example, the Philippines. It is certainly not a sufficient condition, as is suggested by the case of Egypt, which until 1956 received more than twice as much aid from the United States as any other Arab country. Moreover, from U.S. experience with aid in the neutralist countries since 1951, it may be said that aid has not been either a necessary or a sufficient condition for winning or influencing *new* friends. In fact, one of the neutralist countries that has become perceptibly more friendly toward the United States in recent years has been Burma, where our grant aid program was discontinued from June 1953 to June 1956 at the request of the Burmese government. At the least, this experience warrants a certain amount of skepticism toward the view that aid builds up credits in the international goodwill account of the United States. By the same token, it warrants skepticism toward the view that Soviet aid is generally likely to build up the influence of, and goodwill towards, the Soviet Union in the Asian neutralist countries. To say that the Soviet Union may *expect* such influence to result from its aid is, of course, quite different from saying that the Soviet Union is likely to acquire such influence. We sometimes forget that the Soviet Union is at least as prone as the United States to make mistakes in its foreign policy calculations.

The second reason for not elaborating on the influential view is that if there are instances in which the potential influence and good-will realizable from economic aid warrant its reallocation, they are likely to be specific cases involving specific personalities in specific circumstances. General analytical methods have little to say about such cases other than that they will arise and, where they do, will require the exercise of responsible policy judgment which tries to take them into account.

3. Some Consequences of the Instrumental View

If we adopt the instrumental view symmetrically, for Soviet as well as U.S. economic aid, certain reasonable conjectures follow. Thus, Soviet Bloc aid either does or does not provide resources for projects similar to those financed by additional U.S. aid. If it does, Soviet aid will have an economic effect comparable to an equivalent amount of dollar aid. If economic effects constitute some sort of proximate measure of U.S. political returns, then we have gained —assuming, of course, that the comparable U.S. aid was itself appropriately planned. In this connection, a comment by then Deputy Undersecretary of State Douglas Dillon, concerning the $132 million Soviet credit for constructing a one million ingot-ton steel plant in India, is of interest:

"The Bhilai steel project, while small in comparison with steel plants in the United States, is of considerable significance to Indian economic development. This one plant will increase India's present steel capacity by 60 per cent and will result in a savings of foreign exchange to India of some $80 million yearly."[5]

Of course, it does not follow that the Soviet Union has not also gained. Competitive coexistence is a non-zero-sum game. Participants may and do register gains and losses on different scales. On some, the Soviet Union may gain; on others, lose. Rates of exchange

---

[5] Statement on "Economic Activities of the Soviet Bloc in Less Developed Countries" before the Senate Committee on Foreign Relations. Reprinted in *The Department of State Bulletin*, March 24, 1958, p. 471.

To keep the scale in balance, note the following quotation from the London *Economist* commenting on subsequent Indian negotiations for additional Soviet credits:

"Far from rushing to help India over the difficulties it will face in the next few months, the Russians have taken their time about committing themselves . . . which will not ease those difficulties at all."

The *Economist*, "Russia and India: How to Influence People—Cheaply," November 16, 1957, p. 576. As the article's title suggests, the *motives* behind Soviet aid are perhaps less pristine than might be inferred from the *effects* of Soviet aid alluded to by Undersecretary Dillon.

between the scales are unknown or, if known, may differ for different participants. For example, internal communist parties in recipient countries may, as a result of Soviet aid, acquire a new respectability and enhanced political appeal. Or Soviet technical assistance may be larded with increasing numbers of communist organizers or agitators—though it is very likely that neutralist countries will watch this quite closely and try to control it. And there is a question whether increased dependence on Soviet aid and Soviet sources of supply for replacement parts may induce neutralist recipients to become politically more subservient to the Bloc. One reason for doubting this is that the relatively much greater dependence of neutralists on Western aid and Western sources of supply has not seemed to affect their subservience toward the West. Anticipated gains on any or all of these scales may lead the Soviet Union to extend aid even if we (the United States) believe the growth effects in recipient countries will redound to our advantage.

If, on the other hand, Soviet aid is restricted to quite different uses than American aid, it is not clear what the consequences—in terms of payoffs to the United States—may be. Say Soviet aid were to produce sectoral imbalances in recipient economies. This might be done, for example, by using aid to increase the output of subsidized steel faster than demand is rising in other sectors, and hence lowering prices and driving private producers out of business; or by overexpanding transport capacity so that operation of the excess capacity is at a loss.[6] Or Soviet aid might be directed toward less essential projects that a particularly interested ministry in the recipient country had been unable to retain in the country's formal development plan. By giving foreign exchange credits for such projects, on condition that their local currency costs be borne by the recipient country, Soviet aid might contribute to inflation and to the diversion of internal resources from more to less essential uses, thereby actually slowing down growth in the "aided" country. It is by no means impossible, for example, that some of the Soviet aid projects in Burma, such as the sports stadium, hotel, and theater, may have this effect.[7]

---

[6] Clearly, the loss could be eliminated by scrapping the excess capacity provided by Soviet largesse. The recipient, however, may not do so—and may not be expected to—either because it mistakenly estimates that possible future income from the equipment has a present value exceeding the loss, or because it is unaware of the irrelevance of sunk costs.

[7] See Table 37, above.

While such designs are not to be dismissed lightly, there are a number of reasons why they might have quite different consequences from those expected by the Soviet Bloc. For one thing, a clever recipient can usually extract some benefit from aid regardless of the intention of the donor. Substitutability of resources generally permits a recipient to realize the additive effect of aid in a different sector by cutting back its own efforts in the sector to which the aid is directed. And even if Soviet aid does have the intended effect, it is by no means clear that the Bloc will benefit, on balance. There is an asymmetry to the credit-blame consequences of economic aid that tends to discourage a donor from attempting to use it to create imbalances in the recipient economy. When aid is used productively and effectively, credit for its use redounds to the recipient government. When, however, aid creates bottlenecks, surpluses, or other grievances, blame often redounds to the donor government. The blame, of course, is more likely to arise if the imbalances created by aid, because intended, are more frequent or more pervasive.

Incidentally, it might be mentioned that the credit-blame asymmetry provides yet another reason for the skepticism we have previously expressed about the influential view of economic aid, in general. As U.S. experience in the complex business of foreign aid operations has amply shown, the aid relationship, especially in hypernationalistic Southern Asia, is not always a comfortable one. It is bound to be associated with at least occasional disagreements, disappointments, and ruffled dispositions. Nor is this any less true of the aid-*lending* than the aid-*giving* relationship. Polonius' admonitions are as relevant to intergovernmental loans in Southern Asia as to interpersonal loans: "For loan oft loses both itself and friend." There is some evidence that, if the Soviet Bloc was not already aware of this lesson from U.S. experience, or from Shakespeare, it has had an opportunity to learn directly since the beginning of its economic aid "offensive" in 1954.[8]

[8] In 1956, for example, Burma ordered for immediate delivery 60,000 tons of cement—a year's supply—from the Soviet Union under their bilateral trade agreement. The arrival of the shipments at the beginning of the monsoon season, and Burma's lack of storage space to receive it, resulted in substantial losses. The Burmese held Soviet promptness to blame, and this was probably one factor in the subsequent stiffening of Burma's attitude toward the Bloc. Some early examples of Asian disappointment at Soviet Bloc aid deliveries are cited in the *London Daily Telegraph*, July 24, 1956. Nevertheless, Soviet Bloc performance has been generally quite creditable. The occasionally adverse reactions to Soviet aid in the Asian recipient countries are probably neither more nor less frequent than in the case of U.S. aid.

Moreover, it is reasonable to expect that Soviet aid to neutralist countries, regardless of possible Soviet criteria governing its use, will lead to certain repercussions within the Bloc. For example, the claims of China and the Eastern European satellites on the Soviet Union for aid may be expected to depend in part on Soviet aid to non-Bloc countries. While the signs may be less apparent, there is no reason to doubt that the same kind of invidious comparisons that have accompanied U.S. aid will bother the Soviet Union, as a newcomer to the field. If complaints by Bloc claimants are heeded, the Soviet economy may incur some strain.[9] If they are not, the political cohesiveness of the Bloc may diminish.

Besides creating a possible strain between the Soviet Union and other communist *governments* in the Bloc, it is also possible that aid to non-Bloc countries will create some tension *within* the Soviet Union and within other donor countries of the Bloc, as well. Coming in the midst of domestic shortages of consumer goods and of ambitious internal industrial investment programs, aid to non-Bloc countries, if fully publicized, might be less than popular within the Soviet Union and other countries of the Bloc. Providing some support for this conjecture has been the general underplaying by the Soviet press itself of the Soviet Union's aid to non-communist countries. Though scattered reports have appeared concerning Soviet technical assistance and specific commodity aid agreements, articles concerning the over-all scale and detailed composition of extra-Bloc economic aid have been conspicuously absent, not only from the popular press but from the more specialized Soviet foreign trade and financial journals, as well.

It is, of course, true that in a communist state the "popularity" of a policy is hardly a prerequisite to its continuation. Nevertheless, it would be quite wrong to assume that the people of communist countries are inert or that, especially since 1956, the ruling communist elites are insensitive to public reactions to their policies.

---

[9] It is also true that trade with countries outside the Bloc may *reduce* the strain on some sectors of the Soviet economy. If food and other agricultural products were in relatively short supply in the Soviet Union, there would always be an opportunity for a profitable exchange, for example, of Soviet capital goods for Asian rice and raw materials, quite apart from aid. The gains from trade should not be confused with the gains and/or losses from aid. However, it has been argued that recent changes in the relative costs of industrial and agricultural commodities within the Soviet Union may make it quite attractive to the Soviet Union to accept repayment of its aid credits in foodstuffs and raw materials. See Joseph Berliner, *Soviet Economic Aid to Underdeveloped Countries*, New York, 1958, pp. 119-127.

Public opposition to extra-Bloc aid might lead to its diminution or perhaps to a diversion of resources to domestic consumer goods production. The alternative of a forceful repression of such opposition obviously remains, though this would by no means be a costless alternative from the standpoint of the ruling communist elites.

D. SOME IMPLICATIONS OF SOVIET AID FOR U.S. POLICY

The picture that emerges is admittedly not conclusive. If Soviet aid contributes to economic growth in recipient countries outside the Bloc, it may yield payoffs to the United States similar to those associated with the growth effects of U.S. aid. If the Soviet Union tries to use aid to create imbalances in recipient countries, its effort may be circumvented by the substitutability of resources. And if its effort is nevertheless successful, the result may be public blame and hostility directed against the Soviet Union, rather than against the recipient government. There are, too, fair possibilities that Soviet aid to non-Bloc countries might have repercussions within the Bloc, and that these might either place some strain on the economy of the Soviet Union, on relations between the Soviet Union and satellite governments, or on relations between ruling elites and the public within individual countries of the Bloc.

On the other hand, the Soviet Union may also derive benefit from its aid programs. The prestige of communist parties in recipient countries may be bolstered. Goodwill toward and dependence on the Soviet Union may be engendered in recipient countries. And Soviet agents and agitators, packaged along with Soviet technicians and equipment, may go about their work in recipient countries to the benefit of the USSR. For reasons already suggested, these contingencies can be ranked, respectively, as likely, doubtful, and unlikely.

On balance, perhaps all that can be said is that Soviet aid is not simply a threat to U.S. interests as it on first glance appears to be, but that it may also carry with it potential windfall gains for the United States. Consequently, no presumption seems warranted that Soviet aid offers or commitments should be countered by bigger and better American offers. There may be special cases where such counters are indicated, but the general case may indeed be to the contrary.

This is not to say that increased economic aid by the United

States may not be warranted for other reasons. The problem of allocating U.S. resources in the international field is so difficult, as we have seen, that the actual allocation may frequently—perhaps usually—be less than "optimal." If, for example, the success of India's Five-Year Plan represents an indirect but important payoff to the United States, substantial additional aid to India may well be to our advantage—whether or not India is receiving assistance from the Soviet Union. Soviet aid may focus our attention on the need, but it does not create the need. And the need, once recognized, can and should be considered without falling into the challenge-and-response approach to increased aid, where Soviet aid rather than the problems of the recipient country appears as the challenge and our aid the inevitable response.

A further qualification needs to be added to this argument. While Soviet aid may be a windfall rather than a threat to American interests, *given* a substantial U.S. aid effort, this would certainly not be the case if American aid were eliminated or curtailed. On its part, the USSR may be expected to try to exact from recipient countries some political-economic price for its aid, figured in whatever terms the Soviet Union registers its potential gains in this field: political, for example, in terms of support for Soviet foreign policies; economic, in terms of interest and repayment terms. The effect of on-going U.S. aid is to lower the price the Soviet Union can expect. As a monopolist, the Soviet Union could charge a higher price for its aid, or discriminate in the prices its charges different "buyers" of aid so as to maximize its returns. Competition in aid, no less than trade, tends to raise the quantity of aid, and to lower the "price" paid by users.

Of course, the comfort this gives us is not unalloyed. Soviet aid, for the same reason, will tend to lower the price we can charge users, as well. For example, interest rates of 2½ to 3 per cent on Soviet development credits seem to be standard practice in the region, as compared with rates of from 4 to 5 per cent on U.S. government (Export-Import Bank and D.L.F.) loans. Consequently, it is likely that subsidized Soviet rates will tend to lower ours, either in the form of reduced interest rates, longer maturities, or both.[10]

[10] In the case of loans under the Mutual Security Program, the repayment period (up to forty years) is often so long, and the local currency repayment provisions often so "soft," that the loans are probably already at least competitive with Soviet credits. See Howard P. Jones, "U.S. Economic Policy and Programs in the Far East," *De-*

Despite its inconclusiveness, the foregoing argument may have some direct bearing on a number of problems we face in the foreign aid field. It may, for example, help to forestall our being propelled by a fear of Soviet aid offers into precipitate counter-offers; the Aswan Dam and its sequel in 1956 were a case in point. If, as has been suggested here, we can anticipate some of the ways in which Soviet aid may be *both* a threat and a windfall, appropriate actions on our part may enable us to maximize the latter consequences while limiting the former. If we are more aware of the ambivalent character of Soviet aid, we may make more imaginative and effective use of our own aid.

For example, we might consider making an offer to the Soviet Union to share equally with us the costs of the total estimated foreign exchange deficit in India's next Five-Year Plan. Acceptance of the offer might assure the Plan's success and thereby strengthen public confidence in the democratic, moderate, and neutralist Congress Party government. Rejection of the offer would undermine the credibility of the altruistic motives professed by the Soviet Union in its aid offensive.

We might also consider whether a proposal to the Soviet Union to channel its aid through the United Nations, along with a commitment from us to make matching contributions, might, in the perhaps unlikely event it were accepted, remove the possibly adverse consequences of Soviet aid and leave it on balance a gain to the free world. If this proposal were also rejected, the impact on public relations would be unfavorable to the Soviet Union. Moreover, if aid remains on a bilateral basis, we might consider whether and how a judicious allocation of our aid within recipient countries can serve to prevent structural imbalances from arising as a possible result of Soviet aid.

The foregoing discussion may also have some implications with respect to creating potential frictions within the Bloc. If, for example, an opportunity has developed within the satellite countries for some expression of both governmental independence and public opinion, it might be advantageous to encourage the flow of information within the Bloc concerning Soviet aid activities outside the Bloc.

---

partment of State Bulletin, xxxv, No. 904 (October 22, 1956), pp. 640-641. See also this chapter, above, p. 384.

In these matters, of course, we are always uncertain about outcomes. But if we consider the potential gains and losses of possible counteractions by the United States, we can probably characterize some as more likely than others. At the least, we may be in a better position to take advantage of whatever opportunities for gain are afforded us by Soviet aid activities.

E. SOVIET BLOC AID AND SEATO

Another aspect of the Soviet aid offensive which has not been touched on concerns its effect on our Asian allies in SEATO. It is interesting to note, in this connection, how fine the line apparently is in Soviet thinking between "neutralist" countries that are eligible for aid and "committed" countries that are not. Cambodia, for example, which receives military aid from the United States and is within the area covered by the SEATO agreements, though not itself a formal signatory, nonetheless is considered sufficiently neutral to qualify for aid—that is, aid from Communist China. Another explanation for this anomaly is, of course, that China and the Soviet Union may apply somewhat different considerations in deciding on aid recipients.

In any event, the record suggests that an Asian country's formal membership in SEATO is a sufficient condition for disqualifying it from receiving aid from the Bloc as a whole, though not necessarily from entering into bilateral trading arrangements with the Bloc. If, as is not unlikely, the USSR makes aid offers conditional on withdrawal from, or less active participation in, the pact, what will be some of the consequences for American aid policy?

Under these circumstances, clearly, the cost to a SEATO country of its membership rises. Assume, for example, that our *economic* aid to SEATO countries is divided into two components: one component allocated on the same "instrumental" grounds as those on which we extend aid to the neutralist countries; the other, a separate "inducement" component relating to a country's membership in a defense organization benefiting our strategic and diplomatic position in the region.[11] If we think of this inducement component

[11] The distinction does not parallel that previously discussed between "instrumental" and "influential" views of aid. "Inducement," as used in the text, refers to the "price" paid by the United States to pact members in exchange for the strategic or diplomatic value which their membership provides the United States. In terms of the analytical discussion of the preceding chapter, the instrumental component would be the amount

as a subsidy that makes the benefits of membership just exceed the costs, then the effect of a conditional Soviet aid offer is to raise the required subsidy. How far we are prepared to raise the subsidy will depend on how highly we value the strategic or diplomatic benefit of the regional pact.[12] In fact, if the SEATO members knew this limit, they could in theory push us toward it, even in the absence of Soviet aid offers, simply by a firm and credible commitment not to take less. Since they probably do not know this upper limit any better than we, they are only likely to move in this direction under the stimulus of conditional aid offers from the USSR.

There is another way in which Soviet aid is likely to affect U.S. aid to SEATO members. The politically "necessary" rate of growth in any one Asian country depends, in part, on its observation of levels of living in other countries of the region. If people improve their lot in India, the demands of people in Pakistan tend to rise. If Soviet aid to neutralist countries helps them to grow faster and to raise consumption levels, this in itself is likely to boost development targets and resource requirements in the SEATO countries as well. The chances are that the latter's foreign aid needs will rise, and that we will find it in our interest to meet these needs. Stated differently, the "instrumental" component—no less than the "inducement" component—of U.S. economic aid to the SEATO countries is likely to rise as a result of Soviet aid to the Asian neutralists. If the contest proceeds and the Soviet Union is prepared to raise the ante, Asian aid recipients might become increasingly split into two groups: the neutralists receiving all or most of their external assistance from the Soviet Union, and the SEATO members receiving aid only from the United States. That such a cleavage would be hazardous for the United States and the free world should be clear. Bipolarization is obviously least attractive if it gives the adversary advantages of size and time. It is encouraging that the pattern of U.S. economic aid allocation in Southern Asia since 1956 seems to make this prospect appear relatively unlikely.

---

of aid a country receives according to the formal allocation model. The inducement component is an *addition* to the country's allocation, based on a policy judgment intended to "correct" the allocations because of considerations excluded from the model. See Chapter 10, above, p. 371.

[12] And also on how much of a difficulty, for example, in terms of resource burdens on the Soviet Union or intra-Bloc frictions, we think would be created for the Soviet Union if its offer were accepted.

CHAPTER 12

ECONOMIC DEVELOPMENT
AND MUTUAL SECURITY IN SOUTHERN ASIA—
SUMMARY AND CONCLUSIONS

A. SUMMARY

LIKE most major foreign policy problems, foreign aid is one whose serious consideration does not stay within the confines of convenient disciplinary lines. Both analytically and empirically, our discussion has, therefore, ranged widely over political and military, no less than economic, matters. This tendency to ramify is at once a source of interest and of possible confusion. It is also a compelling reason for trying to summarize fairly precisely the ground we have covered.

1. The Background of United States Aid in Southern Asia

In the introduction, the study's focus was described in terms of whether and how the improved allocation of U.S. economic and military aid between countries and programs in a defined region might be approached analytically. To give some feeling for the dimensions of the problem in the particular region of Southern Asia, Part I described the background of United States aid in this region from the end of World War II until 1950. During the transitional period from 1945 until 1947, U.S. aid was largely a response to wartime damage and disruption. Its primary aim was to provide relief for civilian consumption. In the Asian area, such aid was provided through GARIOA, UNRRA, post-UNRRA Relief, and the Philippine War Damage program.

As U.S. relations with the Soviet Union deteriorated, foreign aid underwent a substantial change. With the formulation of the Truman Doctrine and the start of Greek-Turkish aid in 1947, economic and military assistance became major instruments of a foreign policy whose aim was to strengthen the will and ability of free countries to resist communism. During the 1948-50 period, five programs reflected the altered character of U.S. foreign policy and of foreign aid as one of its principal instruments: the European Recovery Program, the China Aid Program, Korean Aid (before and after the communist attack of 1950), the Technical Cooperation

(Point IV) Program in underdeveloped areas, and the Mutual Defense Assistance Program. Though preceding U.S. assistance in Southern Asia, these programs had considerable influence on its objectives, timing, and allocation.

ERP's influence on later aid to Southern Asia arose from the fact that its broad, implicit premise—that political stability in Europe required economic recovery and improvement—invited application in other areas. In addition, the close economic and political ties between Southern Asia and Western Europe increasingly projected Southern Asia into the planning of aid to Europe.

The influence of the China Aid experience lay in the "lesson" that was inferred from it, concerning both the limitations of military assistance in the Asian area and the possible benefits to be derived from economic assistance. The lesson affected both the initiation and the original operating philosophy of U.S. aid in Southern Asia.

The Technical Cooperation Program was, in part, also an outgrowth of the China experience. By establishing assistance for economic development as a national policy of the United States, and by attempting to formulate criteria to assist in the allocation of aid for development purposes, the Point Four Program, in its turn, subsequently affected the objectives and the operations of aid in Southern Asia.

The influence of Korean aid contrasted with that of China Aid and Point Four. By demonstrating that economic and technical aid, even where it was as effective as it had been in Korea, could not counter the threat of external attack, the Korean aid experience altered the allocation of subsequent aid in Southern Asia between economic and military programs, and among the various country recipients.

Finally, the Mutual Defense Assistance Program, beginning in 1949, provided both the organizational framework for later military aid in Southern Asia, and the original stimulus behind the formation of the Southeast Asia Treaty Organization five years later.

2. The Record of Mutual Security Aid in Southern Asia

In Part II, the record of U.S. Mutual Security aid in Southern Asia was reviewed in terms of the international circumstances and aid legislation affecting the programs, and the dollar amounts allocated to particular countries and programs. For the 1951-57 period, total

U.S. economic and technical aid obligations in the countries of Southern Asia under the Mutual Security Program were $1,376 million. The country allocations of economic and technical aid discussed in Part II are summarized in Table 39.

Table 39

FUNDS OBLIGATED FOR UNITED STATES ECONOMIC AND TECHNICAL ASSISTANCE IN COUNTRIES OF SOUTHERN ASIA, FISCAL YEARS 1951-1957

(millions of dollars)

Fiscal Year Country	1951	1952	1953	1954	1955	1956	1957	TOTAL
Afghanistan	.06	.64	2.14	2.51	2.01	18.30	14.39	40.05
Burma	10.80	13.67	6.93	0	0	0	25.00	56.40
Ceylon	.04	.01	0	0	0	5.0	6.08	11.13
India	5.19	52.71	43.58	86.85	84.43	60.88	68.72	402.36
Indochina	21.83	24.60	23.98	24.45	26.77	41.53	65.88	229.04
Cambodia	--	--	--	--	--	(12.20)	(10.98)	
Laos	--	--	--	--	--	(6.61)	(5.96)	
Viet Nam	--	--	--	--	--	(22.72)	(48.94)	
Indonesia	7.98	8.06	3.56	3.91	7.00	11.10	26.72	68.33
Nepal	.04	.20	.45	.74	2.37	1.96	4.35	10.11
Pakistan	.45	10.60	26.80	22.73	71.36	66.68	61.67	260.29
Philippines	15.11	32.10	17.92	14.45	19.64	26.58	33.91	159.71
Thailand	8.88	7.10	6.46	8.73	38.16	34.46	34.50	'138.29
TOTALS	70.38	149.69	131.82	164.37	251.74	266.49	341.22	1,375.71

Sources: Tables 3, 8, 11, 16, 19, 24, 27. The figures in Table 39 exclude surplus commodity assistance under Public Law 480 to Indonesia ($98 million in 1956 [see Chapter 6, p. 221]), Burma ($17 million in 1957 [see Table 27, footnote e]), and India ($290 million in 1957 [see Table 27, footnote e]).

In appraising economic aid allocations, the method used in Part II was to regard the allocations in each year as though they were "optimal," and then to see what further assumptions (concerning the "productivity" of aid, U.S. aid objectives, and the international situation) seemed necessary to validate the optimality premise, and how realistic these assumptions appeared to be. In some cases, we found reasons to believe that, in retrospect, these assumptions may not have been realistic. To the extent that the relevant circumstances actually seem to have remained unchanged, some of the widely varying absolute and relative country allocations in different years must not have been optimal. On these grounds, some of the country allocations shown in Table 39 appeared, perhaps not surprisingly, to be inconsistent with the initial optimality premise; for example, the Indian allocations in 1953 and 1956 in contrast to those in 1954 and 1955, the Indonesian allocations in 1956 and 1957 in contrast to the preceding several years, the Thai allocation in 1954 in contrast to 1955.

Over the same period covered by Table 39, obligations under the Mutual Security Program for what we have called "military support," that is, assistance for military purposes in the form of "soft" commodities, amounted to $1,740 million in the countries of Southern Asia. The country allocations of military support, discussed in Part II, are summarized in Table 40.

Table 40

FUNDS OBLIGATED FOR UNITED STATES MILITARY SUPPORT
IN COUNTRIES OF SOUTHERN ASIA, FISCAL YEARS 1951-1957

(millions of dollars)

Fiscal Year Country	1951	1952	1953	1954	1955	1956	1957	TOTAL
Indochina	–	–	–	678.57	435.82	254.51	272.48	1,641.38
Cambodia						(32.89)	(23.50)	
Laos						(42.04)	(38.48)	
Viet Nam						(179.58)	(210.50)	
Pakistan	–	–	–	–	–	40.88	37.00	77.88
Philippines	–	–	–	–	9.50	2.50	–	12.00
Thailand	–	–	–	–	8.37	–	–	8.37
TOTAL				678.57	453.69	297.89	309.48	1,739.63

Sources: Tables 16, 19, 24, 27.

For various reasons discussed in Part II, military *end-item* aid cannot be presented in a form conveniently comparable to that for non-military aid. Recognizing the non-comparabilities involved, Part II presented the original appropriations for military end-item aid under the Mutual Defense Assistance Program on a *regional* rather than country basis. These data are summarized in Table 41 for fiscal years 1951 through 1957.

Interpretation of the more aggregative military aid data is even less conclusive than interpretation of the more detailed economic aid data. Nevertheless, we noted in Part II some reasons for skepticism concerning the optimality of MDAP allocations as well, in at least a few specific cases. In Indochina in 1952, for example, the effectiveness or "productivity" of MDAP seems to have been fairly narrowly

[404]

Table 41

APPROPRIATIONS FOR UNITED STATES MILITARY END-ITEM
ASSISTANCE, FISCAL YEARS 1951-1957

(millions of dollars)

Fiscal Year Region	1951	1952	1953	1954	1955[a]	1956[a]	1957[a]	TOTAL
Europe	4,413.7	4,818.9	3,128.2	1,910.0	(414.9)	(481.4)	(891.7)	16,058.8
Near East and Africa	339.3	396.3	499.1	270.0	(181.2)	(79.8)	(316.8)	2,082.5
Asia and the Pacific	469.5	535.3	540.8	1,035.0	(583.6)	(455.9)	(784.8)	4,404.9
Latin America	–	38.2	51.7	15.0	(13.0)	(5.1)	(24.2)	147.2
TOTALS	5,222.5	5,788.7	4,219.8	3,230.0	1,192.7	1,022.2	2,017.5	22,693.4

Sources: Tables 5, 9, 13, 16, 25, 28.
[a] For an explanation of the parentheses around the figures for 1955 through 1957, see
Tables 21, 25, and 28.

limited by the type and circumstances of the internal conflict then
underway. Consequently, a point of negligible returns may have
been reached well within the amounts of military equipment that
were provided under the program. The allocation to Pakistan in 1955
offered other grounds for doubt concerning the optimality of MDAP
allocations. In particular, the likelihood of external communist attack
against Pakistan seems too small to have made plausible a large
military aid program with defense against such an attack as a major
objective.

Despite the apparent firmness of MDAP objectives and payoffs,
it seemed clear that they are deeply involved in complex conjectures
concerning the relative probability of various local war contingencies,
the relative "disutility" to the free world of such contingencies, and
the relative ability (productivity) of MDAP in different uses to help
meet or deter these contingencies. Consequently, improved allocation of military aid is, in some respects, an even more difficult task
than improved allocation of economic aid.

3. The Objectives of Economic Aid

Part III then turned to some of the analytically interesting issues
raised in Parts I and II. It was noted that foreign aid is, of course,
an instrument of foreign policy. It is therefore a truism that the
objectives of foreign aid must be *among* the objectives of foreign

[405]

policy. To improve the allocation of aid, the objectives motivating it must be more precisely defined, and, if possible, quantified. In attempting the latter, the best we can hope to do is to formulate proximate, "lower-level" objectives, which might be quantified, in place of the ultimate, "higher-level" objectives, which are bound to remain qualitative. The only way of providing partial insurance against the risks that such a procedure involves is to apply its results with caution, candor, and judgment.

In discussing foreign aid objectives, the approach of Part III was in part descriptive, in part evaluative: descriptive of the objectives that have actually been identified with foreign aid; and evaluative of the usefulness and relevance of these objectives from the standpoint of improving the allocation of aid.

The customary distinction between economic and military aid was then made, according to their respective objectives, *not* their form. The multiple objectives of economic aid were further divided into the familiar political, economic, and humanitarian categories. Among the political objectives, those stressed were: (1) building conditions of internal political strength, "health," and stability in recipient countries; (2) creating or reinforcing U.S. influence in recipient countries and developing friendly and cooperative relations with them; and (3) countering the Communist Bloc economic offensive in underdeveloped areas.

Of these, a central role was ascribed to the first, both as a matter of past fact and present norm. However, for political stability to become more useful as an objective guiding the allocation of aid, it was considered desirable to try to establish a workable way of relating it to aid inputs, or to variables that might be affected by aid inputs. For the political stability objective to affect aid allocations more systematically and explicitly, it would be helpful, to know whether and how stability is related to measurable indicators that can be affected by economic aid.

Two economic objectives that are frequently attributed to economic aid were then discussed: extending the gains from trade, and increasing supplies of strategic materials available to the United States. It was contended that the relation between these objectives and economic aid is too unpredictable for them to be major aid objectives. A statistical test of the unpredictability of this relationship (that is, of the independence of the specified variables) was presented.

[406]

Humanitarian objectives were noted to have influenced both the initiation and allocation of economic aid in fairly special cases. Nevertheless, such objectives were considered not to have influenced, or be likely to influence, the allocation of economic aid in most cases.

4. The Objectives of Military Aid

The broad purpose of military aid in Southern Asia was then described as creating capabilities, and signifying U.S. intentions, to meet the higher-likelihood local wars in the region. Within this broad purpose, the multiple objectives of military aid were discussed in terms of strengthening local defense forces, including both those required for external defense and internal security; providing local military bases, and building military (or joint military-civilian) facilities or infrastructures. The latter two objectives were conceived especially in relation to their contribution to the military effectiveness of U.S. forces which might possibly intervene in particular local war contingencies.

Next, Part III considered the problem of establishing commensurability among these military objectives, and among the differing capabilities (returns) corresponding to them. In principle, the imputed dollar "value" of these capabilities can be regarded as *either* the cost which the U.S. would *have* to pay to provide a substitutable capability through the domestic defense budget, or the cost which the U.S. would be *willing* to pay to provide such a substitutable capability, whichever of the two is lower.

From this standpoint, the returns attributable to larger *internal security* forces in a recipient country are *not* commensurable with the returns attributable to larger *external* defense forces or with the other types of returns usually associated with MDAP. In other words, it is probably fair to say that *no* U.S. defense expenditure can be reasonably construed to buy a product that is comparable to an improvement in internal security in the countries of Southern Asia. The paradoxical conclusion results that one of the most important objectives of "military" aid—strengthening internal security forces—cannot be evaluated in military terms at all. From the standpoint of military aid allocation, the paradox can be resolved by accepting the relatively small requirements for internal security as a *constraint*, rather than a variable, in determining intercountry allocations.

5. *Economic Change and Political Behavior*

Because of the central role and conceptual fuzziness of the political-stability objective of economic aid, the remainder of Part III attempted to express in a testable form some of the intricate connections between economic change and political behavior. A model was formulated relating the notion of political vulnerability to three complex socio-economic variables: economic aspirations, the level of living, and economic expectations. Each of the variables was defined in terms of measurable indicators, and the rationale for selecting these indicators was discussed at length with respect to the particular region of Southern Asia. The implication of the model is that economic development primarily affects political vulnerability by acting on these variables.

Using Indian data, Part III then presented a rudimentary test of the model's predictive power. The hypothesis tested was that vulnerability indices, derived from the model, are of value in explaining the regional distribution of communist voting in the Indian national elections of 1951-52. Though further testing using later data is strongly desirable, the test results shown in Part III tended to support the hypothesis.

6. *An Analytical Approach to Aid Allocation*

In the context of the preceding discussion, Part IV began by considering analytically three problems of allocation which had been repeatedly referred to in the empirical review of the Mutual Security record in Southern Asia: the allocation of economic aid among countries of a particular regional set; the corresponding intercountry allocation of military aid; and the allocation of a given total of Mutual Security assistance in a particular region between economic and military programs.

In considering the first problem, a heuristic model was formulated consisting of an objectives function, a resource constraint, and an allocation criterion. The objectives function related the returns from aid in any country of the region to the amount of aid allocated to it, and to four parameters pertaining to that country: the political-vulnerability parameter, derived from the discussion of Part III; the reciprocal of the country's population; a productivity-of-capital parameter; and a size or scale parameter, each expressed as a relative based on the mean of the set. The resource constraint required that total aid allocated in the region equal total aid available. The allocation criterion stated the allocation problem as one of maximizing the objectives function subject to the resource constraint.

If we assume that the scale parameter is measured in terms of population, two of the parameters cancel out of the model. Under certain plausible simplifying assumptions, an optimal solution of the model then requires aid allocations to recipient countries proportional to the product of the vulnerability and productivity parameters.

To deal analytically with the second problem, we assumed at the outset that aid requirements for *internal* security in each country are small, that they can be regarded as technically "given," and that they represent a first claim on the amount of military aid to be allocated in the region. In considering the use of the *remainder* of regional military aid, the next step would be to draw up a list of the higher-likelihood local wars in the region, together with approximate order-of-battle estimates of the scale of attack involved in each case. It was contended that the number of such wars, at least in Southern Asia, was limited, and hence the computations involved in the subsequent steps of the analysis would be manageable.

The analytical model then required establishing an array of MDAP *cost* functions, showing the relationship between MDAP dollar inputs and specific military capabilities relevant to the higher-likelihood local wars. Corresponding to each capability-cost function, in the countries of the region, would be a *capability-worth* parameter, showing the estimated dollar value to the United States of a unit addition to each of the "relevant" military capabilities. Derivation of the capability-worth parameters was discussed in terms of the alternative-cost technique previously mentioned.[1] With these tools, an objectives function was formulated, expressing the returns from military aid in terms of the MDAP cost functions and the capability-worth parameters. The allocation problem then is to maximize the objectives function subject to the usual resource constraint, adjusted for the previously noted internal security requirements.

Quite apart from the fact that the simplified analytical model conceals an involved, though not unmanageable, empirical and judgmental exercise, an important qualification had to be added to the model. The need for this qualification arose from the fact that the estimation of capability-worths, in accordance with the model, tends to obscure a significant problem. Evaluating a local capability, in

[1] See above, page 407.

terms of the alternative U.S. costs of buying a substitutable capability, overlooks the fact that the U.S. capability may have use in *several* local wars whereas the local capability itself may be confined to a single use. The point requires adding a formal condition to the model: an optimal allocation of mutual defense assistance, as determined by the model, requires that there be no *group* of capabilities among these bought with military aid whose *aggregate* cost exceeds that of a domestic U.S. capability able to substitute for the group as a whole.

Implicit in this formal condition is a general and paradoxical conclusion: it may sometimes be militarily advantageous to use MDAP to buy a seemingly higher-cost, mobile U.S. tactical capability than an apparently cheaper local capability. Despite the more familiar argument to the contrary, MDAP dollars may sometimes be more profitably spent on building more effective local-war capabilities in the U.S. armed forces than in building them abroad.

Finally, the approach adopted in Part IV to the third problem of inter*program* aid allocation was simply an application of the two heuristic models formulated in connection with the inter*country* allocation of military and economic aid. In considering a preferred allocation *between* economic and military programs within a region, the two models can be applied to determine the intercountry allocations that would result from various *possible* combinations of economic and military aid for the region as a whole. Trial pairs of economic and military aid could be arbitrarily chosen, subject to the condition that the sum of each pair equals total Mutual Security aid available for the region. Incommensurability between economic and military aid returns would remain. But the point of the exercise would be to permit—better still, to require—responsible decision-makers to focus judgment explicitly on the desirability of alternative program combinations by considering: (1) what country allocations would result from different military-economic combinations; (2) what country capabilities would be foregone by marginal transfers from military to economic aid; and (3) how economic aid allocations to particular countries would be altered by marginal transfers from economic to military aid.

It should be evident, and should be directly stated if it is not, that the analytical methods discussed in Part IV, and based on the previous discussion in Part III, are not intended to provide answers. The models are too incomplete, and too ruthless in their simplifications, for this to be their purpose. Rather they are intended to stimulate further research and to help focus judgment where it is needed if better allocative decisions are to be made. The models of Chapter 10 are thus intended as an aid to judgment, *not* as a substitute for it.

Moreover, in this significant if limited role, the precise forms of the models used are less important than certain fundamental components of "rational" decision-making in the foreign aid context which the models illustrate. In the case of intercountry allocation of economic aid, these components include explicit consideration of the *productivity* of aid in different uses, the relative *political vulnerability* of recipient countries, and their relative size and importance to the United States. In the case of intercountry allocation of military aid, the components of rational decision-making include the explicit consideration of internal security requirements, the higher-likelihood local wars, the military-aid costs of meeting these contingencies (and hence the "productivity" of military aid with respect to them), and the alternative costs of providing for these contingencies by means other than local forces. And in the case of allocations between economic and military programs, even recognizing the payoff incommensurabilities that are involved, rational decision-making requires, at the very least, explicit consideration of the more prominent allocation choices available, and of the consequences of marginal transfers between the two program categories. Decisions on allocations that have been arrived at *without* explicit consideration of the desirability of marginal transfers between categories can be termed non-rational in a meaningful, rather than simply pejorative, sense of the term.

7. Soviet Economic Aid in Southern Asia

Finally, in the light of the preceding discussion, Chapter 11 considered some of the issues raised for the United States by the Soviet economic offensive in Southern Asia. After briefly summarizing the record of Soviet Bloc economic aid in Southern Asia, we considered whether and in what respects this record posed a threat to U.S. interests, what U.S. responses might be appropriate, and what effects Soviet aid might have on our SEATO allies. For reasons connected with our previous emphasis on the objectives of U.S. aid, and on the political-strengthening potentialities of economic aid, it was suggested that Soviet Bloc economic aid is not *simply* the threat it initially appears to be, but may also carry with it prospective gains for the free world. There are many different dimensions for appraising gains and losses in international affairs. What may be a loss in one dimension, may be a gain in another.

Consequently, we ought not to be too rigid, and hence predictable, in our responses to Soviet aid offers or aid commitments to third countries. In some cases we might even challenge the Soviet Union to join with us in bridging the foreign exchange gap in a country's development plan. India's Five-Year Plan is a possible illustration. More generally, increased U.S. contributions to development aid through the United Nations, if tied to equivalent Soviet contributions, might remove the possibly adverse consequences of Soviet aid and make it, on balance, a clear benefit to the free world. Paradoxically, there also seemed to be some reasons for the U.S. to encourage the flow of information *within* the Soviet Bloc concerning the Soviet Union's economic aid *outside* the Bloc.

B. FOREIGN AID AND FOREIGN POLICY

Underlying this study is the premise that the Mutual Security Program has been, and is, a necessary instrument of American foreign policy in the coexistence era; that it, or a lineal descendant, is likely to continue for an appreciable period in the future; and that, consequently, its current discussion and analysis should focus on how the program's effectiveness—that is, how the relevant returns derived from it—can be increased. Increased effectiveness requires that the objectives we are after in the aid business be clarified and specified. It requires, too, that the relations between these objectives and the various alternative ways that aid can be used be carefully and continuingly analyzed. The problem of increasing the effectiveness of the Mutual Security Program is, thus, synonymous with the problem of improving the allocation of aid funds. This is one reason why the theoretical as well as the empirical parts of our study have stressed aid allocation.

There is also another reason for the attention devoted in this study to the theoretical side of aid allocation besides its possible relevance to improving program effectiveness. Public discussion and Congressional consideration of foreign aid matters have usually been confined to two disconnected levels of discourse. One has involved the assertion and repetition of the broadest principles underlying aid programs. The other has often dealt with specific country programs or projects, and, not infrequently, with particular administrative shortcomings experienced in a few specific cases. The result has too often been a tendency for the public, and its representatives in Congress, to infer that foreign aid is a combination of hopeful principles and hapless administration. Protagonists of foreign aid have usually recited its broad and hopeful principles as corroboration for their support. Antagonists have often lit upon the occasional administrative lapses as corroboration for their opposition. A theoretical approach to foreign aid issues should have something to contribute toward bridging this gap, at least for doing so in the case of that large fraction of the Congress and the public whose minds have not already been irrevocably made up by their previous votes or speeches. Even in a field as complicated as foreign aid, better theory —in the sense of generalizations sufficiently precise and clear that they can be subjected to more or less systematic testing—can perhaps make a useful contribution to public education and understanding.

If there are, thus, reasons for deliberately introducing theory into the discussion of foreign aid, as we have tried to do, we should also be candid in admitting the limitations of theory in this field. It has been cynically remarked that a theorist is one who scrupulously avoids the small mistakes as he sweeps boldly on to a grand fallacy. It would indeed be a grand fallacy to leave the impression that the factors we have tried to take into account in the theoretical sections of this study are the only ones that need to be considered in analyzing the problem of aid allocation. As we have repeatedly observed, there are many other factors than those included in our theoretical models that need to be taken into account in making decisions on allocations. Consequently, decisions on allocations will require always the exercise of policy judgment that tries to take into explicit account factors that simplified analytical models neglect.

Moreover, besides the question of regional aid allocation which we have considered, there is the antecedent, and in many respects more important, question of the desirable size of the *global* Mutual Security Program within which the regional allocation issues arise. This is essentially a question concerning the share of the U.S. national product, or the share of government expenditures, that should be devoted to foreign aid. It involves large and analytically intractable comparisons between the benefits derived from private expenditures and from government aid expenditures, and between the benefits from aid outlays and outlays for other government services.

[413]

Not only do we lack the necessary analytical tools for making these comparisons in any precise way, but, more important, we tend not to be disposed to apply our judgment toward making these comparisons at all.

Yet this is precisely what we, as voters or Congressmen, need to do. Despite the indefiniteness of its duration and the shifting pattern of its location, the grim contest that has been blandly labeled "competitive coexistence" is currently in a critical phase. (Even if this statement seems likely to apply equally well at any time during the next decade, one feels the current phase is perhaps *especially* critical.) Thus, the Soviet Union's recent technological successes present a peaceful challenge to the United States and the free world hardly less than a military one. Communist China's striking and largely unanticipated economic achievements during the period of its first Five-Year Plan seem, on the statistical side, at least, to have exceeded the comparable Indian achievements by a considerable margin. Such achievements by the communist countries have an obvious impact in Southern Asia where economic and technological development is, as we have previously emphasized, a particularly prominent political issue.

It is true, of course, that these developments in the Soviet Bloc have been contemporaneous with others that should strongly suggest to Asian observers the seamier side of communism. In China, the hundred flowers withered in the bloom, and the hundred schools of thought cannot contend because they are not permitted to exist. The Hungarian and Tibetan repressions, the Nagy-Maleter executions, and the "postponement" of Soviet aid to Yugoslavia, provided some other broad hints about the extent of relaxation under de-Stalinized Communism. But, unfortunately, the malefactions of communism do not always offset its accomplishments in Asian eyes. There is frequently an asymmetry, if not an opacity, in the Asian viewpoint in this matter which we need to recognize even though deploring. While technical and economic accomplishments in the Soviet Union and China tend often to be attributed by Asians to the communist *system*, the accompanying political abuses tend too often to be regarded as Soviet or Chinese *national* aberrations which "indigenous" Asian communism might avoid.

This asymmetry, combined with the serious internal problems that the non-communist governments in Southern Asia face, and their only limited success so far in solving them, place the survival of free political systems in Southern Asia in serious jeopardy over the next decade. Probably more so than at any time in the years since World War II, there are credible grounds for according communism a better-than-outside chance of "winning" Southern Asia by peaceful, electoral means. In India, for example, a communist government already came to power by democratic means in the state of Kerala, and there is a considerable likelihood that the national elections of 1962 will bring about a similar result in two other states, Andhra and West Bengal. In Indonesia, too, the Communist Party emerged from the provincial elections of 1957 with the largest vote of any party in Java.

Admittedly and unfortunately, the instruments available to American foreign policy for influencing situations like these—and more generally, for meeting this "peaceful" dimension of the coexistence challenge—are limited. The main requirements in these situations lie instead with internal leadership, resources, and good fortune. But certainly one of the strongest of the foreign policy instruments available to the United States in these circumstances is foreign aid, more especially the "economic" component of foreign aid.

At the same time, we must be wary about purchasing a larger "economic" component at the cost of a smaller military component. In the area we have been primarily concerned with, communism is no less Janus-faced than in Europe or the Middle East. A military push into South Viet Nam by the Viet Minh, with support from Chinese "volunteers," is, for example, a by-no-means remote contingency in Southern Asia. Other local war contingencies in the area are hardly less likely. If we, recognizing the seriousness of the peaceful challenge of coexistence, expand economic aid by reducing military aid, there may be a consequentially heightened risk that these possible local wars will become actual local wars.

Perhaps this is a risk we should take. Perhaps it is a "cost" of expanding economic aid which we should be willing to incur because of the prospective gains to be had by reallocating from military to economic aid. In any event, we need to recognize this cost explicitly in choosing whether and how much to reallocate. Choices have to be made, and the crux of "rational" choice lies in attempting to perceive and compare the gains and costs associated with the alternatives that are available.

This generalization, of course, applies to any problem of choice. It applies to the problem of choosing among alternative ways of using a fixed budget for military aid, and a fixed budget for economic aid. And it applies, as well, to the problem of choosing among different combinations of military and economic aid within a fixed total foreign aid budget.

While these are the problems we have concentrated on in this study, it is clear they are not the only ones, nor are they necessarily the most important ones. To state the point more positively, it is clear that consideration of these problems must be preceded by consideration of another still "higher-level" problem of choice.

The "other" problem is that of judging the global size of the foreign aid program that is appropriate for meeting the requirements of contemporary American foreign policy. To grapple with this question requires that we compare this possible use of national or government resources with alternative uses; that we consider foreign aid as a variable rather than a fixed sum. In doing so, careful consideration of the questions that we have been principally concerned with can help clarify the higher-level question. But consideration of the lower-level questions cannot answer the higher-level question. The question of the appropriate commitment of United States national resources to foreign aid is both a different and, in many respects, more significant question than those we have concentrated on in this study. It is a question that is so affected by the imperfections of our knowledge about the present, as well as by our inevitable uncertainty about the future, that its answer must rest heavily on judgment and intuition. It is, consequently, a question that illustrates one of the perverse facts of life: the more significant the question propounded, the less accurate and reliable the answer to be expected. But even if the answer will be inaccurate and unreliable, and even if it must rely heavily on judgment and intuition, it will be a better answer if the judgment is made explicitly and if intuition is informed by careful consideration of the larger issues of competitive coexistence and of both the peaceful and the aggressive aspects of its challenge to the free world. If we try to take these issues into careful account, our response, as voters or policymakers, may well be to devote a substantially larger share of our national product to mutual security than we are at present doing.

APPENDIX I

THE PROBLEM OF SUBSTITUTABILITY
IN FOREIGN AID

Determination of the "real" impact of aid in a recipient country is an elusive task. One reason is that the *net* goods and services transferred to a recipient through external aid, cannot always be equated with the apparent content of aid. Goods and services are exchangeable directly through foreign trade, and indirectly through a reallocation of domestic factors of production. Imported goods and services provided through foreign aid, ostensibly for a specific purpose, may simply substitute for non-aid sources of similar goods and services.

If the interests of donor and recipient in this purpose coincide, substitutability may facilitate its realization. If, for example, the steel required for a particular aid project were initially overestimated while the trucks required were underestimated, substitutability may permit the miscalculation to be rectified *after* delivery of the steel. The "surplus" steel may be used to substitute for non-aid steel imports that otherwise would have been needed elsewhere in the economy, and the foreign exchange thereby released may be used to buy trucks required for the aid project.

But if the interests of donor and recipient *diverge*, substitutability may permit the recipient to evade the donor's intended purpose. Although obvious, the point is overlooked sufficiently to warrant elaboration.

Assume that an aid program, or a particular project in the program, consists entirely of a specified amount of one good, X_a. Assume further that the recipient country wishes, and is able, to produce domestically and to import from *non-aid sources*, an amount of the same good, X_n. Assume, finally, a divergence of interests between donor, who wants X_a to be a net addition to total $X (= X_a + X_n)$, and recipient, who wants no more of X than X_n.

Empirically, we might set X_n equal to the recipient's *current* non-aid imports and domestic output of X. In fact, this may be convenient rather than accurate. What we really wish to measure by X_n is the amount of X which the recipient *will* want and *will* be able to obtain through non-aid channels. Thus, X_n involves estimating *intentions and future capabilities*, rather than simply noting current imports and production. In practice, it may be preferable to assign a numerical value to X_n based on an explicit and informed judgment of the recipient's intentions and capabilities, rather than simply to equate X_n with the current non-aid supply.

Let us assume, however, that X_n can be estimated, at least approximately. If we now define substitutability as the extent to which X_a can be offset by a reduction in the recipient country's intended imports and/or output of X, we can then distinguish three cases.

If X_n is zero, there is no substitutability (Case 1). X_a is a net addition to the recipient country.

If X_n is positive but less than X_a, there is partial substitutability (Case II). The recipient can reduce domestic output and imports of X, but not by as much as X_a. In part, X_a *must* be a net addition, at least to the extent that $X_a > X_n$.

If, finally, X_n is equal to or greater than X_a, there is complete substitutability (Case III). The recipient can offset the additive effect of X_a in full, by import and output substitutions for X_n.

Case I is perhaps best exemplified by certain military end-items, for example, missiles, advanced radar systems, jet aircraft, etc., which can only be procured through aid channels. Case II applies to most other military end-items, and to the specific (that is, the apparent) commodity content of economic aid in countries where the amount of aid is large relative to the countries' ability to finance substitutable goods, as for instance, in Korea, Formosa, Viet Nam. Either Case I or Case II applies if aid is provided for a specific end-use (project) that the donor is convinced is marginal to the recipient's allocation of non-aid resources. "Marginal" should be understood here in one of two senses: (1) either the project would not have been undertaken at all in the absence of aid; or (2) its scale would have been small relative to the scale undertaken as a result of aid. Case I (no substitutability) applies to (1). Case II (partial substitutability) applies to (2).

Case III applies to all other situations.

In practice, however, substitutability will seldom be complete (Case III), and almost certainly will *not* be complete at the point where $X_n = X_a$. Administrative, and other institutional rigidities, will restrict the actual cutback of imports and redirection of domestic resources to less than the possibilities. Consequently, the degree of substitutability can be considered to be continuous, even for values of X_n greater than X_a. For ordinal comparisons, the *degree* of substitutability of aid commodities for similar non-aid commodities may therefore be expressed as a ratio, $\theta = X_n/X_a$. Generally, the larger the ratio, the greater the degree of substitutability.

If, for example, we consider a given X_a, in one country at different times, or in several recipients simultaneously, substitutability can be considered proportional to θ. The substitution that *actually* occurs will be limited by the degree of substitutability, but not necessarily determined by it. In practice, the limit will be approached only to the extent that the original divergence-of-interest assumption uniformly applies. If donor and recipient interests coincide, θ may be large and substitution may still be zero.

Actually, the relation between donor and recipient interests is more complex than implied by a simple divergence-convergence dichotomy. The interests, goals or objectives of both donor and recipient are numerous. Some coincide, some diverge, and some interests for one party are quite immaterial to the other. The adjustment of a particular divergence of interest with respect to the use of aid is likely to depend on a more or less elaborate bargaining relation between donor and recipient, involving some or all of their other interests as well.

A recipient knows, for example, that his evasion of the intended use of aid may be perceived by the donor. In turn, the donor might retaliate by reducing aid in the future, or in terms of quite a different dimension of the recipient's national interests, say, by non-support of the recipient's border dispute with a neighboring country. Anticipating this retaliatory move, the recipient may be disposed *not* to attempt evasion-by-substitution at all, even if there is ample opportunity for him to do so, that is, even if θ is high. Alternatively, fearing retaliation if *complete* evasion is attempted, the recipient may decide to confine evasion to that extent that he thinks he can get away with, well within the limits set by the degree of substitutability.

The solution, in terms of the recipient's preferred course of action, is not analytically determinate. Instead, it will be arrived at by a bargaining process in which many interests, other than the particular use of aid, are considered, as well as possible exchanges among them. All that can be said with confidence is that θ establishes the amount of substitution that *can* occur, not the amount that does occur.

We should not conclude this discussion of substitutability without noting that substitutions enter foreign aid in numerous ways other than the particular ones we have been concerned with here. In general, we should avoid taking the commodity content of aid as too literal a guide to its intended use, for reasons quite apart from the opportunity for evasion. The preferred factor proportions for achieving an intended and mutually agreed aim may be such that the commodity content of aid seems quite remote from its intended purpose. Consumer goods imports may, for example, be a more efficient way to build dams or expand a local constabulary than, say, imports of bulldozers or guns. While our previous discussion has been concerned with the possible substitution of aid for non-aid sources of the same goods in the context of *divergent* donor-recipient interests, this example concerns the possible substitution of some aid goods for others, in the context of *convergent* donor-recipient interests. If substitutability is a *bête noire* in the former context, because it affords an opportunity for a recipient's evasion of the donor's intent, it is a *bête blanche* in the latter context, because it affords an opportunity for greater *mutual* returns from fixed aid resources.

APPENDIX II

UNITED STATES GOVERNMENT SOURCES USED IN
TABLES ON ECONOMIC AND MILITARY AID ALLOCATIONS

a. Figures obtained directly from the International Cooperation Administration, Office of Statistics and Reports, Washington, D.C.

b. *Mutual Security Program*, Hearings Before the Committee on Foreign Affairs on H.R. 5020 and H.R. 5113, House of Representatives, 82nd Congress, 1st session, Washington, D.C., 1951.

c. *Mutual Security Act of 1951*, Hearings Before the Committee on Foreign Relations and the Committee on Armed Services on S. 1762, U.S. Senate, 82nd Congress, 1st session, Washington, D.C., 1951.

d. *Mutual Security Program Appropriations for 1952*, Hearings Before a Sub-Committee of the Committee on Appropriations on the Mutual Security Program for 1952, House of Representatives, 82nd Congress, 1st session, Washington, D.C., 1951, Part 2.

e. *Mutual Security Appropriations for 1952*, Hearings Before the Committee on Appropriations on H.R. 5684, U.S. Senate, 82nd Congress, 1st session, Washington, D.C., 1951.

f. Foreign Operations Administration, *Mutual Security Program*, Fiscal Year 1953 Estimates, Congressional Presentation Book for the 82nd Congress, 2nd session, Washington, D.C., 1952.

g. *Mutual Security Act Extension*, Hearings Before the Committee on Foreign Affairs on H.R. 7005, House of Representatives, 82nd Congress, 2nd session, Washington, D.C., 1952.

h. *Mutual Security Act of 1952*, Hearings Before the Committee on Armed Services on S. 3086, a Bill to Amend the Mutual Security Act of 1952 and for Other Purposes, U.S. Senate, 82nd Congress, 2nd session, Washington, D.C., 1952.

i. *Mutual Security Act of 1952*, Report of the Committee on Foreign Affairs on H.R. 7005, a Bill to Amend the Mutual Security Act of 1951, House of Representatives, 82nd Congress, 2nd session, H.R. 1922, Washington, D.C., 1952.

j. *Mutual Security Appropriations for 1953*, Hearings Before the Sub-Committee on Appropriations, House of Representatives, 82nd Congress, 2nd session, Washington, D.C., 1952, Part 1.

k. Foreign Operations Administration, *Mutual Security Program*, Fiscal Year 1954 Estimates, Congressional Presentation Book for the 83rd Congress, 1st session, Washington, D.C., 1953.

l. *Mutual Security Act Extension*, Hearings Before the Committee on Foreign Affairs on H.R. 5710, House of Representatives, 83rd Congress, 1st session, Washington, D.C., 1953.

m. *Mutual Security Act of 1953*, Hearings Before the Committee on Foreign Relations on a Bill to Amend the Mutual Security Act of

1951, U.S. Senate, 83rd Congress, 1st session, Washington, D.C., 1953.

n. *Mutual Security Appropriations for 1954*, Hearings Before a Sub-Committee of the Committee on Appropriations, House of Representatives, 83rd Congress, 1st session, Washington, D.C., 1953.

o. *Mutual Security Appropriations for 1954*, Hearings Before the Committee on Appropriations on H.R. 6391, U.S. Senate, 83rd Congress, 1st session, Washington, D.C., 1953.

p. Foreign Operations Administration, "The Mutual Security Program for Fiscal Year 1954," *Monthly Operations Report*, Washington, D.C., December 31, 1953.

q. Foreign Operations Administration, *Mutual Security Program*, Fiscal Year 1955 Estimates, Congressional Presentation Book for the 83rd Congress, 2nd session, Washington, D.C., 1954.

r. *Mutual Security Act of 1954*, Hearings Before the Committee on Foreign Affairs on the Mutual Security Act of 1954, House of Representatives, 83rd Congress, 2nd session, Washington, D.C., 1954.

s. *Mutual Security Appropriations for 1955*, Hearings Before a Sub-Committee of the Committee on Appropriations, House of Representatives, 83rd Congress, 2nd session, Washington, D.C., 1954.

t. *Mutual Security Appropriations for 1955*, Hearings Before the Committee on Appropriations on H.R. 10051, U.S. Senate, 83rd Congress, 2nd session, Washington, D.C., 1954.

u. Foreign Operations Administration, *Mutual Security Program*, Fiscal Year 1956 Estimates, Congressional Presentation Book for the 84th Congress, 1st session, Washington, D.C., 1955, Volume II.

v. *Mutual Security Act of 1955*, Hearings Before the Committee on Foreign Relations on the Mutual Security Program for Fiscal Year 1956, U.S. Senate, 84th Congress, 1st session, Washington, D.C., 1955.

w. *Mutual Security Act of 1955*, Hearings Before the Committee on Foreign Affairs on the Mutual Security Act of 1955, House of Representatives, 84th Congress, 1st session, Washington, D.C., 1955.

x. *Mutual Security Appropriations for 1956*, Hearings Before the Sub-Committee of the Committee on Appropriations, House of Representatives, 84th Congress, 1st session, Washington, D.C., 1955.

y. *Mutual Security Appropriations for 1956*, Hearings Before the Committee on Appropriations on H.R. 7224, U.S. Senate, 84th Congress, 1st session, Washington, D.C., 1955.

z. International Cooperation Administration, "The Mutual Security Program for Fiscal Year 1956," *Operations Report*, Fiscal Year 1955, Issue No. 4, Washington, D.C., 1955.

a'. International Cooperation Administration, *Mutual Security Program*, Fiscal Year 1957 Estimates, Congressional Presentation Book for the 84th Congress, 2nd session, Washington, D.C., 1956.

b'. *Mutual Security Appropriations for 1957*, Hearings Before a Sub-Committee of the Committee on Appropriations, House of Representatives, 84th Congress, 2nd session, Washington, D.C., 1956.

c'. International Cooperation Administration, "The Mutual Security Program for Fiscal Year 1957," *Operations Report,* Fiscal Year 1956, Issue No. 4, Washington, D.C., 1956.

d'. International Cooperation Administration, *Mutual Security Program,* Fiscal Year 1958 Estimates, Congressional Presentation Book for the 85th Congress, 1st session, Washington, D.C., 1957.

e'. International Cooperation Administration, *Counterpart Funds and ICA Currency Accounts,* data as of June 30, 1957, Office of Statistics and Reports, Washington, D.C., 1957.

f'. *The President's Report to Congress on the Mutual Security Program,* for the Six Months ended June 30, 1954, Washington, D.C., 1954.

g'. International Cooperation Administration, *Operations Report,* Fiscal Year 1957, Issue No. 2, Washington, D.C., 1957.

h'. International Cooperation Administration, *Operations Report,* Fiscal Year 1957, Issue No. 3, Washington, D.C., 1957.

i'. International Cooperation Administration, *Operations Report,* Fiscal Year 1957, Issue No. 4, Washington, D.C., 1957.

j'. Foreign Operations Administration, *Monthly Operations Report,* Washington, D.C., July 31, 1954.

APPENDIX III

Table 1

TRADE AND INCOME OF PRINCIPAL WORLD TRADING COUNTRIES, 1955
(dollars and ranks)

Country	Imports[a] (c.i.f. in millions of $)	Rank	Imports Per Capita[b] ($)	Rank	Exports[a] (f.o.b. in millions of $)	Rank	Exports Per Capita[b] ($)	Rank
	1	1a	2	2a	3	3a	4	4a
United States	12,369	(1)	75	(11)	15,553	(1)	94	(12)
Canada	5,156	(4)	328	(1)	4,784	(5)	305	(2)
Brazil	1,306	(15)	22	(14)	1,423	(13)	24	(14)
Venezuela	–	–	–	–	1,912	(9)	330	(1)
Belgium-Luxembourg	2,830	(7)	308	(2)	2,776	(6)	302	(3)
France	4,739	(5)	109	(9)	4,911	(4)	113	(11)
Germany	5,793	(3)	115	(8)	6,135	(3)	122	(10)
Italy	2,711	(8)	56	(12)	1,856	(10)	39	(13)
Netherlands	3,208	(6)	297	(4)	2,688	(7)	249	(5)
Sweden	1,997	(11)	274	(5)	1,726	(12)	236	(6)
United Kingdom	10,867	(2)	213	(7)	8,468	(2)	166	(9)
Australia	2,160	(10)	235	(6)	1,748	(11)	190	(8)
Japan	2,471	(9)	28	(13)	2,011	(8)	23	(15)
Malaya	–	–	–	–	1,358	(14)	223	(7)
Switzerland	1,489	(12)	298	(3)	1,307	(15)	261	(4)
India	1,413	(14)	4	(15)	–	–	–	–
Union of South Africa	1,482	(13)	105	(10)	–	–	–	–

(*continued*)

Table 1 (*continued*)

TRADE AND INCOME OF PRINCIPAL WORLD TRADING COUNTRIES, 1955

(dollars and ranks)

Country	National Income of Principal Importers[c] (millions of \$)	Rank	National Income of Principal Exporters[c] (millions of \$)	Rank	Per Capita Income of Principal Importers[b] (\$)	Rank	Per Capita Income of Principal Exporters[b] (\$)	Rank
	5	5a	6	6a	7	7a	8	8a
United States	324,100	(1)		(1)	1,964	(1)		(1)
Canada	20,717	(5)		(5)	1,320	(2)		(2)
Brazil	11,013	(9)		(8)	188	(14)		(15)
Venezuela	–	–	2,989	(14)	–	–	515	(11)
Belgium-Luxembourg	7,380	(11)		(10)	802	(7)		(7)
France	30,476	(4)		(4)	704	(8)		(8)
Germany	31,862	(3)		(3)	635	(9)		(9)
Italy	17,266	(8)		(7)	359	(11)		(12)
Netherlands	6,216	(13)		(12)	578	(10)		(10)
Sweden	6,840	(12)		(11)	937	(5)		(5)
United Kingdom	42,817	(2)		(2)	840	(6)		(6)
Australia	8,895	(10)		(9)	966	(4)		(4)
Japan	18,189	(7)		(6)	204	(13)		(14)
Malaya	–	–	1,634	(15)	–	–	268	(13)
Switzerland	5,380	(14)		(13)	1,076	(3)		(3)
India	20,190	(6)	–	–	53	(15)	–	–
Union of South Africa	4,171	(15)	–	–	296	(12)	–	–

a *International Financial Statistics*, February 1958, pp. 22-25.

b Per capita figures based on population data in UN *Monthly Bulletin of Statistics*, January 1958, pp. 1-5.

c *International Financial Statistics*, February 1958. National income figures were converted to U.S. dollars at official exchange rates or, where multiple rates were in effect, at the highest legal rate. The French income figure was converted to dollars at the 1957 devalued rate of 450 francs. The Belgian national income estimate is for 1954, combined with a Luxembourg figure for 1955. The Malayan figure is based on data in *The Economic Development of Malaya*, Baltimore, 1955, pp. 13, 21. It should be emphasized that the income figures involve all the usual problems of conversion rates and conceptual and statistical non-comparabilities associated with international income comparisons.

Table 2

UNITED STATES MERCHANDISE TRADE WITH AND NATIONAL AND PER CAPITA
INCOME OF PRINCIPAL U.S. TRADING PARTNERS, 1955

(dollars and ranks)

Country	U.S. Imports[a] (f.o.b. in millions of $)	Rank	U.S. Imports Per Capita of Country of Origin[b] ($)	Rank	U.S. Exports[a] (f.o.b. in millions of $)	Rank	U.S. Exports Per Capita of Country of Destination[b] ($)	Rank
	1	1a	2	2a	3	3a	4	4a
Canada	2,646	(1)	169	(1)	3,134	(1)	200	(1)
Brazil	630	(2)	11	(10)	240	(15)	4	(15)
United Kingdom	615	(3)	12	(8.5)	915	(2)	18	(9)
Venezuela	582	(4)	100	(2)	554	(6)	96	(2)
Colombia	442	(5)	35	(5)	328	(12)	26	(6)
Cuba	417	(6)	68	(3)	452	(8)	74	(3)
Japan	416	(7)	5	(12)	642	(4)	7	(13.5)
Mexico	392	(8)	13	(7)	697	(3)	23	(7)
Germany	362	(9)	7	(11)	587	(5)	12	(11)
Philippines	252	(10)	12	(8.5)	338	(11)	16	(10)
Belgium-Luxembourg	244	(11)	27	(6)	312	(13)	34	(5)
Malaya	234	(12)	38	(4)	–	–	–	–
Netherlands	–	–	–	–	472	(7)	44	(4)
France	–	–	–	–	357	(10)	8	(12)
Italy	–	–	–	–	359	(9)	7	(13.5)
India	224	(13)	1	(13)	–	–	–	–
Union of South Africa	–	–	–	–	260	(14)	18	(8)

(*continued*)

Table 2 (*continued*)

UNITED STATES MERCHANDISE TRADE WITH AND NATIONAL AND PER CAPITA
INCOME OF PRINCIPAL U.S. TRADING PARTNERS, 1955

(dollars and ranks)

Country	National Income of Countries of U.S. Import Origin[c] (in millions of $)	Rank	National Income of Countries of U.S. Export Destination[c] (in millions of $)	Rank	Per Capita Income, Countries of U.S. Import Origin[b] ($)	Rank	Per Capita Income, Countries of U.S. Export Destination[b] ($)	Rank
	5	5a	6	6a	7	7a	8	8a
Canada	20,717	(3)		(4)	1,320	(1)		(1)
Brazil	11,013	(6)		(7)	188	(10)		(13)
United Kingdom	42,817	(1)		(1)	840	(2)		(2)
Venezuela	2,989	(10)		(13)	515	(5)		(7)
Colombia	2,375	(11)		(14)	187	(11)		(14)
Cuba	1,826	(12)		(15)	299	(6)		(9)
Japan	18,189	(5)		(5)	204	(8)		(11)
Mexico	5,989	(8)		(10)	202	(9)		(12)
Germany	31,862	(2)		(2)	635	(4)		(5)
Philippines	3,233	(9)		(12)	148	(12)		(15)
Belgium-Luxembourg	7,380	(7)		(8)	802	(3)		(3)
Mayala	1,634	(13)	–	–	268	(7)	–	–
Netherlands	–	–	6,216	(9)	–	–	578	(6)
France	–	–	30,476	(3)	–	–	704	(4)
Italy	–	–	17,266	(6)	–	–	359	(8)
India	20,190	(4)	–	–	53	(13)	–	–
Union of South Africa	–	–	4,171	(11)	–	–	296	(10)

[a] *Yearbook of International Trade Statistics, 1955*, U N, 1956, p. 701. Figures exclude special category shipments, mostly military aid supplies, which are not reported by country of destination. The corresponding data for 1956, referred to in the text (see above, Chapter 7, pp. 275-276), are from the *Yearbook of International Trade Statistics, 1956*, New York, 1957, p. 609.

[b] Per capita figures based on population data in U N *Monthly Bulletin of Statistics*, January 1958, pp. 1-5.

[c] *International Financial Statistics*, February 1958. National income figures were converted to U.S. dollars at official exchange rates or, where multiple rates were in effect, at the highest legal rate. The French income figure was converted to dollars at the 1957 devalued rate of 450 francs. The Belgium national income estimate is for 1954, combined with a Luxembourg figure for 1955. The Malayan figure is based on data in *The Economic Development of Malaya*, Baltimore, 1955, pp. 13, 21.

INDEX

A

Absorptive capacity, 62-63, 94, 106 (*see* allocation of aid, capital assistance, technical assistance)

Acheson, Dean, 11, 29, 43-44, 46, 49-50, 53, 53n, 58, 59n, 81, 83, 116, 118, 136

Ackoff, Russell L., 356n

Act for International Development, 57-60, 62-64, 66-67, 71-72, 85, 96, 138, 161, 163, 165; allocation criteria of, 64-68, 71-72; appropriations for, 64, 69; Congressional Hearings on, 62-63; economic and technical aid to South Asia authorized by, 145; effect on aid to Southern Asia, 71; intercountry allocations and, 67; objectives of, 58-60, 138; repeal of, 68 (*see also* Point Four, technical assistance)

Afghanistan, 84, 300; aid allocations to economic sectors in (*see* agriculture, industry, transportation, education, community development, military support, health, public administration, labor); Czechoslovak aid to, 386; humanitarian objectives of aid to, 282n; Soviet economic aid to, 207-208, 244, 383, 386, 388, 390; Soviet military aid to, 383n; U.S. aid to, 60, 90, 124, 142, 168-169, 194-195, 216-217, 220, 222-223, 230-231, 244, 268, 390, 403

Africa, MAP appropriations for, 208, 225, 239; MDAP appropriations for, 132, 153, 174, 405

Afro-Asian Conference, 208, 222, 244

Agriculture, aid allocations for, 90, 124, 130, 142, 168, 194, 200, 216, 230

Agricultural Trade and Development Act (Public Law 480), 80, 168, 206-207, 211, 234

Aid (*see also* allocation of aid, economic aid, foreign aid, military aid, individual countries); absorptive limitations and, 94; to China, 84; to Europe, 114; to Formosa, 39; to Japan, 47-48; to Korea, 47-48; from multilateral to bilateral, 31-32; to Nationalist China, 35; objectives in Southern Asia of, 59-60; to Palestine refugees, 62n; production function for, 92-94, 97-98; source of initial funds for Southern Asia, 70, 84; to Southern Asia (*see* individual countries); to Spain, 62n

Aid allocation (*see* allocation of aid)

Aid legislation, relation to aid allocation of, 75 (*see also* Mutual Security Acts, Mutual Defense Assistance Act, Act for International Development, China Aid Act)

Allen, George V., 212, 222n

Allocation (*see also* allocation of aid), between military aid and U.S. defense budget, 286-287; optimality considerations and, 92n, 93, 97-98; as problem of choice, 3

Allocation criteria (*see also* allocation of aid), of Act for International Development, 64-66, 68; of Development Loan Fund, 68, 72; of European Recovery Program, 66

Allocation of aid (*see also* aid, foreign aid, economic aid, military aid), 40, 109, 189, 191, 201; and absorptive capacity, 94, 106; analytical models for, 92n, 93, 108, 253, 258n, 360-382, 408-411; to Asia, 243-244; between "capital" and "technical" assistance, 62n; by China Aid Act, 45-47; among countries (*see also* individual countries), 6, 45, 47, 50, 56-57, 64-66, 70-71, 75-76, 79, 126-127, 359-360; criteria for, 4, 25-26, 64-65, 68, 162, 256; between economic and military programs, 6, 33, 47, 50-51, 57, 70, 107-108, 242, 408, 410-411, 415-416; among economic sectors in Southern Asia, 65, 67-68, 90, 122, 124, 140, 142, 166-169, 181, 192-195, 200, 214-217, 230-231 (*see also* sectoral allocations, agriculture, industry, transportation, health, public administration, education, community development, military support, labor); marginal approach to, 77, 89, 92-94, 96-97, 126, 129n, 220; by obligations, 90, 124, 142, 168-169, 194-195, 216-217; objectives reflected in, 76, 80, 283; optimality and, 62, 66, 77-78, 92n, 93, 97-98, 170, 181, 234, 243, 256; as proposed to Congress, 122, 140, 166-167, 192-193, 214-215; to South Asia, 127; to Southeast Asia, 127; to Southern Asia (*see also* Afghanistan, Burma, Cambodia, Ceylon, India, Indochina, Indonesia, Laos, Nepal, Pakistan, Philippines, Thailand, Viet Nam), 90, 122, 124, 139-140, 142, 166-169, 180, 192-195, 214-217, 230-236

objectives of, 52-53, 71, 93, 101, 103, 109, 159-162, 171, 173, 177-179, 182; in Pakistan, 174, 178-179, 182; in the Philippines, 56, 69, 71, 100, 102-103, 132-133, 152-153, 155, 174, 178; and SEATO, 71, 402; in Southern Asia, 55, 102, 133, 154-155, 173-174, 180; in Thailand, 103, 132-133, 152-153, 174, 178; in Viet Nam, 56, 71

Mutual Security Act of 1951, 114-116, 119-121, 131, 137, 138n, 145, 152, 179

Mutual Security Act of 1952, 137, 138n, 139; economic aid under, 144

Mutual Security Act of 1953, 144, 160-161, 163

Mutual Security Act of 1954, 185-187, 189, 197, 202n

Mutual Security Act of 1955, 210

Mutual Security Act of 1956, 227-229

Mutual Security Act of 1957, 68, 72

Mutual Security Agency, 114, 120, 138, 157, 162

Mutual Security Appropriations, 120, 135, 137

Mutual Security Program, 120-121, 126, 135, 144, 156-158, 170, 179, 181, 184-186, 207-211, 226-228, 232, 252, 280 (*see also* allocation of aid, economic aid, military aid, foreign aid, MAP, MDAP); in Asia, 28, 80, 180, 191, 196-197, 209; economic development and, 131, 179, 261; effect of Lend-Lease on, 12; objectives of, 57, 118-119, 131, 211, 228, 242, 261, 283; in Southern Asia, 131, 179-180, 206-207, 226, 228

Myrdal, Gunnar, 315n

N

Nagy, Imre, 414

National income, and exports, 275-277; and imports, 275-277

Nationalism, in Southern Asia, economic orientation of, 301

NATO (North Atlantic Treaty Organization), 53, 56, 111-112, 135-136, 138n, 156-157, 174-175; effect of Korean War on, 111, 115; suspension of non-military aid to, 157

Nationalist China (*see* China, Nationalist)

Navarre Plan, 170-171, 203

Near East, 132, 153, 174, 202, 225, 239, 405

Nehru, Jawaharlal, 137, 145-146, 219n

Nelson, Richard R., ix

Nepal, 84; Chinese aid to, 387; Soviet

aid to, 383, 390; U.S. economic aid allocations to, 60, 90, 124, 142, 168-169, 194-195, 216-217, 230-231, 390, 403

Netherlands, and Indonesia, 21, 37-38; trade and income data relating to, 424-426

Newell, Allen, 356n

Nitze, Paul H., 108n, 255, 259n

Non-MAP aid, 198, 209 (*see also* economic aid, defense support, military support)

Non-MDAP aid, 159n, 161-162, 173 (*see also* economic aid, defense support, military support)

North Atlantic Treaty Organization (*see* NATO)

Northeast Asia, 20-21, 27

North Viet Nam, 208

Nourse, Edwin G., 23

Nourse Report, 242n

Nurkse, Ragnar, 276n, 317

O

Objectives of aid, 92, 249-254, 296-297, 375, 406-407 (*see also* foreign aid objectives, economic aid objectives, military aid objectives)

Obligations, 76n, 77n

Olds, E. G., 275n, 277n

Opie, Redvers, 12n, 15n, 16n, 22n, 23n, 34n, 47n, 52n, 54n, 96n

Optimality (*see* allocation of aid, analytical models)

P

Pacific area, military aid for, 132, 153, 174, 202, 225, 239, 405

Pakistan, 84, 118, 148-149, 174-175, 204; defense expenditures in, 199; defense support in, 189; development outlays in, 201; force goals in, 178, 240; military aid to, 174, 182, 198, 204; military aid objectives in, 178-179, 182, 226; and SEATO, 175, 179; technical assistance to, 60, 180, 403; U.S. economic aid to, 79-80, 90, 96, 124, 127-128, 142, 145-150, 163, 168-169, 180, 194-195, 200, 216-217, 223, 230-231 (*see also* aid allocation to economic sectors, agriculture, industry, transportation, health, public administration, education, community development, military support, public administration, labor); value parameter and SEATO membership of, 237

OTHER VOLUMES OF RAND RESEARCH

COLUMBIA UNIVERSITY PRESS, NEW YORK, NEW YORK

Soviet National Income and Product, 1940-48, by Abram Bergson and Hans Heymann, Jr., 1954

Soviet National Income and Product in 1928, by Oleg Hoeffding, 1954

Labor Productivity in Soviet and American Industry, by Walter Galenson, 1955

THE FREE PRESS, GLENCOE, ILLINOIS

Psychosis and Civilization, by Herbert Goldhamer and Andrew W. Marshall, 1949

Soviet Military Doctrine, by Raymond L. Garthoff, 1953

A Study of Bolshevism, by Nathan Leites, 1953

Ritual of Liquidation: The Case of the Moscow Trials, by Nathan Leites and Elsa Bernaut, 1954

Two Studies in Soviet Controls: Communism and the Russian Peasant, and Moscow in Crisis, by Herbert S. Dinerstein and Leon Gouré, 1955

A Million Random Digits with 100,000 Normal Deviates, by The RAND Corporation, 1955

HARVARD UNIVERSITY PRESS, CAMBRIDGE, MASSACHUSETTS

Smolensk Under Soviet Rule, by Merle Fainsod, 1958

McGRAW-HILL BOOK COMPANY, INC., NEW YORK, NEW YORK

The Operational Code of the Politburo, by Nathan Leites, 1951

Air War and Emotional Stress: Psychological Studies of Bombing and Civilian Defense, by Irving L. Janis, 1951

Soviet Attitudes Toward Authority: An Interdisciplinary Approach to Problems of Soviet Character, by Margaret Mead, 1951

Mobilizing Resources for War: The Economic Alternatives, by Tibor Scitovsky, Edward Shaw, and Lorie Tarshis, 1951

The Organizational Weapon: A Study of Bolshevik Strategy and Tactics, by Philip Selznick, 1952

Introduction to the Theory of Games, by J. C. C. McKinsey, 1952

Introduction to Matrix Analysis, by Richard Bellman, 1960

Weight-Strength Analysis of Aircraft Structures, by F. R. Shanley, 1952

The Compleat Strategyst: Being a Primer on the Theory of Games of Strategy, by J. D. Williams, 1954

Linear Programming and Economic Analysis, by Robert Dorfman, Paul A. Samuelson, and Robert M. Solow, 1958

THE MICROCARD FOUNDATION, MADISON, WISCONSIN

The First Six Million Prime Numbers, by C. L. Baker and F. J. Gruenberger, 1959

NORTH-HOLLAND PUBLISHING COMPANY, AMSTERDAM, HOLLAND

A Time Series Analysis of Interindustry Demands, by Kenneth J. Arrow and Marvin Hoffenberg, 1959

FREDERICK A. PRAEGER, PUBLISHERS, NEW YORK, NEW YORK

War and the Soviet Union: Nuclear Weapons and the Revolution in Soviet Military and Political Thinking, by H. S. Dinerstein, 1959

PRINCETON UNIVERSITY PRESS, PRINCETON, NEW JERSEY

Approximations for Digital Computers, by Cecil Hastings, Jr., 1955
International Communication and Political Opinion: A Guide to the Literature, by Bruce Lannes Smith and Chitra M. Smith, 1956
Dynamic Programming, by Richard Bellman, 1957
The Berlin Blockade: A Study in Cold War Politics, by W. Phillips Davison, 1958
The French Economy and the State, by Warren C. Baum, 1958
Strategy in the Missile Age, by Bernard Brodie, 1959

PUBLIC AFFAIRS PRESS, WASHINGTON, D.C.

The Rise of Khrushchev, by Myron Rush, 1958
Behind the Sputniks: A Survey of Soviet Space Science, by F. J. Krieger, 1958

RANDOM HOUSE, INC., NEW YORK, NEW YORK

Space Handbook: Astronautics and Its Applications, by Robert W. Buchheim and the Staff of The RAND Corporation, 1959

ROW, PETERSON AND COMPANY, EVANSTON, ILLINOIS

German Rearmament and Atomic War: The Views of German Military and Political Leaders, by Hans Speier, 1957
West German Leadership and Foreign Policy, edited by Hans Speier and W. Phillips Davison, 1957
The House without Windows: France Selects a President, by Constantin Melnik and Nathan Leites, 1958
Propaganda Analysis: A Study of Inferences Made from Nazi Propaganda in World War II, by Alexander L. George, 1959

STANFORD UNIVERSITY PRESS, STANFORD CALIFORNIA

Strategic Surrender: The Politics of Victory and Defeat, by Paul Kecskemeti, 1958
On the Game of Politics in France, by Nathan Leites, 1959
Atomic Energy in the Soviet Union, by Arnold Kramish, 1959
Marxism in Southeast Asia: A Study of Four Countries, by Frank N. Trager, 1959

JOHN WILEY & SONS, INCORPORATED, NEW YORK, NEW YORK

Efficiency in Government through Systems Analysis: with Emphasis on Water Resource Development, by Roland N. McKean, 1958

Lightning Source UK Ltd.
Milton Keynes UK
UKHW021544181021
392409UK00003B/259